Union General
Gouverneur Warren

ALSO BY DONALD R. JERMANN

*Civil War Battlefield Orders Gone Awry:
The Written Word and Its Consequences in 13 Engagements*
(McFarland, 2012)

*Fitz-John Porter, Scapegoat of Second Manassas:
The Rise, Fall and Rise of the General Accused of Disobedience*
(McFarland, 2009)

Union General Gouverneur Warren

Hero at Little Round Top, Disgrace at Five Forks

Donald R. Jermann

McFarland & Company, Inc., Publishers
Jefferson, North Carolina

All photographs courtesy U.S. Army Heritage and Education Center.

LIBRARY OF CONGRESS CATALOGUING-IN-PUBLICATION DATA

Jermann, Donald R., author.
Union General Gouverneur Warren : hero at Little Round Top,
disgrace at Five Forks / Donald R. Jermann.
 p. cm.
Includes bibliographical references and index.

ISBN 978-0-7864-9871-0 (softcover : acid free paper) ∞
ISBN 978-1-4766-2005-3 (ebook)

1. Warren, G. K. (Gouverneur Kemble), 1830–1882—
Trials, litigation, etc. 2. United States—History—Civil War,
1861–1865—Biography. 3. Generals—United States—Biography.
4. United States. Army—Biography. 5. Five Forks,
Battle of, Va., 1865. 6. Trials (Military offenses)—
United States. I. Title.

E467.1.W4J47 2015   355.0092—dc23   [B]   2015027474

BRITISH LIBRARY CATALOGUING DATA ARE AVAILABLE

© 2015 Donald R. Jermann. All rights reserved

*No part of this book may be reproduced or transmitted in any form
or by any means, electronic or mechanical, including photocopying
or recording, or by any information storage and retrieval system,
without permission in writing from the publisher.*

On the cover: Statue of General Warren, Little Round Top,
Gettysburg, Pennsylvania, ca. 1903; Battle of Five Forks,
Virginia, April 1st 1865, Kurz & Allison., ca. 1886 (both
images Library of Congress)

Printed in the United States of America

*McFarland & Company, Inc., Publishers
Box 611, Jefferson, North Carolina 28640
www.mcfarlandpub.com*

To my wife,
Florence

Acknowledgments

I would like to thank my daughter, Mary Jermann Amozig, who provided invaluable assistance in the preparation of this book.

Table of Contents

Acknowledgments vi
Preface 1

1. The Situation Up to Mid-March 1865 — 3
2. Grant's Plan — 6
3. The Fifth Corps — 14
4. An Overview of the Execution of Grant's Plan — 18
5. Why the Separation Between Warren's Divisions? — 30
6. Gouverneur Warren — 32
7. Warren After the War — 47
8. The Court of Inquiry — 50
9. The Testimony — 54
10. More Testimony, Some Confederates Testify — 95
11. Sheridan Responds — 126
12. Some Conclusions — 141
13. The Findings — 143
14. Sherman's Endorsement — 147
15. The Nature of Warren — 150
16. The Aftermath—What Happened to Them? — 155

Appendices:
  A. Sheridan's Official Report — 161
  B. Warren's Official Report — 167
  C. Horace Porter's Narrative — 202

Chapter Notes 210
Bibliography 213
Index 219

Preface

Young Major General Gouverneur Warren was commanding general of the Fifth Army Corps of the Army of the Potomac in March 1865. He had known nothing but success since the very first battle of the war. He was held in such high esteem that he was often looked upon as the logical successor to General George G. Meade as the commanding general of the Army of the Potomac. Now, at the battle of Five Forks, less than a week from the surrender at Appomattox, General Philip Sheridan relieved Warren from command on the battlefield. This was the ultimate disgrace.

The sensitive Warren fought for fifteen years to gain a court of inquiry to establish the facts of the case. Was his relief justified or did Sheridan merely have a grudge against him?

This book documents Warren's rise and fall, and the proceedings of the court of inquiry that followed in an attempt to establish the facts. Was Warren truly an outstanding military leader—or an incompetent in disguise whom Sheridan unmasked? This book will present the facts. You be the judge.

Chapter 1

The Situation Up to Mid-March 1865

Up to March 1864, the war in the East was give and take. The South would appear to be winning, then the North, then the South, and on and on. No end was in sight. Lincoln tried general after general to command the Army of the Potomac; first George B. McClellan, then Ambrose Burnside, then Joseph Hooker, and finally, Meade. None seemed capable of putting down the wily Robert E. Lee once and for all.

In desperation, Lincoln sent to the West for Ulysses S. Grant. Grant had enjoyed success. It appeared that he could succeed where others failed. Lincoln appointed Grant general-in-chief of all the armies. Grant came east, but instead of establishing his headquarters in Washington as might be expected, he chose to establish his headquarters in the field with the Army of the Potomac. Although George G. Meade would remain titular head of the Army of the Potomac, Grant would now give it his personal attention. In order to end the war, he must put down Lee once and for all, and this he proposed to do.

In March 1864, he ordered the Army of the Potomac to proceed south into the Wilderness toward Richmond, and he was never to turn back. From this point forward it was unrelenting bloodshed, a war of attrition. Grant fought Lee in the Wilderness, at Spotsylvania Courthouse, at North Anna, at Cold Harbor. But try as he might, he could not beat his way into Richmond. He finally circled completely around Richmond to the east, crossed the James River, and ended up facing Richmond and its suburb, Petersburg, from the south. We now had the ludicrous situation of the Union Army of the Potomac facing north, and the Confederate Army of Northern Virginia facing south.

Strange as it was, this situation was not all bad for Grant; in fact, it was good. All the major supply lines for Richmond ran in from the south and southwest through Petersburg. If Grant could cut them, Lee would have to evacuate Richmond or starve.

At this point, the nature of the war in the East changed from mobile warfare to siege warfare. As the two contending armies moved south down and around Richmond, the Confederates became ever more adept at "digging in." It soon became evident to both armies that one man, properly dug in, was a match for several in the open. By the time the two armies came to rest south of Petersburg, the Confederates had become masters of the dug-in defense. It was a forerunner of the trench warfare of World War I. While still circling the Confederates east of Richmond, Grant had made a frontal attack at Cold Harbor against the dug-in Confederates and had suffered 7,000 casualties in minutes for no appreciable gain. When he looked at the southern defenses to the south of Petersburg, Grant knew that he could not take them by storm. There had to be another way.

Grant kept extending his siege lines ever farther to the west, thus necessitating a continuous stretching and thinning of the Confederate defense lines, as well as cutting the supply routes into Petersburg one by one.

By mid–March 1865, Grant's siege lines extended as far as the Boydton Plank Road (see map 1). The Weldon Railroad and the Jerusalem Plank Road into Petersburg had been cut and the only other rail lines into Petersburg-Richmond were now the Southside Railroad from the southwest and the Danville Railroad from the south. The two rail lines crossed at a place called Burke, forty-five miles west of Petersburg (see map 2).

By mid–March 1865 the siege had been in progress for ten months; the Confederate entrenchments were still too strong to storm, and the public was tiring of a war that, it appeared, could go on forever.

While the siege of Petersburg-Richmond was in progress, the Confederates suffered disasters in other theaters. General Sheridan, the Union commander of the Shenandoah Valley Army, had decisively defeated his Confederate opponents, cleared the valley for

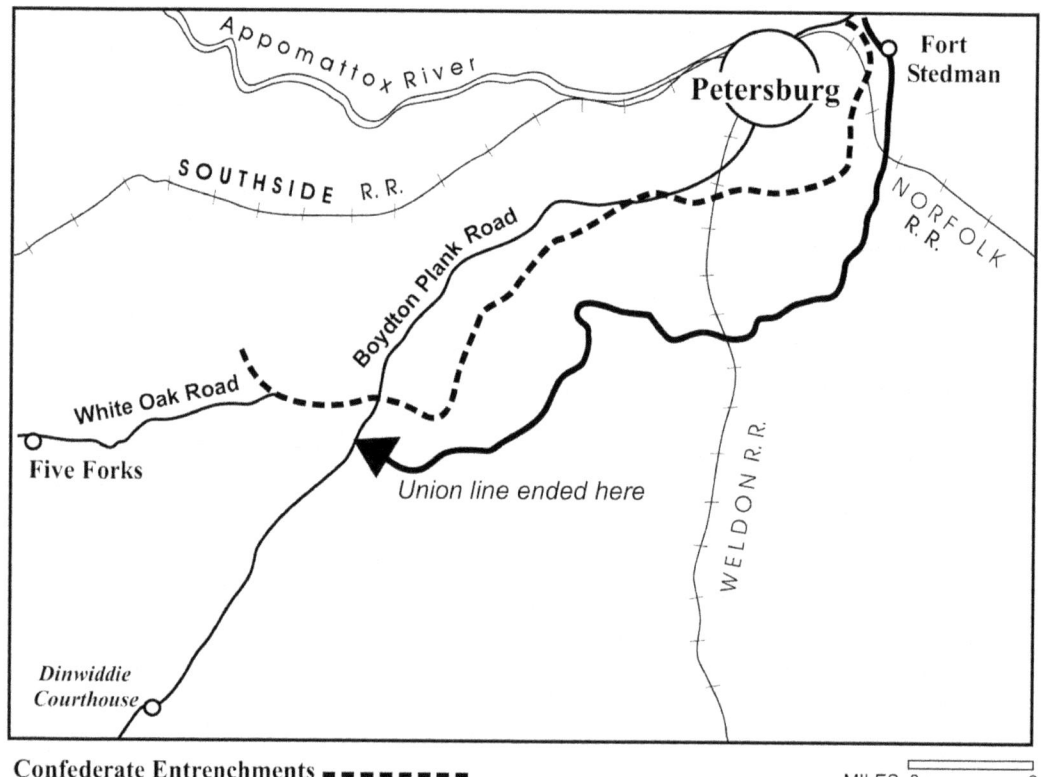

Map 1. Situation to mid–March 1865.

1. The Situation Up to Mid-March 1865

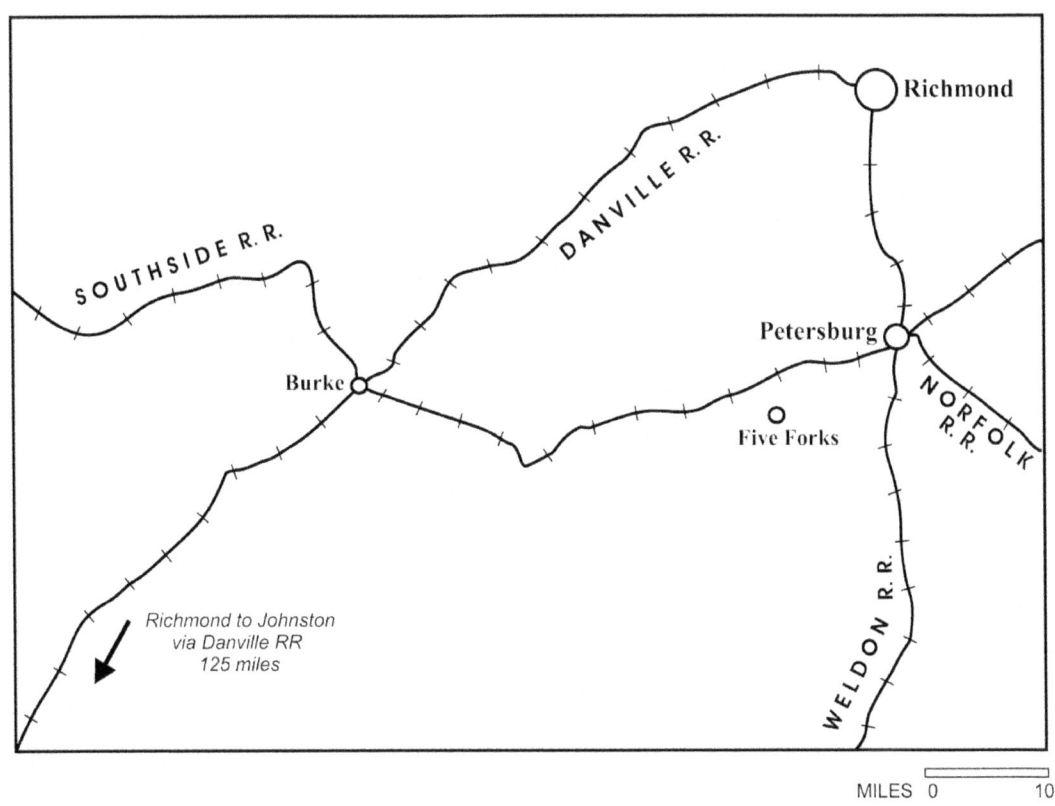

Map 2. Rail lines into Richmond from South and West, the connection to Johnston.

the Union once and for all, and was now en route to join Grant. Farther west, the Union army under John Schofield grievously wounded the Confederate army under John B. Hood at Franklin, and Union General George Henry Thomas completed its destruction at Nashville in December 1864. General William T. Sherman's Union army had crossed Georgia from west to east and was now pushing up the Atlantic coast through the Carolinas to join Grant. The only major Confederate fighting force still in the field between the Atlantic Ocean and Mississippi River, besides Lee's army, was a scratch army under General Joseph Johnston that was attempting to arrest Sherman's progress through the Carolinas (see map 2).

There was one last hope for Lee—slight, but possible. If Lee could disengage from Grant, that is, slip away and steal a march and be transported by the remaining railroads and join Johnston, the combined armies of Lee and Johnston just might be able to defeat Sherman. The combined Confederate armies could then turn to deal with Grant. Grant was very much aware that as long as the rail lines were open to Lee, Lee might be able to pull the rabbit out of the hat. Grant thus had two good reasons for cutting the last rail connections with Richmond: to starve out Lee, and to prevent Lee from uniting with Johnston.

Chapter 2

Grant's Plan

In March 1865, the country had been at war for four years. Casualties had increased each of the four years and there was no reason to believe that the trend had ceased. Hardly an extended family in the North was without a casualty. The country was tiring of the war.

On March 27, 1865, Major General Philip Sheridan, the commanding general of the Army of the Shenandoah, reported to General Grant at City Point. Sheridan had succeeded where all of his predecessors had failed. He had destroyed the Confederate Army in the Shenandoah Valley once and for all. The Shenandoah was now Union for good. Sheridan and his army were now available for a new assignment.

Grant now thought he at last had all the resources necessary to bring the war to an end. He understood that he could not break through the massive Confederate defenses before Richmond-Petersburg if they were fully manned. The Confederates had perfected earthwork defenses to the extent that one man properly dug in could hold off several in the open. Grant knew that to break through the Confederate defenses, he had to radically thin out their ranks. Furthermore, he had to do so soon. Once spring advanced and the dirt roads hardened, Lee could move. It was just possible that he and his army would slip out of their defenses, steal a march on the Union army, proceed south by rail, and unite with the Confederates of Joseph Johnston then facing Sherman. Just perhaps, the combined Confederate armies would defeat Sherman and turn on Grant.

Grant believed he had to act, and to act now. He could not allow Lee a chance at victory. Grant formulated his plan. It was four-fold:

Major General Philip Sheridan, U.S. Volunteer Army, Grant's protégé and Warren's nemesis.

(1) He would have the Army of the James, currently north of the Appomattox River, dig in so as to free troops for transfer to the Army of the Potomac south of the Appomattox. These troops would relieve the Fifth and Second Corps of the Army of the Potomac for mobile operations.

(2) The Fifth and Second Corps would then slide westward below the front, beyond the current westward terminus of the Confederate defense line at the White Oak Road. This would compel the Confederates to thin their defenses in order to transfer troops westward to extend their line beyond the White Oak Road.

(3) Concurrent with the above, he would augment the two cavalry divisions that Sheridan brought from the Shenandoah Valley with the cavalry corps of the Army of the Potomac and place this 10,000 man all-cavalry strike force under Sheridan. This force would proceed westward, south of the Fifth Corps and Second Corps force, but roughly parallel to it, so as to threaten to cut the last remaining rail links with Lee southward. The purpose of this movement was not actually to cut the rail links, but to draw a large Confederate force out of their defense line to move southward to protect them. This would further thin out the Confederate defenses.

(4) Once 2 and 3 above had succeeded in thinning the Confederate defense line, Grant would attack and break it, seize Petersburg and Richmond, and complete the destruction of Lee's army (see map 3).

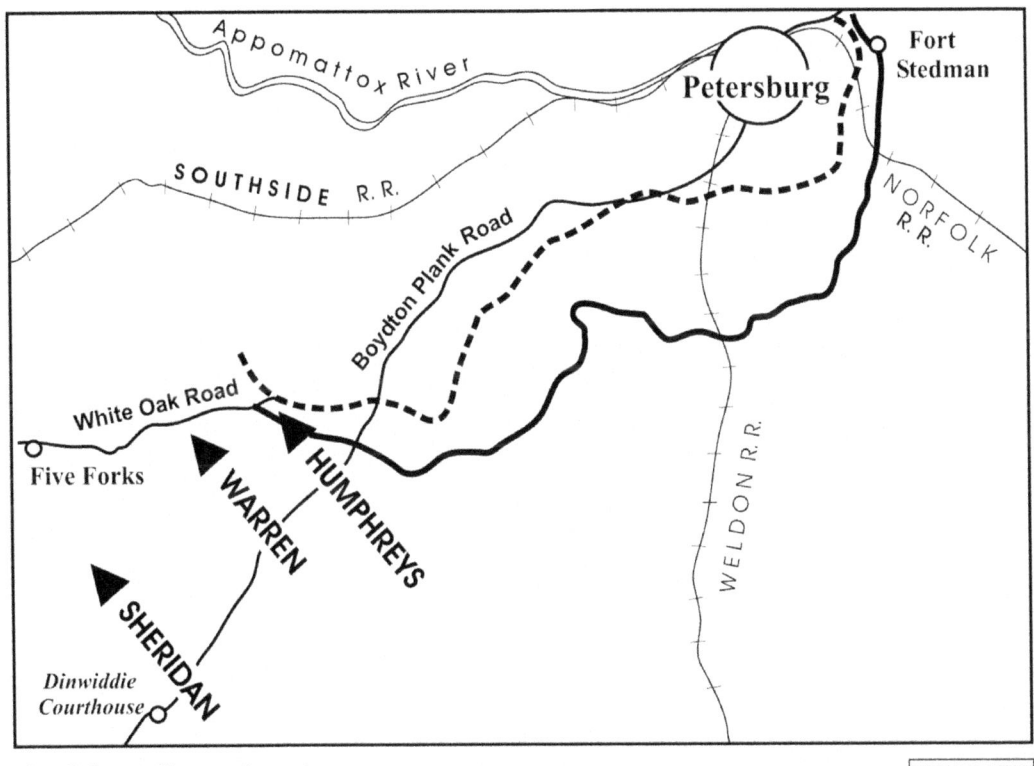

Map 3. Grant's plan.

Maps

The maps available for the forthcoming campaign were so outrageous that it is now hard to believe. Let us start with General Gouverneur Warren's (commander of the Fifth Corps) description of the map provided to him:

> The map which we possessed of the county into which the 5th Corps was about to operate, was known as the Dinwiddie county map, prepared many years ago, and republished for our use on a scale of one inch to the mile. It gave no topography except the main streams and main roads. The names of the occupants of the houses did not now correspond to those on the map; some of them too had disappeared, and others erected in places not noted. The map contained no distinction of the forest and clearings or swamps, all of which have ever played a most import part in the Virginia Campaigns.[1]

When a junior reported a position to a senior via telegraph, or a senior directed a junior to a position, map coordinates were never used. Such usage would have insured that both correspondents were talking about the same position. Rather, positions were invariably described in relation to names on the map. For example, "Just east of Dabney's" or "at Mrs. Butler's." This provided a huge opportunity for sender and receiver to be looking at different points on their maps.

The area of operations was rural with wide separations between dwellings. As generation followed generation, families tended to spread out in the area, and there could be numerous places with the same name. For example, on Warren's map were a W. Dabney, an S. Dabney, two plain Dabneys without an initial, two separate A. Dabneys, a Dabney and Boisseau, a Miss Hargrave and a Mrs. Hargrave, and many more similarly named points.

Many roads on the map bore no names and the actual roads usually bore no signs. The area of operations was deep in Rebel territory and if a Yankee were to ask a local resident (usually a Yankee hater) for information, as likely as not he would be purposely misled.

Although major streams were indicated on Warren's map, the map gave no indication of their width, depth, or fordability for wagon or man. When a corps commander reported the position of his forces to the army commander, unless specifically stated, when the army commander plotted their positions, he would have no idea whether they were in an open field, an impenetrable forest, or an impassable swamp.

When one considers the maps and communications then available, the marvel is that things worked out as well as they did.

Telegraph Communications

Telegraph was used throughout the war, but radio had not yet been invented. Telegraph required a wire between the correspondents. Radio did not. Messages were transmitted by Morse code—that is, by dots and dashes with a unique group of dots and dashes representing each letter and digit. The transmission rate was limited to the capabilities of the least experienced operator in the conversation.

The sending of Morse code was a highly skilled profession and, at the outbreak of the war, the only individuals having the necessary skills were civilians. The army attempted to come up with a substitute system that could be quickly mastered by army recruits and, as a result, came up with the so-called Beardslee system. Under the Beardslee system, the operator simply dialed the desired digit or letter and it appeared on the dial of the recipient. However, the Beardslee system proved even slower than Morse code, and by the time of the siege, the army was again using Morse, usually with civilian operators. Typically, the rate of transmission of Morse code was twelve to twenty words per minute. Inasmuch as a person normally spoke at a rate at least ten times as fast, the rate, and thus the capacity, was low.

By March 1865, each Union army corps and army headquarters was equipped with a telegraph wagon that contained a Morse terminal and operator. As the units moved, wire was laid to keep the corps wagons connected with the army wagon. The wagons could not, of course, be located at the front where they were subject to destruction or capture, and thus were usually deployed some miles to the rear of combat.

Aside from its slow rate and corresponding low capacity, Morse telegraphic communications possessed one even more serious drawback for battlefield management. In the case of radio communications, the circuit could terminate directly in the hands of the battlefield commander wherever he may be located. In the case of telegraphic communications, the circuit terminated at the operator in the wagon. Here the message had to be given to a courier to deliver to the commander, or the commander had to be at the wagon. Obviously, he could not be at the front managing the battle or miles in the rear at the wagon receiving the message at the same time.

Consequently, telegraphic Morse communications were a mixed blessing for battlefield management. The sending of a large number of messages to a corps commander engaged in combat could actually decrease his effectiveness. This is precisely what happened in the crucial seventy-two hours from March 29 through 31, 1865, in the case of the Fifth Corps. In these seventy-two hours, Fifth Corps Commander Warren received over forty messages from headquarters, many of which required responses. In Warren's words: "The receiving of dispatches and giving necessary orders had kept me almost continuously engaged at my headquarters so that I had no opportunity to examine the condition of affairs personally along my front."[2]

Roads and Railroads

Grant's plan called for moves from east to west. All major roads in the area, however, led from south to north, as might be expected; that is, from rural areas into the metropolitan area of Petersburg-Richmond. Roads east to west merely led from one rural area to another.

All east-to-west roads were unpaved (dirt) and were thus seasonal. During the spring thaw and spring rains they turned into mud, and between December and April were largely unusable for wheeled vehicles.

The only useable roads from south to north in all seasons were the Jerusalem Plank Road and the Boydton Plank Road. By March 1865, the Jerusalem Plank Road was already in Union hands, and the Boydton Plank Road was just beyond their grasp. A plank road was just what the name implied—a road paved with wood. Plank roads were common in 1865. The locals paved roads with whatever was available, and nothing was more available than wood.

Plank roads were constructed with planks that were eight feet long, one foot wide, and two to four inches thick. The planks were laid in the direction of the road and nailed to four inch square cross beams that were laid perpendicular to the road. Plank roads were generally twelve feet wide to permit the passing of two horse drawn wagons. They usually had wooden curbs and invariably had drainage ditches on either side.

Plank roads tended to deteriorate quickly and were in constant need of repair. The Boydton Plank Road, which is central to our story, was laid between 1851 and 1853 and as of 1865 was obsolete and in need of major repairs. However, it was still infinitely superior in the spring season to its alternatives, dirt roads.

The other type road we will encounter in our narrative is the corduroy road. Corduroying was a way of making an existing mud road passable for horses and wheeled vehicles. Corduroying consisted of placing small sized tree trunks tightly side by side at right angles to the direction of the road. The road thus, literally, looked like corduroy. Corduroying could be accomplished with axes alone and a corps sized unit could corduroy several miles in a single day. The area of recent operations was heavily wooded, so that necessary material was readily at hand. The ride on a corduroy road was bumpy, but it served its purpose. Horse drawn vehicles could move.

Now let us look at railroads. If Lee were to remain in Petersburg-Richmond or evacuate it and join Johnston to the south, he must have railroad access. By mid–March 1865, Grant's continuous push west had cut all rail lines but two. These were the Southside Railroad from the southwest and the Danville Railroad from the south. The two lines crossed at a place called Burke, forty-five miles west of Petersburg (see map 2). The Danville then ran on into Richmond and the Southside first to Petersburg and then up to Richmond. Under Grant's plan, Sheridan's force was heading toward Dinwiddie Court House, on to Five Forks, and then just four miles up Ford Road to the Southside Railroad.

Supply

The Army of the Potomac south of the Appomattox consisted of over 100,000 men and over 65,000 horses. Since as one horse ate as much as eight men, feeding the horses was the biggest problem. From the time Grant crossed the James in the fall of 1864 and began besieging Petersburg-Richmond from the south, he set up his main supply base at City Point. City Point was an insignificant town at the confluence of the James and Appomattox Rivers.

The Union had absolute control of deep water, and within months City Point grew, tonnage wise, into one of the great ports of the world. It had numerous docks, acres of warehouses and administrative buildings and an enormous army hospital. It proved easy to get supplies, waterborne, as far as City Point. The problem grew, however, as Grant extended his siege lines westward, ever farther into the interior. The east-west dirt roads alone simply could not support Grant's westward movement.

2. Grant's Plan

In answer to the problem, Grant ordered the construction of the City Point Military Railroad. The railroad was constructed just behind the Union siege lines, and continued to be extended to the west as the siege lines extended west. In March 1865, the line was twenty-one miles long and terminated at the north-south Weldon Railroad (see map 4).

The City Point Military Railroad looked like a regular railroad but was not quite so. Its gauge was the same as other railroads and it used the same rolling stock. There the similarity ended.

The construction of the railroad was done on an expedited basis and the surface preparation did not meet the standards of other railroads. Instead of cutting through protuberances to establish a level road bed, the track was simply laid on the ground as is. Consequently, the trains could not maintain the same speeds, nor pull the same loads as other railroads, and the ride was bumpy. Nevertheless, it served its purpose and by March 1865 had twenty-five locomotives and 275 cars, and made eighteen trips per day to the end of the line.

The distance from the railroad's westernmost terminus to Five Forks, where Grant's campaign was headed, was ten air miles and perhaps fifteen road miles. This distance had to be covered by horse-drawn wagons on dirt roads.

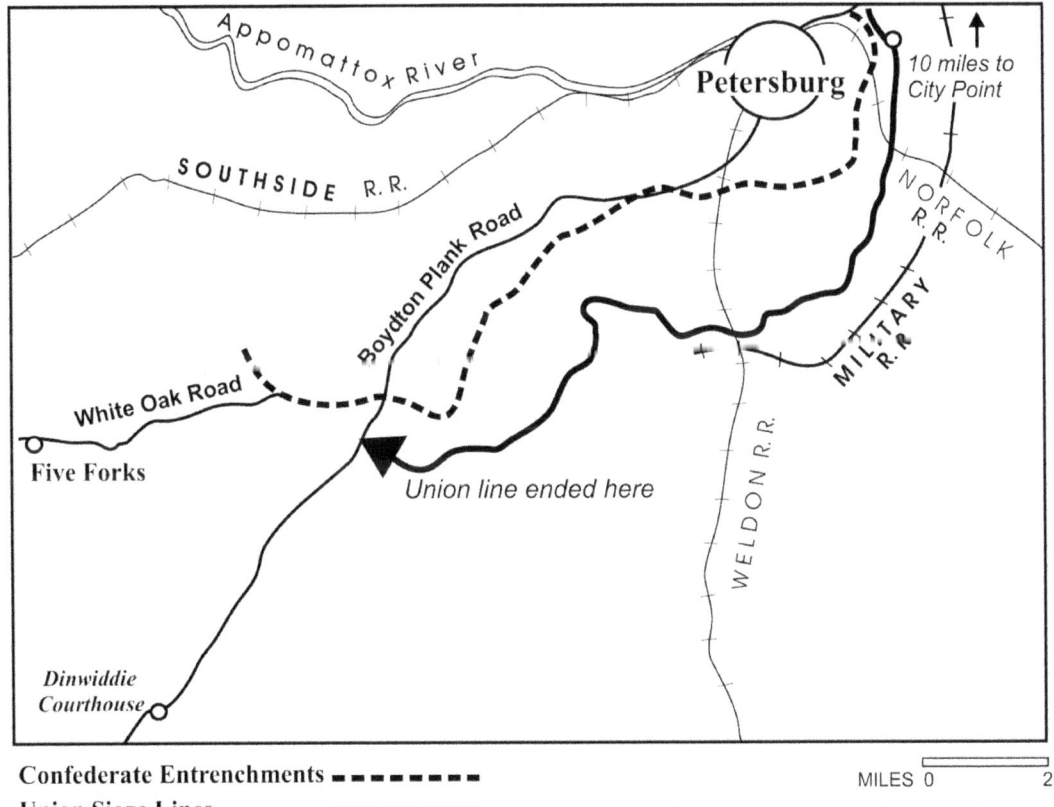

Map 5. Military Railroad, situation to mid–March 1865.

The Weather

Another critical factor affecting Grant's plan was the weather. In the part of Virginia where Grant proposed to campaign, the soil was such that, when saturated, it could not support a wheeled vehicle or a horse. The wheeled vehicle would sink up to its axles and the horse up to its belly.

The critical period was between December and early spring, when the combination of melting frost and spring rains saturated the soil. It was not safe to begin campaigning before mid–April. However, Grant feared that Lee might give him the slip once the roads dried, and he was determined to prevent it. Grant elected to begin his campaign on March 29, in the hopes that this year the spring rains were over. March 29 was a sunny, warm spring day. The violets and daffodils were blooming and there was no hint of rain. The dirt roads were drying and passable. But Grant could not foresee that more rain was to come.

Command

When Sheridan reported in to Grant on March 27, 1865, Sheridan was not part of the Army of the Potomac and hence not subordinate to Meade. In the forthcoming

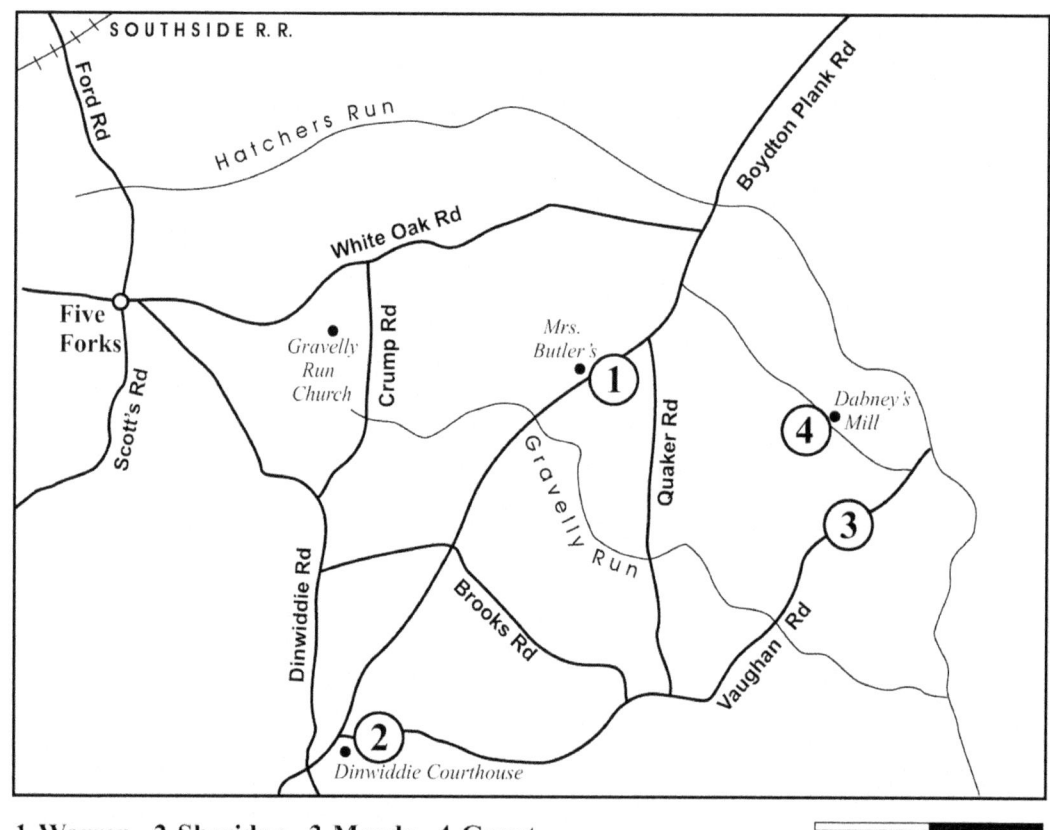

1-Warren 2-Sheridan 3-Meade 4-Grant

Map 5. Headquarters and Area of Operations, March 31–April 1.

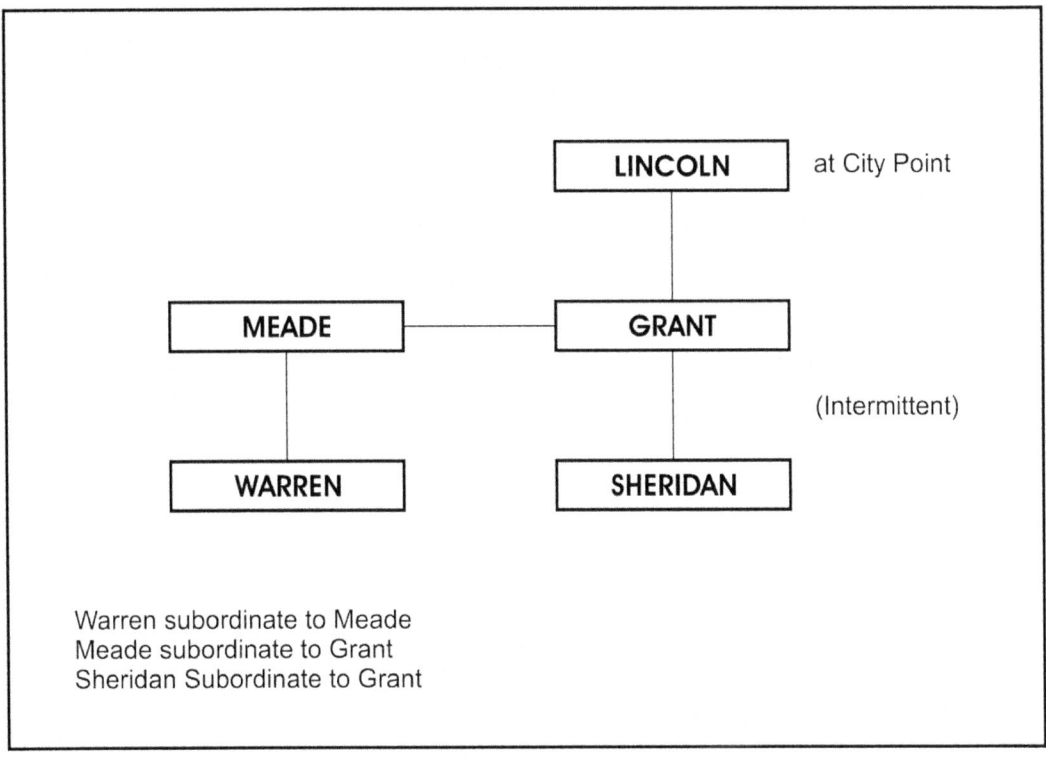

Figure 1. Five Forks—telegraphic connections of the Union.

operation, Sheridan's force was under the command of Grant, while the force of Warren and Andrew A. Humphreys would operate under the command of Meade. Hence, Sheridan's telegraph was connected to Grant's headquarters, while Warren's was connected to Meade's. At no time during the operation were Grant's and Meade's headquarters in the same place, but they were connected by telegraph. As the plan proceeded, both Meade and Grant moved their headquarters closer to the scene of action. The locations of the various headquarters the crucial night of March 31 are as indicated on map 5.

There were no wire connections between Warren and Sheridan, Warren and Grant, or between Meade and Sheridan. The wire connections were as indicated in figure 1.

Despite the fact that the movements of the Sheridan force and the Warren-Humphreys force were almost always within five miles of each other, the written operation orders for each called for no collaboration, cooperation, or contact. It was only on the eve of March 31, after Sheridan reported that he was confronted with a force larger than he could cope with, that Warren was ordered to send assistance to Sheridan.

Chapter 3

The Fifth Corps

At the outset of the Civil War, the U.S. Regular Army was tiny and the largest component was the regiment. A regiment was composed of twelve companies of one hundred men each. The regiment was commanded by a colonel and the companies by captains.

With the creation of the huge new U.S. Volunteer Army to put down the rebellion, it was immediately evident that the new army required a new organizational structure. Regiments were modified. The new volunteer regiments consisted of ten rather than twelve companies. As before, a regiment was commanded by a colonel and the companies by captains.

The regiments were then gathered into brigades. A brigade consisted of at least three regiments and was commanded by a brigadier general. The brigades were then gathered into divisions. A division consisted of at least three brigades and was commanded by a major general. The divisions were then gathered into an army, which in the North was commanded by a senior major general and in the South by a full general. Why the difference? The North still adhered to the tradition that no officer could be senior to George Washington, and George Washington was not a full general but a lieutenant general. Consequently, the top hierarchy of the Union army consisted of major generals of varying seniority.

The U.S. Volunteer Army at the beginning lacked an intermediary organization between division and army level, that is, the corps. Corps had become common in European armies since the time of Napoleon, but the young general in chief of the U.S. Volunteer Army, George B. McClellan, resisted their establishment for some time. He was reluctant to put so much authority in the hands of a subordinate, fearing that if the wrong man were chosen for the job, he could bring disaster on the whole. However, it soon became evident that corps were essential and they first appeared in 1862, de facto and finally de jure.

A corps usually consisted of three divisions: an artillery component, a cavalry detachment, and detachments of engineers, medical personnel, and transportation. In short, a corps was a self-sufficient unit, a smaller replica of an army. As of the time of their original formation in the volunteer army in 1862, a corps contained about 25,000 men. Thus, a corps commander was indeed an important figure, and many corps commander's names are familiar to this day, even to those who are not Civil War buffs. "Stonewall" Jackson, James Longstreet, and Winfield Scott Hancock were all corps commanders.

Now let us look at some of the advantages of the corps. If Meade's U.S. Volunteer Army at the time of Gettysburg were advancing on a single road, it would extend for over fifty miles. Sufficient supplies could not be brought up the road to feed it, and if it were attacked in front, it could not reinforce itself from the rear for two days. Corps, being self-contained units of all arms, could advance or retreat, subsist by different routes, and only unite to fight.

Another great advantage of the corps is that it greatly simplified an army commander's problem of controlling his forces. It did this by limiting the number of individuals who had direct contact with the army commander. He could now issue orders and receive reports from three, four, or five subordinates versus nine, twelve, fifteen, or more. Let us cite some specific examples of the advantages of the corps.

In 1862 during McClellan's Peninsular Campaign, his supply base was at White House north of the Chickahominy River, and Richmond, his objective, to its south. When the main theater of operations moved to the south of the Chickahominy for McClellan's attack on Richmond, he considered it necessary to detach a force to operate north of the river to protect his supply base. The size and nature of the force required was more than two divisions plus artillery and cavalry. Had there been no corps, he would have had to create an ad hoc corps of disparate units that had never worked as a single entity, and its senior officer and commander would have a staff that had no experience in controlling more than his own division. As it were, McClellan simply dispatched the Fifth Corps for the task. (See figure 2.)

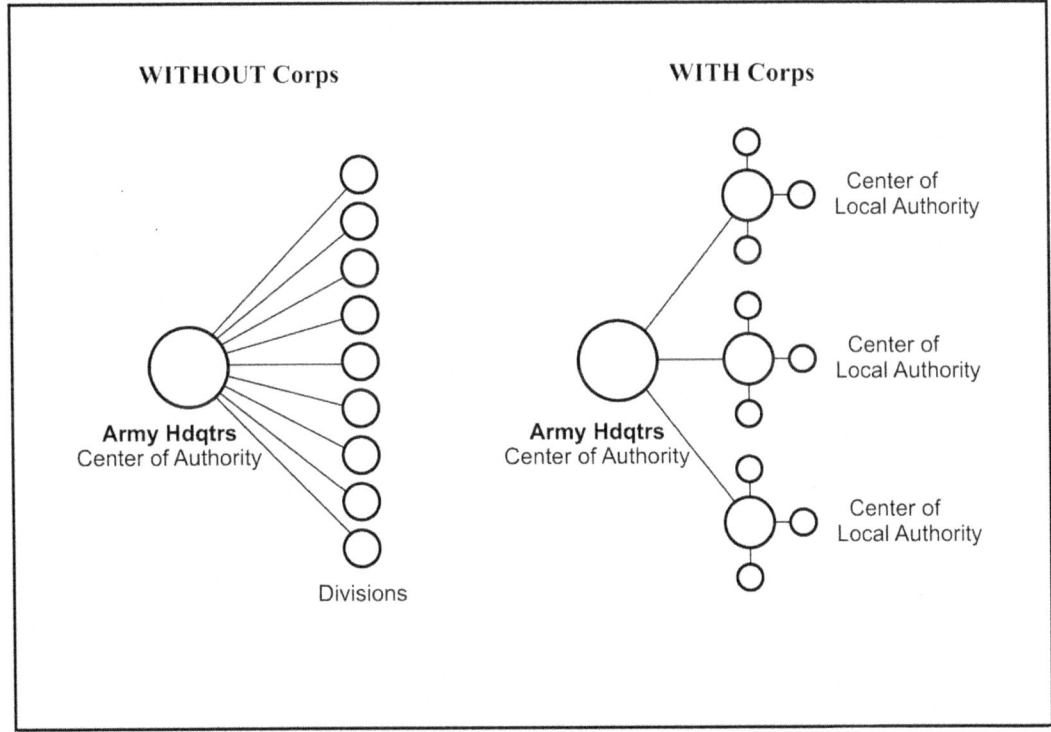

Figure 2. The Advantage of Corps.

Had there been no corps at Gettysburg, General Meade would have had the following reporting directly to him: nineteen division commanders, three cavalry commanders, and seven artillery brigade commanders. Inasmuch as there was little telegraphy use at Gettysburg, and commands and reports were by courier, each courier would have had to cover the distance from his unit to army headquarters rather than to a nearby corps headquarters.

For a third example of the necessity of corps, let us look at the Fifth Corps' battle at the White Oak Road, which is covered in this book. The Fifth Corps headquarters telegraph was connected to Meade's army headquarters by wire, and Meade controlled the battle by telegraph. Even this single circuit was often overloaded. What if there had been no corps and Meade had to control the three divisions that composed the Fifth Corps each directly? This immediately poses a number of questions. Would there now be a separate telegraph wagon at each division connected to headquarters? If not, and there was but a single field telegraph wagon connected to headquarters, whose would it be? Where would it be?

The Fifth Corps of the Army of the Potomac was permanently established on May 18, 1862, as "V Corps Provisional." On July 22, 1862, the "provisional" was dropped and the War Department confirmed it as "The V Corps of the Army of the Potomac."

The Fifth Corps' original composition incorporated almost the entire peace time army of the United States. Thus, it was more professional than the other corps and was looked upon as a model for all others.

The Fifth Corps participated in McClellan's Peninsular Campaign, the second battle of Bull Run, the battles of Antietam, Fredericksburg, Gettysburg, Bristoe Station, and all the battles of Grant's final campaign from the Wilderness to Appomattox. Its final commander, General Charles Griffin, was present in Wilmer McLean's house at the surrender.

The Fifth Corps had a number of Civil War luminaries as its commander, including General Fitz John Porter and General Meade, but the general who served the longest was Gouverneur Warren, who was commanding general just short of one year. The full complement of the corps at the time Warren assumed command was about 25,000, but the number was reduced to about 17,000 or less by the time of Five Forks due to unreplaced casualties.

When General Hooker assumed command of the Army of the Potomac in the spring of 1863, he assigned each of the corps a symbol to be worn on each man's uniform. This was to enhance esprit de corps. The symbol assigned to the Fifth Corps was the straight-edged variant of the Maltese Cross (see figure 3).

The corps underwent a series of reorganizations during the years, but for Warren's entire tenure, it consisted of three infantry divisions and an artillery brigade. The artillery brigade consisted of six four-gun batteries. Two batteries were three-inch rifles and four were twelve-pound smooth bores (Napoleons). The three infantry divisions were commanded by Brigadier Generals Charles Griffin (1), Romeyn B. Ayres (2), and Samuel W. Crawford (3). The artillery brigade was commanded by Brigadier General Charles Wainwright. Crawford was the senior division commander and hence second in command to Warren.

Warren, Ayres, and Griffin all knew each other as young men and were at West

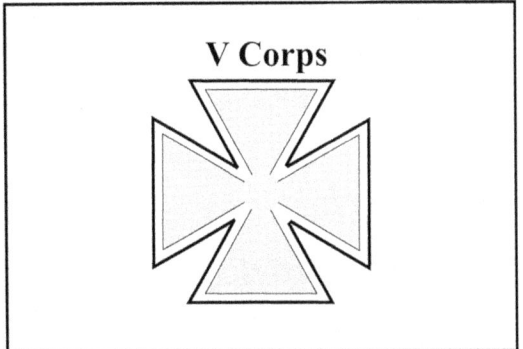

Above: **Figure 3. Fifth Corps Symbol, The Maltese Cross.** *Right:* **Colonel Fred T. Locke, U.S. Volunteer Army, longtime chief of staff, Fifth Corps.**

Point at the same time. Ayres and Griffin graduated in the class of 1847 and Warren in the class of 1850. Crawford and Wainwright did not attend West Point.

Strangely enough, Warren was junior to all three of his subordinate division commanders in the regular army. When the war ended and the U.S. Volunteer Army was disbanded and all reverted to their regular army ranks, the situation would be reversed and Warren would become the junior.

One other important person in the Fifth Corps that we have not mentioned is Colonel Fred Locke. Locke had been the chief of staff of the Fifth Corps since its inception and was an outstanding staff officer. It was Locke and not Warren who normally signed the orders to Griffin, Ayres, Crawford and Wainwright.

There is one last oddity regarding the Fifth Corps that we will mention. The two most famous courtroom dramas involving Union Civil War generals were the court-martial of Fitz John Porter and the court of inquiry of Gouverneur Warren. Both were serving as commanding general of the Fifth Corps at the time of the incidents that produced the courts.

Chapter 4

An Overview of the Execution of Grant's Plan

To determine whether Warren was done an injustice by being relieved on the battlefield of Five Forks on April 1, 1865, one must have an intimate knowledge of the events unfolding between March 29, when the campaign started, and its culmination at Five Forks on April 1. To gain such an understanding, we will start by presenting a simplified overview and then address the details.

Up to March 27, the Union siege forces and Confederate defense forces south of the Appomattox River were in a deadlock. The Confederate earth defenses, although manned by inferior numbers, were simply too strong to be broken by direct assault. The Confederate defense line naturally extended farther west than the opposing Union lines, so as to prevent the Union forces from simply flanking the Confederate position. The extension of the Confederate line beyond the Union line was approximately four miles, and almost midway in this extension, the Boydton Plank Road entered the Confederate line from the south. The retention of this road by the Confederates was important inasmuch as the Boydton Plank Road was the only paved road, and hence all-weather road, still entering the Confederate line from the south.

On March 27, Grant acquired additional troops while the Confederates had to make do with what they had. The new troops consisted of 35,000 to 40,000 troops from General Edward Ord's Army of the James and Sheridan's troops from the Army of the Shenandoah.

Ord's troops were to relieve the Fifth and Second Corps from their positions in the line, freeing them for mobile warfare. The Fifth and Second Corps were then to march west and extend the Union line beyond the present terminus of the Confederate line, forcing the Confederates to make a commensurate extension of their line, which could only be accomplished by thinning its ranks. In the meantime, Sheridan would command an all cavalry force that would move west, parallel but south of the Fifth-Second Corps force, so as to threaten the railway connections entering the Confederate line from the south. This would compel the Confederates to send troops south, outside of their earthwork defenses, to stop Sheridan. This would further thin the Confederate defenses.

The Union plan was of such magnitude that it could not escape the attention of the Confederate commander, General Lee. He knew its general thrust from the start and took measures to counter it. He planned to stop the western movement of both Union forces before they reached the White Oak Road (see map 3). He would do this by thinning the line to accumulate two mobile forces that would operate south of the main Confederate defense line. The first of these, headed by himself, would be located on the White Oak Road just south of the Confederate defense line, and stop the westward movement of the Warren-Humphreys force before it hit the White Oak Road. The second force would be commanded by General George E. Pickett and would be located four miles farther down the White Oak Road at Five Forks and would stop Sheridan short of the railroad and hopefully destroy his force. The crucial day would be Friday, March 31, 1865.

There was one great danger in Lee's Plan. The northern force on the White Oak Road commanded by him and the southern force commanded by General Pickett were separated from each other by four miles and connected only by cavalry vedettes. If the northern force failed to stop the westward movement of the Warren-Humphreys force, and it crossed the White Oak road, the southern force under Pickett would be isolated from the main Confederate defense line.

The kickoff date for Grant's plan was to be Wednesday, March 29, 1865. Warren would move out first at 3 a.m. Warren commanded the forward force and would necessarily do most of the fighting and suffer most of the casualties. The last we encountered Humphreys, he was Meade's chief of staff. However, Hancock, the normal commander of the Second Corps, was again infirm and Humphreys substituted for him. Of the two friends, Warren and Humphreys, Humphreys was a generation older than Warren and far senior to him in the regular army. However, Warren was senior to Humphreys in the Volunteer Army, and that is what counted as long as the war continued.

The kickoff time for the operation was 3 a.m., March 29, 1865, when the Fifth Corps was scheduled to move out. Reveille, of course, was at least an hour earlier, so that the troops got little if any sleep that night. It was commonly known that they were going into action and if there was any sleep, it must have been fitful, as each man knew that he may be heading for his last sunrise.

The starting point for the march was near where the City Point Railroad met the Weldon Railroad. Here was a supply dump, and it was to here that the corps' supply wagons must return for reloads once they had exhausted their cargoes. A beautiful spring day dawned warm and pleasant. The roads were drying, the violets and daffodils and forsythias were blooming, and it appeared that, weather-wise, Grant had won in picking the start date.

There was no single east-west road that Warren's troops could follow to extend their lines westward beyond that of the Confederates. They had to use what was available to move westward, that is south-west, north-west, etc. When Warren's troops departed, they were accompanied by six batteries of artillery, wagons carrying one hundred feet of bridging material, plus ambulances and supply wagons. They used most of their bridging material to cross Rowanty Creek early in the morning. By late morning, they were heading northwest up the Quaker Road, which angled into the Boydton Plank Road just about one mile south of the presumed location of the main Confederate defense line (see map 6). About noon they came to a place where the Quaker Road crossed Gravelly Run, a small stream, but the bridge was down. The infantry were able to scramble across

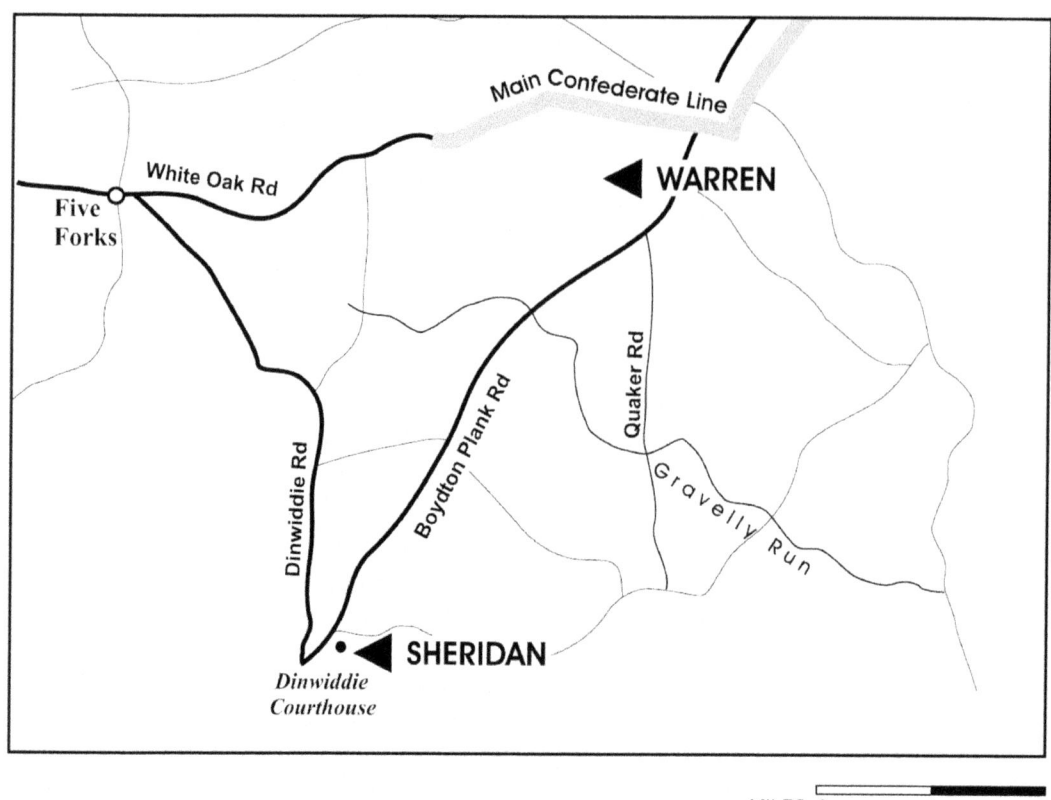

Map 6. Dark, March 29, 1865.

the stream, but Warren had to use the remainder of his bridging to permit the artillery to cross. They were now within less than two miles from where the Quaker Road merged with the vital Boydton Plank Road. As yet they had encountered no real opposition, only an occasional single shot from a picket here and there.

Between 3 and 4 p.m. Warren encountered the enemy in line of battle across the Quaker Road just before it entered the Boydton Plank Road. Here was a real fight for the first time, and it continued for almost two hours until the enemy withdrew up the Boydton Plank Road to the safety of their main line. Warren's casualties were 370 killed and wounded.

Warren's men entered the Boydton Plank Road and, from this point to the end of the war, it was of no further use to the Confederates. Warren determined that the main Confederate line crossed the Plank road just a short distance north of where he had entered it from the Quaker Road. He also ascertained that the bridge on the Plank Road over Gravelly Run, just a short distance south of him, had been destroyed. His next move was to continue on to the west parallel to the main Confederate line so, at the time, he made no attempt to repair the bridge. It was now getting dark and he prepared to hunker down for the night. He deployed Crawford's division across the road facing the main Confederate east-west defense line, and kept Ayres's division in reserve on the Quaker Road where it could quickly reinforce either of the others. The fatigued troops

4. An Overview of the Execution of Grant's Plan

now looked forward to a hot meal and a well-earned rest. As the evening progressed, it began to drizzle, then rain, and then to pour unrelentingly. It was to be a miserable night.

As the rain poured down, Gravelly Run, which lay between Warren's and Sheridan's forces, began to rise. The downed bridge on the Plank Road became ever more important. Come morning, in accordance with the plan, Warren intended to continue sliding west to the point where the White Oak Road turned from east-west to south-west. This was approximately the point where the main Confederate defense line terminated and precisely the point where Lee intended to stop Warren. It was only about one and one half miles away (see map 7). The total Fifth Corps casualties for Wednesday, March 29, were 381, including fifty-three killed.

Sheridan's Movements on Wednesday, March 29

General Sheridan's command on the morning of Wednesday, March 29, consisted of the first and third cavalry divisions that he had brought from the Shenandoah, both under the command of General Wesley Merritt, and the second cavalry division, which

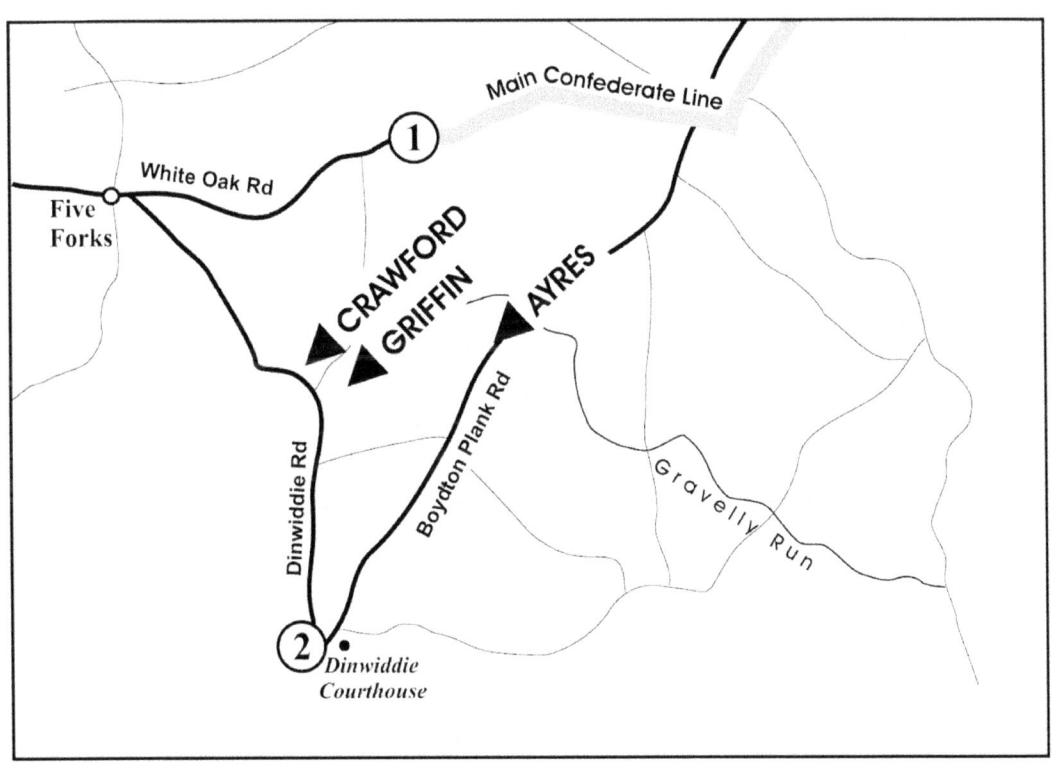

1-Battle of White Oak Road
2-Battle of Dinwiddie Courthouse

Map 7. Night of March 31–April 1, Transfer of Fifth Corps to Sheridan.

had been serving as part of the Army of the Potomac. The total force was about 9,000. Sheridan operated directly under the command of Grant, while Warren's force operated under the command of Meade. Even though the two forces were on parallel courses westward, with Sheridan to the south, and usually no more than five miles apart, there was no requirement for either collaboration or even communications between the two.

Sheridan's starting point was close to that of Warren; that is, near the junction of the City Point Military Railroad and the Weldon Railroad. Sheridan's command was camped to the east of the Weldon Railroad and Warren's to the west.

Each of Sheridan's men carried five days' rations, thirty pounds of forage, and forty rounds of ammunition. Any replenishment had to come from the wagon train that followed the troops. The carrying of forty rounds of ammunition in one's cartridge box was more or less standard. When one considers that when in combat in line of battle, an individual could easily get off two shots a minute, forty rounds could last as little as twenty minutes.

Sheridan reached Dinwiddie Courthouse on the Boydton Plank Road at about 5 p.m. without having encountered any significant opposition. Thus, as of this time both Sheridan and Warren were on the Plank Road, with Warren about five miles north of Sheridan and the two separated by the downed bridge over Gravelly Run.

Sheridan went into bivouac at this point, with his troops deployed to cover all roads intersecting at Dinwiddie Courthouse, including the road to Five Forks, on the White Oak Road, his next destination.

Warren's and Sheridan's Movements on Thursday, March 30, 1865

Warren's and Sheridan's troops woke up on Thursday, March 30, to what can be best described as a mess. It had rained all night and was to continue all day. Little movement was possible, and much time and effort was devoted to corduroying roads.

General Merritt stated, "The roads were in a horrible condition, and it was found impossible for the wagon trains to reach the point made by the cavalry during the day, in fact the wagon trains did not get up until the third day, it being necessary to corduroy almost the entire road over which the march was made."[1] Lieutenant Colonel Theodore Lyman of Meade's staff said: "Heavy rains ... reduced the roads, already poor, to a hopeless, Sunday pudding! Gravelly Run was swelled to treble its usual size."[2] And lastly, Grant sent the following to Lincoln: "The quicksands in this section exceed anything I have ever seen. Roads have to be corduroyed in front of team and artillery as they advance. We were 50 hours moving 600 teams five miles with 1200 men to help them."[3]

Little movement was possible on Thursday, March 30, 1865. Warren's and Sheridan's tired troops suffered in that they could not light fires to provide a hot meal or even a cup of coffee.

To the north, Warren pushed his corps slowly westward with Ayres in the lead. By late in the day, Ayres could plainly see the White Oak Road as it turned off to the southwest, away from the main east-west Confederate defense line. Ayres observed Confederate troops marching down the White Oak Road toward Five Forks. These, of course, were Pickett's infantry, which had been dispatched to join Fitzhugh Lee's cavalry at Five Forks.

To the south, Sheridan sent Merritt's cavalry off on the road from Dinwiddie Courthouse to Five Forks. Merritt quickly encountered Confederate cavalry, and in the ensuing skirmishing suffered 150 casualties. Warren's total casualties for the day were thirteen, four killed and nine wounded.

The Union troops were dog tired and miserable. Warren's had little to no sleep on the night of 28–29, marched and fought during the day of the 29th, spent the night of 29–30 in the rain and mud, moved little on the 30th but were unable to light fires because of the rain to make a hot meal, and would now spend another night in the rain and mud. Both Warren's and Sheridan's supply trains lagged far behind as the roads were slowly corduroyed before them. Tomorrow, March 31, boded ill for the Union forces north and south, as both forces had now reached the point wherein Lee had decided they would go no farther.

The rain continued during the morning of Friday, March 31, 1865. Warren slowly organized his forces for a move to the White Oak Road, just at the point where it turned to the southwest away from the main Confederate defense line. At about 10:30 a.m. his three divisions were in echelon with about one half mile separating the line of battle of each division. Ayres was closest to the White Oak Road, next came Crawford, and then Griffin. Griffin's position was the strongest because it was posted behind a branch of Gravelly Run. They were prepared for advance, but the enemy struck first.

Ayres was routed, then Crawford. But Griffin held and Ayers and Crawford rallied and formed behind Griffin.

Preparations were at once initiated by Warren for a counterattack. Although his losses were significant, they had not been disastrous, and Warren considered that the situation was no worse than he had experienced several times previously in the war.

By 1:45 p.m. the rain had stopped and the counterattack was delivered. It succeeded and by about 3 p.m. Warren had pushed almost 300 yards beyond the White Oak Road. Pickett's force to the south was now isolated from the main Confederate defense line.

Surprisingly, it was Warren's handling of his troops during the attack by the Confederates and the counterattack by Warren that dissatisfied Grant and ultimately caused him to allow Sheridan to dismiss Warren. Grant thought Warren should not have allowed the Confederates to attack his divisions one after the other; Warren should have brought all three divisions into action at the same time. Up to this time, Warren's operations were completely independent of those of Sheridan.

Shortly after 5 p.m. Warren heard the rattle of musketry to his south. It was clear that Sheridan was engaged by the enemy. The sound of the musketry trailed off to Warren's southeast, and it was clear that Sheridan was being pushed back. At this point, Warren, on his own initiative, ordered one of his brigades to proceed due south overland to strike in the flank and rear the Confederates that were pushing Sheridan back. Warren had no sooner issued the order than he received one from Meade ordering him to do just that.

Now, let us turn to see what was transpiring with Sheridan, five miles to the south of Warren, during the day of March 31. Sheridan's wagon train had still not arrived at Dinwiddie on the morning of the 31st. Desultory fighting between the Union and Confederate cavalry before Five Forks continued throughout the morning. During the afternoon, Confederate infantry entered the fray and pushed Sheridan back to Dinwiddie Courthouse. In Sheridan's account of the action, he incorrectly concluded that the infantry that now appeared on his front was the same that had driven Warren back, and hence was available to march the four miles down the White Oak road and confront him. In fact, the infantry that drove Warren back was separate and distinct from Pickett's force at Five Forks.

Between 6 and 7 p.m. when fighting ceased for the day, Sheridan sent Grant a report of the day's fighting. Up to the last three lines, it was self-serving and appeared that he had nothing but success. However, the last three lines read: "This force is too strong for us. I will hold out to Dinwiddie Court House until I am compelled to leave. Our fighting today was all dismounted."[4]

The bottom line was that Sheridan had been pushed back and needed help. Up to this point, we had two distinct operations under two commanders: Warren-Humphreys under Meade, and Sheridan under Grant. Now it was clear that Sheridan needed help and it could only come from Warren-Humphreys. The thinking and consultations of Grant and Meade gradually evolved from "How can we save Sheridan?" to "How can we destroy Pickett?" Initially it was decided to send one of Warren's divisions down the Boydton Plank Road to help Sheridan. This evolved into a decision to send Warren's whole corps down to Sheridan to unite under Sheridan and destroy Pickett. The plan was thus: inasmuch as Pickett had pushed Sheridan back to Dinwiddie Courthouse, he was actually east of Warren above him. The plan then was to send one division down the Boydton Plank Road to join Sheridan and to send the other two divisions straight south so that they would appear in Pickett's rear. Thus, Pickett would be sandwiched in between the two forces and destroyed (see map 7).

Having finalized the plan in his mind, Grant sent the following message to Sheridan:

Dabney's Mill, Mar 31 1865 10:05 p.m.

Major General Sheridan:

The Fifth Corps has been ordered to your support. Two divisions will go by J. Boisseau's and one down the Boydton road. In addition to this I have sent MacKenzie's Cavalry which will reach you by the Vaughn Road. All these forces should reach you by 12 tonight. You will assume command of the whole force sent to operate with you, and use it to the best of your ability to destroy the force which your command has fought so gallantly today.

U. S. Grant[5]

The supposition that Warren's divisions would arrive at "12 tonight" was total fantasy. This was in no way possible. The division that was to march down the Boydton Plank Road had to cross Gravelly Run and the bridge was down and the grossly swollen creek impassable without it. Warren had to rebuild the bridge during the night and he had no bridging material. To get the materials, he had to disassemble a house before he even started on the bridge.

The other two divisions that were to march to the southeast and appear in Pickett's rear were bedded down within sight and sound of the enemy. They had to disengage, and that without the aid of bugle or drum.

Once disengaged, they had to proceed to the southeast, through the mud, without benefit of a surfaced road, in the dark for four to five miles. To exacerbate the situation, they were already exhausted and hungry, not having the benefit of a good night's rest nor a hot meal since the campaign began.

Although Warren had received the order to move the two divisions before 11 p.m. on the 31st, he did not order the move to begin until after daylight on April 1. Warren's three divisions reported in to Sheridan on the Dinwiddie Road the morning of April 1. We were now ready for the battle of Five Forks.

The Battle of Five Forks

The Confederates in front of Dinwiddie, detecting Union forces coming down from the north in their rear, withdrew to Five Forks. At Five Forks, they established a defense line about three-fourths of a mile along the White Oak Road with the vital Ford Road radiating out to the north from the center of the defense line. One mile up the Ford Road was Hatchers Run, which ran roughly parallel to the White Oak Road. An additional one mile up the Ford Road was the vital Southside Railroad, which Pickett was directed to protect.

Pickett refused the left flank of his line on the White Oak Road. That is, he bent it back at roughly a right angle to protect the flank. The length of the refuse was roughly 300 feet. Pickett's men then threw up a barrier along the main line and the refuse. The barrier consisted of earth and logs and was roughly waist height. They also cleared the foliage in front of the line and refuse for about fifty feet to give the men behind the barrier a field of fire. Pickett placed his five brigades of infantry behind the barrier in the following order from west to east: Montgomery D. Corse, Joseph Mayo, George H. Steuart, William H. Wallace, and Matthew W. Ransom. He placed W.H.F. Lee's cavalry division on his right flank and that of Thomas T. Munford on his left flank; that is, the one with the refuse. He moved his wagon train up the Ford Road to the far side of Hatchers Run, and he placed Thomas L. Rosser's cavalry division there to protect it.

About noon, Rosser invited Pickett and Fitzhugh Lee, the two senior Confederate officers, to a shad bake at his headquarters. Both accepted, and were thus north of Hatchers Run and out of touch with events when the battle erupted.

Before we treat the Battle of Five Forks, let us look at the terrain over which it was fought (see map 8). The main feature was woods. The entire area was covered with woods except for four cleared areas, two south of the White Oak Road, and two north of the White Oak Road.

Of the two cleared areas south of the White Oak Road, we come first to the area around Gravelly Run Church. Here was a cleared area sufficiently large to hold the entire Fifth Corps deployed in line of battle. The area was just south and east of the left flank of the Confederate line, but was not visible to the Confederates because of trees. The other cleared area south of the Confederate line on the White Oak Road was the Gillian farm. The Gillian farm was located south of the opposite end of the Confederate line. The so-called Gillian field extended northward to the Confederate line, and eastward to the Five Forks junction. North of the Confederate line on the White Oak Road, that

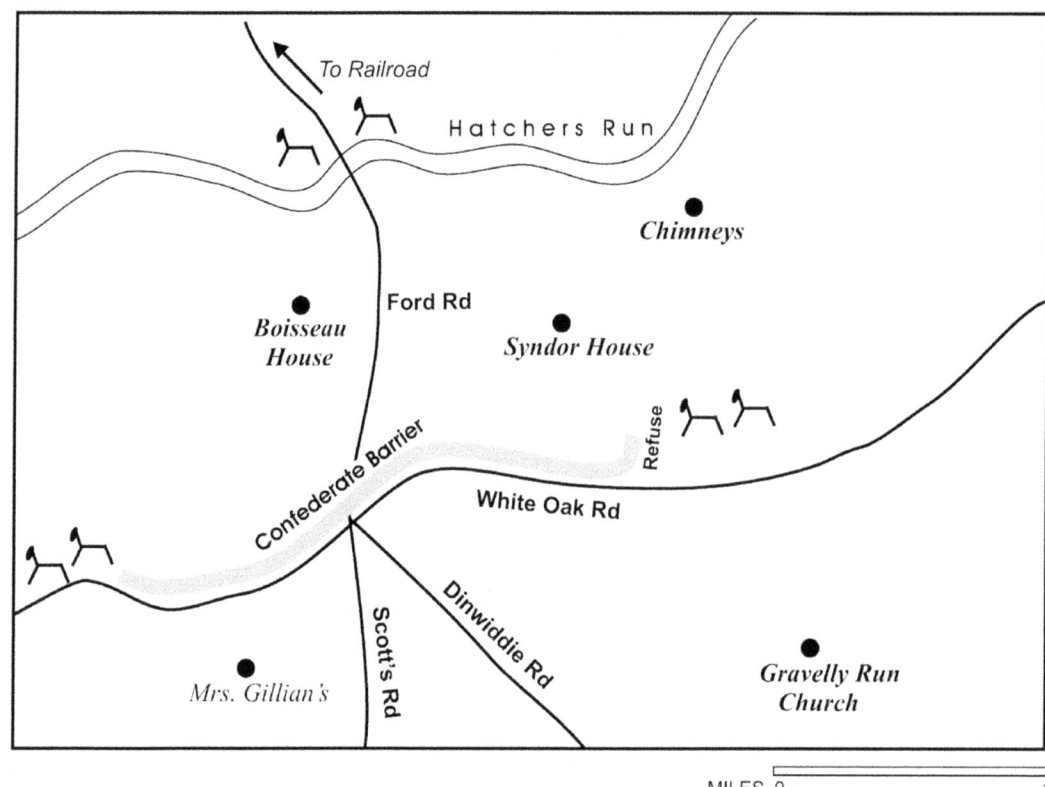

Map 8. Five Forks Battlefield.

is, between the White Oak Road and Hatchers Run, were two farms. One, the so-called Syndor or Snydor farm, was to the east of the Ford Road, and the other, the so-called Boisseau farm, was to the west of the Ford Road. Each farm house was surrounded by a cleared area of about one hundred acres. One last feature on the battlefield was the so-called "Chimneys." This was the remains of a house to the northeast of the Syndor house.

Sheridan's cavalry followed the retiring force of Confederates down to Five Forks and then took up a position paralleling the Confederate defense line.

The entire Fifth Corps arrived at the Five Forks–Dinwiddie Road and reported to Sheridan the morning of April 1. Sheridan now had his entire augmented force—his own cavalry division and the three infantry divisions of the Fifth Corps. This gave him a total force of 22,000 men. This was two to three times the number of men Pickett possessed. Sheridan now developed his plan of attack. He would keep his cavalry facing the line along the White Oak Road. He would gather and deploy the Fifth Corps in the open space at Gravelly Run Church. Gravelly Run Church was just beyond the refuse in Pickett's line, but out of sight because of the trees. He would deploy the Fifth Corps as shown in figure 4, with Ayres on the left and Crawford and Griffin on the right.

The corps would march obliquely to the angle of the refuse and Crawford and Griffin would strike it. The corps would then wheel so that it was perpendicular to the White Oak Road and roll up the Confederate line. In the meantime, his cavalry would attack from the front (see figure 5).

Things turned out differently than planned. The Fifth Corps marched off to the attack at about 4 p.m. This gave Sheridan less than three hours to complete his destruction of Pickett's force before darkness. When the Fifth Corps hit the White Oak Road, there was nothing there. Sheridan had been misinformed as to where the Confederate line with its refuse was. It was several hundred feet to the left. The Confederates in the refuse fired into Ayres' flank (see figure 6). Ayres's division alone wheeled, confronted the refuse, charged, and carried it. Meanwhile, Crawford, followed by Griffin, marched off to the northeast, away from the battle.

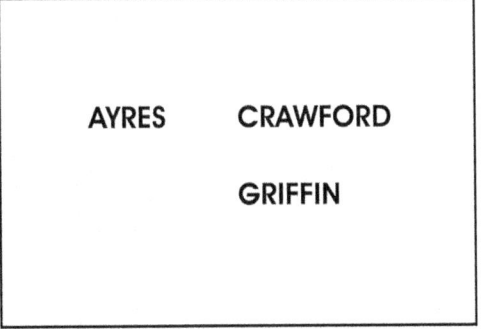

Figure 4. Deployment of Ayres, Crawford, and Griffin.

Sheridan was furious. Both he and Warren sent staff members chasing after Crawford and Griffin to re-orient them back to the battle area. Warren finally chased after them in person while Sheridan remained with Ayres at the fighting.

Griffin was soon turned back and formed an extension of Ayres's line. Crawford made a wide circle all the way up to Hatchers Run and was finally turned down the Ford Road to strike the Confederates in the rear (see map 9).

The Confederates made three organized attempts to stop the Union onslaught as Ayres, aided by cavalry, marched down the White Oak Road rolling up the Confederate line. First, the Confederates pulled Steuart's brigade out of line and formed it perpendicular to the White Oak Road just east of Five Forks to stop the

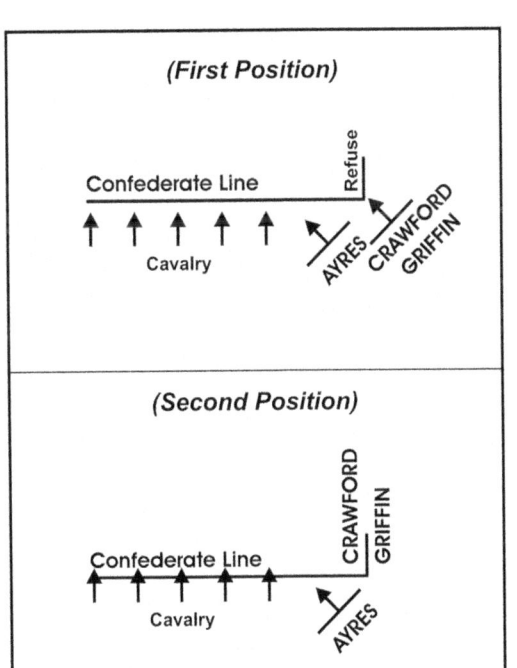

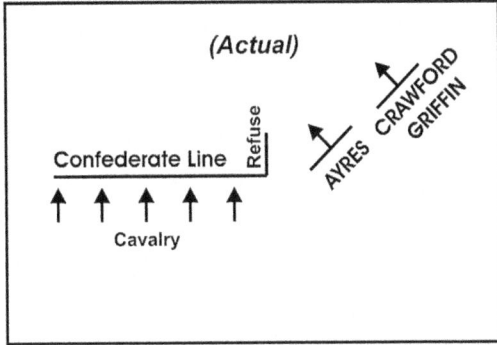

Left: **Figure 5. Planned first and second positions.** *Right:* **Figure 6. Actual position.**

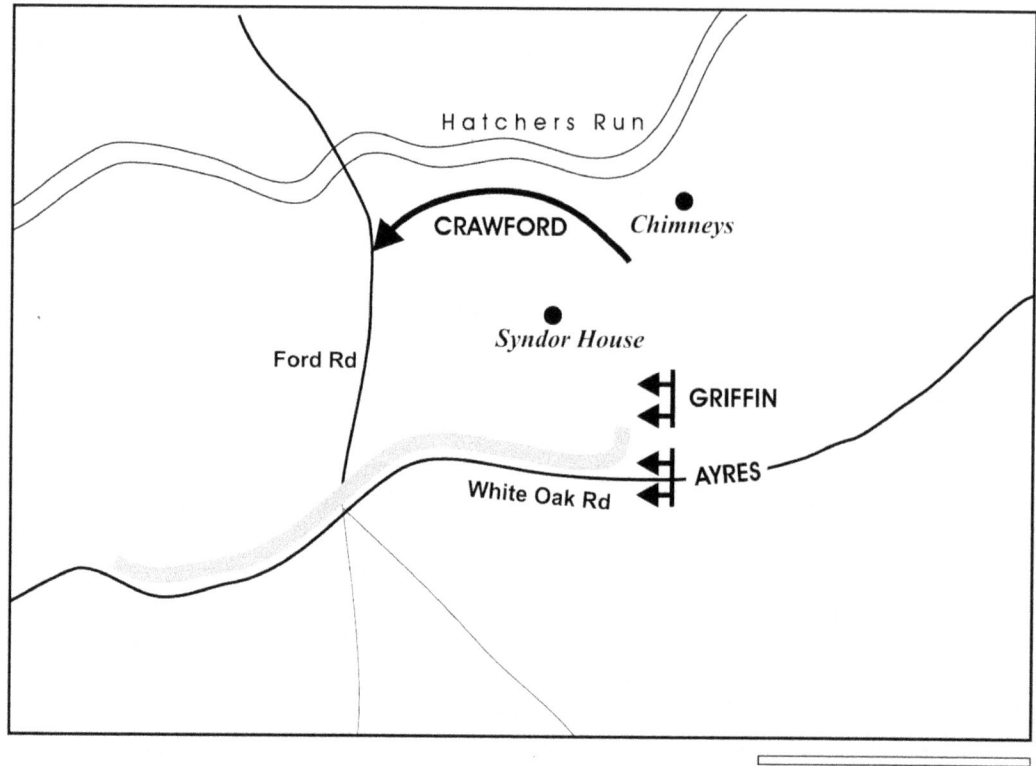

Map 9. Movements of Crawford, Griffin, and Ayres in the Battle of Five Forks.

Union onrush. It held for about an hour, but it soon was receiving fire from three sides—from the cavalry to the south, from Ayres's augmented by cavalry from the east, and from Griffin, who overlapped Steuart's line to the north. Steuart's line then collapsed. The next, and perhaps simultaneous, attempt to preserve the Confederate position involved Mayo's brigade. He was pulled out of line and sent up the Ford Road to stop the oncoming Crawford in the Confederate rear. His line collapsed before it was fully formed. The last attempt was by Corse's brigade, which formed west of Five Forks perpendicular to the White Oak Road. It too quickly collapsed. In short, the Confederates were simply overwhelmed by the greatly superior Union forces (see map 10).

The total battle lasted less than three hours, from about 4 p.m. to shortly after 6:30 p.m. The outcome was predictable—a Confederate disaster. The result was inevitable. The Confederates were outnumbered by two or three to one and the position that they were required to hold was poorly selected. Defeatism had already permeated the rebel ranks, and desertions had increased alarmingly. The final casualties were: Union, 830; Confederates, 2950, the great majority prisoners.

Sheridan spent his entire time during the battle with Ayres's force, fighting its way through the refuse and thence down the White Oak Road. Warren spent his entire time during the battle first overtaking Griffin and re-orienting him to the battle, and then overtaking Crawford and accompanying him down the Ford Road to strike the Confederates in the rear.

4. An Overview of the Execution of Grant's Plan

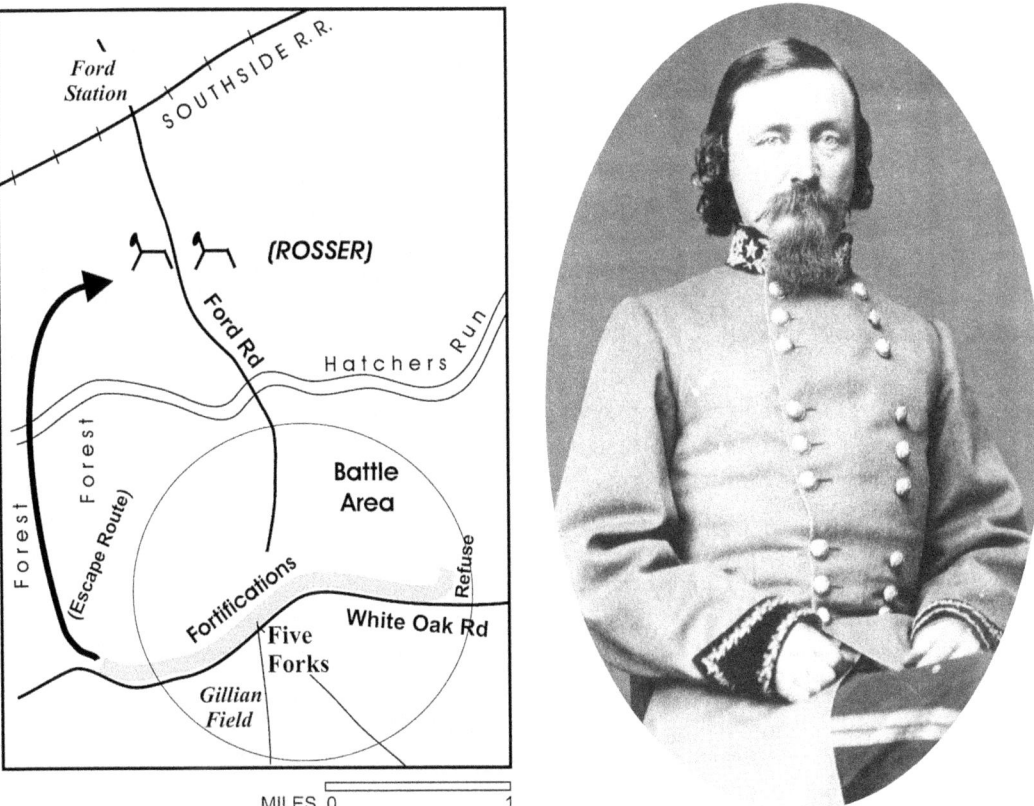

Left: **Map 10. Confederate retreat route at Five Forks.** *Right:* **Major General George Pickett, Confederate commander at Five Forks.**

It was after 6 p.m.—when the battle, to all intents and purposes, had already been won by the Union—that Sheridan sent a message to Warren by courier to the effect that Warren had been relieved of command.

General George Pickett, the Confederate commander, missed most of the battle. Prior to noon he had been invited to a shad bake at General Rosser's headquarters. At the time, Rosser was entrusted with protecting Pickett's wagon park, which was located up the Ford Road beyond Hatchers Run, one to two miles from the battle area. The sound of battle failed to reach Pickett and Rosser, and the Confederate force was already in its death throes when Pickett finally reached the scene. Pickett himself eluded capture and managed to return to Lee's lines.

Pickett thus became the central figure in the two greatest fiascoes of the Army of Northern Virginia: Pickett's Charge at Gettysburg and then at Five Forks. In both instances, Pickett himself managed to emerge unscathed. One would thus expect that history would treat him unkindly. However, largely as a result of the propagandizing of his young widow, who survived him by over fifty years, he has come down to us as the "Gallant Pickett."

Chapter 5

Why the Separation Between Warren's Divisions?

It is certain that Ayres, Griffin, and Crawford all understood Sheridan's plan. They were to form up with Ayres on the left and Crawford on the right in the front line with Griffin behind Crawford. The corps was then to advance obliquely to the White Oak Road with Crawford, followed by Griffin, hitting the angle of the refuse and main Confederate defense line on the White Oak Road. The corps was then to wheel to its left so as to become at a right angle to the White Oak Road and roll up the main Confederate line. Why then did the divisions become separated once they hit the White Oak Road with Crawford, followed by Griffin marching off to the north, and Ayres alone storming the refuse?

The corps' front, once it advanced, was almost three-fourths of a mile long. It is evident that, once it wheeled to the left, the man on Ayres's left would have little distance to cover and could move slowly, and the man on Crawford's right would have a large distance to cover and would have to move fast.

The end of the Confederate line, with its refuse, was not where Sheridan assumed it to be, but several hundred yards to the west. Consequently, the entire Fifth Corps hit the White Oak Road to the east of the refuse, and Ayres received a withering fire into his left flank from the refuse. Accordingly, he, who was to wheel slowly, was compelled to wheel rapidly so as to face the refuse.

Sheridan further assumed that there were no Confederate troops east of the refuse. He was wrong. General Munford's cavalry division was deployed to the east of the refuse, in the woods on the far side of the White Oak Road but parallel to it. Consequently, Crawford hit Munford head on and was thus unable to wheel fast to his left without exposing his flank to Munford. In summation, the left end of the Fifth Corps' front, which was supposed to wheel slowly, had to wheel fast; and the right end of his line, which was supposed to wheel fast, had to wheel slowly (see figure 7).

Now let us look at the problem of the individual brigades being required to keep "closed up" to the left (see figure 8). Upon crossing the White Oak Road, the entire formation entered a forest. Each man in line could see no farther than five to ten men at most on either of his sides. The distance between Ayres's and Crawford's front lines was far greater than that. John Kellogg's leftmost man could not see James Gwynn's rightmost man. Farther back in the formation, things got worse. It was over one-fourth of a mile between Richard Coulter's leftmost man and Frederick Winthrop's rightmost man. And farther back yet, there was absolutely no one at any distance on J.L. Chamberlain's or E.M. Gregory's left.

In short, the brigades on the right could not close on the brigades on the left by sight, in that they could not see them. In some cases, there was no brigade to the left to close on. Whatever shortcomings occurred in the execution of the plan were the fault of Sheridan and not Warren. It was the cavalry's responsibility to fix the position of the enemy, and the cavalry reported to Sheridan and not to Warren.

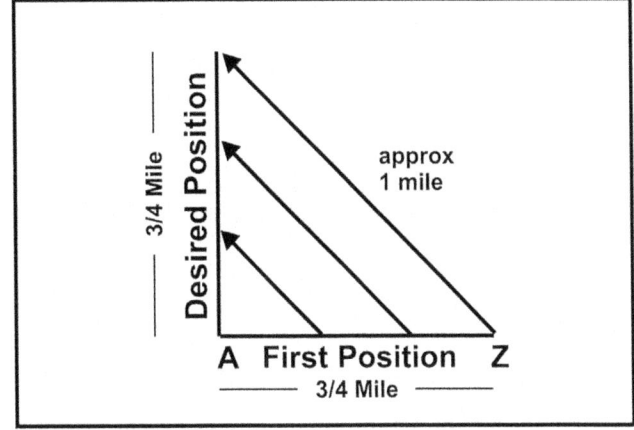

Top: **Figure 7. Changing Front.** *Right:* **Figure 8. Deployment at Gravelly Run Church.**

Chapter 6

Gouverneur Warren

On April 1, 1865, at the time of the battle of Five Forks, Gouverneur Warren was a thirty-five year old major general in the U.S. Volunteer Army and the commanding officer of the Fifth Corps of the Army of the Potomac. An army corps was the largest organizational unit short of an army, and at the time consisted of about 20,000 men.

Warren was not only a corps commander but, then and now, considered one of the best in the Union Volunteer Army. Thus, as of April 1, 1865, Warren was an important figure of national standing.

A number of Civil War corps commanders' names are readily recognizable today even to those who are not Civil War buffs. For example, what well-read person has not heard of "Stonewall" Jackson or James Longstreet? However, when the name Gouverneur Warren is mentioned to someone other than a Civil War buff, one is likely to draw the response, "Who?" Warren's personality was such that he just did not "click" with the national press.

Warren entered West Point in 1846 at the age of sixteen and quickly established himself as an unusually bright young man. He graduated in 1850, ranking second in a class of forty-four. Because of Warren's exalted academic standing, he was commissioned a second lieutenant in the prestigious Corps of Topographical Engineers. Warren's first superior in the corps was Captain Andrew Humphreys, a man almost twenty years older. Despite the age difference, Humphreys recognized the talent of his young subordinate and the two became lifelong friends. This friendship was to serve Warren well in later years.

The young Warren excelled in whatever assignment he received. He was entrusted with responsibilities including heading an exploration of the Badlands of

Major General Gouverneur Warren, commanding general of the Fifth Corps.

the Dakotas that now seem remarkable for a man of his age and rank. Warren even impressed the then secretary of war, Jefferson Davis, to the extent that Davis publicly commended him. This was, of course, the same Jefferson Davis who was to become the president of the Confederate States. Warren's greatest accomplishment in these pre-war years was probably the mapping of Nebraska and the Dakotas. Warren even succeeded in having a geographic feature named after him, the glacial "River Warren." This naming, however, was accomplished after Warren's death.

As war was brewing, and after nine years of topographic engineering work, Warren was assigned as mathematics professor at West Point. While at West Point, and while the U.S. Volunteer Army was being recruited to put down the rebellion, Warren assisted in recruiting a volunteer regiment called Duryees' Zouaves, and officially, the Fifth New York. Naturally, Abram Duryee, a prominent and wealthy New York businessman, was appointed its colonel, but Warren was appointed its lieutenant colonel. Warren, still a lieutenant in the regular army, received permission from the War Department to occupy the position of lieutenant colonel in the U.S. Volunteers.

Abram Duryee, the titular colonel, was not a professional army officer and left Warren to act as the de facto commanding officer. Now Warren, at the age of thirty-one, was the de facto commander of a 1,000 man unit. This is all the more remarkable when we look at the status of promotions in the pre-war regular army. There was no compulsory retirement system and promotions only opened up when a senior died, and sometimes it seemed that they never did. Colonels were invariably gray haired, and most career officers never reached that exalted rank at all.

Warren was more than up to the task. He excelled in all aspects of command—discipline, training, and supply. His regiment was soon recognized as one of the premier regiments of the volunteer army.

The Fifth New York participated in the first battle of the Civil War, that of Big Bethel on the York Peninsula. It was of a tiny scale but seemed big at the time. It was a Union disaster, although Warren was not at fault and performed well. Here, Warren was first to show the characteristics that ultimately proved his downfall. He was quick to criticize others and to offer unasked for advice. In the vernacular, Warren was a "know-it-all."

Warren's regiment was incorporated into McClellan's Army of the Potomac and conspicuously participated in McClellan's Peninsular Campaign. McClellan was impressed by Warren and the feeling was mutual.

Warren went from success to success. He participated prominently in the battle of Gaines Mill, where he was wounded. He was next a central figure in the Second Battle of Bull Run, where he was moved up from regiment to brigade command; he participated in the battle of Antietam and, at the age of thirty-two, was promoted to brigadier general in the U.S. Volunteers. Warren then participated in the battle of Fredericksburg, where he temporarily served as division commander.

When Hooker took command of the Army of the Potomac in 1863, he recognized Warren's talent as an engineer and appointed him chief topographer of the army, and later, chief engineer of the army. It was in this capacity that Warren made one of the greatest contributions to Union victory of his thus far illustrious career.

On the second day of the battle of Gettysburg, Warren, while inspecting the Union position, noted that Little Round Top was the key to the battlefield, was unoccupied, and was being approached by the Confederates. Had the Confederates occupied the hill, the whole Union defense line on Cemetery Ridge would be untenable and the prospects for a Confederate victory would move from good to excellent. Warren, although in command of no combat unit as a staff officer, ordered the nearest Union brigade to divert from its assigned mission and occupy the hill. This was accomplished moments before the Confederates arrived; the Union line held and went on to final victory the next day. Today, a giant statue of Warren stands on Little Round Top to immortalize the event.

General Meade took command of the Army of the Potomac from General Hooker just before the battle of Gettysburg. Meade, recognizing the young Warren's talents, offered Warren the position of his chief of staff. Warren declined, indicating that he preferred a combat command. As luck would have it, Meade later appointed Warren's old friend and mentor, Humphreys, who was now a major general of volunteers, to the position. It was inevitable that the relationship between the acerbic Meade and the sometimes insolent and arrogant Warren would be rocky, but now, with Humphreys, Warren would always have a "friend in the front office."

General Hancock, the commander of the Second Corps, was wounded in the battle of Gettysburg, and Meade, in response to Warren's request for a combat command, appointed Warren commander until such time as Hancock would return. Warren was so successful as corps commander that, when Hancock did return, Warren was appointed commander of the Fifth Corps. It was in this capacity that Warren met his Waterloo.

We will cover Warren's relationship with Meade further in the next section. First, let us look at a climactic event for the Army of the Potomac, the arrival of General Grant.

General Grant was promoted to lieutenant general and general in chief of all the armies in March 1864. Normally in this capacity, he would make his headquarters in Washington. However, Grant decided otherwise; he considered the most important theater of operations was that of the Army of the Potomac, and he would make his headquarters in the field and accompany that army.

Here we must digress with a bit of explanation as to the future relationship between Grant, the overall commander, and Meade, the commanding general of the Army of the Potomac. Some tend to think of it as an Edgar Bergen–Charlie McCarthy relationship. Grant stands beside Meade, and when his lips move, Meade speaks. This was not so. To understand the relationship, we might consider a naval analogy.

An admiral commands a number of ships but he and his staff reside in one, the so-called flagship. The admiral and staff are separate and distinct from the ship's crew and play no role in the internal operation of the ship. The admiral and staff have a separate bridge, communications center, intelligence center, and even mess. In short, the flagship is treated no differently than the other ships the admiral commands. As in the case of all others, the admiral's commands come only to the captain.

Although Grant travelled with the Army of the Potomac, he always maintained a separate staff and a separate headquarters, and he did not interfere with the internal affairs of the Army of the Potomac anymore than he did with the internal affairs of his other armies. His orders were always addressed to the commanding generals, and theirs to their subordinates. Grant's headquarters were often miles from those of Meade. From his own headquarters he issued orders to all the armies.

Of course, inasmuch as Grant considered the Army of the Potomac the crucial theater and travelled with it, he devoted the greater part of his attention to its activities and the commands closely collaborating with it. These included the Army of the James, for a time the Army of the Shenandoah, and for a time the Ninth Corps. The Ninth Corps was a unique situation. It was transferred from the western theater to augment the Army of the Potomac but since its commander, Burnside, was senior to Meade, for a time it operated directly under Grant.

Warren had known nothing but success up to the arrival of Grant. Warren's fate now entered a period of jeopardy and was sealed with the arrival of Grant's protégé, Sheridan.

Warren's Relations with Meade, Grant, and Sheridan

George G. Meade was fifteen years older than Warren and, as of July 1863, was forty-eight years old. When we look at pictures of Meade today, he looks much older than his age. He is cadaverous, has sunken eyes with large black circles and, in short, looks very much like someone who suffers from ill health. His temperament matched his appearance. He was referred to by his contemporaries as "Old Snapping Turtle."

Grant summed up Meade thusly:

> General Meade was an officer of great merit, with drawbacks to his usefulness that were beyond his control. He had been an officer of the engineer corps before the war and consequently had never served with troops until he was over 46 years of age. He never had, I believe, a command of less than a brigade. He saw clearly and distinctly the position of the enemy, and the topography of the country in front of his own position. His first idea was to take advantage of the lay of the ground, sometimes without reference to the direction we wanted to move afterwards. He was subordinate to his superiors in rank to the extent that he could execute an order which changed his own plans with the same zeal he would have displayed if the plan had been his own. He was brave and conscientious, and commanded the respect of all who knew him. He was unfortunately of a temper that would get beyond his control, at times, and make him speak to officers of high rank in the most offensive manner. No one saw this fault more plainly than he himself, and no one regretted it more. This made it unpleasant at times, even in battle, for those around him to approach him even with information. In spite of this defect he was a most valuable officer and deserves high place in the annals of his country.[1]

Major General George G. Meade, commanding general, Army of the Potomac.

Upon taking command of the Army of the Potomac, Meade offered the young Warren the position of his chief of staff, which Warren declined. Meade had stormy relations with Warren, but when calmed down, always came down on Warren's side. Meade appointed Warren head of Hancock's Second Corps while Hancock recuperated from a wound and later named him head of the Fifth Corps.

After Gettysburg, Meade was under great pressure from the administration to push on into Virginia and complete the destruction of Lee's army. This led to the Mine Run Campaign. Meade crossed the Rapidan River and prepared to attack the Confederates. He and Warren examined the ground on the eve of battle and agreed that Warren would deliver the main attack at dawn. When Warren examined the position at dawn, he found that the situation had radically changed and to execute the ordered attack would be suicidal. It would be Pickett's Charge in reverse. Warren flat out declined to obey his orders. Later he stated, "I would sooner sacrifice my commission than my men."[2]

Meade had to sheepishly re-cross the Rapidan and go into winter quarters, to the chagrin of the administration. Meade was initially furious with Warren but, when calmed down, admitted that Warren was right.

As a result of his actions at Mine Run, Warren acquired a respect and even affection from his men that he never before enjoyed. Here at last was a general willing to sacrifice his own career rather than waste the lives of his men.

In the spring of 1864, Meade decided to reorganize the Army of the Potomac from five corps to three. This meant that two corps commanders had to go. The end result was that the First and Third Corps were broken up and integrated into the remaining Second, Fifth, and Sixth Corps. Their commanding generals were: Second, Hancock; Fifth, Warren; Sixth, Sedgwick. Had Meade wanted to rid himself of Warren, this was the opportunity. Warren stayed.

On March 5, 1864, Meade, in a conversation with Warren, stated that he had recommended to Grant that Warren be nominated for a vacant brigadier general's position in the regular army.[3] For whatever reason, Warren did not get the appointment, but Meade's recommendation still attests to his high regard for Warren at this late date.

Even after Warren's battlefield relief by Sheridan, Meade tried to help him. On April 18, 1865, Meade wrote to Grant pointing out the necessity of appointing a permanent commander of the Fifth Corps. Meade wrote, "Should you be disposed to reassign General Warren I shall make no objection thereto."[4]

Long after the war, in 1882, a Decoration Day ceremony was planned to take place in the Gettysburg battlefield. Warren was unable to attend but wrote to his old division commander, General Crawford, who intended to attend: "Don't let the name of General Meade be forgotten nor any note of detraction go unsilenced on that field."[5]

Thus we can see that although Meade was choleric and Warren could be insolent and overbearing, the two managed to retain a positive relationship based on mutual respect and perhaps even a modicum of friendship.

When Warren reported in to Philip Sheridan on the morning of April 1, 1865, he moved beyond the help of Meade. He was now subordinate to Sheridan, who was directly subordinate to Grant.

Now let us consider what Grant thought of Warren. Grant's initial impression of Warren was favorable. As late as the end of the battle of the Wilderness, Grant considered

Warren to be the logical successor to Meade, should Meade become incapacitated. This is the more remarkable when we consider that Warren was the youngest of Meade's three corps commanders. In Grant's words, "At that time my judgment was that Warren was the man that I would suggest to succeed Meade should anything happen to that gallant soldier to take him from the field. As I have before said, Warren was a gallant soldier, an able man, he was beside thoroughly imbued with the solemnity and importance of the duty he had to perform."[6]

As time went on, however, Grant began to see more limitations in Warren's capabilities, although he still considered him a talented officer. Of particular interest is the fact that Grant, looking at Warren's performance from above, and Lieutenant Colonel Lyman, Meade's aide de camp, looking at Warren's performance from below, independently noted the same deficiency. First let us look at Grant's assessment:

> Warren's difficulty was twofold: When he received an order to do anything, it would at once occur to his mind how all the balance of the army should be engaged so as to properly cooperate with him. His ideas were generally good, but he would forget that the person giving him orders had thought of others at the time he had of him. In like manner, when he did get ready to execute an order, after giving most intelligent instructions to division commanders, he would go in with one division, holding the others in reserve until he could superintend their movements in person also, forgetting that division commanders could execute an order without his presence. His difficulty was constitutional and beyond his control. He was an officer of superior ability, quick perceptions, and personal courage to accomplish anything that could be done with a small command.[7]

Lieutenant Colonel Lyman, Meade's aide de camp, frequently served as a go-between for Meade and Warren, knew Warren well, and frequently observed him in action. After the Battle of the Wilderness, Lyman wrote in his journal: "Warren is not up to a corps command. As in the Mine Run move, so here, he cannot spread himself over three divisions. He cannot do it, and the result is partial and ill concerted and dilatory movements."[8]

Grant and Lyman agreed. Warren suffered from the same deficiency that many young men who were suddenly thrust into high places in the Civil War suffered. He could not delegate authority. He felt that each action could be best accomplished by him. He might make a good division commander, but as a corps commander over multiple divisions, he was at a level beyond his capabilities. At this level he could not do it all himself.

In June 1864, Grant was provided an opportunity to be rid of Warren without punishing or humiliating him. The position of head of the Department of West Virginia suddenly opened up and had to be filled. Grant considered nominating Warren. This would be a step up and Warren would be effectively "kicked upstairs." However, before submitting the nomination, Grant decided to run it by his protégé, Sheridan. Grant proposed Warren as first choice and, if not Warren, then Humphreys. Sheridan responded that he preferred Gibbon, and if not Gibbon, he preferred Humphreys to Warren. None of the above actually received the position, but this gave an indication of Sheridan's feelings toward Warren. Warren remained commander of the Fifth Corps, Army of the Potomac.

Now let us look at Sheridan's view of Warren. It is perfectly clear that Sheridan did not like Warren. When and how this began we do not know. It may have begun as early as Sheridan's West Point days. When Sheridan entered West Point in 1848, Warren was already an upperclassman. It is just possible that Sheridan had some altercation with his nerdy senior.

When Sheridan was first called east by Grant in 1864, he initially assumed the position of chief of the cavalry of the Army of the Potomac. As such, he and Warren were both subordinates of Meade. Beginning with the Battle of the Wilderness, Warren, as was his wont, leveled several criticisms of Sheridan's actions to Meade. This undoubtedly exacerbated whatever ill feelings the thin skinned and hair trigger tempered Sheridan may have already harbored toward Warren.

If there was still any doubt as to Sheridan's ill feelings toward Warren, it evaporated on the morning of April 1, 1865, the day of the battle of Five Forks. The first of Warren's Fifth Corps units to report in to Sheridan that morning was Joshua Chamberlain's brigade. When Chamberlain met Sheridan, he began with the usual courtesies. Sheridan responded, "Why did you not come before? Where is Warren?" Chamberlain responded, "He is at the rear of the column." Sheridan replied, "That is where I expected to find him. What is he doing there?" "General," said Chamberlain, "we are withdrawing from the White Oak Road where we fought all day. General Warren is bringing off his last division, expecting an attack." At this point General Griffin, Chamberlain's superior, arrived, allowing Chamberlain to extricate himself from this embarrassing conversation.[9]

During the afternoon of the 31st, Warren was ordered to send a brigade to Sheridan's assistance, then, during the night of March 31–April 1, to send first a division and then the remaining two divisions to Sheridan's aid. Finally, at 6 a.m. on the 1st, Warren was specifically ordered to report to Sheridan and to subordinate himself and the Fifth Corps to Sheridan. The message was as follows: "General Meade directs that in the movements following your junction with General Sheridan you will be under his orders and will report to him. Please send in a report of your progress."[10]

General Warren was within three miles of Sheridan's headquarters at Dinwiddie when he received this message but did not appear before Sheridan until five hours later at approximately 11 a.m. Sheridan did not divulge his displeasure at the meeting but this episode certainly did not reflect positively on Sheridan's feelings toward Warren.

Whether or not we agree with Sheridan's act of relieving Warren later that date, if we put ourselves in Sheridan's shoes, his action is understandable. By early afternoon of April 1, Sheridan saw that he had an unprecedented but brief window of opportunity. Grant could not break the strong Confederate defense line guarding Petersburg unless he could thin the line by drawing a large number of the Confederates out of the defenses and into the open. He had now done so. About one-fourth of Lee's available fighting men now stood outside of the defense line before Sheridan.

Sheridan's cavalry alone could not defeat these Confederates. However, with the addition of Warren's corps of infantry, he would outnumber Pickett's force by more than two to one and victory should be all but certain.

The window of opportunity for Sheridan would close at darkness on the 1st. If he had not destroyed the Confederate force by that time, he would have to retire to the high ground at Dinwiddie Courthouse to provide fodder for his horses, to replenish his ammunition, and to provide a suitable bivouac site for his exhausted troops. When he would return to resume the conflict on the morning of the 2nd, all could be radically different and all the variables were against him.

Lee's main defense line was just four miles up the White Oak Road from Pickett. The intervening four miles were only lightly held by Union cavalry. It was possible that during the night Lee would gather sufficient force to re-occupy the four miles of the White Oak Road and reunite with Pickett. In that case, there would be no open flank at Five Forks to attack in the morning.

Another nasty possibility was that Pickett would withdraw one mile down the Ford Road during the night and take up a new position behind Hatchers Run. In that case, any attack on Pickett on the 2nd would have to proceed down the single Ford Road, with mud on both sides, and then cross Hatchers Run under fire before even reaching Pickett's defense line.

Even if the Confederates exercised neither of these options and remained where they were, they could be expected to spend the night furiously engaged with ax and spade strengthening their position. They could build stronger barricades with mud and logs, lay down abbattis before their defense lines, and do whatever else was necessary to strengthen their position. Near certain victory for Sheridan on the 1st would recede to chancy possibility on the 2nd.

Things seemed to move in slow motion on the 1st as Sheridan prepared for the attack. Warren's exhausted troops moved toward their deployment area at what seemed like snail's pace as the sun inched across the sky.

Sheridan was a tempestuous, high strung man. He had been incorrectly led to believe that Warren's troops would begin arriving at Dinwiddie by midnight, but the first of Warren's men did not arrive until dawn. For the attack to succeed on the 1st before dark terminated the fighting, the attack had to be delivered not later than 4 p.m.

Noon came and went, and then 1, 2, and 3 p.m. as Warren's exhausted men slowly moved into position. According to Grant's aide, Horace Porter, "Sheridan chaffing with impatience and consumed with anxiety, became as restive as a racer when he nears the scene to make the start. He made every possible appeal for promptness, he dismounted from his horse, paced up and down, struck the clenched fist of one hand into the palm of the other; and fretted like a caged tiger. He said at one time: This battle must be fought and won before the sun goes down. All the conditions may be changed in the morning. We have but a few hours of daylight left us."[11]

When the attack was finally launched at about 4 p.m. things did not go exactly as planned, as they seldom do in wartime. Crawford's division of Warren's corps marched right beyond the woods-concealed refused flank of Pickett's line and off into the distance and out of the action. It had to be overtaken, turned, and brought back. It was, however, and participated in the final rout and destruction of Pickett's force.

When victory was all but complete, Sheridan's pent up emotions finally imploded and the logical target was Warren.

We have covered Meade and Warren's rocky but positive relationship, Grant's ambivalent feeling toward Warren, and Sheridan's ill feelings toward Warren. What about Warren's view of Grant? After all, it was Grant who took the unusual step of authorizing Sheridan to relieve Warren. It was Grant who was ultimately responsible for Warren's humiliation.

Warren looked askance at Grant's method of warfare. Prior to Grant taking charge, it was much sparring and only occasional bloody combat. Now it was continuous and unrelenting bloodletting. It was now a war of attrition—total war.

Warren long considered that Grant showed favoritism to the generals he had brought from the west. He also believed that Brigadier General John A. Rawlins, Grant's chief of staff, was instrumental in turning Grant against him. Warren, in a letter to his brother, referred to Rawlins as "a personal coward in danger, but a bold liar and firm believer in the value of a lie and was the active principle on Grant's staff against him."[12] So Warren thought Rawlins a liar and a coward. What did Grant think of Rawlins? Grant was so impressed with Rawlins that, later, when he was elected president, he appointed Rawlins as his secretary of war. Whose judgment of Rawlins was correct, Grant's or Warren's?

Major General John Rawlins, U.S. Volunteer Army, Grant's indispensable chief of staff.

Warren's true feelings toward Grant were revealed later in a letter to his wife that discussed President-elect Grant's cabinet selections. Warren wrote: "I believe it is the success and flattery and adulation that attends Grant, who is nothing but a worthless drunkard, that is causing so much mischief."[13]

The U.S. Volunteer Army

At the start of the Civil War, the regular U.S. Army consisted of a little over 16,000 men. It soon became evident that a vastly larger force would be required to put down the rebellion. The answer was the U.S. Volunteer Army. The U.S. Volunteer Army was ultimately to grow to over one-hundred times the size of the pre-war regular army.

The volunteer army was largely created by the individual states raising regiments that were then incorporated into the federal army. Thus we see regiments in the U.S. Volunteer Army with names such as the First Wisconsin and the Fifth New York. The numbers were assigned in the sequence the regiments were recruited. Once a regiment was recruited, the governor would appoint its colonel, usually a prominent person who was instrumental in raising the regiment. The members of the regiment would usually elect their officers. Once the regiment was complete, it would be "federalized," that is, inducted into the U.S. Volunteer Army. From this point, the federal government picked up the pay and cost and determined the rules and promotions.

Initially, it was unclear what role regular army officers would play in the volunteer army, but it was soon accepted that one could retain his rank in the regular army and at the same time accept a much higher rank in the volunteer army.

Promotions in the regular army proceeded at a glacial pace. There was no compulsory retirement and one could only be promoted when a vacancy was created by death or resignation. In the volunteer army, however, promotions could be meteoric. Lieutenants and captains in the regular army were being jumped up to colonel and general in the volunteer army.

As long as the war continued and the volunteer army existed, the rank that one held in the volunteer army was the one that counted. The incumbent received all the pay, authority, privilege, and responsibility of that rank. However, all knew that someday the war would end, the volunteer army would be disbanded, and the career officers would revert to their regular army ranks. Thus, regular army officers serving in high ranks in the volunteer army valued whatever promotions they received in the regular army even though they had no immediate effect.

Some general officers in the volunteer army, who held low rank or even no rank in the regular army, performed so impressively in the volunteer army that they were given high level positions in the regular army as slots became vacant. These included Grant, Sherman, and Sheridan.

One anomaly of the dual rank system is that, upon dissolution of the volunteer army and the resumption of the regular army ranks, a general in the volunteer army could suddenly find himself subordinate to his chief of staff or even his aide de camp.

At the time Sheridan relieved Warren of command on April 1, 1865, Warren was a major general in the volunteer army, but only a major in the regular Army Corps of Engineers with a date of rank of June 25, 1864. Upon the dissolution of the volunteer army and the resumption of regular army ranks, Warren would find himself junior to all three of his division commanders.

Warren the Man

Warren was a small, slightly shorter than average man weighing about 140 pounds. He was unimpressive in appearance and could easily go unnoticed in a crowd of three. His general demeanor could not be described as either cheerful or affable, but was nearer to dour. At times he could be arrogant.

Warren was a democrat and indifferent to abolition. If war had to be made, he preferred it on the light or McClellan style, and not on the Grant or attrition style. He was a devoted son, and when his beloved father died in 1859, he took on the support of his mother and the education of his younger sisters, to whom he became almost a father figure. Warren married for the first and only time in 1863 at the age of thirty-three. To all appearances the marriage was happy, and bore a son and a daughter.

Warren was an ardent follower of Dennis Mahon, a West Point professor and leading military theoretician of his time. Warren absorbed and applied the art and mechanics of nineteenth century warfare. He not only concerned himself with battlefield management but with the disciplining, training, and supplying of his men. His bravery and gallantry in battle were beyond dispute. He was wounded three times and had a horse shot out from under him. He was particularly adept in evaluating the lay of the land to provide his men the maximum advantage in battle. This, of course, is not surprising because of his training and experience in topographical engineering.

Warren lacked the charisma of McClellan, the panache of J.E.B. Stuart, or the elan of Sheridan, but this was counterbalanced by the knowledge of his troops that he would not waste their lives. Warren did not possess the even temper or imperturbability of Lee or Grant, but could flare up in anger and be unreasonably harsh on a subordinate for a defect real or imagined.

Warren had two deficiencies as a leader. The two deficiencies were really two manifestations of the same quality. Warren was far smarter than average, knew it, and acted accordingly. Consequently, when receiving an order, he tended to believe that he had a better assessment of the situation, and modified it. When executing an order, he tended to believe that he could do it better than his subordinates and hence was reluctant to delegate authority.

One might compare Warren with Confederate corps commander Leonidas Polk. Polk always "knew better" and tended to look upon orders as suggestions. There was, however, a fundamental difference between Warren and Polk. Warren was competent and Polk was not.

Inasmuch as Warren always felt that he understood the situation better than others, he was quick to criticize his fellow generals to their common superior. This too was not appreciated, nor designed to cement friendships. When Warren finally ran into Grant and Sheridan, he met a general who did not like his orders modified, and another who did not like to be criticized.

A good source of information on Warren the man is the diary of Brigadier General Charles Wainwright. Wainwright was Warren's chief of artillery. Wainwright did not attend West Point, was not a career officer, and was not a member of the regular army. He entered the volunteer army at the beginning of the war and served until its dissolution at the end. Prior to the war, he was a prosperous farmer, and to this he returned at the end. Wainwright served as an artillerist throughout, and in this capacity he was highly regarded. His private diary was apparently not intended for publication and was published by his brother only after his death. His descriptions of Warren appear to be reasonably objective in that he recorded the good as well as the bad. Following are some extracts from his diary that describe Warren the man.

Diary Entry Tuesday, May 10, 1864

The following quote describes Warren during the battle of Spotsylvania Courthouse:

> The Third Division in particular is said to have acted abominably, breaking all to pieces, so that Warren was obliged to rally them himself, colours in hand. I believe these reports, for when I went out with Stewart's battery I found the Pennsylvania Reserves forming away to the rear of Griffin, and not two hundred yards from the knoll where Cooper and Walcott belonged, while Warren still grasped the staff of his corps flag. He held it short, for it had

been shot in two in his hand just before. The little general looked gallant enough at any rate. Mounted on a great tall white horse, in full uniform, sash and all, and with the flag in his hand, he must have made a prominent mark at any rate.[14]

Diary Entry, Thursday, May 12, 1864

The last three days I should have had very little to do under any circumstances; but General Warren has shown no disposition to treat me differently, though he has not reiterated his order about remaining with the reserve. I have found no previous commander who did not show me more consideration, though he made so good a commencement. I have talked the matter over with Patrick, in whom I have great confidence. He confirms me in my determination to grin and bear it until this campaign is over, and then ask to be relieved, unless matters change for the better.[15]

Diary Entry, Wednesday, May 18, 1864

Since leaving the Alsop House, Warren seems to have got over the freak he had of fighting the artillery through his aides, and today has allowed me to attend to my own business. I know nothing as to what put such a notion into his head; and am willing to forget it all, if he chooses to treat me decently hereafter. I fear though, that he is apt to take freaks, and when excited does not consider much what he does.[16]

Diary Entry, Monday, May 23, 1864

The conversation in the following entry relates to Warren's interrogation of a prisoner after the battle of Jericho Mills:

Warren put a few sharp questions but got no answer. He then again offered to send him, under guard, to look for his brother, and on refusing this offer, ordered him to the rear, saying that he was a fool or something of that sort. The fellow at once replied that "he heard on their side that Warren was a good general but no gentleman." I heard Warren murmur, "If they only think me a good general I don't care to be considered a gentleman," which I believe to be true.[17]

Diary Entry, Saturday, May 28, 1864

Warren laid out the lines here himself, and for once were made with some knowledge. The men and many of the officers too looked with wonder at the great openings he left in the re-entering angles. He liked the work and was consequently in good humor, so that I had a very pleasant time aiding him.[18]

Diary Entry, Tuesday, May 31, 1864

General Warren has been in one of his pets all yesterday and today. One would suppose that a man in his position would be ashamed to show that kind of temper. When I reported to him the result of my efforts, he grumbled to himself something of which I could only catch a few words, to the effect that he could get nothing done.... He has pitched into his staff officers most fearfully, cursing them up and down as no man has a right to do, and as I wonder that they allow. I would certainly not stand for it one instant; and as he may let out on me, I have thought much as to just how it would be best to act and what I should say, did he try it.[19]

Diary Entry, Friday, June 3, 1864

The day has been a rather pleasant one to me, as I have been free to move around from one battery to another without any unreasonable demands being put upon me. I mention this, as I feel that I am standing on the edge of a volcano which may burst out at any moment, and in the spot least looked for. This evening I saw it in its fury though its lava did not reach me. General Warren went over to Burnside's headquarters before dark, leaving no orders whatever for the night, and did not return until 10 or 11 o'clock. His staff were yawning around a fire under some trees on the plain, where he had his tents up last night, but were afraid to put a tent or even order the supper without his consent. I had established my headquarters about a hundred yards off, where we had our supper, and were all ready to put up tents, but waited to learn whether we remained here all night or not. I was talking with some of the Corps staff when the general returned, and seeing no preparations for the night, he ripped out at his staff generally and poor little Marvin in particular. I used to think the Charleston hackmen the most profane in the world. Our army swears as badly as did Uncle Toby's in Flanders. I have heard Meade in one of his towering passions. But I never heard anything which could begin to equal the awful oaths poured out tonight; they fairly made my hair stand on end with their profaneness, while I was filled with wonder at the ingenuity of invention and desperate blackguardism they displayed. So as soon as I gathered that we were to remain, I called my staff and went home; far enough off, fortunately, to be out of hearing.[20]

Diary Entry, Monday, June 6, 1864

General Warren still keeps his headquarters around the Leary House, though it is a wretched spot, being right at the corner of two roads where trains are all the time passing, and covering them with dust. The general will not move. He appears to have sunk into a sort of lethargic sulk, sleeps a great part of the time, and says nothing to anyone. I think that these fits of his must be the result of a sort of insanity; indeed that is perhaps the most charitable way of accounting for them.[21]

Diary Entry, Thursday, July 14, 1864

The following was written while the Fifth Corps was building defensive works in the Union line south of Petersburg.

General Warren is now in his element: so far as I can learn he is his own officer of the trenches, and commander of the working parties. There is nothing that he likes so much as overseeing work, and consequently is in a most agreeable humor. I spent some hours with him yesterday in the large redoubt, which one might easily believe he had undertaken to build by contract, and certainly has pushed forward with most wonderful rapidity. It is an immense work, five hundred feet front I believe, and perfectly square. Bigelow and Breck are to move their guns into this work, as soon as it is ready for them, and I was much surprised to have the general expressly leave the selection of position for the different pieces entirely to me, as also the building of the platforms and magazines. He is a queer mixture: one might have thought that he had the greatest confidence in his chief of artillery, who heard him today explaining all his plans about this work, and consulting most confidentially with him. I am becoming more than ever convinced that he has a screw loose, and is not quite accountable for all his freaks.[22]

Diary Entry, Sunday, October 23, 1864

This entry was written just after Warren returned from a leave during which he married.

General Warren returned on Friday; ten days with his wife does not appear to have sweetened his temper at all, from what I hear. I see very little of him myself, except when obliged to officially. Our notions are not at all similar, so I deem it best to keep on the most punctilious terms with him.[23]

Diary Entry, Wednesday, March 29, 1865

The episode described in the diary occurred late in the evening of March 29. Warren's troops had forced their way off Gravelly Run on the Quaker Road and had reached the Boydton Plank Road. It was dark and fighting for the day had ceased. At this point, Warren left his staff behind, without instructions, and rode over to General Meade's headquarters for consultation.

The staff did not know if they were to set up camp where they were or await Warren's return, which might bring them instructions to move on, they did nothing. The headquarters wagon was lagging somewhere behind and had not yet reached the location of the staff. The diary records Warren's reaction upon his return, discovering that headquarters camp has not been set up, and his supper was not ready.

> Corps headquarters wagon was not up for some unknown reason, and when Warren came back from Meade's headquarters there was a scene. I was just near enough to catch a word now and then: they fell on Locke and everyone around, and were fearful, worse if anything than that night at Bethesda Church. The devil within him seemed to be stirring all day, and I presume something had been said at army headquarters which he did not like.
>
> Presently Locke came over to me, and asked me to invite the General to supper with me. This I had already resolved to do, but thought that it would sound most easy, and as if I had not heard any of the goings on, did I wait until just as it was being served.
>
> Accordingly, when all was ready, I walked up and said, "General I am lucky enough to have a pair of broiled chickens for supper tonight, and as I see your wagon has not yet arrived, should be glad if you will come over and help me eat them." He, however, refused, and for him, politely; but could not help damning his staff. "If a corps commander could not get his own supper" he did "not see why they should sponge on their subordinates, and he would be damned if he would." I did not attempt to reason, but tried to tempt him by praising my supper, and saying that Fitz Hugh was absent, and I should have to eat it almost alone; but could get nothing more out of him.
>
> Later and just before I turned in, I again tried him with the offer of a bed, but it was the same answer; If I can't sleep in my own tent, I'll be damned if I sleep in anyone else's; and the last thing I heard as I went to bed were his mumbled oaths as he sat under a tree, in the same spot he had been in for two hours. I have not put this down so particularly save as proof what I have been for some time convinced, viz: that these awful fits of passion are a disease with Warren, and species of insanity, over which he has no control.[24]

A general's official family is his staff. When in the field, it is with these that he eats, sleeps, and sometimes dies. It is beyond question that Warren's two antagonists, Grant and Sheridan, treated their staffs with greater consideration than did Warren. It is beyond doubt that Warren often bullied his while his antagonists seldom if ever did so to theirs and, in fact, were idolized by theirs.

We will conclude our assessment of Warren by citing what Lieutenant Colonel Lyman, Meade's aide de camp, wrote in his journal when he heard of Warren's removal by Sheridan:

> Poor Warren! A man of marked ability and valor, too rapidly promoted, and now cast down at the turning point of this great war. In his day he was wont (like many young men) to make severe criticisms on others, but this humiliation he did not deserve. Warren's military ability, which was great, did not exactly take the direction of command of troops. He seemed unable to "spread Himself" over more than one division, and he had the incorrigible error of trying to do each thing himself, putting no faith in his subordinates. It was this that ruined

him; for Sheridan (who disliked him before) seeking to give him some orders for the attack by his corps, found that he had gone off to look for the 3D Division, and after the fight, relieved him. His great strength was as a field engineer and perhaps chief-of-staff, to discern proper routes, put troops in position; discriminate points of attack and defense. He was a man of sleepless energy, activity, and study—his mind never still; a master of his art, and of a daring spirit; but promotion was too rapid and in the wrong direction.[25]

Chapter 7

Warren After the War

Warren resigned his commission as major general in the U.S. Volunteer Army in May 1865, and resumed his rank as major in the regular army in the Corps of Topographical Engineers. Warren, had he been an optimistic man, had much to look forward to. It was now peacetime. He was again in the field he loved and where he was appreciated. His superior was again his good friend Andrew Humphreys and, even as a major, he was solidly established in the upper middle class. Last but not least, for the first time he could establish a normal family life with his wartime bride.

It was not to be. Warren was a naturally dour, pessimistic individual, and he could not break with the past. During the four years of war, he had risen to national prominence. He had testified before Congress, interacted with the president, and commanded more men than in the peacetime army. He was a central figure in earth shaking events, advised army commanders, and contributed significantly to the final Union victory. His four years of triumph had ended in disgrace within days of the end of the war. He had suffered the ultimate disgrace. He was relieved of command on the battlefield, and that within sight and sound of his subordinates. Warren was barred from active participation in the final days of the war. While his tormentors, Sheridan and Grant, basked in the glow of Appomattox and then went on to further glories, he had to look on from the sidelines. Warren, a proud man, could not put the humiliation behind him and continue on with the many plusses he had. He had to seek vindication.

Warren's postwar career must have been one of intense humiliation. Although he was never to rise higher than lieutenant colonel in the postwar army, all of his fellow corps commanders in the volunteer army did better. Humphreys was named commander of the Corps of Engineers with the rank of brigadier general. John Parke rose to the rank of colonel and became superintendent of West Point. Wright was ultimately promoted to brigadier general and chief engineer.

If that were not enough, his three wartime division commanders were to surpass him in the peacetime army. Ayres and Griffin rose to colonel and Crawford to brigadier general.

To add to the humiliation, Warren's wartime staff surpassed him in peacetime. Frederick Locke, his chief of staff, rose to colonel; his aide de camp and brother-in-law Washington Roebling became rich and famous as a bridge builder, among whose many accomplishments was the Brooklyn Bridge. To the proud Warren, all that remained was his wartime reputation.

Warren's case is often compared to that of Major General Fitz John Porter. Porter, like Warren, had earlier commanded the Fifth Corps of the Army of the Potomac. Porter, at the peak of his popularity, was relieved of command after the Second Battle of Bull Run and charged with disobeying an order. Porter was tried by court-martial, convicted, and sentenced. His sentence was that he be dismissed from the army without rank and be forbidden forever from holding any position of trust with the government.

Porter, like Warren, felt he had been done an injustice and spent a lifetime seeking vindication. He finally succeeded, had the conviction overturned, was restored to his full rank, was lionized in the eyes of the public, and when he died, was buried with full military honors.

When we look closely at the Warren and Porter cases, however, we see that there is a fundamental difference. Warren, unlike Porter, was not only never convicted of committing a crime; he was never even accused of committing one. The real instigator of Warren's downfall was Grant. It is a certainty that Sheridan would never have relieved Warren had not Grant gratuitously given him permission to do so. Whether or not Grant did the correct thing is arguable. That he had the right to do so is not. It was, in fact, Grant's job to put the round pegs in the round holes. In general, Grant enjoyed great success in this responsibility. In a number of cases, he obviously replaced an incompetent with a supremely competent individual. Once a leader had gained Grant's confidence, he was wont to give him a blank check as to how to accomplish his tasks. When Warren appeared before Grant on April 1, 1865, Grant did not shout at, berate, or condemn Warren. He merely re-assigned him.

Warren sought a court of inquiry for the next decade and a half to restore his reputation. A court of inquiry is not a trial. It is not a court-martial. It is a judicial fact-finding body. Its purpose is not to try but to establish the facts. Its proceedings have many of the appearances of a trial. It calls witnesses and it takes testimony. However, there is no defendant and no sentencing.

One can readily see why Warren's attempt to have a court of inquiry called was an uphill battle. A person charged with a crime in the military is entitled to a trial. No one is entitled to a court of inquiry. Let us say that the purpose of the court of inquiry that Warren sought was to determine if there was justification in relieving him. Any finding in favor of Warren must necessarily be a finding against Grant. If Warren were unjustifiably relieved, it was Grant and Sheridan who were responsible for his unjustifiable relief.

Warren's attempt to gain a court of inquiry would have to go through the army, and Grant and his supporters controlled the army for the next generation. Grant himself was general in chief until he assumed the presidency for two terms beginning in 1868. Grant was to be succeeded as army chief by Sherman, and Sherman by Sheridan.

If Warren believed he had been done an injustice and his reputation thus damaged, he had other means of redress. One obvious means was the press. After the Civil War ended and the Confederate Army and the U.S. Volunteer Army were disbanded, the public acquired a voracious appetite for Civil War press articles. The celebrities of the times were the generals, both North and South. Battles were now re-fought in the press. Most generals quickly cashed in on this appetite. Articles written by Civil War luminaries regarding their experiences appeared almost daily in newspapers, magazines, and books.

Many were self-serving, putting the author in the best light. Some were continuing controversies over who was responsible for disasters such as the Crater, Chickamauga, and the Confederate failure at Gettysburg. There were continuing controversies as between Generals James Longstreet and Jubal Early, and Generals William Rosecrans and Thomas J. Wood.

Warren made a very limited effort to clear his name through the press. A few well written articles might easily have restored his reputation and enriched him in the bargain.

Warren continued his efforts to seek his court of inquiry as his health deteriorated. His chance finally came in 1877 when Grant left the presidency and was succeeded by Rutherford B. Hayes. Hayes, unlike Grant, Sheridan or Warren, was neither a professional soldier nor a member of the West Point clique. He rose to become a general solely on the basis of his leadership capabilities and battlefield gallantry. He was not a member of the Grant coterie and owed nothing to Grant or Sherman. Hayes approved the convening of a court of inquiry to look into the Warren dismissal.

Warren knew that once it came time for the court to call witnesses, the Fifth Corps, almost to a man, would rally to his side. The rank and file knew that they were being led by a competent and conscientious man who would never rashly expose their lives for his own glory. This feeling even extended to Colonel Locke and Warren's staff, whom he sometimes abused in fits of anger.

Warren died on August 8, 1882, at the age of fifty-two from complications of diabetes. At the time of death, he was still on active duty in the rank of lieutenant colonel. He left behind a widow and two children. The results of the court of inquiry had still not been published, but Warren knew of their content. He died an embittered man, and requested that he be buried in civilian clothes.

Chapter 8

The Court of Inquiry

The court of inquiry was finally approved on December 9, 1879, almost fifteen years after the battle of Five Forks and Warren's removal. Warren's tenacity in seeking it for so long is as remarkable as is President Hayes's approval of it.

For most crimes and civil judicial actions there is such a thing as a statute of limitations. Such a statute requires that the proceedings commence within a prescribed time after the event. The reason is that witnesses' memories fade and are contaminated by later discussions of the event, and that a fair procedure will no longer be possible.

Courts of inquiry were usually convened to investigate some disaster, to determine who, if anyone, was at fault. If it so determined, charges were filed against the presumed culprit and he was then tried before a court-martial. No charges or court-martial could emanate from the Warren Court of Inquiry, inasmuch as the time stipulated for their filing had long since expired under the statute of limitations. Consequently, the conducting of a court of inquiry at this late date made no sense. It made even less sense when we consider that there was no disaster to investigate. The battle of Five Forks was a resounding Union victory, one of the greatest of the war.

The court of inquiry was to investigate events of April 1, 1865, and occurrences leading up to that date to ascertain if Warren was justifiably relieved of command. This lapse far exceeded any statute of limitations.

The Union suffered over 800 casualties at the battle of Five Forks and it is doubtful if any of these casualties, or the thousands that remained unscathed that day, gave any thought, at the time or since, to Warren's reputation. Warren's reputation was probably important only to Warren. The battle itself was a swirl of confusion in the forest, and the happenings were probably only dimly understood even by those in charge. There were no adequate maps of the area at the time.

In the intervening fifteen years, the battle was dissected again and again in the press. Accurate maps were produced and the events were clarified with ever greater precision. The minds of the veterans were undoubtedly contaminated and they now understood clearly what they did not understand at the time. With this contamination of minds, how would it be possible, after fifteen years, to recreate what they thought, heard, or saw at the time?

An added complication was the fact that many of the key players were now dead and thus not available for interrogation. Griffin, to whom Sheridan handed command after relieving Warren, died in 1867. Meade, Warren's superior, died in 1872; George

Armstrong Custer, a prominent participant, died at "Custer's Last Stand" in 1876; and their opponent, Pickett, died in 1875.

Other main players of the fateful day of April 1, 1865, had since experienced earth shaking events, which would have caused events of that date to recede into insignificance. Grant, for example, had completed two terms as president of the United States.

To think that, after fifteen years, one could accurately reconstruct the words, deeds, and events of that day was unrealistic. To complicate matters further, this was not a trial to reach an objective truth, guilty or innocent. It was to investigate a judgment—justified, not justified, partially justified, etc. It was not a matter of black and white but of gray.

Whether or not Warren should have been removed was not a matter of fact but a matter of judgment. A military organization operates on the premise that a senior's judgment is superior to that of a junior.

Now, in the court of inquiry, juniors were tasked with evaluating the judgment of the senior. Furthermore, these juniors were not there when the event happened. They would be looking on from a vast time distance. They would not have all the facts the senior had at the time of the decision.

The court was to determine if Warren was justly removed. If the court so determined, it would necessarily follow that Sheridan unjustly removed him. At the time of the activation of the court, Sheridan was the second senior general in the army, second in rank only to Sherman. Furthermore, it was anticipated that Sheridan's relief of Sherman was imminent. Of necessity, Sheridan would be senior to whoever was appointed to serve on the court.

In a court of inquiry, the members of the court in effect serve as a jury. In any judicial proceedings, the jury must be impartial. Either side in the proceeding may challenge any prospective juror. If a prospective juror has any relationship to either the prosecution or defense, he will be denied seating. In the case at hand, the members of the court were, in effect, judging their own superior. They lacked the power to either remove him or even censure him. They were merely able to criticize him. To conclude, it was Warren's criticism of Sheridan that got him into trouble in the first place.

The court of inquiry in the case of Warren should never have been approved. We can argue that it was a waste of money; it proved to be just that.

The following officers were appointed members of the court: Major General W. S. Hancock, U.S. Army; Brigadier General C. C. Augur, U.S. Army; and Colonel Z. B. Tower, Corps of Engineers. Major James McMillan of the 2nd Artillery was appointed recorder.

We have encountered General Hancock before. He too was a corps commander in the Army of the Potomac and his fate was twice intertwined with that of Warren. It was Hancock's Second Corps that repulsed Pickett's charge at Gettysburg, and in the process, Hancock was seriously wounded. Thus, Hancock and Warren became the two Union heroes of Gettysburg: Warren for saving Little Round Top on the 2nd and Hancock for repulsing Pickett's charge on the 3rd. Their fates were intertwined again when Warren was chosen to replace Hancock as the commanding general of the Second Corps until such time as Hancock returned. Warren, in fact, enjoyed excellent relations with Hancock, and was pleased with Hancock's selection as president of the court. Furthermore, Hancock was not a member of Grant's coterie from the west and could be depended upon to render a just appraisal.

Brigadier General C. C. Augur, U.S. Army, was nine years older than Warren and had graduated from West Point in 1843, seven years before Warren. Augur was not a member of the Corps of Engineers. He had served ably in the Mexican War and in the pre–Civil War Indian campaigns. He participated in various actions in the east in the Civil War until he was seriously wounded at the battle of Cedar Mountain. Upon his apparent recovery, he participated in Bank's campaign in Louisiana to seize Port Hudson on the Mississippi. This campaign, of course, was the one wherein Grant's army from the north attempted to seize Vicksburg, and Nathaniel P. Banks's army from the south attempted to seize Port Hudson and thus gain complete control of the Mississippi and sever the Confederacy in two. Augur ultimately accepted the surrender of Port Hudson.

At this point, Augur's old wound flared up and he was precluded from any further field service for the duration of the war. He was assigned the backwater position of the Department of Washington. In this capacity, he provided replacements and supplies to both the Army of the Potomac and Sheridan's Army of the Shenandoah. For his excellent performance, he was commended by both Sheridan and Grant. Thus Augur's only connections with Sheridan and Grant were tangential. He never had any direct association with either.

Warren knew Augur only by sight. During Warren's tenure as professor of mathematics at West Point, Augur was commandant of the Cadet Corps. Warren had no objection to Augur serving on the court.

We need not go into the background of Colonel Tower, as he never served a day on the court. He became sick before the court convened and was replaced by Brigadier General John Newton. Newton was a contemporary of Augur and graduated in the same class of West Point, that of 1843.

Newton had much in common with Warren. Both graduated second in their respective classes and each entered the prestigious Corps of Engineers. Each spent their entire prewar and postwar years as engineers, and Newton ultimately rose to replace Humphreys as head of the corps.

Newton's wartime career also paralleled that of Warren to a degree. Both rose to the rank of major general in the volunteer army, both served in the Army of the Potomac, and each rose to corps command; Newton to the commander of the First Corps and Warren to the commander of the Second Corps. However, when the Army of the Potomac was reorganized in 1864 and five of the corps were consolidated into three, Newton was one of the odd men out while Warren stayed. Newton ended up in the backwaters of the war as commander of the District of Key West, Florida. Warren had no objection to the selection of Newton as a member of the court.

Hancock called the court into session for the first time on December 11, 1879. No one at the time had any idea that the proceedings would drag on almost three years before the findings were published, or that Warren would be dead before they were.

There was yet to be one more major perturbation in the court's composition before it arrived at its findings. On June 28, 1880, General Hancock received the nomination for president by the Democratic Party in the 1880 race against Republican candidate James Garfield. Hancock requested that he be relieved as president of the court of inquiry, and his request was granted. Regulations precluded the appointment of a new court member inasmuch as testimony had already been taken. Consequently, Augur moved up into the chair, and now Warren's future was in the hands of Generals Augur and Newton.

The court initially convened on Governor's Island in New York Harbor, but later moved to Manhattan. It called a distinguished list of Civil War luminaries from both the Union and the Confederacy. These included Sheridan, Grant, and General Merritt from the Union side, and General W.H.F. Lee and Fitzhugh Lee from the Confederate side.

The proceedings were plagued with delays, interruptions, and postponements from the beginning. These were caused by illnesses, tardy arrival of witnesses, and summer heat. Warren, already in questionable health, suffered from stress, long separations from his family, and a progressive deterioration of both his physical and financial situation. He was compelled to mortgage his home to pay his lawyer's fees. He finally died on August 8, 1882, at the age of fifty-two, approximately four months before the original publication of the findings of the court.

Regulations required that the findings be published as a three-fold document; the findings, an endorsement by the judge advocate general of the army, and an endorsement by the commanding general of the army. In response to a plea by Warren's attorney, complaining of the excessive delays already encountered, the findings were originally published without the endorsements, in November 1882, but the full three-fold document quickly followed.

Chapter 9

The Testimony

Despite the fact the court convened in December 1879, the first testimony was not taken until April 1880. It was intended and desired that the first to testify be General Sheridan. However, because of other commitments and illness, Sheridan was not available prior to May 1880.

Captain E. R. Warner

The first to testify was Captain E. R. Warner. He was moved to the head of the list because he would become unavailable after April.

As of April 1, 1865, the date of the battle of Five Forks, Warner was a member of the staff of General Meade serving in the capacity of inspector of artillery. As dawn broke, Meade's and Grant's staffs were camped separately a few miles distant, Grant at Dabney's Mill. For efficiency in the battle that was obviously imminent, Meade decided to consolidate his camp with that of Grant, and the two were united at Dabney's Mill shortly after breakfast.

At this point, General Henry Jackson Hunt, Meade's chief of artillery, sent for his subordinate, Captain Warner. Hunt directed Warner to proceed to the Fifth Corps headquarters (Warren's) and ascertain the status and deployment of Warren's artillery. He further directed that, before proceeding, Warner report to Grant's chief of staff, General Rawlins, to see if Rawlins had any additional tasks for Warner. Rawlins expanded upon Hunt's tasking and directed Warner to determine the location and status of the entire Fifth Corps.

Warner did not know precisely where the Fifth Corps was, much less its headquarters. At some time between 8 and 9 a.m., after an hour or so searching, he sighted what was obviously the Fifth Corps' headquarters compound. It consisted of the headquarters' wagons and an artillery park. General Warren, however, was not present. The senior Fifth Corps officers present were Colonel Locke, the chief of staff, and Brigadier General Wainwright, the Fifth Corps chief of artillery. Locke advised Warner that Warren was with a portion of his command on the Boydton Plank Road and that they had to repair a downed bridge before they could proceed and join Sheridan. Warner could not recall the name of the stream the downed bridge was over, but said he knew it at the time. The stream was, of course, Gravelly Run.

Warner returned to Grant and Meade's headquarters, arriving about 10 a.m. He reported to General Rawlins with Grant standing by within earshot but not a participant in the conversation. When Grant overheard Warner say that Warren was stopped at a downed bridge on his route to join Sheridan, Grant took it to mean that this was the situation at the present and that as of 10 a.m. on the 1st, Warren had still not joined Sheridan. As previously noted, Grant had sent Sheridan a dispatch that he could expect Warren by midnight on March 31. In actuality, Warren had long since repaired and crossed the bridge and had already joined Sheridan.

Grant took umbrage at Warren's presumed dilatory movement and said something to the effect that he previously wanted to remove Warren but Meade had talked him out of it, and he was now sorry that he had not done so. Grant then turned to Horace Porter of his staff, who was about to be sent to Sheridan, and said, "Tell Sheridan if he has any occasion to relieve General Warren, not to hesitate to do so."[1]

Grant's immediate motivation to authorize the relief of Warren was this mistaken belief that Warren had still not joined Sheridan as of 10 a.m. on April 1.

The Testimony of Lieutenant General Philip H. Sheridan

The big day was Tuesday, May 4, 1880. The place was Governor's Island in New York Harbor. It was this day that Lieutenant General Philip Sheridan was called upon to testify. General Sheridan was only the third man since George Washington to receive the exalted rank of lieutenant general. The testimony this day, it was hoped, would determine the validity of Warren's charges.

The testimony of General Sheridan was broken into two pieces. First, he read a prepared statement covering the critical days of March 31 and April 1, 1865. After the statement was read, he was subject to questioning by Warren's attorney, Albert Stickney.

Sheridan began by presenting a presumably accurate map of the field of operations that was drawn up after the event. He next testified that during the day of March 31, he was attacked by a superior enemy force that drove him back from the direction of Five Forks to a short distance from Dinwiddie Courthouse. During the evening, as the final assault of the enemy was taking place, he sent his brother and aide de camp, Captain Michael Vincent Sheridan, to General Grant's headquarters to report the state of affairs. On his way to Grant's headquarters, which was at Dabney's Mill, some eight and a half miles up the Boydton Plank Road, he stopped off at General Meade's headquarters nearby to ask directions. While at Meade's headquarters, he was questioned by General Meade as to the status of Sheridan's force. As a result of this questioning, Meade sent the following two dispatches to Grant via telegraph.

Lieutenant General Grant:

>Headquarters of the Army of the Potomac
>March 31 1865 7:40 p.m.

Captain Sheridan from Sheridan's cavalry is here and is directed to you by a staff officer. He reports that General Sheridan is just north of Dinwiddie Courthouse having been repulsed by the enemy's infantry on the dirt road running northwest from north of Dinwiddie. General Sheridan states that if he is forced to retire it will be on the road. The staff officer leaves here to report to you.

>G. G. Meade Maj. General[2]

Shortly thereafter, upon reflection, Meade sent the following dispatch to Grant. It was this second dispatch that triggered all that followed.

Lieutenant General Grant:

> Headquarters of the Army of the Potomac
> March 31 1865 9:45 p.m.
>
> Would it not be well for Warren to go down with his whole corps and smash up the force in front of Sheridan? Humphreys can hold them to the Boydton Plank Road and the refusal along with it. Bartlett's brigade is now on the road from G. Boisseau's running north where it crosses Gravelly Run, he having gone there down the White Oak Road. Warren could go at once that way, and take the force threatening Sheridan in rear, or he could send one division to support Sheridan at Dinwiddie, and move on the enemy's rear with the other two.
>
> G. G. Meade Maj. General[3]

(This was the plan that was ultimately implemented. Warren was to the north of the Confederate forces. One of his three divisions would proceed down the Boydton Plank Road to join Sheridan facing the Confederates and the other two would drop down in the Confederates' rear. The Confederates would be boxed in between the two forces and captured or destroyed.)

Grant readily accepted Meade's proposal and at 10:15 p.m. sent him the following: "Let Warren move in the way you propose," and added, "urge him not to stop for anything."[4] Sheridan continued, it will be observed that General Meade said that "Warren could go at once."

Meade transmitted the implementation order to Warren. Although the dispatch contained no time of origin, we know that Warren received it at 10:50 p.m. It read:

> Headquarters of the Army of the Potomac
> March 31 1865
>
> Major-General Warren,
> 5th Corps:
>
> Send Griffin promptly as ordered by the Boydton Plank Road but move the balance of your command by the road Bartlett is on, and strike the enemy in the rear who is between him and Dinwiddie. General Sheridan reported his last position as north of Dinwiddie Court House near Dr. Smiths, the enemy holding the cross-roads at that point. Should the enemy turn on you, your line of retreat will be by J. M. Brooke's and R. Boisseau's on Boydton Plank Road; see one inch map. You must be very prompt in this movement, and be at the forks of the road at J. M. Brooke's before the enemy, so as to open the road to R. Boisseau's. The enemy will probably retire towards Five Forks, that being the direction of their main attack this day. Don't encumber yourself with anything that will impede your progress, or prevent your moving in any direction across the country. Let me know when Griffin starts and when you start. Acknowledge receipt.
>
> G. G. Meade Maj. General[5]

Sheridan, pointing to the phrases in the order requiring promptness, alleged that Warren disobeyed the order. Specifically he cited the phrases "send Griffin promptly," "You must be very prompt" and "Don't encumber yourself with anything that will impede your progress, or prevent your moving in any direction across the country."

Warren indeed immediately ordered Ayres (who was on the Boydton Plank Road instead of Griffin as assumed by Grant, Sheridan, and Meade) to proceed to Dinwiddie

Courthouse. However, the other two divisions which were ordered to drop down in the Confederate rear were ordered to mass where they were.

Sheridan said nothing about the downed bridge over Gravelly Run that was between him and Ayres. He merely stated that Ayres was met in the morning by one of his staff officers who conducted him to the desired position. The Sheridan narrative continued that the other two divisions (Griffin's and Crawford's) only moved after daylight in accordance with orders from Warren, who thus disregarded Meade's orders to move promptly.

Sheridan then returned to the night of March 31–April 1. Once Grant and Meade had agreed on a course of action and Meade had sent the necessary directive to Warren, Grant sent a message to Sheridan advising him of the plan. The message was as follows:

> Dabney's Mills
> March 31st, 1865 10:05 p.m.
>
> Major General Sheridan
> The Fifth Corps has been ordered to your support. Two divisions will go by J. Boisseau's and one down the Boydton Road. In addition to this I have sent MacKenzie's cavalry which will reach you by the Vaughan Road. All these forces except MacKenzie's cavalry will reach you by 12 to-night.
> You will assume command of the whole force sent to operate with you, and use it to the best of your ability to destroy the force which your force fought so gallantly today.
>
> U. S. Grant
> Lieut. General[6]

Sheridan contended that he waited and waited and, when nobody reached him by midnight, did what he considered to be the next best thing. He sent a message to General Warren dated April 1, 3 a.m. ordering him to attack the Confederates at daylight.

The enemy retired from Sheridan's front toward Five Forks during the night. Warren's force not only did not arrive at midnight, but did not arrive in order to attack at daylight as specified in Sheridan's message. Sheridan contended that as of the time of his 3 a.m. message, Griffin and Crawford had not moved and were still in bivouac at the place where Warren had placed them the night before, and only after 3 a.m. did they begin to move.

Sheridan did not state the precise times each of the three divisions of Warren joined him, but stated that it was about 11 a.m. when Warren personally appeared before him. He concluded: "I felt that there were no circumstances in existence during the night which should have prevented the movement of these two divisions in obedience to the order, and not enough to justify the delay at the bridge by the other division as the creek could have been forded."[7]

Sheridan then directed Warren to hold fast at J. Boisseau's house, refresh his men, and be ready to move to the front when required. In the meantime, Brigadier General Ranald MacKenzie's cavalry had arrived and Sheridan ordered MacKenzie and command to rest in front of Dinwiddie Courthouse until further orders. While Warren and MacKenzie waited, Sheridan's cavalry pressed the enemy back to Five Forks, where they took a stand.

At 1 p.m. Sheridan ordered Warren to move the Fifth Corps to the area of the Gravelly Run Church and put it in line of battle, two divisions in front and one in column of regiments behind the right division. This was oblique to and but a short distance from the White Oak Road, and about one mile from Five Forks. Sheridan found the Fifth Corps moving to its deployment position very slowly. He became very anxious, as the sun was getting low. They had to fight before sundown or go back. The distance from the resting location of the Fifth Corps to the Gravelly Run Church was but two miles and the corps was not formed in line of battle until 4 p.m. Three hours had elapsed from the time Warren received the order until the Fifth Corps was deployed and ready to attack. Three hours to move two miles and deploy. Sheridan stated: "I did not know then, nor do I know now, of any special effort General Warren made to bring up his corps."[8]

The corps was to swing to the left upon reaching the White Oak Road, placing it perpendicular to the Confederate line, the two divisions being closed up. Ayres's division (that to the left), obeyed the order and hit the enemy in its flank. Crawford's division, to Ayres's right, became detached and marched off angling away from the enemy. This not only put it out of the action but created a situation that could have resulted in disaster.

Sheridan stated: "I do not recollect that General Warren was present anywhere near the line on this occasion or any efforts he made to bring Crawford's division into the position contemplated in the orders."[9]

Finally, Sheridan gave his explanation as to why he relieved Warren after the battle was substantially won. He believed that although the battle had been won the emergency was not over. His troops were isolated from the main Union army. He was, in fact, closer to Lee's line than to the Union line, and Lee might yet attack his detached force. Consequently, Sheridan concluded: "I deemed it after due deliberation, to be in the best interest of the service to relieve him, which I accordingly did and I put the corps under the command of General Griffin."[10]

The Questioning of Sheridan

It was now Warren's turn. His counsel, Albert Stickney, subjected Sheridan to a seemingly endless series of questions—some incisive, some silly and, in the early phases, definitely weighted toward the ridiculous.

Stickney began by asking a series of questions about the maps and documents Sheridan used. The only new fact that this questioning elicited was that Sheridan had access to information on Warren's situation other than what he received from messages from Grant and Meade. He also received information from approximately sixty scouts.

Stickney then shifted to asking questions about what information Sheridan received from Meade, Warren's superior, the night of March 31–April 1. It turned out that when Meade issued the order to Warren to join Sheridan, he also forwarded a copy of the order to Sheridan by courier. Stickney pursued this matter by asking useless questions, such as how long it took the courier to ride from Meade's headquarters to Sheridan, and asking about everything but the color of the horse.

Stickney then latched onto a new subject. Grant's message to Sheridan advised Sheridan that Warren would join him by midnight. When Warren (Ayres) did not appear,

Sheridan finally sent a staff officer to ride up the Boydton Plank Road until he found Ayres to tell him which road to turn off when he finally approached Dinwiddie. Sheridan sent the staff officer off at about 4 a.m. Stickney queried that, if Sheridan really expected Warren to arrive at midnight, why did he wait until 4 a.m. to dispatch the staff officer? Sheridan replied that he waited, waited, waited, and by 4 a.m. had moved his force and sent the staff officer to find the approaching Ayres and to tell him where to turn off the Boydton Plank Road.

And so it went, on and on. Stickney often pressed Sheridan for details that he was unlikely to know even fifteen years in the past. This brief exchange was typical of the whole:

> Q. This report of General Ayres is dated April 12; you cannot undertake to say that there was any error in that?
> A. No; I have nothing to say about it.
> Q. Then if you recollect, where were you at the time you received that 10:05 dispatch?
> A. I was at Dinwiddie, behind my lines in front of Dinwiddie Courthouse.
> Q. Can you recollect what you did with the original?
> A. No, sir.
> Q. When did you last see the original?
> A. I don't know.
> Q. Have you any reason to believe that the original is in existence anywhere?
> A. No, sir.
> Q. Did you turn it over to the War Department?
> A. I don't know.
> Q. You are familiar with the handwriting of most of the officers at General Grant's headquarters, I suppose?
> A. No, sir; I knew General Grant's handwriting; I could not at this time identify the handwriting of any officer, except General Grant's.[11]

None of this had any relevance to the matter at hand. It appeared that much of the questioning was designed to embarrass General Sheridan. Sheridan maintained his composure remarkably well and usually addressed Stickney as "sir."

One of the more ridiculous sequences of questions related to Grant's message of 10:05 p.m. the night of March 31 when Grant advised Sheridan that Warren had been ordered to join him. To recall, the message read: "The Fifth Corps has been ordered to your support. Two divisions will go by J. Boisseau's and one down the Boydton Road ... all the forces should reach you by 12 to-night. You will assume command of the whole force."[12]

As visualized by Grant, the two divisions coming down via Boisseau's would drop in Pickett's rear, and the division coming down the Boydton Plank Road would join Sheridan in Pickett's front. Pickett would thus be boxed in and eventually destroyed. Sheridan would, of course, command the whole Union force in the battle.

Stickney attempted to make the outlandish point that the two divisions assigned to cut off Pickett from Five Forks could not possibly reach Sheridan by midnight as stated in the dispatch of Grant, as they would have to fight their way through Pickett's force to do so. Stickney actually thought that he had trumped Sheridan and Grant by this ludicrous interpretation of Grant's dispatch. Thus, the day's testimony came to an end.

The court reconvened on Governor's Island on Wednesday, May 5, 1880, at 11 a.m. The interrogation of Sheridan by Stickney continued. Stickney made the point that until Warren reported in to Sheridan, he was under Meade's command, and any messages exchanged between Meade and Grant were thus not strictly relevant to the case.

The testimony this date related entirely to the question of whether or not Warren did all he could to move his force to join Sheridan on the night of March 31–April 1. It appears that the two divisions assigned to drop in Pickett's rear could have arrived earlier than they did. Now, let us look at the situation of the third division, that of General Ayres. Ayres was to proceed down the Boydton Plank Road to Dinwiddie but was stopped by a downed bridge over Gravelly Run. Stickney believed this was sufficient reason for the delay. Sheridan thought it was not.

It had rained torrentially all day on the 30th but had stopped by evening and did not rain at all on the 31st. Sheridan testified that on the evening of March 30, after the rains stopped, he had personally ridden across Gravelly Run just above where the downed bridge was, and the water did not reach his stirrups. He further testified that the bottom was firm, that it was not muddy and he had absolutely no trouble in crossing.

Stickney countered that the run could have been deeper twenty-four hours after the rain had stopped. Sheridan responded that the crest depended on the length of the run, the run was short, and he doubted that it would have been as high.

The court reconvened Thursday, May 6, 1880, at 11 a.m. Stickney's interrogation of Sheridan continued. The questioning was devoted entirely to events of April 1, 1865, the day of the battle.

In this instance, Stickney's questioning was greatly improved and followed a logical sequence. In many instances, Sheridan answered that he could not remember. In judging Sheridan we must remember that, although this was the climactic day in the life of Gouverneur Warren, it was not so for Sheridan. The war ended on April 1, 1865, for Warren, but not for Sheridan. It continued for eight more days of furious combat and pursuit in which Sheridan was a central figure. Then, while Warren settled down to the sedate life of an engineer, Sheridan presided over the Indian wars.

Let us see if we can summarize Sheridan's answers to Stickney in a logical sequence: Warren's corps did not arrive until the early morning of April 1. By this time, it was too late to cut off Pickett's force from retreating to Five Forks. Warren himself did not report to Sheridan until about 11 a.m. Sheridan ordered Warren to put his troops in bivouac to rest and await further orders. Sometime later, MacKenzie arrived and reported to Sheridan. Sheridan ordered MacKenzie's cavalry into bivouac at Dinwiddie Courthouse to await further orders.

In the meantime the Confederates, pressed by Sheridan's cavalry, withdrew to Five Forks and there took their stand. By 1 p.m. Sheridan had formulated his plan of attack. Sometime before, time unspecified, General Babcock from Grant's headquarters arrived with the message that Sheridan could relieve Warren if he so desired. This was unusual but not unprecedented. In at least one instance that Sheridan could recall, he was given similar authority.

At about 1 p.m. Sheridan advised Warren of his plan and ordered Warren to bring his corps up to the vicinity of Gravelly Run Church and form in line of battle. The distance from Warren's bivouac area to Gravelly Run Church was approximately two miles.

It took three hours, from 1 p.m. at the time the order was delivered to Warren, until 4 p.m. for the troops to move the two miles and form in line of battle. Sheridan was desperate to complete the battle before nightfall, and considered Warren's movements excessively slow. Sheridan complained to Warren about the slowness of the movement but could not recollect the words that he used. He did remember that he was patient and said nothing disagreeable. Sheridan was asked specifically whether he, at any time, had any prejudice against General Warren. Sheridan said that he did not.

Sheridan's plan was basically as follows: The Confederate line ran for about one mile along the White Oak Road and then ended with a refuse. A refuse is a turn in the line (approximately a right angle in this case) to protect the flank. The plan was for the cavalry to demonstrate in front of the Confederate line to hold the Confederates in place. The Fifth Corps would deliver the punch. Its objective point was the refuse. The Fifth Corps would hit the refuse obliquely, wheel, be at right angles to the Confederate main line and march down the line, hitting it in front, flank, and rear.

Warren's corps lined up as follows: Ayres to the left joined by Crawford to the right and Griffin following Crawford. MacKenzie's cavalry would first occupy the White Oak Road and then operate to Crawford's right.

Warren's corps marched off at 4 p.m. assuming the refuse was but a short distance ahead. It was not. The Confederate line with its refuse ended some hundreds of yards to Warren's left. This caused confusion when Warren hit the White Oak Road with the Confederates firing into Ayres's flank. In the confusion that followed, Sheridan and Ayres rode out ahead to reorient the line. Sheridan expected Warren to be out there helping, but noticed him behind the Union line.

This was the third time he became dissatisfied with Warren. The first was on being late in arriving the night of March 31–April 1, the second on being slow in forming his corps for the attack at Gravelly Run Church, and the third for exerting less effort than he expected in straightening out the situation at the outset of the battle. In the confusion, Crawford, followed by Griffin, became detached from Ayres and marched off to the northwest, away from the battle and the Confederate line.

Ayres and the Union cavalry won the battle by late afternoon. Sheridan considered his position precarious and anticipated fighting ahead. Consequently, with the battle won, he sent a staff officer to find and advise Warren that he was relieved. He, in turn, advised Griffin that he was in charge. Warren later appeared before him and he ordered Warren to report to General Grant. Sheridan could remember none of the details of the conversation between him and Warren, but said that he did not consider this a punishment but merely a matter of seeking more effective command for future operations.

Score for the day: Sheridan 1, Warren 0.

The court resumed the questioning of Sheridan on Friday, May 7, recessed Saturday and Sunday, May 8 and 9, and continued Monday, May 10 and Tuesday, May 11 and concluded Wednesday, May 12. During this period, Stickney did score points for Warren to the detriment of Sheridan.

During the day of March 31, 1865, Warren and Sheridan were operating independently, Warren some five to ten miles north of Sheridan. Warren, while reaching for the White Oak Road, was struck by the Confederates and temporarily pushed back. He was then reinforced, recovered all the lost ground, and pushed on beyond the White Oak Road.

Later that date, Sheridan was attacked by the Confederates and pushed all the way back to the Dinwiddie Courthouse. In later writings, Sheridan attributed this setback to Warren. He contended that once Warren was pushed back, this made Confederate troops available, who then marched down the White Oak Road, joined those already there, and pushed Sheridan back to Dinwiddie Courthouse. Stickney demonstrated that the Confederate forces facing Warren and Sheridan were separate and distinct and that Warren's temporary embarrassment had nothing to do with Sheridan's defeat.

Stickney then returned to the actual battle of Five Forks. As we have previously noted, early in the battle Crawford's division became separated from that of Ayres, and Crawford marched obliquely away from the Confederate line and the action. Sheridan had opined that since Warren was the corps commander, he was responsible for the actions of all three of his divisions and that this action reflected poorly on his capabilities.

Stickney established that, unknown to Sheridan to this day, Crawford was confronted with a Confederate cavalry division commanded by General Munford that seriously affected his ability to change directions. Stickney also pointed out that Crawford suffered more casualties that date then either of the two other divisions of the corps.

Sheridan did not see Warren—from early in the beginning of the battle, when he saw Warren behind Ayres's lines, while he (Sheridan) was out in front trying to rally the troops—until after the battle. He did not know that Warren went after Crawford to reorient him. He did not know that Warren sent a detachment of the Fifth Corps to seize the ford on the Ford Road to cut off the Confederate retreat. He did not know that Warren successfully reoriented Crawford so as to attack the Confederate line in the rear, and he did not know that Warren had personally led the final attack.

Stickney asked: "As far as I understand, you had no knowledge at the time of what General Warren did do in this battle after you parted with him at the beginning of the attack?" Sheridan answered: "No, I had no knowledge."[13]

The attention then turned once again to the downed bridge over Gravelly Run the night of March 31. Sheridan once again contended that the run was easily fordable and as evidence pointed to the fact that not only he, but Colonel Horace Porter, General O.E. Babcock, and General James W. Forsyth at different times all crossed the run one or more times between late afternoon of the 30th and the afternoon of the 1st without trouble.

The questioning of Sheridan continued until May 12. One of the last areas of questioning related to the performance of the Fifth Corps for the last eight days of the war, after Warren had been released. It had been superb. The significance of this is often lost on the reader and perhaps also on the court. The function of any general is not only battle management, but the training and disciplining of the troops before they enter battle. The fact that the Fifth Corps was highly trained and disciplined can be attributed to none other than its long term commander, Gouverneur Warren.

Frederick C. Newhall

We now come to Wednesday May 12, 1880, and the next person to testify. This was Frederick C. Newhall. Newhall was not a member of the regular army but served in the volunteer army throughout the war. As of April 1, 1865, Newhall was a lieutenant colonel serving as assistant adjutant on Sheridan's staff. Newhall was either at, near or a participant in each transaction involving Sheridan and Warren that critical day. Newhall also happened to be the author of *With Sheridan in the Final Campaign Against Lee* published in 1866.

Newhall acknowledged at the outset that the account of the battle of Five Forks in his book was based entirely on the reports and writings of Sheridan and, hence, the book itself could not stand the test of impartial objectivity. Newhall's memory was not good and, to the great majority of questions, answered that he could not remember or did not know, or variants of the two.

The first meeting of Sheridan and Warren occurred at approximately 11 on the morning of April 1 when Warren reported in to Sheridan. Newhall stated that, although he was nearby, he heard none of the conversation but saw that the meeting was very brief.

Newhall next saw Sheridan and Warren together near Gravelly Run Church as Warren's corps was moving up and forming in line of battle. Newhall estimated that this was at about 2 or 3 p.m. Sheridan waited with Warren until the advance of the Fifth Corps began. This was perhaps one and a half hours. They were sometimes standing and sometimes sitting down, but Newhall could not recollect any special activity on the part of either, except at times he observed Sheridan pacing up and down impatiently. Newhall heard some of the conversation between them, could not recollect the words; there was an urgency, but Newhall heard nothing disagreeable.

After the Fifth Corps marched to the White Oak Road, the action commenced, and Ayres's division became confused. Newhall was sent by Sheridan to notify Warren that the divisions on the right (Crawford followed by Griffin) were becoming disjointed and separated from the battle. Newhall found Warren on the south side of the White Oak Road behind Ayres's division, gave him the message, rode back to Sheridan, and moved on with Ayres's division. About fifteen minutes elapsed and Sheridan again sent Newhall to Warren to notify him that the troops of Crawford and Griffin were going entirely away from the battle and "ruining the whole thing."[14] Newhall found Warren at a place called "The Chimneys" and delivered the message. Warren was sitting on his horse. Newhall told him that General Sheridan was exceedingly anxious that there was a very long interval between Crawford-Griffin and Ayres. Newhall urged Warren, as strongly as he thought proper, to get those troops to Ayres's support. Warren responded that it had been attended to.

Newhall then returned to Sheridan. Sheridan was now standing inside where the Confederate line had formerly been. Less than an hour had elapsed since the Fifth Corps had left Gravelly Run Church and it was getting dark. Newhall further attested that Sheridan was angry when he sent him to Warren the first time and more angry when he sent him the second. However, in Newhall's recollection, he saw nothing that indicated the anger was directed at Warren. Newhall had no recollection of the words Sheridan used. He did say that Sheridan was very emphatic in telling him to find Warren at once and deliver the message.

And so ended the testimony of Frederick Newhall and the day.

Major W.H.H. Benyaurd

The court reconvened Thursday, May 13, 1880, at 11 a.m. The next to testify was Major W.H.H. Benyaurd. Benyaurd was an officer in the regular army and, at the time of the battle of Five Forks, a first lieutenant and brevet captain. He proved to be an excellent witness with an unusually good memory.

As of March 1865, he was an engineer on the staff of General Meade. At the outset of the current campaign, Meade temporarily transferred him to the staff of Warren to serve as Warren might desire.

Benyaurd testified that, on the night of March 31, he had already gone to sleep but was awakened and told to report to Warren. Warren told him that the bridge on the Boydton Plank Road over Gravelly Run was down, and that he was to go and see if it could be repaired or replaced.

Benyaurd, accompanied by Captain Wadsworth of Warren's staff, proceeded to the site and determined the bridge could not be repaired. Benyaurd checked the depth of the water with a stick in several places and found it to be over four feet deep and decided that the river was not fordable. He selected a site just below the old bridge for the new. This would require constructing a road from the Boydton Plank Road down to the bridge and then, once the bridge was complete, a road back from the bridge to the Boydton Plank Road. He decided that he could construct the bridge and the necessary connecting roads in an hour if he had the help of the entire headquarters escort. He so reported to Warren, was given the escort, and proceeded back to the site. When he began, the road leading to the bridge was empty.

Benyaurd completed the bridge and connecting roads on schedule and, on returning to the road, encountered General Ayres at the head of his division. He asked Ayres how long he had been waiting to cross, and Ayres replied that it had only been minutes, as he was just arriving.

Upon questioning, Benyaurd further testified that, even if Ayres had to wait two hours or so for the bridge to be complete, in the end, he would have made better time with the bridge than without it in his march to Dinwiddie. Benyaurd said the waters in the tributaries to the northwest of Gravelly Run were so high that, earlier in the day, he had to build a bridge over one of the tributaries. He estimated that when the water of all the tributaries ran into Gravelly Run, the water would be deeper at the bridge on the night of the 31st than it was on the 30th.

Questioning now shifted to the day of April 1, 1865, the day of the battle. More specifically, the questioning shifted to the activities of Warren and the Fifth Corps from the time the Fifth Corps went into bivouac at J. Boisseau's after reporting in to Sheridan until the end of the battle.

Sheridan ordered the Fifth Corps to proceed from J. Boisseau's to Gravelly Run Church and to form a line of battle. From this time until the end of the battle, Major Benyaurd was either with Warren or on a mission dispatched by Warren. Benyaurd measured the distance between J. Boisseau's and Gravelly Run Church and it came to two and three-sixteenth miles.

Warren and staff, including Benyaurd, were at the head of the column. The sequence of march was Crawford, Griffin, and last, Ayres. As far as Benyaurd could recollect, it moved at a respectable pace. At one point, Warren asked Benyaurd to proceed to Ayres at the end of the column to speed him up. Ayres replied that he already was.

The corps stepped off for the nearby White Oak Road and action at about 4 p.m. It was hit in the flank and Warren ordered Benyaurd to carry a message to Colonel Winthrop, the commander of the brigade on the far left that was in the heat of the action. Benyaurd told Winthrop which way to face and to march in the direction of the sun.

Later, Warren ordered Benyaurd to proceed to Crawford and "get Crawford in." Benyaurd did not know where Crawford was, but found him near the Ford Road and delivered the message. It was now almost 5:30 p.m. and Crawford was in action. Benyaurd noticed that after Crawford turned down the Ford Road, Warren was proceeding towards Crawford.

Benyaurd next encountered Captain Allen from Sheridan's staff. Allen had a written message for Warren. He told Benyaurd that Sheridan had relived Warren from command.

The questioning of Benyaurd continued Friday, May 14, 1880, but elicited nothing new.

James W. Wadsworth

Next to testify was James W. Wadsworth. This was the same Captain James W. Wadsworth of Warren's staff who accompanied Major Benyaurd to the downed bridge on the night of March 31, 1865. Wadsworth was not a regular army officer, but had served in the Volunteer Army during the war. At the time of his testimony he was comptroller of the State of New York.

As of the night of March 31, 1865, Wadsworth was aide de camp to General Warren. He was sent down to check on the bridge by General Warren at about 10 p.m. He reported back and Warren sent for Benyaurd.

Wadsworth distinctly remembered an incident when he first went to the downed bridge. There was a picket there and they heard the clatter of horses' feet on the far side of the run. They assumed it was the enemy and lay down. The picket challenged the horsemen and it turned out to be a friendly cavalry patrol. Wadsworth called over and asked if an officer was there. There was an affirmative reply. Wadsworth requested that the officer cross over and report to General Warren. Wadsworth noted that the horse sank so deeply into the water that he assumed that it was swimming as it crossed.

Wadsworth confirmed that there was no one on the pike at the bridge at the time he and Benyaurd returned to build a bridge. He returned to headquarters before Benyaurd and there was still nobody on the pike. Wadsworth thus affirmed Benyaurd's story that the downed bridge played absolutely no role in Ayres's late arrival to Sheridan. Ayres did not arrive until the bridge was complete.

Wadsworth also pinpointed the location of Warren's headquarters the night of March 31. It was at the Wilson house, which was located approximately one half mile up the Boydton Plank Road from the bridge.

About daylight, Warren, accompanied by staff and Wadsworth, vacated his headquarters at the Wilson house and rode a fraction of a mile to the west to the vicinity of R. Butler where Crawford's and Griffin's divisions were congregated. It was just about break of day when they arrived. The two divisions began a movement to the southwest almost immediately. They marched to J. Boisseau's, where they encamped. It was now about 7 or 8 a.m.

Interrogation now shifted to the morning of April 1. Crawford and Griffin, who had come down overland, were now camped at J. Boisseau's; Ayres, who had come down the Boydton Plank Road, was camped about one-half mile closer to Dinwiddie Courthouse and farther away from Five Forks. General Warren himself had come down with Crawford and Griffin, and now proceeded up the road toward Five Forks to report in to General Sheridan.

Wadsworth received an order, he believed from Colonel Bankhead of Warren's staff, to go back and bring up Ayres. It was now about noon. Crawford, Griffin, and Ayres were now all marching toward Gravelly Run Church. Wadsworth was with Ayres. Ayres's division was about one half mile behind Crawford and Griffin. Wadsworth stated that the division marched as fast as it could, but the road was very muddy. He noticed no delay in the marching of the division. Ayres arrived at Gravelly Run Church when Crawford and Griffin were already forming up.

Questioning now jumped to the actual battle. After the corps marched from Gravelly Run Church to the White Oak Road and entered into combat, General Warren sent Wadsworth to Ayres to find out how he was getting along. Ayres told him to tell Warren that the troops were doing well and moving steadily forward. Wadsworth then spent the next three-quarters of an hour looking for Warren to give him Ayres's report. He finally found Warren in an open field three-quarters of a mile north of the White Oak Road. It was not at the Chimneys but near the Ford Road.

Warren, accompanied by Wadsworth, then moved to the Ford Road. Wadsworth was next sent by Warren to find General Griffin. He rode due west about one-half mile, ran into Rebels, and turned back. Wadsworth finally found Warren to the east on the south side of the White Oak Road. By that time, the battle was winding down and there were only a few scattered shots. Warren was in Mrs. Gillian's field when Wadsworth found him. It was now already dusk, about 6:30 p.m.

James W. Forsyth

Testimony continued that date. The next to be called was Lieutenant Colonel James W. Forsyth. As of April 1, 1865, Forsyth was Sheridan's chief of staff and was with him the day of the battle and for several days preceding.

The battle with Pickett on March 31 ended after dark, Forsyth said in testimony. Immediately after hostilities that date, Captain M.V. Sheridan was sent to Grant's headquarters to report the state of affairs. About 8 or 9 p.m. General Philip Sheridan set up his headquarters at the Dinwiddie Hotel, but it is doubtful that Sheridan or any of the staff slept that night. Colonel Kellogg of Sheridan's staff was also sent to Grant's headquarters that night. As far as Forsyth could recall, the round trips of these two were the only personnel to transit from Sheridan's headquarters to Grant's that night. Forsyth could not recall any officers bringing dispatches from Meade's headquarters that night. Forsyth was prompted to recollect that an officer was sent up the Boydton Plank Road, at time unspecified, to meet the oncoming Ayres and direct him to turn off toward Five Forks before reaching Dinwiddie.

The staff vacated the Dinwiddie Hotel at the break of day and headed up the road toward Five Forks. The Confederate force had been withdrawing during the night and early morning toward Five Forks as Sheridan's cavalry followed them. There was some skirmishing and some heavy fighting. By 1 p.m. the sides were facing at Five Forks where the Confederates made a stand.

Forsyth was with Sheridan when Warren reported in to him. Forsyth's recollection was that Warren stated that he had come up with two of his divisions. Sheridan ordered Warren to let the two divisions now halted at J. Boisseau's, plus Ayres's division, which was one-half mile closer to Dinwiddie, rest where they were. Forsyth also recollected that, in the conversation between Sheridan and Warren, there was some mention about a delay in moving up because of a downed bridge. He attributed this comment to Warren. The meeting took place close up to Five Forks just behind the cavalry command.

Forsyth recollected that the Fifth Corps moved off from Gravelly Run Church toward the enemy position at about 4:30 p.m. Sheridan and staff, including Forsyth, were continually with Ayres's line of battle. Sheridan was moving to and fro along Ayres's front continuously, from start to finish. The battle was substantially ended at sundown. Forsyth himself did not recall giving any orders or instructions during the battle, but knew that Sheridan was giving orders to find Crawford's division and "get them in." Sheridan had a habit of repeating orders, sending one officer and then another five minutes later. Forsyth could not recall seeing either Crawford's or Griffin's divisions once action started. At one point during the battle, Forsyth's horse bolted and almost ran into the Rebel lines. He distinctly heard a Rebel yell, "Here come the Yankee sons of bitches."[15]

Forsyth did not see Warren during the battle. After the battle was won he was given a written order to deliver to Warren. He found Warren near the intersection of the White Oak Road and the Ford Road. The message was that Warren was relieved of command of the Fifth Corps and was to report to General Grant. It was after this that Sheridan personally advised Griffin that he was now in command of the Fifth Corps.

Forsyth had been with Sheridan earlier in the day when General Babcock of Grant's staff came and advised Sheridan that he had the authority to relieve Warren if he so desired. This occurred shortly after Warren reported in to Sheridan. From that time up until the moment Forsyth was handed the order to relieve Warren, Sheridan had said absolutely nothing about relieving Warren. He did express impatience at the forming up of the Fifth Corps prior to the attack, but up until the actual relief, Sheridan had controlled whatever feelings he may have harbored and said nothing derogatory about Warren.

The court adjourned and reconvened on Saturday, May 15, 1880, at 11 a.m. The interrogation of Lieutenant Colonel Forsyth continued. It shifted to the events before the battle. It turned out that Forsyth himself had written and delivered the 3 a.m. dispatch of April 1 to Warren (this was the so-called "attack at dawn" message). Sheridan dictated the message, Forsyth wrote it, and Sheridan signed it. Forsyth then set out for his horse. It was about 3:15 a.m. when he began up the Boydton Plank Road from Dinwiddie to

Warren's headquarters. Forsyth rode alone without escort, always fearful that he would run into Confederates. When he arrived at Gravelly Run, he encountered pickets. They told him that another horseman had crossed earlier that night and pointed out the place. This was very near the road. Forsyth believed he reached Warren's headquarters a little after four. He was shown into Warren's room. Warren was lying on a camp bed but arose and read the dispatch, in fact, read it twice, and endorsed the message with the time of receipt. It was received at 4:50 a.m. Warren then sent for some aides and assured Forsyth that Sheridan's orders would be carried out. After just a few minutes, Forsyth set out on the return journey.

By the time Forsyth reached Gravelly Run, there was just a glimpse of daylight. He watered his horse in the middle of Gravelly Run. Forsyth saw no new bridge and believed that, had there been one then, he would have seen it. He experienced no delays on his return ride. It took somewhat over one hour to ride from Warren's headquarters to Sheridan's. Forsyth did not see Ayres on either the up or return rides.

Just as Forsyth was returning, an officer from Sheridan, name un-remembered, was sent up the Boydton Plank Road to advise Ayres to turn off in the road to the west before he reached Dinwiddie. Sheridan and staff were moving out of the hotel and proceeding toward Five Forks just as Forsyth returned. It was now the gray of the morning.

Questioning now returned to the battle itself. Forsyth's memory was somewhat different than it had been when questioned earlier. He now recalled being sent to turn the diverging division of Crawford back to the main battle scene. He encountered two brigade commanders of Crawford, and both, not knowing him, declined his order to reorient their brigades toward Ayres in what appeared to be the main conflict.

Forsyth arrived at a road he did not recognize (the Ford Road). He met two women and asked the name of the road. They refused to give him any information. Forsyth next came upon Warren. Warren was also seeking Crawford to reorient him. Warren did not recognize Forsyth and erroneously assumed that he was commanding Crawford's troops in the area. Forsyth identified himself and assured Warren that he was also attempting to reorient Crawford. Warren then rode off rapidly.

The enemy fleeing down the Ford Road toward Hatchers Run to escape ran into Crawford's troops, whom they did not expect to find there, and there was a sharp fight. Around that time, Forsyth had his horse shot out from under him. He acquired another. He eventually met Sheridan on the White Oak Road.

Captain Michael Vincent Sheridan

Captain M. V. Sheridan was the youngest brother of General Sheridan, being nine years his junior. Unlike his brother, he did not attend West Point, but entered the Volunteer Army at the outset of the war.

At the time of the Civil War, nepotism was the norm. Numerous generals had relatives on their staffs. As of April 1, 1865, young Sheridan was aide de camp to his famous brother. By that time, he had participated in numerous battles, was cited for gallantry, and was a seasoned veteran.

On the eve of March 31, at the termination of fighting that date, General Sheridan dispatched him to proceed to General Grant's headquarters and report the state of affairs. He carried no written message as the report was to be verbal. Young Sheridan departed about 6:30, before General Sheridan and staff settled in the Dinwiddie Hotel. He set out on the Vaughan Road, not knowing exactly where Grant's headquarters were. He came upon General Meade's headquarters and stopped to ask for directions. Meade questioned him and they consulted maps by lantern light. Meade asked Sheridan if a force coming down the Boydton Plank Road would not come in at the flank and rear of the enemy. Sheridan said that he thought it would. Meade said that he would send such a force. The time was almost half past 7 or 8 p.m. Young Sheridan then proceeded on to Grant's headquarters. It was on this side of Hatchers Run and hence he did not have to cross. He must have crossed Gravelly Run en route, but had no recollection and did not know if there was a pontoon bridge over it or not.

Captain Sheridan said he believed that it was about 8 p.m. when he arrived at Grant's headquarters. He spent as much as two hours there, much of it waiting for General Rawlins to send information back to Sheridan.

While young Sheridan was at Grant's headquarters, Colonel Kellogg from Sheridan's staff arrived. He bore a written dispatch from Sheridan. It was the one that began, "The enemy attacked me at about 10 o'clock today on the road coming in from the west of Dinwiddie Court House" and ended with the words, "This force is too strong for us. I will hold on to Dinwiddie Court House until I am compelled to leave." This message was delivered to Grant about nine or half past nine.

Captain M.V. Sheridan then left with the verbal assurance that troops would be sent to General Philip Sheridan's support that night. He could not recollect if it had yet been decided if the troops would be Warren's or someone else's. At least some of the troops would come down the Boydton Plank Road. Others would approach so as to hit the enemy in the rear.

Young Sheridan departed Grant's headquarters about 9 or 9:30 p.m. He did not stop off at Meade's headquarters but cut across country. He arrived at the Dinwiddie Hotel about 10 or 10:30. He found the staff singing and playing the piano as he delivered his report.

A courier came from General Grant that night at about 11 p.m. He brought a written message to the effect that assistance would be sent to them that night.

General Sheridan and staff, including Captain Sheridan, left the hotel just as it was beginning to get light the morning of the 1st and headed toward Five Forks. When near the front, a messenger was sent to find the oncoming General Ayres on the Boydton Plank Road and advise him to turn off the pike on the road leading westward before Dinwiddie. Captain Sheridan supposed the messenger was General J. W. Forsyth, but later found out that it was not. It was already daylight when the messenger left.

The questioning now shifted to the afternoon of the 1st. The Fifth Corps formed up at Gravelly Run Church and moved out to the attack at about 4 p.m. Sheridan and staff were with Ayres on the left. The line of battle proceeded but a short distance and the skirmish line fell to the ground and began shooting in the air; that is, there was no enemy in sight. Captain Sheridan witnessed no similar experience to date and was astonished. This occurred well before the skirmish line reached the White Oak Road. Because of this, Captain Sheridan was sent to General Merritt, Sheridan's chief of cavalry, to stop his attack. The plan had been for the cavalry under Merritt to attack the Confederate line in front just as the Fifth Corps hit it in the flank.

Captain Sheridan found Merritt near the intersection of the White Oak Road and the Dinwiddie Courthouse road. He directed Merritt to withhold his attack, as the Fifth Corps was not behaving well, until the Fifth Corps executed its attack.

Captain Sheridan returned, the problem appeared to have been resolved, and the Fifth Corps had moved off and was nowhere in sight. He met General Horace Porter of Grant's staff and asked him where General Sheridan was. Porter pointed towards the White Oak Road, where the young Sheridan found his brother. The fighting was already dying down, the battle won, and young Sheridan remained with his brother the remainder of the day. Captain Sheridan believed that it was about 5:30 p.m. when he joined his brother. He thought that he saw General Warren with General Sheridan after the engagement, but could provide no details.

Colonel John A. Kellogg

Crawford's division was composed of three brigades. Colonel Kellogg commanded the first, General Henry Baxter the second, and General Coulter the third. When the division lined up at Gravelly Church for the attack on the afternoon of April 1, Colonel Kellogg's brigade was on the left, General Baxter's on the right, and General Coulter's behind as support. Ayres's division was to the left of Crawford's and Griffin was behind Ayres in support. Although Ayres and Kellogg-Baxter were all in a line, there was a brigade-sized gap in the line between Kellogg and Ayres as they moved forward.

Before the corps moved out, Warren explained the plan utilizing a hand drawn diagram. Warren, Kellogg, Crawford, Coulter, and probably Baxter were present. As Kellogg understood it, they were to advance until they hit an east-west road (the White Oak Road). After hitting the road, they were to change front, so that the sun was in their eyes; that is, they were to swing around so as to be perpendicular to the Confederate line on the White Oak Road, and then advance.

When Kellogg reached the White Oak Road, Ayres was nowhere in sight to his left. Kellogg swung around to what he thought was perpendicular to the White Oak Road and advanced.

Kellogg recollected two encounters with General Forsyth of Warren's staff as he advanced. Kellogg did not know Forsyth and just before Forsyth appeared the first time, Warren had reiterated his orders to Kellogg. Kellogg was receiving a very light fire when Forsyth first appeared. Up to that that time, he had suffered only one man wounded. Forsyth approached the leftmost regiment of Kellogg's first line and gave it some order. Kellogg could not recall precisely what it was. He immediately rode over to Forsyth and told him that he commanded the brigade and, if any orders were to be given, they were to be given to him. Forsyth then stated, "Your orders are to move into action,"[16] or something to that effect. Forsyth said that the orders were from General Sheridan. Kellogg then informed Forsyth that his brigade was the first pivot for the change of front and that the other brigades had been ordered to guide on his right.

Kellogg felt that he was in a dilemma and did not know whose orders to obey. After a brief reflection, he decided to obey Forsyth and swung around to the left, that is, more to the west. He noticed that no one was on his left flank and he noticed that Baxter was not on his right flank. They were now passing a house to his left that was occupied by the enemy who were firing into his flank. He detached a battalion to deal with the Rebels in the house.

Kellogg continued on to the Ford Road, where he again changed his front toward the rear of the rebel main line. Here, he again met Colonel Forsyth. Forsyth was of great help in moving the troops at that point, exposed himself recklessly, and performed in a very gallant manner. Kellogg now turned down the Ford Road toward the enemy line.

They struck a breastwork. It is not clear if this was the original breastwork along the White Oak Road, or another one parallel but facing to the rear. Here, he had a severe fight that lasted about ten minutes. Kellogg lost about seventy-five men. Here, he saw General Warren again. Warren was in an open field near the breastworks with several officers and holding the corps colors. Warren must have been about twenty rods ahead of Kellogg's troops, and he was urging them on. It was now nearly night.

Kellogg drove through the Confederate breastworks and reoriented his line at a right angle to the Confederate line on the White Oak Road. The battle was now over.

The questioning then shifted to the eve and night before the battle. After the battle of White Oak Road during the day of March 31, Warren, in response to Meade's directive to send troops to Sheridan, ordered his troops back from their hard won gains preparatory to sending them to Sheridan. Kellogg's brigade was pulled back to the vicinity of Mrs. Butler's house, although he could not recollect the name. This was less than one mile southwest of Warren's headquarters in the Wilson house on the Boydton Plank Road. The brigade bivouacked on the field without tents. At the grey of the morning on April 1, the brigade was roused and moved overland southward to the vicinity of J. Boisseau's, where they camped. The distance from Mrs. Butlers' to J. Boisseau's as the crow flies is a little over two miles. They arrived at J. Boisseau's around 8 or 9 a.m. It was from here that they were ordered to Gravelly Run Church to form up for the attack. Kellogg believed that Warren accompanied the division during the move.

J. L. Chamberlain

The next witness was Brigadier General Joshua Chamberlain. Chamberlain was the hero of Gettysburg who so resolutely defended Little Round Top. It was also Chamberlain who was given the honor of accepting the surrender of Lee's army after Appomattox. As of March 31, 1865, Chamberlain was the commanding officer of the First Brigade in Griffin's division, and the commander of the Second Brigade also reported to him.

Chamberlain participated prominently in the battle of White Oak Road on March 31. He described the ground they fought over as exceedingly rough and in spots marshy. It was very wet, having been soaked with rain.

By between 5 and 6 p.m. on March 31, the Confederates had been pushed back across the White Oak Road, Chamberlain was firmly ensconced, and the battle had been won.

About this time, Warren and Chamberlain heard the sound of firing to their south. It was receding to the east. They rightly concluded that Sheridan, who was operating to the south of them, was being pushed back. Warren unilaterally decided to send help. He dispatched Bartlett's brigade of Griffin's division that had not been engaged to proceed overland to the South and strike Sheridan's pursuers in the flank and rear. Warren and Chamberlain were together as Bartlett departed. It was not later than 6 p.m. when Bartlett left.

That evening General Warren received the following from General Meade:

> You will, by direction of the major-general commanding draw back at once to your position within the Boydton Plank Road. Send a division down to Dinwiddie C. H. to report to General Sheridan. This division will go down the Boydton Plank Road. Send Griffin's division. General Humphreys will hold to Mrs. Butlers.[17]

In response to this message, Warren sent the following:

> HdQtrs 5th Army Corps
> 9:35 p.m. March 31st, 1865
>
> 1. General Ayres will immediately withdraw his division back to where it was yesterday, near the Boydton Plank Rd.
> 2. General Crawford will follow General Ayres and mass his troops behind the entrenchments near Mrs. Butlers.
> 3. General Griffin will immediately withdraw General Bartlett to his present position, then move back to the plank road, and down to Dinwiddie Court-House and report to General Sheridan....[18]

At the time of receipt of this message, Bartlett was detached from Griffin and it was some time before he could be brought back. Consequently, Warren ordered Ayres in place of Griffin to proceed down the Boydton Plank Road to report to Sheridan.

He ordered Griffin and Crawford to abandon their newly, hard won position on the White Oak Road and pull back to their previous positions near Mrs. Butler's, which was just off the west side of the Boydton Plank Road and near his headquarters at Mrs. Wilson's. At this time, all feared that the Confederates would attack as they withdrew. Crawford brought up the rear.

Griffin and Crawford bivouacked near Mrs. Butler's, ready to move at a moment's notice with Griffin awaiting Bartlett's return. Ayres headed for the Boydton Plank Road and the march down to Dinwiddie Courthouse.

It was about 5 a.m. when Crawford and Griffin got the orders to move out from Mrs. Butler's and proceed overland to join Sheridan. Griffin moved first with Crawford following. Chamberlain was at the head of Griffin's division.

At about 7 a.m. Chamberlain ran into Sheridan's group heading from Dinwiddie to Five Forks and almost fired into it. Chamberlain related the conversation he had with Sheridan as best as he could recollect it: Sheridan asked where Warren was. Chamberlain replied that he understood that Warren was at the rear of the column with the rear division. Sheridan replied, "That is where I should expect him to be,"[19] and then said something to the effect about them not coming up sooner. Chamberlain told him that they had a heavy engagement the evening before and that they were moving off in line of battle and had to be cautious as they distanced themselves from the enemy. Sheridan appeared to accept this, and he became much more pleasant. He then moved off toward Five Forks.

Chamberlain believed that the march from their bivouac at Mrs. Butler's until they met Sheridan near Boisseau's consumed about two hours and was as brisk as possible. After the meeting with Sheridan, Griffin camped where he was for five or six hours. Crawford came down shortly and camped to Griffin's left, that is, closer to Five Forks. Ayres, of course, arrived by a different route and camped about one half hour closer to Dinwiddie Courthouse.

At about 1 p.m. Griffin received orders to proceed to Gravelly Run Church. As he was beyond Crawford, he had to wait about one half hour until Crawford took to the road. The march to Gravelly Run was a good, brisk march with no delays, considering that the road was mud.

As the corps moved toward Gravelly Run, Warren's time was consumed in receiving instructions from Sheridan and passing them on to his subordinates. These included Griffin, Chamberlain, Crawford, and all subordinate commanders who happened to be there. The meeting lasted a good half hour. In the meantime, they were waiting for General Ayres, who was camped farther down the road, to come up. Ayres and everyone else knew an engagement was pending and there certainly was no lacking of zeal or celerity. The men were exhausted, were thoroughly soaked, and had suffered great losses.

Attention had been called to the apparent apathetic and indifferent manner of Warren, but Chamberlain insisted that was merely his way. Chamberlain stated:

> I should say that those who do not know General Warren's temperament might think him to be negative when he was deeply intent. General Warren's temperament is such that he, instead of showing excitement, generally shows an intense concentration in what I call important movements, and those who do not know him might take it to be apathy when it is deep, concentrated thought and purpose and it would not be unnatural that a stranger, looking at General Warren and not seeing indications of excitement and resolution on his face, might judge him to be apathetic, when in fact that conclusion might be far from the truth.[20]

The court then adjourned to resume Monday, May 17, 1880, at 11 a.m. The first witness that date was Joseph P. Cotton.

Joseph P. Cotton

Joseph P. Cotton was not in the army and was not present at the events of March 31–April 1, 1865. He was a civil engineer of fifteen years' experience who was engaged in producing a detailed map of the battlefield as it appeared at the time of the battle. His map indicated the terrain, vegetation, and defensive lines as he believed existed. Cotton spent sixteen days examining the battlefield beginning December 26, 1879, over fourteen years after the battle.

Questioning related to the terrain, the foliage, the soil, and similar details. The battle itself was a welter of confusion. It seemed that fifteen years later the court was attempting to measure a cow flop with a micrometer. Cotton's testimony appears unrelated to the question of whether the relief of Warren was justified.

Romeyn B. Ayres

The next to testify was Colonel Romeyn B. Ayres, a key player in this unfolding drama. As of March 31, 1865, Ayres was a brevet major general in the Volunteer Army, and the commanding general of the Second Division of Major General Warren's Fifth Corps. Ayres's division was by far the smallest of the three divisions in the corps. By April 1, 1865, by attrition, it had been reduced to just 2,400 men.

Ayres started by identifying his key subordinates. General Winthrop commanded his First Brigade, Colonel R.N. Bowerman his Second Brigade, and General Gwynn his Third Brigade.

On March 31, Ayres, Crawford, and Griffin, in that order, were operating in the crotch between the White Oaks Road and the Boydton Plank Road. Ayres was ordered to make a reconnaissance of the Confederate position. He advanced and was pushed back upon Crawford, who was pushed back upon Griffin. The combined Fifth Corps, then supported by the adjacent General Humphreys, pushed the Confederates back. At the end of the day, Griffin was camped on the far side of the White Oak Road, and Ayres and Crawford just on this side of it.

Ayres next described the nature of the terrain they had advanced over, retreated over, and again advanced over. He described it as exceedingly rough, cut full of little ravines. In fact, he described it as the most difficult you could find—difficult during the day and near impossible at night.

Major General Romeyn B. Ayres, U.S. Volunteer Army; Second Division commander, Fifth Corps.

After dark on March 31, Ayres received a dispatch from Warren dated 9:35 p.m. The dispatch directed that he retire from his White Oak position to the position that he occupied on the preceding day. While still rationing his men and replenishing their ammunition, he received another dispatch which amplified upon the earlier dispatch. This one was dated 11 p.m. and directed that Ayres continue on to the Boydton Plank Road and proceed down the road to Dinwiddie to reinforce Sheridan.

Ayres estimated that it would require at least three hours to draw in his pickets and cover the rough ground to the Boydton Plank Road. The march to the road was exceedingly enervating but was accomplished as quickly as humanly possible.

The march down the Boydton Plank Road passed Warren's headquarters at the Wilson house. Ayres checked in with Warren to find out the situation, but in no way delayed the march. Warren advised Ayres that Sheridan had been attacked, pushed back, needed help, and that Ayres should get there as quickly as possible.

Ayres had no distinct memory of crossing Gravelly Run. He knew he crossed on a bridge and did not ford the run. He had no recollection of a downed bridge, a new bridge, or of any significant delay. He had no recollection of meeting Captain Benyaurd and no idea of the time he crossed the run. However, an endorsement on a dispatch that night by a telegraph operator indicates that he was crossing at 2:40 a.m., April 1.

Ayres continued on south past the intersection of the Brooks Road. The Brooks Road angled off the Boydton Plank Road to the southwest until it hit the Dinwiddie–Five Forks Road. The intersection was between the Dinwiddie Courthouse and Five Forks.

When Ayres reached a point on the plank road about one mile south of the Brooks Road intersection and one mile north of Dinwiddie Courthouse, he met an oncoming member of Sheridan's staff. Ayres believes that it was Colonel Forsyth. The staffer apologized and said that Sheridan desired that Ayres turn off on the Brooks Road in order to hit the Five Forks Road behind the enemy. Thus, two miles of marching were wasted and Ayres had to countermarch back to the Brooks Road.

Dawn was just breaking as Ayres, at the head of his column, turned down the Brooks Road. Here he met what was obviously a Confederate picket who jumped on his horse and rode off, undoubtedly notifying the Confederate commander of Ayres's approach. Any chance there was of cutting off any Confederates that night thus evaporated as the Confederates expedited their march from Dinwiddie to Five Forks.

As Ayres approached the Dinwiddie–Five Forks Road, they were met by Sheridan and his staff. The conversation with Sheridan was pleasant. There was no inference that Sheridan blamed Ayres for the late arrival. Sheridan directed that Ayres bivouac his men where they were, breakfast, and await orders. Sheridan then rode off toward Five Forks.

In the afternoon, Ayres received an order to move up the road to Gravelly Run Church. This was a distance of about three miles. The road was crowded with wagons and horses, and Ayres was camped farther away than Crawford and Griffin. Ayres estimated that, considering the condition of the road, the marching to and forming up at Gravelly Run Church would probably require a couple of hours. He considered that he marched as fast as possible under the circumstances, but the going was slow.

Ayres arrived last at the church. His division formed to the left of the road with his right resting on the road. As Ayres formed his line of battle, the Second Brigade was on the left (Colonel Bowerman), the Third Brigade was on the right (General Gwynn), and the First Brigade was in the rear (General Winthrop). General Crawford, the Third Division, was on the other side of the road, in line with Bowerman and Gwynn, and Griffin was behind (see figure 9).

The corps entered a wood before reaching the White Oak Road. This greatly obscured visibility. The Rebels had only cleared a belt of some fifty feet deep in front of their works and suddenly one burst out of the woods, and there they were. The position of the Rebel line was not quite where Sheridan assumed it to be, and Ayres hit the White Oak Road some 200 yards beyond the refuse of the Rebel line. He was enfiladed and taking fire in his left flank. He had to change his front so as to face the rebels in the refuse, and he had to do it quickly. He had to turn to his left so as to not only face the Rebels in the refuse, but to be at right angles to the main Rebel line along the White Oak Road.

About this time, Colonel Bowerman was hit and Ayres himself took command of Bowerman's brigade. Ayres did not observe the confusion described by others wherein some of his men allegedly dropped to the ground and fired into the air. The only confusion Ayres observed was brief and quickly rectified. It occurred when the shooting started. Gwynn, to Bowerman's (Ayres's) right, ordered his men double quick forward when he should have been wheeling to the left to face the enemy in the refuse.

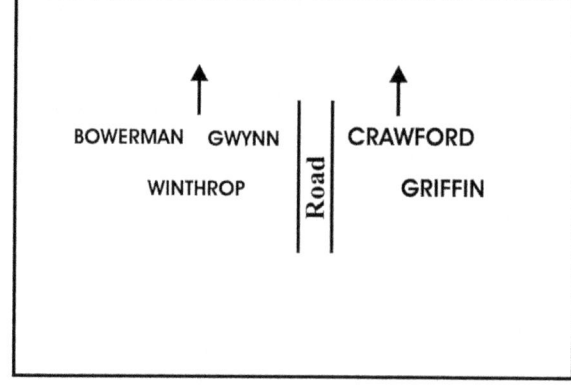

Figure 9.

Winthrop and Bowerman faced the enemy in the refuse. Gwynn was beyond it. Crawford disappeared during the change of front and was nowhere in sight. It was Winthrop and Bowerman who stormed the refuse and, in effect, won the battle.

Sheridan was with Ayres's division throughout, riding to and fro. Several times he expressed the view that Ayres had changed his front to the left too soon and was firing into the flank of their own cavalry, who were assaulting the main Rebel line along the White Oak Road from the front. This was not so.

Warren gave Ayres detailed instructions before the corps moved into action after leaving Gravelly Run Church. Ayres did not see Warren afterward during the battle. Griffin rode up while Ayres was advancing toward the Confederate refuse. According to Ayres, the following conversation ensued:

GRIFFIN: Ayres, what is up?
AYRES: There is nothing new, Griffin: Crawford has taken his division away and left me to fight alone. The same old story.[21]

At this point, Griffin disappeared back into the woods, and so ended Ayres's story. The battle was soon over, as it was getting dark.

General Chamberlain, Captain Sheridan, and General Ayres were all recalled by the court for further questioning. The questioning elicited nothing new concerning whether Sheridan was justified in relieving Warren—with one exception. Chamberlain was asked—that on the night of March 31 when all three divisions were bivouacked near the White Oak Road after the battle and Ayres was ordered to proceed to the Boydton Plank Road and march down to Sheridan—how long would it have required Ayres to reach the Boydton Plank Road. Chamberlain replied that, because of the nature of the terrain and the darkness of the night, it would have required three hours. This was precisely the estimate Ayres had given.

If it required three hours even to reach the road before turning south to Dinwiddie, there is no way possible for Ayres to have reached Sheridan by midnight, as Grant stated, or even earlier than he did. Furthermore, it had been established that the downed bridge over Gravelly Run played no role in the timeliness of Ayres's march.

Colonel W. W. Swan

At the time of the battle of Five Forks, Colonel W.W. Swan was a captain and the adjutant general of General Ayres. The night of March 31, 1865, Ayres's division was camped near the White Oak Road near the enemy. They withdrew in two stages. They moved a considerable distance and then halted. Rations were issued. This was before they received the order to proceed to Dinwiddie Courthouse. Most thought it a day and went to sleep. They then received the order to proceed to Dinwiddie Courthouse. Swan did not recollect the time. He had no recollection of any delays or run crossings on the way to Dinwiddie.

It was a dark night, the road was muddy, and they were all much fatigued. It was difficult to rouse the troops after they had been issued rations and the second order to move arrived. They marched down the Boydton Plank Road through the night and, when nearing Dinwiddie, were met by a staff officer from Sheridan. Swan thought he was one of the two Forsyths on Sheridan's staff, but apparently he was not. In any event, the staffer was impressive.

In the three minutes or so that the staff officer was with them, he told them that they were already beyond the place where Sheridan wanted them to turn off. Explaining why he had not come earlier, before they had crossed the road where they were to turn off, the staffer explained that Ayres had made better time than the general (Sheridan) expected. Swan, when pressed on this point, was adamant that this was the substance of what the staffer said. He was certain.

Ayres then retraced his route, returned north to the turn-off road, and turned off to the southwest. This was the Brooks Road that ran into the road between Five Forks and Dinwiddie.

The day broke, and as they approached the Five Forks Dinwiddie road, they heard bugles and a band. It was Sheridan's staff. Sheridan met Ayres and the two conversed, but Swan could not hear what they said. Ayres's division remained where it was. The other two divisions of the corps came down nearby and the corps was united.

Ayres's division camped, built fires, cooked breakfast, and awaited orders. They spent several hours there. Swan remembered that they moved up to Gravelly Run Church that afternoon, but could recall no details. When at Gravelly Run Church, the corps lined up in line of battle for an advance. They formed up at the edge of a wood—Ayres on the left, Crawford on the right, and Griffin a little in the rear. Swan saw Sheridan and Warren together talking. He also saw Ayres and Griffin together in the rear of Ayres's division. Then he saw Warren go over to them. He could not hear what was said.

The corps then moved forward. The order for Ayres was for the men to advance and keep the sun on their left shoulder. Swan did not have the least idea which point of the compass this was. He assumed that they were going to strike the enemy line head on. He knew nothing about the refuse at the end of the enemy line and nothing about "wheeling."

They passed through a wood and into an open field. Swan rode to the left of Ayres's line. He somehow realized that the enemy was in the woods to their left. He could not recollect how he sensed this, as the firing had not yet begun, but was certain that they were there.

Swan rode back to Ayres and told him that he was convinced that the enemy was in the woods to their left and that they (Ayres) were passing by. Ayres directed Swan to ride back to General Winthrop, who was following behind Bowerman and Gwynn, and order him to keep a sharp watch to the left. When Swan returned, he noticed that not only were the divisions of Ayres and Crawford being separated, but that there was a significant gap between Ayres's leading two brigades, those of Bowerman and Gwynn.

Swan was pretty well in front of the two brigades in the gap between them, when General Sheridan and several staff officers rode up from the right of Ayres's lines. Sheridan said, "What in the hell are you doing there?"[22] Swan felt that this was uncalled for and felt deeply offended. Forsyth, who was with Sheridan, tried to smooth it over by telling Sheridan that it was all right. Swan told Sheridan that he did not think that any enemy was in front of them, but rather, to the left. Suddenly, they drew fire from the left and the battle was on.

By this time, Gwynn was moving a little ahead of Bowerman. When Swan reached Winthrop in the rear, Winthrop was already facing the enemy and Bowerman was also wheeling to face the enemy.

When Swan returned to Ayres, Ayres told Swan to send someone to Gwynn and tell him to "go in." Swan sent an officer named Yardley. Swan then went off to find General Griffin. He found Griffin to the north, already turned toward the enemy and heading toward an extension of the enemy line (the refuse).

By the time Swan returned to Ayres, the enemy, in large numbers, was already coming out with their hands up—swarms of them. Ayres had already carried the works (the refuse).

Swann did not see Warren and he was not sure if he saw Sheridan after their initial unpleasant encounter.

(When the Sheridan staffer met the oncoming Ayres on the morning of April 1, he stated that Sheridan did not expect him so early. This directly contradicted Sheridan's statement that he expected Ayres by midnight on the 31st.)

Colonel R. M. Brinton

As of April 1, 1865, Brinton was a captain and aide de camp to Major General Griffin. Brinton testified to the futility of trying to establish with precision what was not even known precisely when it occurred fifteen years earlier. He repeatedly answered that he did not know or could not remember. He could seldom place a time on an event.

Brinton first described the situation the night of March 31, after the battle of the White Oak Road. He testified that Griffin's division passed the night in a field between the White Oak Road and Gravelly Run that they called the Negro house. They fully expected to move during the night. They stayed up all night with orderlies holding their horses. Bartlett's brigade had left earlier, but Brinton could not recall or did not know if it returned during the night.

Brinton was unaware of the context of any orders, but was under the impression that they were to go down to Dinwiddie during the night. As he understood it, the orders were countermanded and Ayres went instead. He presumably saw no orders.

Very early the next morning, that is April 1, the division departed for J. Boisseau's.

They moved cross country with no particular problems and arrived at about 7 a.m. There they met General Sheridan.

About 2 p.m. the division began a move to Gravelly Run Church. Again, Brinton did not see the orders and did not know their exact nature. Brinton thought that it was about 3 p.m. that the corps moved across the White Oak Road into action. Before the corps moved out, Brinton saw Sheridan marking the action in the ground but could not hear what he said. Brinton did not know the intended movements of Griffin's division when they moved out. He did not notice any separation between Ayres's and Crawford's divisions as they moved across the White Oak Road, as the woods were quite thick.

Griffin noticed that they were getting quite far from the firing (Ayres's) and began turning toward the action. Warren then arrived and the division was reoriented toward the action. Warren then departed in the presumed direction of Crawford.

The court recessed and resumed Friday May 21, 1880. Brinton continued his testimony. After Ayres had succeeded in overwhelming the refuse and the battle was essentially won, Brinton, General Griffin, and other unidentified officers met Sheridan on the White Oak Road. Sheridan was coming up from the south and they were coming down from the north. Sheridan said "Smash 'em." He then said, "Where is Warren?" No one answered. He then said, "General Griffin, I place you in command of the Fifth Army Corps."[23]

Brinton again saw Warren after Griffin was given command of the corps. The Confederate defense along the White Oak Road had fallen. Confederates were retiring to the north, up the Ford Road and west of it, and Crawford was coming down from the north. The two met at a large open field and the Union troops were reluctant to cross it in the face of fire. Brinton saw Warren at the head of the troops encouraging them on.

Colonel E. B. Cope

As of April 1, 1865, Cope was a major and aide de camp to General Warren. Cope's testimony was unique in that most of it was not dimmed by time. Immediately after the battle, he prepared a detailed written account of his involvement and, on April 13, 1865, submitted it to General Warren. He submitted a certified copy of this account to the court and it was admitted in total as testimony. Of further interest, Cope was a trained cartographer and, in the days after the battle, he, with Warren's assistance, prepared a map of the battlefield. The distances between important points consisted of actual measurements. Herewith is Cope's written account:

> Petersburg
> April 13, 1865

To Major-Gen'l Warren:

General: I beg leave to submit statement of operation of Fifth Army Corps on April 1st, 1865 at the battle of Five Forks as seen by me.

About 8 o'clock on the morning of the 1st I started out from headquarters to join you on the White Oak Road near the Dabney house. I reached there at 8:30 a.m. and found the troops in motion; they marched in a southwest direction, and in one mile came to the

Dinwiddie Court-House road, near Dr. Boisseau's; then proceeded down this road to its junction with Ford's road. This point was reached by the 1st and 3rd divisions about 9:30.

The 2nd division had come up by the Boydton Plank road the night before and were massed ½ mile beyond.

The cavalry were passing on Ford's road toward Five Forks.

About 12 o'clock the corps was ordered to move in the direction of the Five Forks, the first division leading, followed by the third, then came the 2nd in two and a half miles; the head of the column turned to the right, and proceeded to the vicinity of Gravelly Run Church; the troops were then formed in the following order:

The 3rd division on the right of a road leading north by the church and crossing the White Oak road; the second division on the left, and the 1st in reserve. Here each division commander was furnished with a plan and written explanation of the movement about to be made.

About 4 o'clock all being ready, the line was ordered to advance; in ¼ of a mile it crossed the White Oak road, wheeled to the left perpendicular to the road; this movement brought the 1st and 3rd divisions in the woods, and as the line advanced they went too much to the right, and lost the connection with the 2nd division. After the line had passed through the open fields to the edge of timber, the 2nd division became engaged with the enemy's skirmishers, you sent me to General Griffin with an order to bring his division toward the White Oak road, by the left flank, in order to be in better supporting distance to the 2nd; also to inform Gen'l Crawford that he was going somewhat too far to the right. I found Generals Griffin and Crawford to the right of the burned chimneys, and gave them your orders; at this time the enemy had a line of skirmishers running from left of their line of works by the Sidney house to Hatchers Run. You came to where General Griffin was, and then returned to the White Oaks road, where I joined you a few minutes after; this part of the enemy's line, where you were, had been carried by the 2nd division, and you sent me again to General Griffin with this information, and with an order to push forward as fast as possible; he had already reached the Sydney house, and was pushing forward across the field; I delivered your order, and gave him the direction to advance, which was about west. Bartlett's brigade struck the enemy on the flank, behind their works, and drove them steadily before him. Crawford's division had gone into the wood on the extreme right. It soon reached the Ford's road north of Five Forks; wheeling and advancing south he came up in rear of the enemy's line, at the same time cutting off their retreat in this direction, and capturing wagons, artillery and a large number of prisoners.

The enemy finding themselves pressed in front, flank and rear made but a feeble resistance; the line then swept on down the enemy's works carrying everything before it, capturing prisoners by hundreds. The brigades that had been in reserve followed up by the flank on the White Oak road. I joined you again at the Five Forks, and remained with you through the evening.

The enemy having been driven out of their entire line of work, two miles long, were followed up until dark, and the troops were withdrawn to the large fields at Willisburg house, where they encamped for the night.

I am general, very respectfully, your ob't sert

E. B. Cope

A true copy[24]

Questioning returned to March 31, the day before the battle. As we will recall, in the late afternoon of March 31, Warren heard gunfire to his south, concluded that Sheridan was in trouble, and unilaterally dispatched Bartlett's brigade south to strike Sheridan's opponent in the flank and rear. Questioning related to this transaction.

Cope was ordered to accompany Bartlett. They departed around 5 o'clock, Cope believed, although he had no watch. The order was to proceed to the sound of the gunfire. At the time of the order, Bartlett was near the junction of the White Oak and Claiborne Roads. The firing was believed to be initially in the area of Gravelly Run Church and then moving eastward toward Dinwiddie Courthouse.

Captain Gentry of Warren's staff was sent ahead to assess the situation. He was fired upon at Boisseau's and returned and reported the facts to General Warren. Cope led the brigade to the vicinity of Dr. Boisseau's and found that the area was occupied by enemy skirmishers. Bartlett deployed his troops. It was now about six or half past six p.m. A squad of Sheridan's cavalry that had been cut off by the enemy advance rode in and reported to Bartlett. It was now nearly dark. They saw a long line of men and campfires about three-quarters of a mile to the south. This was the enemy. At this time, pickets of each side were firing at one another. Cope departed, rode back to Warren, and reported the situation. It was 7 or, probably, 8 o'clock, when he reached Warren. It took about one-half hour to get back.

That evening, orders were received from Meade that General Griffin's division should join Sheridan at Dinwiddie. Bartlett's brigade belonged to Griffin's division, and Warren sent Cope off to bring Bartlett's brigade back to join Griffin so that the full division could proceed to Dinwiddie. Cope departed for Bartlett about 9 or 10 o'clock. Griffin told Cope to take a company of infantry because of the danger. Cope got lost in the dark in the woods en route and wasted perhaps twenty minutes. When Cope finally reached Bartlett, Bartlett had to draw in his picket line, which consumed additional time. Bartlett did not rejoin Griffin until about midnight. Cope first reported to Griffin that Bartlett had rejoined the division and then headed for Warren's headquarters. This was in the Wilson house on the Boydton Plank Road. Cope then turned in and went to sleep.

When he awoke in the morning, General Warren was gone. Cope rode over to where Griffin's division had been, and it was gone. He was informed that they all had gone south toward the Boisseau house. Cope rejoined Warren somewhere in that area. The time could have been as late as 9:30 a.m.

Cope could not recollect exactly what he did after that, but he was away for a time and, when he returned, the troops had already departed and moved up to Gravelly Run Church. He did recall running into an enemy picket line where he was fired upon and his horse was killed. He returned to the Gravelly Run Church where the corps was forming up and his written narrative picks up at that point.

Major Cope's paper brought out one point that was becoming increasingly clear. Although it was not intended, General Crawford's wide swing to the north, and then his turn south down the Ford Road, was not all bad. In fact, it was good.

The Confederates, routed out of their line on the White Oak Road, tended to retire to the north; that is, up the Ford Road. Had they been permitted to do so, they might have formed a new defense line on the north bank of Hatchers Run. Had they done so, this new defense line would have been far more formidable than the original one along the White Oak Road. It would have been much less vulnerable to a flank attack such as had occurred to their original position. Crawford, coming down the Ford Road from the north to the south, cut off their retreat and sealed the Union victory.

Lieutenant Colonel W. J. Denslow

At the time of Five Forks, Lieutenant Colonel W.J. Denslow was a member of the Ninety-first New York Volunteers, of Kellogg's brigade of Crawford's division. They participated in the battle of White Oak Road on the 31st and slept on their arms just south of the White Oak Road on the night of March 31–April 1.

When the corps formed up at Gravelly Run Church the afternoon of the 1st, Denslow's regiment was in the right rear of Crawford's division. The Ninety-first was an unusually large regiment containing 1,400 men.

Upon advance, the division crossed the White Oak Road, swung left, and passed the "Chimneys" with part of the regiment passing on each side. While passing the Chimneys, Denslow was wounded slightly. At that time, the regiment was substantially engaged with the enemy directly in their front.

After passing the Chimneys, they swung left again with the left of their regiment passing about 300 yards north of the Syndor house. The Confederates occupied the Syndor house and fired into the flank of the passing Yankees. General Kellogg ordered Denslow to take four companies and drive them out, which he did. The division moved westward and Denslow and his group overtook it and rejoined. When they reached the Ford Road, they swung left again and proceeded down toward the main enemy line. By this time, the left of Denslow's regiment was in Gillian field to the west of the Ford Road.

At this point they were subjected to a sharp fire from the west that drove them back, and they lost quite a number of men. It was here that General Warren appeared. He took his corps colors and rode ahead in the direction that the fire was coming from. Denslow asked his men if they were going to allow the corps commander to attack alone. They shouted "No" and followed. Denslow estimated that his regiment lost about 250 killed and wounded that date.

So closed Denslow's testimony, and the court adjourned.

Brigadier General H. C. Bankhead

In March–April 1865, General H.C. Bankhead was a lieutenant colonel of volunteers and assistant inspector general of the Fifth Army Corps. As such, he was on the staff of General Warren.

On the night of March 31–April 1, Bankhead was with Warren at Warren's headquarters in the Wilson house on the Boydton Plank Road. During the night, he was engaged with Warren in receiving and issuing orders. Towards morning, he fell asleep. When he awoke General Warren was gone. He proceeded down the Boydton Plank Road and the Five Forks–Dinwiddie Road, where he initially encountered General Ayres. It was early in the day, but Bankhead had no recollection of the time.

After passing Ayres's division, he proceeded on to General Griffin's and Crawford's divisions where he finally encountered Warren at a camp fire. He understood that the corps had been ordered to rest where it was.

Sometime around 11 a.m. General Warren asked Bankhead to ride over with him to see General Sheridan. This was the first time that Bankhead saw Warren and Sheridan together.

Bankhead observed Sheridan and Warren talking but was sitting off to the side with some staff members and could not hear what they said. Finally, Sheridan left Warren, mounted his horse, and rode off toward the front. Bankhead heard no firing at this time. Some fifteen minutes later, an officer from Sheridan's staff brought an order. Bankhead did not know what the order was, but immediately afterward, Warren directed Bankhead to bring up the corps at once. Warren gave Bankhead the destination and indicated the order of the march. It was in the order they were camped; that is, Crawford first, then Griffin, and then Ayres. Bankhead was to lead the troops and meet Warren at the indicated destination, Gravelly Run Church.

The road was extremely muddy and there were many led cavalry horses on the road that encumbered the march. However, it was as fast as possible. Bankhead met Colonel Forsyth of Sheridan's staff and complained of the cavalry horses. Forsyth in turn ordered them off the road.

Upon arrival at his destination, Bankhead found Sheridan and Warren sitting together on a log or bench. He approached and sat near them. The corps was forming in line of battle, and this appeared to Bankhead to occur as fast as possible; he saw no delay. Bankhead thought that he saw Warren draw a sketch and then submit it to Sheridan for approval. He believed that Sheridan approved it, although he could not hear what was said.

Sheridan seemed to be annoyed at what he thought were delays, and he overheard Sheridan say something to the effect that it would probably be after dark before they got into action. About this time, Bankhead departed.

Bankhead was again with Warren as the corps moved forward across the White Oak Road. After crossing the White Oak Road, Warren sent Bankhead to Crawford twice, telling him to close in on Ayres. Crawford seemed to be exerting himself to do so as the gap between the two widened.

The first time Bankhead was sent off to Crawford, he met Colonel Forsyth from Sheridan's staff, who was trying to do the same thing; that is, to get Crawford to close on Ayres. Crawford marched near where the Chimneys were. Bankhead then rode from Crawford to Griffin. Griffin's division, instead of following Crawford, had diverged and was heading toward an extension of Ayres's line.

By the time Bankhead joined Griffin, Ayres had already captured the angle with large numbers of prisoners. Near the White Oak Road, Sheridan rode up to Griffin. Colonel Porter of Grant's staff and Forsyth of Sheridan's staff were also there. Bankhead heard Sheridan ask Griffin if he knew where Warren was. Griffin replied that he did not. Sheridan then said something to the effect that "You take command." At the time, Bankhead did not interpret this as Sheridan's transferring command of the Fifth Corps to Griffin.

Then Sheridan became preoccupied with another matter. He was afraid that some of the Fifth Corps were firing into his cavalry.

Bankhead rode along with Griffin and first Ayres, and then Colonel Locke, Warren's chief-of-staff, came up. Locke asked Bankhead what was the problem between Sheridan and Warren. Bankhead answered that he did not know. Very soon after that, Warren came galloping past. General Sheridan was some distance off. The Bankhead group was on the White Oak Road and Warren did not stop but continued on past. Bankhead next saw Warren leading an attack against some enemy cavalry across an open field on the far side of Ford Road.

Warren joined Griffin and Bankhead. He said that there was nothing but Confederate cavalry in their front. He told Bankhead to go back to Sheridan for further instructions. Bankhead rode back and met Sheridan on the White Oak Road. Bankhead reported that Warren was waiting for instructions. Sheridan replied that he had already sent Warren instructions by an aide de camp. It was now quite dark.

Thus ended Bankhead's testimony.

Brevet Brigadier General Richard Coulter

At the time of the events under review, Coulter was a colonel in the U.S. Volunteers and commanding officer of the Third Brigade in Crawford's division. The First Brigade was commanded by Colonel Kellogg and the Second Brigade by Brigadier General Baxter.

Coulter recalled that on the night of March 31¬–April 1, his brigade spent the night lying on their arms without tents and without fires within sight of enemy works on the White Oak Road.

On the morning of the 1st, the brigade moved southwest by several short marches to a place where they had a long halt. In the afternoon, they moved to Gravelly Run Church. There were led horses on the road to Gravelly Run Church but, as far as he could recall, they did not delay the march. At Gravelly Run Church, the corps formed up for battle. Crawford was on the right in the front line. Crawford's division formed as follows: Kellogg on the left, Baxter on the right, and Coulter in the center of the rear of the two (see figure 10).

Prior to the corps moving forward, the commanders met with General Warren. He exhibited a diagram and explained the forthcoming movement to them. General Warren's directions were that they should keep the sun upon their left until they reached the White Oak Road. Then they should make a change so as to become perpendicular to the road. Then they were to move west, keeping as nearly as they could to the line of the White Oak Road. The intention was that Ayres should advance to the south of the road and parallel to it, and Crawford should move the north of the road and parallel to it. They would thus roll up the enemy line. General Warren explained the plan very fully and precisely.

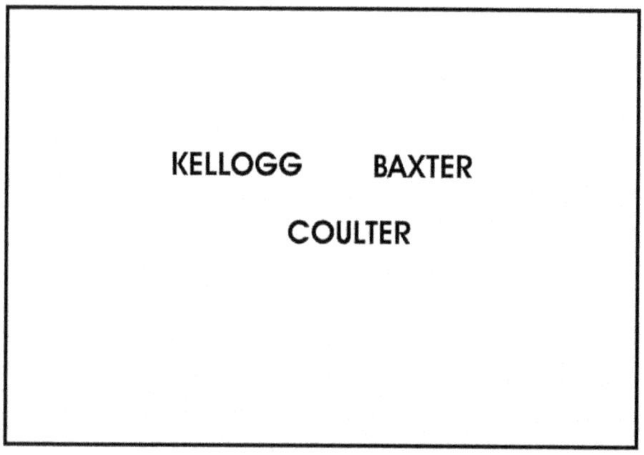

KELLOGG   BAXTER

COULTER

Figure 10. Formation of Crawford's Division.

After Warren detailed the plan to the brigade commanders, Coulter went back and explained it to his regimental commanders. By the time the advance began, Coulter believed that no man in the command was ignorant of the plan.

As soon as Coulter crossed the White Oak Road, there was some skirmish firing. Before they reached the first wood, Coulter had his horse shot out from under him, and he saw some of his men injured and one or two killed. The firing at this point consisted largely of Rebel sharpshooters picking off officers.

As soon as the brigade crossed the White Oak Road, Coulter began wheeling to the left. Because of Coulter's position in the middle, behind Kellogg and Baxter, he had no one touching his left and no one touching his right. Much of the move was in the woods where visibility was limited.

Coulter encountered some of General Crawford's orderlies and commandeered a horse from one of them. He recollected passing the Chimneys, but had no recollection of passing the Syndor house, which, according to other witnesses, was occupied by Rebels who fired in their flank.

Coulter's brigade passed about 150 yards south of the Chimneys and headed west. Shortly before hitting the Ford Road, they encountered severe fire from the woods. The brigade proceeded south down the Ford Road and encountered three enemy cannon. The enemy got off no more than two or three shots before the cannon were captured. Both Crawford and Warren were present at the time, and it was apparently Warren who was giving orders for the capture of the cannon. Coulter only realized later that the cannon were probably retreating up the Ford Road to presumed safety beyond Hatchers Run.

Some of the heaviest fighting for the brigade occurred late in the day in Gillian field as it was getting dark. This came as a surprise, as the rank and file thought it was all over. Warren was again present. The brigade suffered 146 casualties on the 1st.

Coulter never saw General Sheridan that date, with one possible exception. In one instance he saw a general and staff in the distance on the White Oak Road, but did not know if it was Sheridan.

Major Richard Esmond

On March 31–April 1, 1865, Major Richard Esmond was a first lieutenant and the assistant adjutant general on Richard Coulter's staff.

Esmond was with Coulter on the afternoon of April 1 at Gravelly Run Church when Warren gave instructions for the forthcoming movement. Prior to the movement, Esmond walked down one line of the brigade and Coulter the other, passing the instructions to each officer. General Warren wanted every man to know the intended movement. Kellogg's brigade was in front. Coulter was in the rear of the first line.

Just as the brigade was crossing the White Oak Road, they suffered their first casualty: Colonel Farnham was wounded. Upon reaching the White Oak Road, the order was given "left half wheel." The corps entered the woods and Esmond saw no more of Kellogg's brigade, which they thought they were following.

After passing through the woods, they came out on an open field. Esmond testified that he never saw the "Chimneys." Apparently, they were in the Syndor field. Esmond saw a house but did not know if it was the Syndor house. They were receiving some firing. It was coming from the southwest side of the field. He heard that Colonel Coulter was hit, but it proved to be only his horse. As they crossed the field, the house was to Esmond's right. Esmond recalled passing down the Ford Road, capturing the cannon, crossing the Confederate works, and turning west into Gillian field.

Asked why the brigade did not keep closed up to Ayres's brigade on their left as they crossed White Oak Road, Esmond correctly pointed out that, inasmuch as their brigade was in the middle behind Baxter and Kellogg, there was no one in sight to their left or right when in the woods.

Esmond described the final action in Gillian field and stated that Warren was there. He had no recollection of seeing Sheridan at any time.

Brevet Brigadier General Frederick T. Locke

At the time of the battle of Five Forks, Frederick T. Locke was a lieutenant colonel in the volunteers and chief of staff to General Warren. Locke's testimony should prove of particular value, as he was the man closest to Warren. As his chief of staff, he ate with him, lived with him, and was of necessity his closest confidant. Locke was of particular value to Warren as he brought continuity to the job. He had been assistant adjutant general of the Fifth Corps almost back to its inception and remained as such until the end of the war.

The eve of March 31, Locke was with Warren at Warren's headquarters at the Wilson house on the Boydton Plank Road. The two had been busily occupied receiving and issuing orders. At midnight, Warren ordered Locke to go to bed while he continued working. When Locke awoke, Warren was gone, and Locke received orders to dismantle the headquarters and to join Warren.

Locke proceeded down the Boydton Plank Road, down Brooks Road, up the Five Forks–Dinwiddie Road to Gravelly Run Church, where he finally encountered Warren talking to Sheridan. He saw no troops, as they had already moved off to the White Oak Road and battle. Shortly, Sheridan departed, and Warren, Locke and staff proceeded across the White Oak Road where they were subjected to heavy fire. By the time they reached a point just northeast of the Confederate line, Warren had become increasingly concerned with the movement of Crawford's division. The gap between Ayres and Crawford widened as Ayres confronted the Confederates in the refuse (at right angles to the main line) and Crawford moved off to the northwest, away from the battle.

Warren sent staff member after staff member to find Crawford and to bring his movement into Warren's original plan. Finally, there were only two staff members remaining—Locke and one other, unnamed. Warren ordered Locke to go find Crawford and turn him back toward the desired position; that is, the right of Ayres. Locke set out in the woods and, at times, could not even see the sun to orient himself. Finally, as the gunfire from Ayres's encounter in his rear receded, he was able to follow the sound of gunfire to the northwest, which led him to Crawford. At the time Locke located him, Crawford was just east of the Ford Road near the Boisseau house (about three-fourths of a mile north of the main Confederate line on the White Oak Road).

Locke delivered his message and Crawford advised him that that was precisely what he was trying to do. Shortly after Locke's arrival, Warren himself arrived. Within just a few minutes, Warren ordered Locke to carry a message to Sheridan. The message was that Warren had gained the enemy's rear, had taken over 1,500 prisoners, and was pushing forward a division as fast as he could. While Locke was proceeding south toward the Confederate line, he met Captain Melcher of his staff, and Melcher accompanied him. Melcher knew of Sheridan's approximate location, and the two encountered Sheridan on the White Oak Road to the east of the Forks.

Locke could see that Sheridan was excited and angry. Locke delivered his message. Sheridan, in turn, raised his right hand and said, "Tell General Warren, by God; I say he was not at the front. That is all that I have got to say to him."[25] That was Sheridan's only message for Warren. Locke wrote it down and later verified the exact words by reading it to Melcher. It was now late in the afternoon. The main battle at the angle was over and it was mainly a matter of rounding up some diehards.

Locke found Warren and repeated Sheridan's words to him. It was afterward that Warren led the charge across Gillian field. Locke learned later that Sheridan had relieved Warren. He learned this from Warren himself. It was now dark.

Brigadier General C. E. LaMotte

At the time of Five Forks, Brigadier General C.E. LaMotte was a lieutenant colonel and division inspector of the second division of the Fifth Army Corps. That is, LaMotte was on General Ayres's staff. Much of LaMotte's questioning demonstrated the futility of attempting to establish with precision what had transpired fifteen years earlier.

As of the night of March 31, the men of the Fifth Corps had spent the night of the 30th in the mud in a driving rain, and during the day of the 31st had been engaged in the battle of the White Oak Road. LaMotte had laid down to sleep the night of the 31st between 9:30 and 10 p.m. was awakened, and the division (Ayres's) put in motion to move down the Boydton Plank Road to join Sheridan at Dinwiddie. The night was moonless and black, and LaMotte kept falling asleep in the saddle. He only vaguely remembered crossing Gravelly Run at an unspecified time, and of later meeting Sheridan's representative in the blackness, who told them that they had already marched too far and should return to and turn down the Brooks Road. LaMotte could not see him, did not recognize him, and knew nothing of the Brooks Road. The division countermarched, went down the Brooks Road, and there enjoyed a long halt. Precisely where and why was unknown to LaMotte.

That afternoon, they moved up to the Gravelly Run Church. There was no delay encountered. At the Gravelly Run Church, the corps formed into a line of battle. LaMotte saw a diagram of their intended movement but did not recall hearing any oral explanations.

Ayres's division crossed the White Oak Road and immediately swung to the left. They were quickly subject to fire from the left. LaMotte observed no confusion on the left and only a slight, momentary confusion on the right. The left was in the woods and one could not see any enemy until it burst into the open, just fifty feet from the enemy fortifications. The right, however, swung out into an open space and was subject to a fire, both from the front and from the north (their right). Some of the men feared they were flanked, but the officers quickly established order and the advance continued. LaMotte minimized the confusion as momentary and local. In fact, he stated that the confusion "was hardly worth mentioning."[26]

LaMotte noticed General Sheridan about this time. He was not out to the front. In fact, he rode along the rear of LaMotte's line, waving his hat and shouting. LaMotte thought he was calling to General Ayres but could not hear what he was saying.

LaMotte last saw Crawford's and Griffin's division just as Ayres began to change front. He noticed Griffin after Ayres had carried the refuse and was realigning his men for further advance. Ayres then continued his advance, rolling up the Confederate main defense line along the White Oak Road all the way to the Ford intersection and beyond. Warren was with Ayres as they crossed the White Oak Road.

LaMotte inspected the Confederate fortifications after they were captured. He said that they were well constructed of earth and logs, were revetted, and there were periodic traverses so that an enemy entering them could not shoot down the length of the embankment.

LaMotte's account is at considerable variance with the often accepted view that Ayres's division was in total disarray and Sheridan was gallantly out in front rallying the troops.

Lieutenant Colonel Walter T. Chester

The next to testify was Lieutenant Colonel Walter T. Chester. In April 1865, Chester was a captain in the volunteer army and serving on the staff of General Crawford as mustering officer.

Early on the morning of April 1, that is, the morning after the battle of the White Oak Road, Crawford began drawing in his skirmish line preparatory to moving south to join Sheridan. This was just at daybreak, before sunrise. The corps then marched to the south a distance of four or five miles. They marched cross country, through fields most of the way, and completed the march on a road that proved to be the Crump Road. There, in the vicinity of Dr. Boisseau's house, they came to rest for two or three hours. Crawford's division was in the rear of the march, to the south; the last to separate from the enemy.

Later, the division moved up to Gravelly Run Church. Crawford's division was now first in the line of march, and Crawford and Chester were at the head of the column. There was no delay in the march. When the division deployed at the church, Chester was assigned to accompany Baxter's brigade. Kellogg and Baxter were in front, side by side, and Coulter was behind in the middle.

As the division moved forward across the White Oak Road, it was subjected to picket firing, and Colonel Farnham of Baxter's brigade was struck in the chest and seriously wounded. Chester took charge of Farnham, helped him from the saddle, acquired a stretcher, and took him to the rear. Chester spent about one-half hour caring for Farnham and then set out to find and rejoin Baxter's brigade.

Chester passed the Chimneys to his right, turned westward, and finally overtook Crawford's division just to the west of the Ford Road, on a level with the Boisseau house, which was to the west of the road. He hit not Baxter's brigade but Coulter's, which somehow moved up into a gap between Baxter and Kellogg. Chester met Crawford, and soon Warren appeared. Warren consulted with Crawford and the division reoriented to the south and proceeded down the Ford Road toward the rear of the enemy line on the White Oak Road.

Crawford's division captured enemy troops fleeing north on the Ford Road, and also several cannon. The Rebels had managed to get off several shots but then abandoned the artillery.

Chester later met General Sheridan on the White Oak Road and reported to him that Crawford had captured some prisoners and that there was an enemy line of works. Sheridan then directed him to tell Crawford that he knew all about that line of works and that "we were going to take them, by God."[27]

Chester then rode on down the White Oak Road to the west, past the Ford Road intersection, where he met Warren at the northeast corner of the Gillian field. It was now dusk, the sun was down, and it was probably fifteen or twenty minutes after sundown. Chester noticed the enemy retreating across Gillian field.

Just then, General Warren, holding the corps flag in his hand, started out across the field toward the enemy. Chester and other Fifth Corps troops followed him. They followed the enemy a couple of miles and then halted as Union cavalry came up and took up the pursuit. The pursued Confederates never made a real stand. They would sometimes turn and fire a shot, but there was nothing like a real volley.

The court met on Wednesday, May 26, 1880, but dealt with procedural matters and did not call anyone to testify. The next testimony to be taken occurred Thursday, May 27, 1880.

Lieutenant Colonel James P. Mead

Lieutenant Colonel James P. Mead was a captain in the volunteer army and an aide de camp on the staff of General Crawford at the time of Five Forks. The night of March 31, 1865, Crawford's division was sleeping on its arms in sight of the enemy entrenchments after the battle of White Oak Road. Mead could not point out the exact location, but it was in the vicinity of the juncture of the White Oak Road and the Boydton Plank Road. This was about five miles north of Sheridan's battle at Dinwiddie Courthouse. The division slept in battle formation. There were no fires and no tents.

Mead said that at about 10 p.m. they received an order that the division was to be ready to move at once. He carried the order to Baxter's brigade. It was extremely dark, the exhausted men lay about wherever they could, and he feared that his horse would step on someone. It was a good half hour before Mead reached the brigade and the officers spread the word among the tired men. Since the campaign began three days ago, the men had been marching, fighting, and attempting to sleep in a driving rain. As of the 31st, however, the rain had stopped.

Between 11 p.m. and 12 a.m., probably closer to 12, they received another order that the troops were not to march but to remain where they were. As far as Mead could recollect, Baxter's brigade had not yet moved when the second order came in. He could not vouch for the other brigades.

Very early the next morning, Warren appeared and the division began to move south in line of battle. Mead saw the corps flag and could attest that Warren was ahead of them in the direction of the enemy. The movement was made under the personal supervision of Warren. Coulter's brigade was the last to withdraw from the face of the enemy. They moved southwest, across Gravelly Run to the vicinity of Dr. Boisseau's, where they came to rest.

That afternoon, the entire corps moved up to Gravelly Run Church, where they formed up for battle. Crawford was to the right in the front line with Ayres on the left. Crawford's division formed with Kellogg on the left, Baxter on the right, and Coulter in the center in the rear.

General Sheridan and General Warren were together at the church with General Sheridan drawing a diagram of the plan of battle in the ground with a stick. At the time, Colonel Newhall, General Warren, Colonel Locke, Mead himself, and several other officers were present.

Sheridan's diagram gave the general location of the roads, the position of the enemy, the position of the cavalry, and the location where the Fifth Corps was forming. The Fifth Corps was to wheel upon crossing the White Oak Road so as to face the enemy in the refuse and be at right angles to the main enemy line along the White Oak Road. They were then to advance, break through the refuse, and roll up the main enemy line.

General Warren then passed instructions to his division commanders. Once across the White Oak Road, every man was to keep the sun on his left shoulder and move westward. Mead did not recall what the cavalry was supposed to do.

Mead accompanied Baxter's brigade as it crossed the White Oak Road. They entered a wooded area of pine trees. The branches were low so that they inconvenienced the men. One could see but a short distance, but could not see the formation and, at times, one could not see the sun. While in the woods, Colonel Farnham was wounded. Mead stayed a short time to help Farnham and then set out to overtake Baxter. In all, he was separated from Baxter for about fifteen or twenty minutes.

Mead found Baxter's brigade just to the southeast of the Chimneys. Coulter's brigade was to the left of Baxter's where Kellogg's brigade had been, and Kellogg was nowhere in sight.

Here Mead met a staff officer of General Warren. He believed that it was Benyaurd. Benyaurd asked Mead where General Crawford was. Mead replied that he did not know. General Warren then appeared. He seemed excessively annoyed that Baxter was so far to the right and indicated that he must change direction and keep more to the left. Mead then went to Baxter and helped him to bring the brigade around to the west. They reached the Ford Road near the Boisseau house. There was skirmish fire throughout and they lost several men.

Mead, with Baxter's brigade, ultimately passed down the Ford Road and through the abandoned rebel works on the White Oak Road. There, he saw General Crawford and rode up to report to him that Baxter was coming up solidly and well. Just as he arrived, Crawford said, "Mead, where have you been all day?" Mead replied, "I have been on the right."²⁸ Just then, Mead was hit. Crawford jumped off his horse and held him up. Mead recovered sufficiently to remount his horse. He later saw Warren lead the charge across Gillian field. He thought that but a small number of men followed him.

Colonel Ellis Spear

At the time of Five Forks, Colonel Ellis Spear was a major in the Volunteer Army and was temporarily assigned to General Bartlett's staff as an aide. Bartlett's brigade was assigned to Griffin's division. Thus, it was the Third Brigade of the First Division of the Fifth Corps. Spear mentioned the surprising fact that Bartlett's brigade was larger than Ayres's division. It consisted of nine regiments and over 3,000 men.

As we have previously noted, Warren heard receding gunfire to the south on the afternoon of March 31. He assumed that it was Sheridan being pushed back toward Dinwiddie by the Confederates and sent Bartlett's brigade to assist Sheridan by attacking the Confederates in the flank and rear. Now let us hear from Colonel Spear.

It was late in the afternoon of March 31 when the brigade moved some three or four miles to the southwest to the Boisseau house and an open field beyond. A skirmish line was then thrown out towards the west and southwest. It was now dark and picket fires of the enemy were visible in those directions. The brigade stayed there until about midnight. At that time, they received orders to move back. They returned substantially over the same ground. It took between one and two hours to return to Griffin's division. In the return, the brigade moved slowly, as it was very dark and the roads muddy.

In the early morning of the 1st, the whole division moved to the southwest over much the same ground. Spear could not recollect exactly where the division came to rest, but it was in the same vicinity that the brigade was in the night before.

Later, the brigade and the entire corps moved over to the Gravelly Run Church, where they formed up. Griffin's division formed up behind Crawford's, as far as Spear could recollect, and Bartlett was on the far right.

Spear saw General Griffin the last time shortly after the formation moved out and crossed the White Oak Road and entered the woods. He did not see Griffin again until dark, after the battle was over. As the brigade advanced through the woods and beyond, it swung constantly to the left as the plan required. The swing to the left began when the brigade hit the White Oak Road. Spear could see Crawford's division ahead of them but lost sight of it once they entered the woods and did not see it afterward.

Spear did not recollect seeing the Chimneys and felt that he probably passed to the right of them. There was occasional light fire from their front and from the west as they moved to the Ford Road. Spear noticed two regiments to his right that he believed were from Bartlett's brigade but had wandered too far to the right. Spear rode over and redirected them farther to their left.

The brigade proceeded down the Ford Road. Spear had not seen Bartlett himself since they crossed the White Oak Road. Spear met General Warren on the Ford Road. He rode up and told him of the two regiments he had redirected. Warren directed Spear to take the two regiments, place them across the Ford Road, and face them to the rear; that is, toward the north toward Hatchers Run. Warren feared that there was a body of the enemy to his rear and that he must be prepared for an attack from that quarter. Spear placed the two regiments and then returned to Warren, who was proceeding down the Ford Road toward the rear of the main enemy line along the White Oak Road.

(Warren was not entirely wrong when he feared that a body of the enemy was in his rear farther up the Ford Road. When Pickett set up his defenses along the White Oak Road, he moved his entire wagon train, guarded by General Rosser's cavalry brigade, up the Ford Road beyond Hatchers Run for safety.)

General Warren directed Spear to return up the Ford Road to the two regiments, take them farther up the road to Hatchers Run, determine if there was a bridge across Hatchers Run and, if so, protect it. Spear proceeded as directed and, upon reaching Hatchers Run, determined that there was no bridge but a ford. As they approached the ford, the enemy on the far side of the run opened fire on them.

Spear established a picket line on his side of the run, put two battalions in position, and rode back to report to Warren. He found Griffin in command instead of Warren and reported to him. He then proceeded to the junction of the Ford Road and the White Oak Road, where he finally encountered Bartlett's headquarters and Bartlett.

Captain Charles F. Sawyer

Charles F. Sawyer was a captain of volunteers in the First Maine Sharpshooters of Bartlett's brigade of Griffin's division as of March 31–April 1, 1865. The First Maine was not a regiment but a battalion of six companies. The battalion had joined Bartlett's brigade just days before Five Forks.

Sawyer recollected that the brigade moved south to Dr. Boisseau's on the afternoon of March 31, and then, at midnight, was ordered back to their division to the north. They rejoined the division at about 3 a.m. on the 1st. Before they had breakfast or coffee on the morning of the 1st, the division was ordered back south and the battalion ended up at the same place they had vacated just hours earlier. They later moved up to the Gravelly Run Church where the corps formed up for battle. Sawyer did not know the larger plan or where the enemy was, but knew that they were to wheel to the left and presumed that they were going to hit the enemy in the flank.

When they formed up at Gravelly Run Church, Bartlett's brigade, being unusually large, struck out to the east beyond the other, and Sawyer was at the easternmost end of the brigade. Sawyer's unit was the farthest east unit of the entire corps. They set out on a giant wheel and, in the Syndor field, Sawyer's battalion and the regiment next to them "snapped off," being on the outside and unable to keep up.

It was here that they encountered "General" (Sawyer misstated his rank) Spear. Spear ordered Sawyer to take two companies and move up the Ford Road (away from the main Confederate line on the White Oak Road) to Hatchers Run and to take possession of the bridge over the run.

As Sawyer approached Hatchers Run, he noted two or three Confederates who mounted up and rode across the ford to warn their comrades. Upon arrival, Sawyer noted that there was no bridge, but a ford. It was now twilight and visibility was limited.

When Sawyer reached a point about fifty feet from the run, he was subjected to fire from the far side. The firing increased to a full volley and Sawyer estimated the enemy as at least a brigade. They exchanged fire and, after the second volley from the enemy, General MacKenzie, the cavalry brigade commander, rode up. He said that he believed that Sawyer's unit was firing on their own men. Sawyer assured him that they were not. The two sides were so close that there had been talking between the men. Before the firing, someone called across and claimed that they were our troops. Sawyer asked them who was in command of the Fifth New York Cavalry. A voice replied with the correct answer. He asked who the major was. The correct answer came back. Sawyer then asked the name of the adjutant. The reply came back that "he is talking to you." In actuality, the adjutant was Sawyer's brother. Sawyer now was certain that he was dealing with the enemy.

Shortly thereafter, General MacKenzie departed. It was already 10 or 11 p.m. And so ended Sawyer's testimony. What all this had to do with Warren's generalship is hard to say.

Captain E. G. Sherley

As of March 31, 1865, Captain E.G. Sherley was a first lieutenant in the Ninety-first New York Volunteers. On the evening of March 31, he was detailed on the staff of Colonel Kellogg, who commanded the First Brigade of the Third Division, as aide de camp.

Sometime during the night of the 31st, hour unremembered, they received an order to get ready to move immediately. Sherley carried the order to his own regiment. The orders were later changed, and they did not move until morning.

Questioning now jumped to Gravelly Run Church on the afternoon of April 1. Sherley was assigned by Colonel Kellogg to assist his own regimental commander in the advance. Kellogg's brigade lined up to the left of Baxter's and in line with Bowerman's and Gwynn's brigades of Ayres's division to their left.

Kellogg's brigade formed in two lines. Sherley's regiment was in the rear and the other two in front. Sherley's regiment was unusually large, and overlapped the two in front together. Although the regiment had between 1,200 and 1,400 on its roster, Sherley thought that no more than 800 were present when it stepped off that afternoon. Sherley noted with pride the alignment as it crossed the White Oak Road and entered the woods. Sherley then heard a loud command, apparently form Colonel Kellogg, to wheel to the left. It was then that things began to deteriorate.

They were receiving what was apparently firing from a skirmish line in their front, and Sherley's horse was hit in the front. They quickly lost connection and sight with the other brigades. Sherley did not recollect seeing Baxter's brigade to their right or Ayres's brigades to the left.

Sherley remembered coming out of the woods into an open field, but could not remember seeing the Chimneys. As they got to the Boisseau house (just to the west of the Ford Road and a little over a half mile north of the Confederate fortifications along the White Oak Road), they swung around to the southwest; that is, toward the rear of the enemy line.

Most of the casualties they took that day were in the vicinity of the Boisseau house. The New York Ninety-first suffered six killed and forty wounded that day. Sherley thought that the two regiments in Kellogg's front line must have suffered more severely.

CHAPTER 10

More Testimony, Some Confederates Testify

Testimony resumed on Governor's Island on Friday, May 28, 1880, at 11 a.m. The first witness was M. D. Corse.

M. D. Corse

At the time of the battle of Five Forks, M. D. Corse was a brigadier general in the Confederate Army and commander of a brigade in Pickett's division. Corse arrived at Five Forks from the west end of Lee's line on the afternoon of the 30th. On the 31st, the Confederate force under Pickett succeeded in pushing Sheridan back to Dinwiddie Courthouse. As one may recall, apologists for Sheridan attempted to attribute the blame for Sheridan's temporary defeat this day to Warren. Warren was operating five miles to the north and was temporarily pushed back by the Confederates. It was alleged that this momentary defeat of Warren allowed the Confederates to transfer troops to Pickett, and that this augmentation allowed Pickett to prevail over Sheridan. Corse debunked this by testifying that the Confederates at Five Forks–Dinwiddie received no reinforcements on the 31st.

At midnight on the 31st, Pickett called a meeting of his commanders. He said that Sheridan was being reinforced by infantry and that they would have to move back to Five Forks. Corse could only recollect that they were told that Sheridan was being reinforced, but not where. Corse thought that the Fifth Corps was mentioned as the reinforcement.

The retirement to Five Forks commenced before daylight. Corse could not recollect any particular pressure on the retiring Confederates. They were deployed at Five Forks by about 9 a.m. and began erecting barriers of logs and earth along the White Oak Road. Corse said that the troops were dead tired and he quickly fell asleep.

Corse testified that only three of Pickett's brigades were present. These were commanded by himself, William R. Terry, and Steuart. Pickett had a fourth brigade commanded by Hunton, but it had been diverted just before the move to Five Forks. Johnson's division, commanded by Ransom, was also at Five Forks, as were cavalry units commanded by W.H.F. Lee, Rosser, and Munford, and artillery commanded by Pegram.

Pickett's division held the western end of the White Oak Road line. Corse was on the far west, except for W.H.F. Lee's cavalry that was on his flank. Corse was deployed along the northern end of the Gillian field. Terry was next, just to the east of Corse, and then came Steuart. Ransom's men then took over to the eastern end of the line with Fitzhugh's cavalry (commanded by Munford) on their flank.

According to Corse, his brigade as of the 1st had only about 800 men, Terry's somewhat less, and Steuart's somewhat more. He thought that Pickett's entire division at Five Forks only numbered about 2,500. He had no idea as to the size of Ransom's division or of the cavalry or artillery.

During the late morning and early afternoon, there were several cavalry feints at Corse's position, but nothing worthy of attack.

A real attack began against the eastern end of the line (Ransom's) in the afternoon. Corse admitted it could have been at 4:30 p.m. but thought it was earlier. Terry was called out of line to move to the east to stem the attack. This left a void and Corse had to thin his line to fill Terry's space.

Late in the afternoon (about 6 p.m.), Pickett told Corse that he would have to change front from along the White Oak Road to perpendicular to it. This Corse did. His right now rested on the north side of the White Oak Road at the western end of the Gillian field and his left extended about seventy yards toward the north. Confederate cavalry extended the line to the south of the White Oak Road. Corse held this position until dark and then slipped away cross country through the woods. He estimated that he salvaged about 600 of his 800 men to fight another day. He had no idea what Pickett's total loss for the day was.

Colonel Harrison Adreon

Colonel Harrison Adreon was a major in the Fourth Maryland Volunteers at the time of the battle. His regiment was assigned to Bowerman's brigade of Ayres's division of the Fifth Corps.

The night of March 31–April 1, his division marched from the scene of the battle of the White Oak Road to the vicinity of Dinwiddie Courthouse. Aside from the darkness of the night, he could recall no impediments that delayed the march. He made no mention of crossing Gravelly Run or of a downed bridge. His regiment brought up the rear of the march. As they neared Dinwiddie Courthouse, they learned that they had passed the road on which Sheridan intended them to turn off. That is, the Brooks Road. The column turned about and Adreon's regiment was now in the lead. It was about one half mile back to the Brooks Road.

As they turned down the Brooks Road, which was to the southwest, it was just starting to get light. They met Sheridan near the intersection of the Brooks Road and the Five Forks–Dinwiddie Courthouse road. Here, they were ordered into bivouac. Later that day, around 2 p.m. the whole corps was ordered to Gravelly Run Church, where they formed up for battle. Adreon described the march down the plank road to Dinwiddie as fast as could be expected, and the later march to Gravelly Run Church as "very prompt."[1]

When they deployed, Ayres's division was to the left in the front line. Bouverman's brigade, to which Adreon's regiment belonged, formed on the left. Each brigade formed in two lines, and Adreon's regiment was on the right of the rear line. Adreon's regiment was as indicated in figure 11.

While forming up, they were hurried along by commands from both Warren and Ayres, such as, "General Warren directs to hurry up the formation of the line."[2]

The enemy fire commenced even before the division reached the White Oak Road. They began to wheel to the left almost immediately. They then went to the "flank" to expedite the change of front while under fire. The fire became very heavy as they moved around to face the enemy in the refuse.

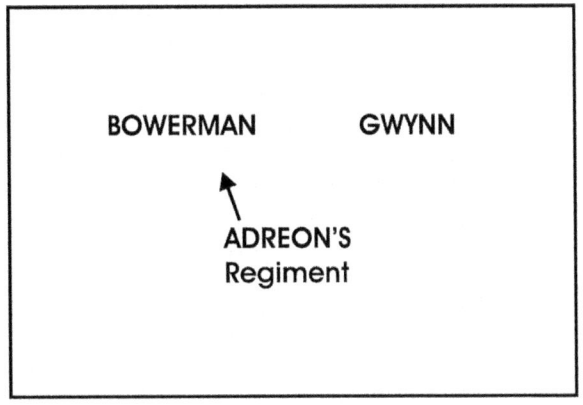

Figure 11. Adreon's Regiment.

When realigned and before charging the enemy in the refuse, Sheridan, followed by his staff, appeared on Adreon's right and rode down the line between Adreon's line and the enemy. He held his hat in hand and was cheered by the troops as he moved along. (A previous witness described Sheridan's trot down the line before the battle but stated that Sheridan was *behind* the line. Could they both be right? Adreon testified that each brigade was deployed in two lines and that his regiment was in the rear line. Could Sheridan, then, have ridden between the lines?)

The rush on the enemy line along the refuse was a complete success. It was up and over and they took over 2,000 prisoners. Adreon was so concerned that so many Confederates were behind him with rifles lying about that he sent men to the rear to manage the situation. Adreon's regiment continued the advance down the White Oak Road but was met by Sheridan, who ordered him to return to the captured refuse and remain there. Adreon's regiment and elements of the two New York regiments, perhaps 500 or 600 men, were ordered to remain in the refuse. These troops took no further part in the fight.

Why did Sheridan order Adreon to remain in the refuse? It had something to do with Sheridan's cavalry. Adreon noticed Union cavalry appearing on his left and charging down the White Oak Road. It would appear that Sheridan was concerned with Adreon firing into the Union cavalry or vice versa. About 6:30 when the battle was essentially over, Adreon's regiment was permitted to march down the White Oak Road to its bivouac for the night.

The next to testify was Lieutenant Colonel West Funk. His testimony had little if anything to do with the issues at hand. Consequently, we will skip to the next, who proved to be a key individual in the happenings of March 31–April 1, 1865.

Thomas T. Munford

Munford's testimony was taken on Governor's Island on Saturday, May 29, 1880, beginning at 11 a.m.

At the time of the battle, Munford was a brigadier general in the Confederate Army in command of a brigade in the cavalry division of General Fitzhugh Lee. However, inasmuch as Fitzhugh Lee served as the overall commander of cavalry in Pickett's force on the crucial days of March 31–April 1, Munford commanded Fitzhugh's division. In all, there were three cavalry divisions in Pickett's command. These were commanded by W.H.F. Lee, Thomas Munford, and General Rosser. Each cavalry division was composed of two brigades.

Munford devoted much time to describing the battle of Dinwiddie Courthouse on March 31. However, inasmuch as this had nothing to do with Warren's generalship, we will move on to April 1. Munford clarified the composition of Pickett's force as of the 1st. In addition to the three cavalry divisions and Pegram's artillery, Pickett had five infantry brigades. Three were of Pickett's own division and two were of General Johnson's division. The three of Pickett's divisions were those of Corse, Terry, and Steuart. However, Terry was wounded on the 31st and,

Brigadier General Thomas Munford, always reliable Confederate cavalry commander.

as of the 1st his brigade was commanded by Colonel Mayo. The two brigades of Johnson's division were those of Wallace and Ransom. Ransom was senior and commanded the two. The lineup from west to east was W.H.F. Lee's cavalry, Corse, Mayo, Steuart, Wallace, Ransom, and Munford's cavalry. Ransom commanded in the crucial refuse. Rosser's cavalry division was located up the Ford Road on the far side of Hatchers Run, guarding the wagon train. The deployment was as in map 11.

Munford also testified that Ransom had an artillery battery. It was called McGregor's battery, and it was posted at the northeastern corner of the angle. Munford asked Ransom if he could borrow it. Ransom declined.

Munford formed a skirmish line parallel to the White Oak Road. Its right connected with the north end of the refuse. The men were all dismounted, as the ground was not suitable for cavalry operations. Munford had to leave his horse artillery in the wagon park north of Hatchers Run because of the wetness of the ground. Munford's total command consisted of about 1,500 men. However, inasmuch as the men were dismounted, he had to devote one-fourth of the total force as horse holders. It took one man to hold four horses.

The held horses had to be protected, yet kept close enough to be quickly retrieved in case of necessity. Munford had them slowly moved up a farm road that extended from the White Oak Road to the Boisseau house just beyond the Ford Road.

Munford confronted the oncoming divisions of Crawford and Griffin and, later, Crawford alone, with just a skirmish line. He did not have enough men to form a line

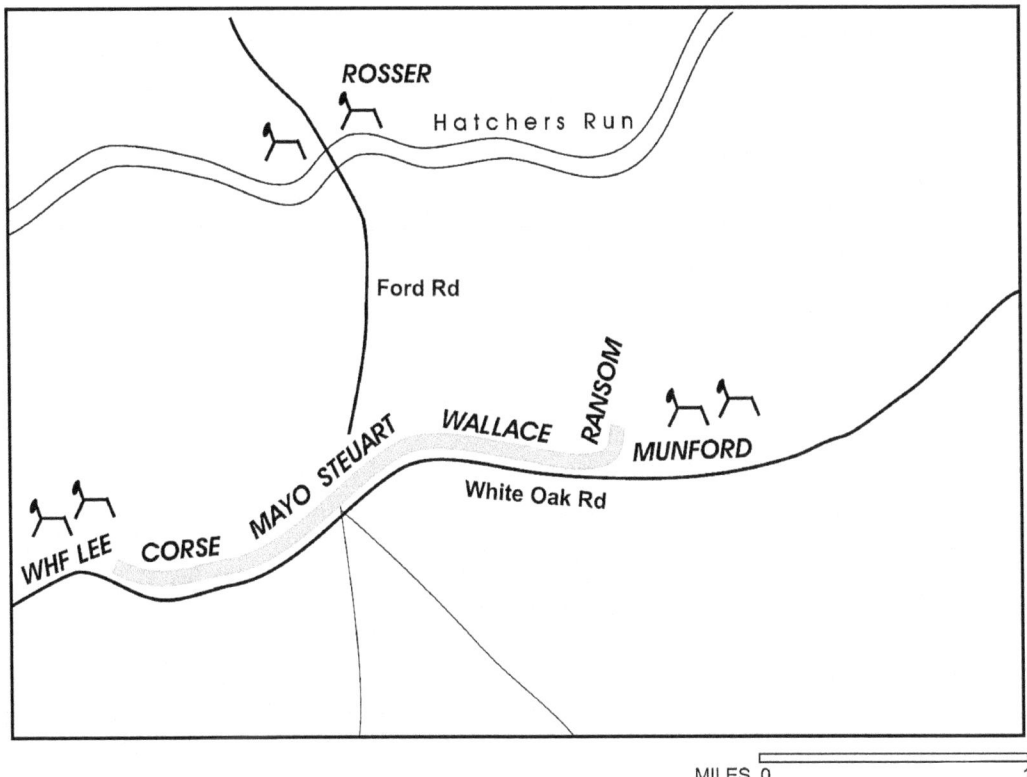

Map 11. Munford's version of Pickett's deployment.

of battle. A skirmish line consists of a thin line of men who are allowed to seek whatever cover is available, such as trees and boulders. A line of battle consists of two rows of men, shoulder to shoulder, with one line directly behind the other. While the first row shoots, the second loads, and they are then reversed. Munford's skirmishers proved particularly effective in the woods, where they inflicted more casualties than they took.

Munford was continually pushed northwest and then west in a giant arc, always fearful that the Yankees would overlap his left. At one point, the Yankees swept so close to Hatchers Run that they were fired upon by Rosser's men on the far side of the run.

After two miles of retreat, Munford was pressed back to the Ford Road at a point about halfway between the White Oak Road and Hatchers Run. He wanted to move up the Ford Road, cross Hatchers Run, and join Rosser, but could not. He had to continue to retreat to the southwest of the Ford Road.

While on the Ford Road, Munford met Pickett. Pickett had been with Rosser on the far side of Hatchers Run at a shad bake when the enemy struck and, now that the battle was substantially over, he was just now arriving at the scene of the disaster. Munford declined to say what he said to Pickett.

Munford retreated through the same woods as Corse to the west of the battle and managed to salvage most of his command. He estimated that 1,200 of his original 1,500 lived to fight another day.

Captain Holman S. Melcher

At the time of the battle, Melcher was postmaster on the Fifth Corps staff. It is extremely difficult to establish the substance of Captain Melcher's actual testimony. At least three-quarters of the verbiage consisted of long, leading questions by the attorneys (Stickney for General Warren and Gardner for General Sheridan), to which Melcher often replied that he did not know or could not remember. We are, of course, only interested in what Melcher testified that he knew, not in what the attorneys thought. To make matters more complex, the attorneys jumped from one time to another without any attempt to maintain a logical sequence. This is the substance of Melcher's testimony in correct time sequence.

General Chamberlain's brigade was fiercely engaged the afternoon and evening of March 29. The trains did not come up that night and the corps spent the night of the 29th–30th without shelter and without food. It rained throughout the night and the troops were miserable. On the 30th, it rained all day and they spent the entire day in the mud. The night of the 30th they finally got their tents pitched and got some rest. On the 31st, the general (Warren) called his staff and they rode together to the front just beyond Gravelly Run on the Boydton Plank Road. Here they found the second and third divisions heavily engaged near the White Oak Road. The fight continued until late at night. Warren remained at the front until about 9 p.m. and then returned to his headquarters at the Wilson house. Two of the Fifth Corps' divisions (Ayres and Crawford) had been pushed back behind the first (Griffin), which was on the north bank of Gravelly Run to the west of the Boydton Plank Road. Here they rallied. Helped by some troops from the Second Corps, they pushed the enemy back across the White Oak Road. Here, the ranks came to rest. When Melcher returned with Warren to his headquarters, the three division commanders had not yet established their headquarters for the night.

At about 11 p.m. on the 31st, Warren called for Melcher and sent him to Griffin with a sealed order. Melcher did not know what it contained. With much difficulty, Melcher found Griffin near where he had last seen him. In all, Melcher spent over an hour finding Griffin and returning to headquarters. Griffin was by a campfire, just about to mount his horse, when Melcher handed him the order. Griffin told him that the enemy campfires in front of him had just been extinguished and he feared that the enemy was about to attack. He directed that Melcher report this to Warren.

Melcher returned to the Wilson house and gave Griffin's message to Warren. In the meantime, Warren had sent out other couriers with messages for other generals. About 1 a.m., Warren called Melcher and sent him out with another message of unknown content. This one was for Crawford. While heading for Crawford, Melcher passed a column of marching troops. It was Ayres heading for the Boydton Plank Road. In fact, the head of Ayres's column may have already reached the road and turned south toward Dinwiddie.

Melcher found Crawford about where he had last seen him, and there was no evidence of a pending move. Melcher also passed Griffin and, likewise, Griffin's division gave no evidence of an impending move. Melcher returned to Warren's headquarters in the Wilson house at about 2 a.m. on the 1st. General Warren directed Melcher to turn in and get some rest.

Melcher awoke about 8 or 9 a.m. on the 1st. Warren was no longer there but had proceeded on to the front during the night. At about 10 a.m., Melcher set out to join Warren. He proceeded down the Boydton Plank Road, down the Brooks Road and up the Five Forks–Dinwiddie road where he found Warren at the Gravelly Run Church. It was now about 11 a.m. or 12 p.m. on the 1st and troops of the Fifth Corps were getting into battle formation in the open space near the church. When the troops moved forward, Warren was accompanied by Melcher and staff. They rode just behind the skirmish line and in front to the main body of troops.

After Ayres's division moved in to storm the angle, General Warren sent Melcher to Crawford with a message. Crawford was already out of sight and Melcher found him by the sound of gunfire. He found Crawford in Syndor field to the east of the Ford Road. He was heavily engaged and Crawford himself was just behind the front. The message was simply to tell Crawford to push forward.

On the way back, Melcher discovered that the refuse had been taken. There was much confusion and crowds of prisoners. Melcher proceeded westward along the now captured defenses along the White Oak Road until he met Colonel Locke. Colonel Locke asked him if he knew where Sheridan was. Locke had a message for Sheridan from Warren.

Locke and Melcher rode westward along the White Oak Road, passed a captured battery and, near the intersection with the Ford Road, came upon Sheridan. Locke delivered his message to Sheridan. When asked what Sheridan said, Melcher said that, although he could not recollect the exact words, it was to the effect that all Sheridan had to say was that Warren was not at the front where he belonged and that Locke could tell him just that. This astonished Melcher. The two rode on to find Warren. They saw him sitting on his horse at the northeastern corner of Gillian field looking across the field, and reported Sheridan's message to him. Warren turned, seized the headquarters flag out of the hands of the sergeant, leaped his horse over the ditch in front of the woods, and led a charge against the enemy at the far side of the field. Melcher then headed for their bivouac for the night, which was to the east of the angle in the Confederate line.

Fitzhugh Lee

Fitzhugh Lee was a major general in the Confederate Army and in charge of a division of cavalry. However, in the Five Forks campaign, he was put in command of all three cavalry divisions then serving Pickett, and his own division was commanded by Brigadier General Munford.

At a meeting with General Robert E. Lee at Petersburg before Fitzhugh Lee left for Five Forks, the senior Lee told him of Sheridan's campaign to threaten the Southside Railroad, and advised the young Lee that the best way to break it up was to attack Sheridan.

Pickett's infantry forces and Lee's cavalry were transferred down to Five Forks on March 29–30, and Fitzhugh Lee was the third to testify that Pickett received no reinforcements afterwards. Fitzhugh Lee estimated that Pickett's total force was about 8,200 and was composed of 3,200 cavalry and about 5,000 infantry. This conformed closely to Pickett's own estimate.

Pickett's force attacked Sheridan on the 31st and pushed him all the way back to Dinwiddie Courthouse. At the close of the day, Pickett was deployed across the Five Forks–Dinwiddie Courthouse Road within one half mile of the courthouse. Fitzhugh Lee testified that he could plainly see the courthouse, and that Pickett intended to renew the contest at daylight.

By 10 p.m. the night of the 31st, Pickett and Lee learned that Union infantry were marching down to reinforce Sheridan. They decided to move all wheeled vehicles back at once. These included cannon, ambulances, and ammunition wagons. These started to the rear by 11 o'clock that night and all were gone by daylight. The cavalry were ordered to begin to withdraw at 4 a.m. and the infantry before that. It is possible that the movement of the infantry and cavalry behind them did not actually start by 4 a.m. but, rather, at first light.

The withdrawal was not vigorously followed by the enemy, and it appeared that they were merely following to see where Pickett was going. The entire Confederate force arrived at Five Forks by 8 or 8:30 a.m., but it was sometime later before they were fully deployed. There were rudimentary fortifications at Five Forks along the White Oak Road and the arriving Confederates set out to improve them. Lee testified that the three cavalry divisions were deployed as follows: W.H.F. Lee on the right flank of the Confederate line (that is, to the west), Munford on the left flank (to the east at the refuse), and Rosser's up the Ford Road across Hatchers Run to protect the wagon train. Lee's listing of the deployment of the five infantry brigades differed from that of the other witnesses and was probably incorrect. The deployment of Pickett's force according to Lee was as indicated in map 12.

Lee testified that about 12 o'clock, everything being quiet, he rode up the Ford Road, crossed Hatchers Run to see General Pickett, and then passed farther down to where the wagons were to see General Rosser in regards to rations and ammunition for his men.

(The generally accepted belief is that Pickett and Lee did not cross Hatchers Run on business but, rather, to attend a shad bake at the invitation of General Rosser. In any event, they were unable to get back, as Crawford hit the Ford Road. Both Lee and Pickett were cut off from the battle. Pickett managed to get back just before the finale at Gillian field, but Lee never succeeded in getting back before the end. The battle of Five Forks was fought without Confederate leadership. While Pickett and Fitzhugh Lee feasted on shad, their command was annihilated.)

Lee testified that, after the battle wound down, he moved off to the west to unite with the retreating Confederates, but then, considering that his main mission was to protect the Southside Railroad, moved back to the ford. There he remained the night of the 1st, where he received reinforcements from the main Confederate line.

(Lee lived long enough to re-establish his reputation. Pickett did not.)

W. W. Wood

W. W. Wood was another Confederate. At the time of Five Forks, he was a lieutenant colonel in command of the Fourteenth Virginia Infantry in Steuart's brigade of Pickett's division.

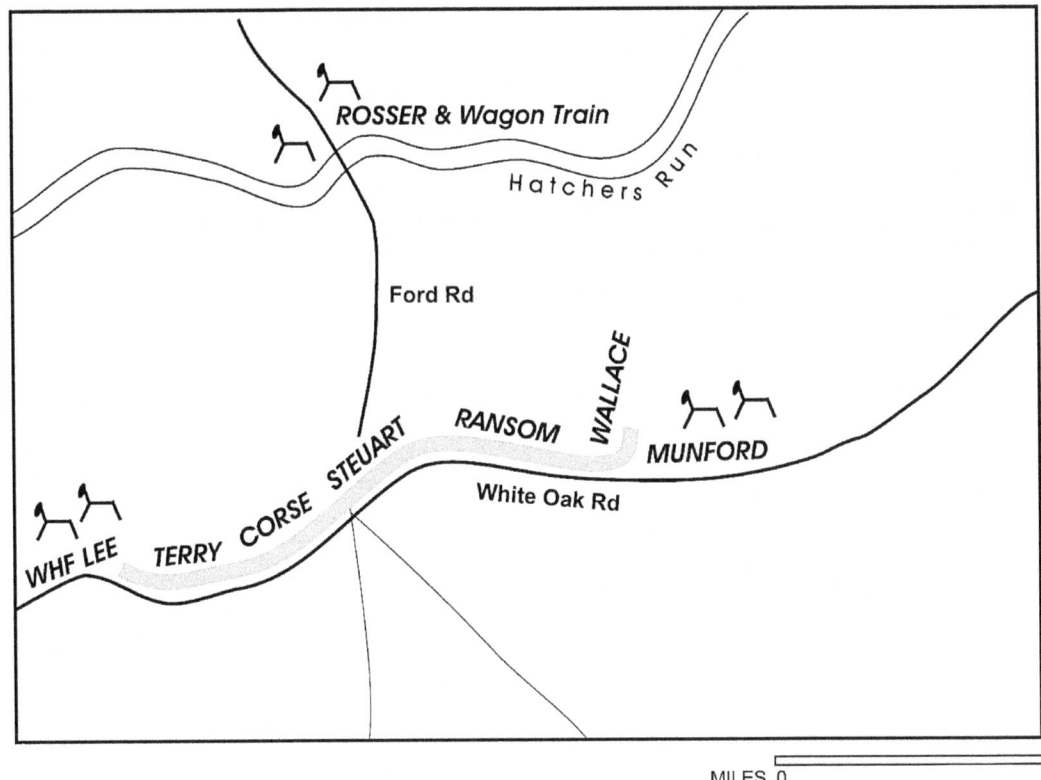

Map 12. Fitzhugh Lee's version of Pickett's deployment.

A little before noon on March 31, Pickett's force, including Wood's regiment, moved out of Five Forks to confront Sheridan's cavalry in the battle of Dinwiddie Courthouse. When combat stopped the night of March 31, they had pushed back Sheridan to Dinwiddie Courthouse and were camped across the Five Forks Road one-half mile from the courthouse.

Wood was not informed of the approach of Union infantry until just before they were ordered to move back. The move started at first light. Wood's regiment brought up the rear of the infantry and acted as skirmishers, although there was Confederate cavalry behind them.

In their retirement, the Confederates were not molested and there was no shooting. The action of the Union cavalry can be better described as "following" rather than "pushing."

The Confederates reached Five Forks between 8 and 9 a.m. There were rudimentary barricades along the White Oak Road prepared by them at their earlier stay. They now set to work to improve the barricades. It was soon table-high with traverses.

Steuart's brigade, to which Wood's regiment was assigned, was placed in the line along the White Oak Road with its left facing south on the Forks (the Ford Road). The complement of the brigade was estimated to be 1,200, and Wood's regiment between 300 and 400. Wood's regiment was on the far left of the brigade; that is, closest to the return. The deployment of the force as described by Wood was as indicated in map 13.

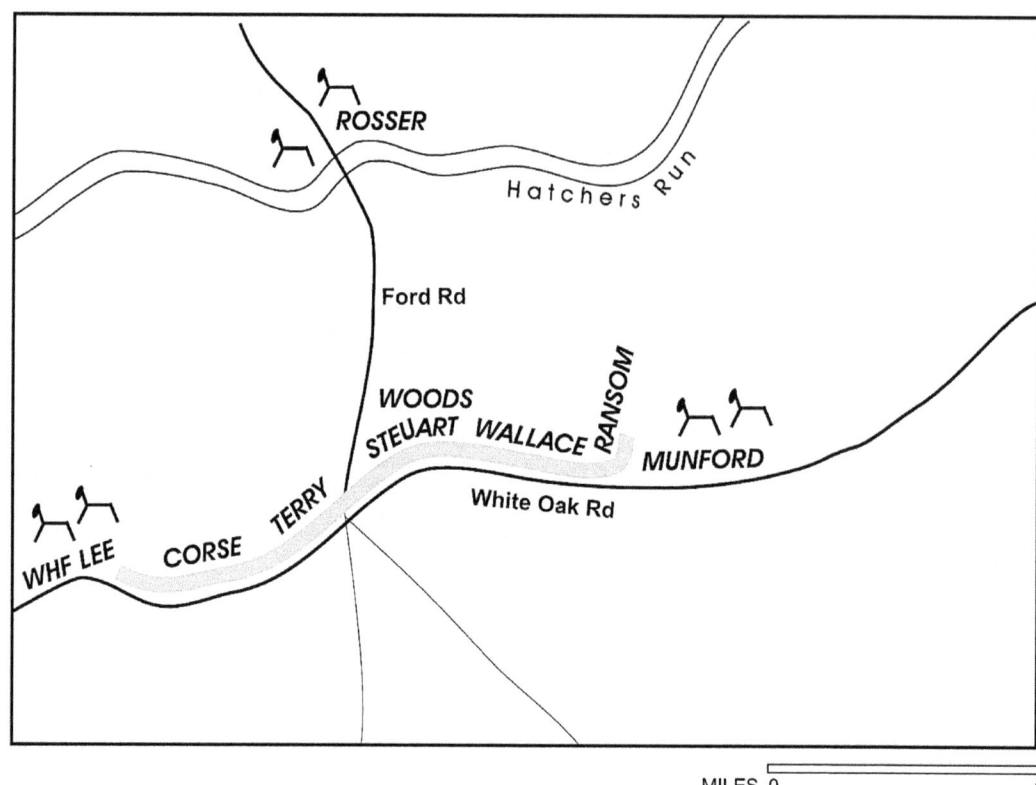

Map 13. Colonel Wood's version of Pickett's deployment.

Wood initially reversed the location of Wallace and Ransom, but later corrected it. After arriving at Five Forks, and after eating breakfast and working on the barrier, his brigade was charged by a small force of cavalry, perhaps seventy-five to one hundred troops. Some leaped over the barrier. The brigade easily disposed of their attack and killed, wounded, or captured all. This was the only enemy action until late in the afternoon. Not a gun was fired until then.

Wood knew little of Pickett's artillery placement. The only friendly artillery he knew of was Pegram's battery located at the Forks.

In the late afternoon, the time of which Wood could not recollect, there was a vigorous and rapid attack at the refuse. It was not accompanied by any attack from the front. It was but a very short time after the attack on the flank began that Wood was engaged.

The first information on the attack was brought to him by a dismounted cavalryman from Munford's division with whom Wood was acquainted. He greeted Wood and informed him that the enemy was in their rear. Almost simultaneously, what apparently were marching men appeared in Wood's rear, proceeding from the direction of the attack in the east, along the White Oak Road heading to the west.

Within minutes, General Ransom himself rode up and asked Wood if he was in charge. Wood replied in the affirmative. Ransom said that the apparent marching column consisted of troops who were vacating their positions without orders. Ransom directed

Wood to reform his position from along the White Oak Road to perpendicular to it. The purpose was to stop the rout and the enemy that was pursuing them.

Wood swung his regiment around so that the right now rested on the White Oak Road and the left extended to the north. The brigade that was to his right, Terry's, then moved up the White Oak Road to fill the void left by Wood.

By the time Wood established his new line, at least half the routed soldiers of Ransom's and Wallace's brigades had passed. Wood's new line consisted of his own 300 to 400, plus another 500 to 600 he acquired from the routed force of Wallace and Ransom.

Wood's new line was barely formed when the enemy was upon him. Wood's men were on slightly higher ground than the charging Fifth Corps troops, which gave him some advantage. Wood was sure that his line was inflicting serious harm on the attacking Federals. Wood believed that he held his own as much as one and a half hours. He was then overlapped on both flanks and overwhelmed.

Some of Wood's men surrendered, and others ran down the White Oak Road to the west. Wood hoped to join Pegram's artillery at the Forks and there attempt another stand. However, when he got to the Forks, Pegram was dead and the cannoneers were abandoning their weapons. Wood continued down the road and past Corse. It appears that, as of this time, the perpendicular line across the road that Pickett ordered Corse to form was not yet in place.

The only resistance that the fleeing Wood noticed occurred in Gillian field by W.H.F. Lee's cavalry.

Wood felt that the entire force attacking him was infantry. He noted no cavalry, but could not exclude the possibility that some of what appeared to be infantry could have been dismounted cavalry.

By the time Wood reached the woods to the west and turned north toward the railroad to safety, he counted twenty-seven survivors of his regiment.

Joseph Mayo

Joseph Mayo was another Confederate. As of the day of the battle, he was a colonel in command of Terry's brigade of Pickett's division. Terry himself had been wounded in the operations of March 31, 1865.

Mayo's description of events on March 31 cast no new light on the case, so we will jump to April 1, 1865, the day of the battle.

Pickett's force retired without molestation from Dinwiddie Courthouse to Five Forks on the early morning of the 1st. Mayo's brigade was posted along the White Oak Road west of the intersection with the Ford Road. Three guns of Pegram's artillery were posted at the intersection. To the east of the intersection along the White Oak Road, Steuart's brigade was posted. On Mayo's other side (to the west) was the brigade of Corse. Gillian field was to the south of Corse. Mayo, at this time, after the losses of the 31st, had about 1,000 men in five regiments.

Upon arrival at the White Oak Road and being posted, Mayo's men, as well as the men of the other brigades, constructed a defensive barrier of logs and earth.

There was no enemy activity until about noon. At that time, some enemy cavalry slipped into a break in the skirmish line between Steuart and Mayo and captured some of Mayo's skirmishers. Peace then returned until late in the afternoon.

That morning, after the fortifications were constructed, Pickett called the brigade commanders, just in the rear of the guns at the Fork. He showed them a map indicating how they were deployed, told them to strengthen their positions, and rode off with General Fitzhugh Lee (this was apparently to the shad bake). It was Pickett's opinion that if any infantry attack came, it would be at the west end of their line; that is, in the sector occupied by Corse's and W.H.F. Lee's cavalry.

Late in the afternoon, at a time Mayo could not recollect, the skirmish firing became very heavy in front, and there was loud musketry to Mayo's left. (Actually, it was now about 4:30 p.m. Mayo said that from that time until dark, two to two and one-half hours later, he was engulfed in a swirl of activity, during which he could not place a time to any event.

The fire to Mayo's left grew alarming. Soon thereafter, Mayo was advised that Steuart, who was to his left, wanted to see him. He met Steuart at the intersection by the three guns. Steuart said that General Ransom, who was at the far left, was in trouble and wanted Steuart to send his entire brigade to help. Steuart told Mayo that he could not do this, but would send two regiments if Mayo would send one. Mayo agreed and sent off one of his regiments. He never saw it again.

Shortly thereafter, Major Pickett, General Pickett's brother and adjutant, rode up. He said that Pickett had ordered that Mayo leave one regiment in the fortifications and bring the other three up the Ford Road to him. Mayo had not moved more than 200 yards up the Ford Road when he met Pickett himself. Pickett said: "Colonel, the enemy are in our rear, and if we do not drive them out, we are gone up."[3] Pickett then directed that Mayo file off the road to the left and, with his right resting on the road, continue up the road until he met the enemy.

Mayo never even succeeded in putting all three regiments in line of battle before he was overwhelmed by the enemy from the north and the east. This all occurred in minutes, and Mayo was sent reeling back toward Five Forks. His fifth regiment was still holding the front on the White Oak Road. He gathered up what troops he could and continued to flee to the west beyond Corse. Corse at the time was just in the process of reorienting his line from along the White Oak Road to perpendicular to it. Mayo entered the woods heading west and then turned north toward the railroad. It was now night. He joined Pickett's other survivors at the railroad on the 2nd. At this time, he had 250 survivors of the 1,000 that had been at Five Forks.

W. Gordon McCabe

W. Gordon McCabe was yet another Confederate officer. At Five Forks he was a captain and adjutant in Pegram's battalion of light artillery.

Pegram's battalion had twenty guns. On the 30th they moved six of the twenty guns to Five Forks, leaving the remaining fourteen at Burgess Mills. They arrived about 5 p.m.

On the 31st, they engaged in the battle of Dinwiddie Courthouse. At about 2 a.m. on the 1st, they pulled out from the vicinity of Dinwiddie and returned to Five Forks. They arrived at sunrise. The infantry arrived later and took position along the White Oak Road. The six guns were placed as follows: three at the intersection of the Ford Road and the White Oak Road about the center of the line and three at the far west end of the line, that is, at the far end of Corse's brigade. The three at the far end swept Gillian field. The three at the intersection faced woodland.

From daylight to 8:30 a.m., when infantry and artillery were in position, there was no firing. There was some before noon, but it did not amount to much. There was no attack. The artillery fired only two or three rounds.

During the morning, Colonel Pegram and Captain McCabe rode over to the guns on the far right of the line. There they witnessed a spectacle. Some of Sheridan's cavalry and some of W.H.F. Lee's cavalry were making a race to seize the Gillian house in the field before them. Sheridan's men arrived first, but Lee's men drove them out. Finally, the enemy formed some troops in the back of the field. One of Pegram's guns fired a single shot at them. It burst right over their colors and they fell back into the woods. That was all.

When the big attack came, Pegram and McCabe were still at the guns at the far end. Pegram was sleeping and McCabe was reading a copy of *The Richmond Examiner*. McCabe woke Pegram up and the two leaped on their horses and rode to the guns at the intersection. They piled up canister at each gun and commenced a brisk fire; at first to the front, and then to the southeast.

Before they got out, they heard a hullabaloo on their left. Men were streaming back. At first they were not concerned, as some men always deserted the front in battle. Just as Colonel Pegram gave the order "Fire your canister. Low men,"[4] he tumbled out of the saddle. He was shot through his arm and right under the heart. He said that he was mortally wounded. At this time, McCabe noticed that bullets were not only coming from the east, but from the north and south as well.

McCabe told the doctor to bring an ambulance down the Ford Road, and McCabe got the litter corps men to carry Pegram to the ambulance. However, the gunfire was now so intense that the litter corps men lay down and McCabe had to threaten them to get them to carry Pegram. McCabe guessed that it was now about a half hour since the attack began. He moved off in the ambulance with Pegram up the White Oak Road to the west, after giving the gunners final instructions. The men at the guns were still working the guns, firing canister, and seemed cheerful enough.

McCabe in the ambulance passed Corse's brigade. Corse was in the process of reorienting his brigade from along the White Oak Road to a right angle with the road. McCabe took the three guns on Corse's right with him as he passed into the woods beyond Corse. McCabe arrived at Ford's Station on the railroad that night where he rejoined with other Pickett survivors. In the meantime, Pegram had died.

(In McCabe's narrative, he said nothing about McGregor's battery of artillery. General Munford had previously mentioned it as being attached to Ransom's command and located at the northeastern end of the refuse. When asked about it by Sheridan's counsel, McCabe replied that he had heard about it since, and thought that McGregor had a couple of guns of horse artillery. In any event, it was not part of Pegram's battalion. The

Colonel Theodore Lyman

Next to testify was a Yankee, Theodore Lyman. In March–April 1865, Lyman was a lieutenant colonel and volunteer aide de camp to his good friend General Meade.

Lyman kept a detailed, day by day journal of events, so his answers to questions were usually quite precise and not affected by a fifteen year lapse. Incidentally, his journal became a major source for this book.

Inasmuch as Warren was transferred to Sheridan the night of March 31–April 1 and Meade played no role in the actual battle, Lyman's testimony related entirely to events before the battle. First, let us quote Lyman's description of the weather in the days leading up to the battle.

> Wed Mar 29, 1865 a mild day, with violets in bloom, but no small leaves yet on the trees. The marching troops threw away their overcoats because of the heat....
> March 29 10:30 p.m. heavy rain
> Thursday Mar 30 Heavy rain still which reduced the roads, already poor, to a hopeless pudding. Gravelly Run was swollen to treble its usual size, and Hatchers Run swept away its bridges and required pontoons.[5]

Lyman's journal had another entry on the 30th, which read:

> So terrible were the roads, and so questionable the possibility of getting up supplies, that the generals began to speculate on the necessity of drawing back. The chief quartermaster said it was the worst time to move trains he ever had seen. It took 1000 engineers 56 hours to get a train of 600 wagons 5 miles.
> Friday, 31st. The sun came out at 10 a.m.[6]

Although Lyman did not say so, the sun stayed out. April 1, 1865, the day of the battle, was a beautiful spring day.

As of daylight on the 31st, Grant's headquarters were at Dabney Mills. Meade's were near Gravelly Run on the Vaughan Road. Meade's headquarters were about five miles from Sheridan's at Dinwiddie; Grant's headquarters were about an additional mile farther. If one wanted to go from Sheridan's headquarters to Grant's by road, he had to pass Meade's.

Lyman presented the following chronology of events for the day of March 31, centered on Meade's movements:

0930	Meade consulted with Humphreys at Humphreys' headquarters
1000	Meade consulted with Grant at Grant's headquarters
1330	Warren's Second and Third Divisions had been pushed back from the White Oak Road in disorder, upon his First Division (Griffin's). Meade consulted with Warren in the field. He then ordered Griffin to advance and rode over to General Humphreys. He directed Humphreys to order Miles's division to aid Warren by striking the advancing Confederates in the flank. Humphreys had anticipated Meade and had already done so.

1430	Meade went to the Butler house where he had a long consultation with Grant.
1630	Meade and Grant could hear heavy firing from the direction of Sheridan.
1700–1800	Warren, aided by Miles of Humphreys' command, pushed the Confederates back and secured a lodgment on the far side of the White Oak Road.
1700–1800	A major or lieutenant colonel of cavalry attached to Sheridan approached Meade and reported that he had been cut off from Sheridan and that Sheridan had been pushed back by a large enemy force of infantry. Lyman could tell by the demeanor of the officer that he considered the situation serious. Lyman was sure that the officer was not Captain Sheridan of Sheridan's staff. Lyman did not know of any other envoy from Sheridan arriving and talking to Meade on the 31st.

When asked if Meade had made any derogatory comments to Warren concerning Warren's initial retreat that day, he replied that Meade did not.

The court reconvened on Governor's Island on Tuesday, June 8, 1880, at 11 a.m. The morning was taken up with procedural matters. It then called the next witness.

The Reverend Edmund R. Sanborn

Edmund R. Sanborn was another Yankee. At Five Forks, he was first lieutenant of the Twentieth Maine Regiment, command company E, the right company of the regiment. The Third Maine was attached to the Third Brigade (Bartlett's) of the First Division (Griffin's) of the Fifth Corps.

It will be recalled that, on the afternoon March 31, Warren sent Bartlett's brigade to assist Sheridan. The brigade was later recalled to join its division, and the division was then sent to exactly the same place from which Bartlett had been withdrawn. Thus on the 31st, Bartlett marched from Griffin to Dr. Boisseau's, from Dr. Boisseau's back to Griffin, and then Griffin's division, including Bartlett, marched back to Dr. Boisseau's. We will now turn to Sanborn's story.

About 5 p.m. on March 31, Bartlett's brigade moved out from Griffin's division. The division was still on the White Oak Road where the day's hostilities ceased. The brigade reached the vicinity of Dr. Boisseau's after dark. This was near the Five Forks–Dinwiddie Road in the rear of the main body of the enemy that was deployed across the road before the Dinwiddie Courthouse. It was a miserable night, very dark, and it began to drizzle. The brigade was ordered to make no noise and light no fires. Sanborn was assigned picket duty and he deployed some but not all of the pickets.

Sanborn could not see the enemy in the dark but he could clearly hear their conversations. The noise level was considerable. He estimated the number of enemy in the immediate vicinity was large. Captain Bartlett of General Bartlett's staff was with Sanborn and periodically carried back reports to headquarters. The snatches of Confederate conversation that Sanborn heard indicated that the Confederates were either throwing up temporary works or were preparing to leave.

Somewhere around midnight, the brigade was ordered to withdraw and return to the division. The pickets, including Sanborn, were called in. Basically, the return route was the same as the advance route. Much of it was cross country, and the going was difficult in the dark.

The brigade reached the bivouacked division at about daybreak. It was but a short time before the division moved out and Sanborn did not even have time for breakfast, much less sleep. The division marched back to the vicinity of Dr. Boisseau's without pause. The Confederates were no longer there but had moved back to Five Forks.

Sanborn's story picked up after the division moved up to Gravelly Run Church that afternoon and deployed for battle.

As the corps moved out, Sanborn, being of low rank and lacking a staff position, knew nothing of the overall plan or of the overall deployment of the corps. Basically, he had a worm's eye view of what subsequently transpired and gave confusing or often incoherent answers regarding the location and movements of his regiment.

Sanborn did not recollect crossing the White Oak Road when they moved out. The first major resistance they met was near the White Oak Road. This must have been Steuart's brigade that was deployed at a right angle to the road. There was much confusion on both sides. After sharp volleys, the enemy gave way and they took many prisoners. They continued on to the Ford Road, where they captured a cannon (this must have been one of Pegram's three cannon that were supporting Steuart).

Sanborn did not see Griffin or Bartlett, but he did see Sheridan and staff. Apparently, this was in front of Steuart's line. Sanborn heard Sheridan say something to the effect: "Get over the works and give them hell boys."[7]

It was getting dark and the fighting died down. Bartlett's brigade crossed to the south side of the White Oak Road to the west of the Ford Road and went into bivouac.

W.H.F. Lee

W.H.F. Lee was the son of Robert E. Lee and in command of a cavalry division at Five Forks. His division normally consisted of three brigades: those of Barringer, Beale, and Robertson. Robertson was left behind and Barringer and Beale arrived at Five Forks on the eve of March 30.

The division participated in the battle of Dinwiddie Courthouse on March 31, during which they drove Sheridan back. During the night of March 31, Lee received orders from Fitz Lee to return to Five Forks. The infantry retired first and W.H.F. Lee covered the rear. He retired the same way he had come; that is, the southern route via Chamberlain Creek. The division stopped to feed and water their horses and eat breakfast at Chamberlain's Creek, and did not arrive at Five Forks until 11 a.m. The infantry was already there and constructing a barricade along the White Oak Road. There was no fighting of significance during Lee's retreat.

Upon arrival at Five Forks, Lee took up a position on the far west end of the Confederate line beyond General Corse. Pickett requested Lee dismount one of his brigades to extend Corse's line. This Lee did. It was the brigade of Beale. Corse's line ran to the north of Gillian field.

Lee also ordered the regiment that had suffered the most casualties at Dinwiddie to guard the trains that were parked beyond Hatchers Run on the Ford Road. He apparently did not know that Rosser had already been given this assignment.

Lee originally had about 1,700 to 1,800 mounted men, but the demounting of one brigade, the losses at Dinwiddie Courthouse, and the assignment of a regiment to guard the trains reduced his mounted force to about 600 to 700.

McGregor's battery of horse artillery belonged to Lee. He stated that part of the battery was with him. He gave no explanation as to how the other part ended up with Ransom's infantry brigade at the other end of the line.

Lee's division was not significantly involved in the battle until its final phase. It was about 5:30. Ayres had already seized the refuse, Steuart's line was broken, and Crawford was coming down the Ford Road when Pickett rode up. He said that his lines were broken. Immediately after, Beale rode up and said that the enemy was to their rear.

Lee directed Beale to re-mount his men. He said that he would protect their flank and rear the best he could. The action took place in the Gillian field and its environs. It was Lee's cavalry against Sheridan's. The action only ended when darkness brought it to a halt.

Lee, with his entire command, escaped to the west. He said that his losses were "slight." He came to a road that was roughly parallel to the Ford Road and headed north. He reached the railroad that night. Lee did not see Corse form up across the White Oak Road. However, he later heard that Corse also got out to the west and north.

We have now heard the testimony of thirty-four witnesses. All, with the exception of Captain Warner and General Philip Sheridan, were requested by Warren. Warren requested an additional nineteen witnesses before he himself would testify. However, the testimony was becoming redundant, so we will just treat the testimony of two of the nineteen before turning to the testimony of Warren himself. These two are Major General Crawford and Samuel Gillian. Crawford was a central figure in the events of March 31– April 1, 1865. Gillian was the only civilian to testify. It was on his farm that certain of the events of April 1 unfolded, and his testimony was of human interest only. We will conclude the chapter with Warren's testimony and then turn to the witnesses requested by General Sheridan.

Major General Samuel Crawford

General Samuel Crawford was in command of the Third Division of the Fifth Corps. He was next in seniority to Warren and, as such, would normally assume command of the corps if Warren were incapacitated.

Crawford's testimony began with the events of March 31, 1865. As will be recalled, at the time the Fifth Corps was sliding westward across the main Confederate defense line before Petersburg. The Confederates attempted to stop the movement at the White Oak Road where it turned off at roughly a right angle to the main defense line. Sheridan's operations were five miles to the south. The situation was as indicated in map 14.

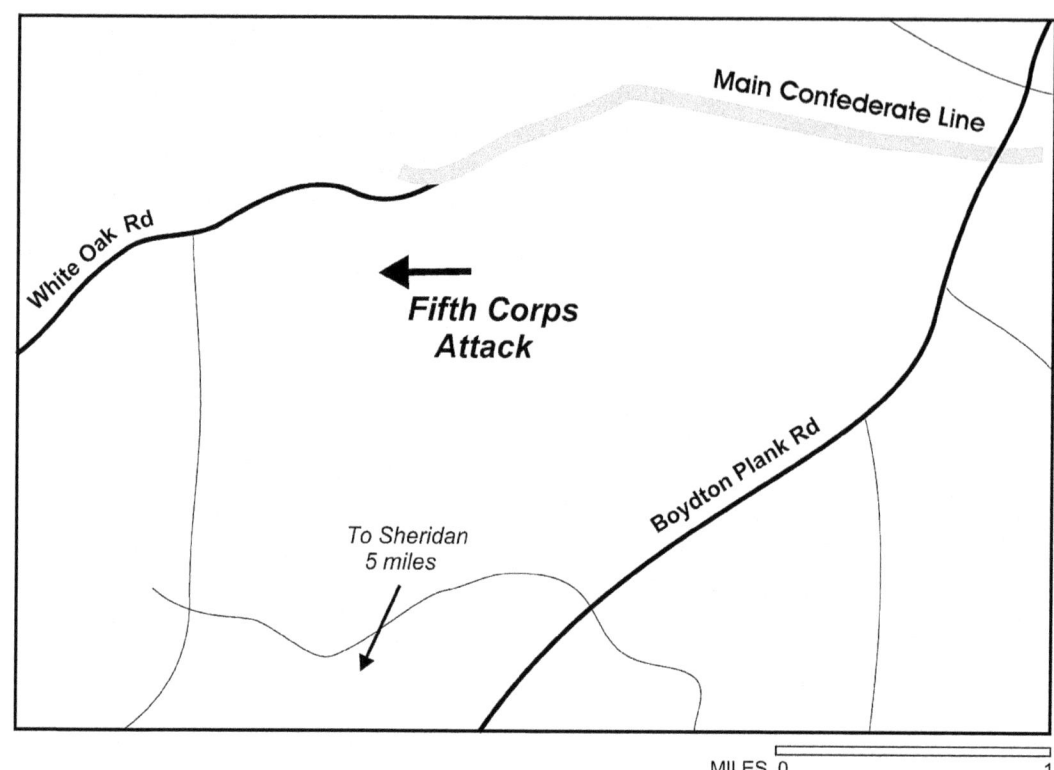

Map 14. Situation on March 31.

As of the 31st, Crawford's division numbered between 4,700 and 5,000 men. Most were veterans from the now disbanded First Corps. During the morning of the 31st, Ayres, who was closest to the enemy, was ordered to make a reconnaissance of the enemy position on the White Oak Road. Crawford was ordered to support Ayres. Crawford rode over to Ayres to ask Ayres how he could help. Before they could do anything, the enemy attacked. Ayres's division was routed and thrown upon Crawford's, and the two were swept back upon Griffin's, which was farther to the rear.

When asked if Warren was with Crawford at the time, Crawford replied that, in

Major General Samuel W. Crawford, Third Division commander, Fifth Corps physician and soldier.

action or pending action, he saw Warren so constantly that he could not say positively just when he saw Warren last.

Ayres's and Crawford's divisions rallied upon Griffin's. It was now about noon. The corps began an advance about 2:30 or 3:00 p.m. About this time, the Confederate force confronting the Fifth Corps was hit in the flank by the adjacent Union Second Corps. Crawford, however, knew nothing of this attack. The combined Fifth and Second Corps troops drove the Rebels back to the White Oak Road and at some points beyond. When the fighting ended at dark, Crawford was just to the south and east of the White Oak Road, with the enemy in plain sight.

Crawford spent the night in the field in a tent. He thought, but could not fully recollect, that his troops remained in line of battle. He did not know where Warren's headquarters were, but his staff knew and they remained in contact.

That night, Crawford received an order from Warren via courier dated 9:35 p.m. It was not handed to him until 10 or 10:30 p.m. It directed Crawford to mass his division and move to his previous position. They were close to the enemy, silence was essential, and it took time to disseminate the order, probably around three-quarters of an hour.

A second courier arrived with a new order directing that they were to remain where they were when the order reached them. There they remained for the night.

Warren himself arrived at daylight. He ordered that the division move to the southwest to aid Sheridan. The division was underway by 5 a.m. Early in the morning they reached Dr. Boisseau's, where they were to halt and rest for several hours (see map 15). There they rested for several hours until ordered up the road to Gravelly Run Church. Crawford, who was farthest to the west, led the march. Then the complete corps formed up for battle. Perhaps one and a half hours were spent at the church. Ayres was the last to arrive.

Here Warren gave detailed instructions to his division commanders for the pending movement. He then provided each with a drawing of the impending movement.

The formation moved forward at around 4 p.m. Kellogg was on Crawford's left, Baxter on his right, and Coulter behind. They did not move due north but to the northwest. Crawford's orders never specifically called for him to connect with Ayres to his left, but he believed that was what he should do. He lost contact with Ayres in the woods and sent a courier to Warren to ask what he should do. When he came out of the woods, Kellogg was no longer to Baxter's left and Coulter moved up from behind. They inclined to the left and, when at the Chimneys, swung due west. His line of battle was then north-south. While crossing Syndor field, he received orders first from Sheridan and then from Warren to come farther left and continue on.

This he was unable to do, as he was receiving fire directly from his front. In his own words: "I should have made the decided attempt to get to the left if it had not been for that decided fire…. The men turned around and faced the fire. I could not have got a flank movement from them."[8] Crawford's problem is portrayed in figure 12. Had Crawford come farther to the left as the orders called for, Munford would be firing into his flank, which would have been fatal.

Crawford, of course, did not know if he was facing infantry or dismounted cavalry. Munford's men tended to stay in the trees and, at times, their fire appeared more like a thin line of battle rather than a skirmish line.

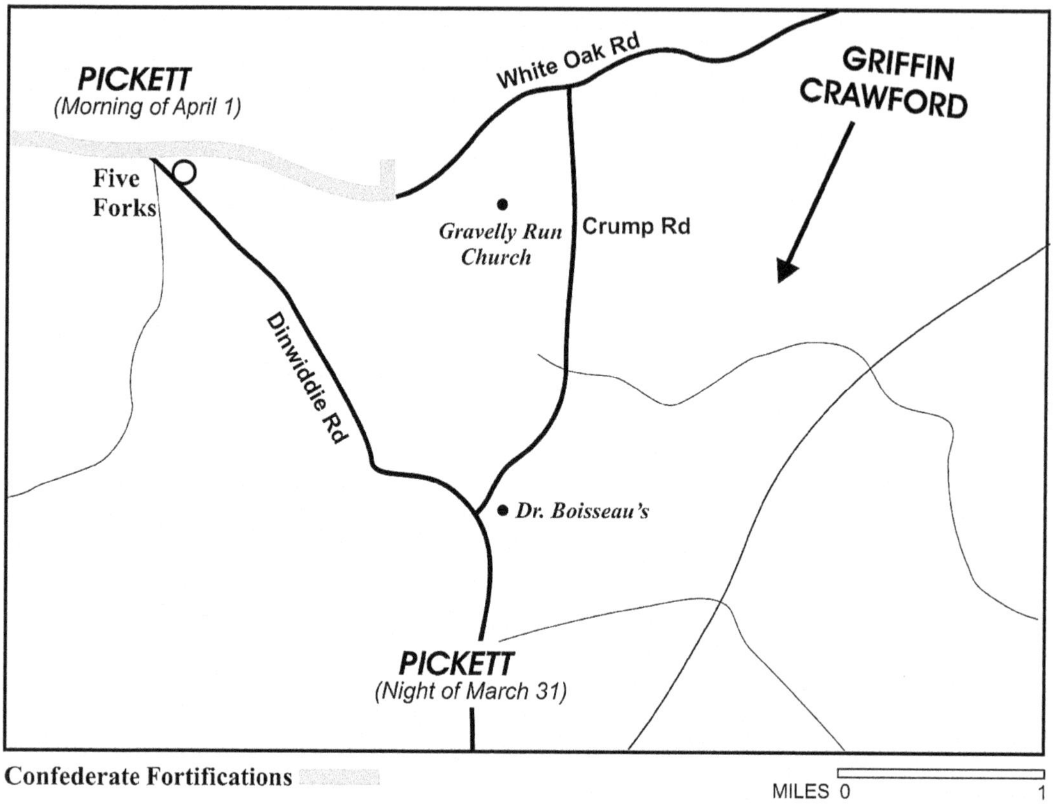

114   Union General Gouverneur Warren

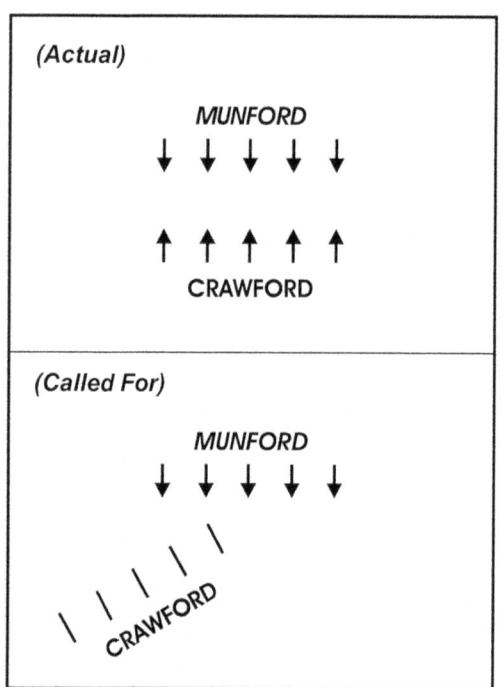

Map 15. April 1, Griffin and Crawford Move from Battle of White Oak Road to Dr. Boisseau's.

Baxter rejoined before Crawford hit the Ford Road. There they encountered Warren, who directed they proceed south down the Ford Road toward the rear of the enemy line. This they were able to do. Here they met an enemy force deployed across the road, which briefly kept them at bay. This undoubtedly was Mayo, whom Pickett had ordered up the Ford Road to stop the advance of the enemy in their rear.

Crawford continued down the Ford Road and turned right at the intersection of the White Oak Road, where he witnessed the termination of the battle at sunset in the Gillian field. Crawford did not see Warren's famous or infamous charge across Gillian field.

Figure 12. Crawford's actual position at the Battle of Five Forks.

Samuel Y. Gillian

The testimony of Samuel Gillian was given at Governor's Island, N.Y., on Tuesday, June 29, 1880. Gillian and Joseph P. Cotton were the only civilians to testify. At the time of Five Forks, Gillian was sixteen years old and lived in the Gillian house with his mother and sister. He had lived there his entire life. He did not mention a father but said that his mother owned the property. The entire property was 2,680 acres.

The Gillian house and complex of outbuildings was one mile south of Colonel Corse's position on the White Oak Road at the west end of the Confederate line. Between the house and the road was the Gillian field. This was an eighty-five acre cleared, open space. It was ideally suited for cavalry charges and also provided an open field of fire for the Confederate cannon to Corse's right.

The young Gillian had been familiar with firearms and was a hunter since the age of nine. He was intimately familiar with the territory between the Southside Railroad and Dinwiddie and, upon General W.H.F. Lee's arrival on the 30th, volunteered his services as a guide. He remained with Lee more or less continuously until Lee managed to successfully withdraw his troops from the battle to the Southside Railroad the night of April 1.

Gillian was questioned extensively about the terrain, which contributed little if anything to our understanding of what transpired. He was with Lee at the battle of Dinwiddie on the 31st but, inasmuch as this did not relate to Warren, we will not cover it.

Lee's command returned to Five Forks during the night and early morning of April 1. They came by way of the southern route, that is, by Chamberlain Creek. Inasmuch as they camped en route, Gillian did not arrive home until about 10 a.m. He breakfasted in his own home. In his absence, he noted that the Confederates had constructed fortifications along the White Oak Road and established a picket or skirmish line to the south and parallel to the road. He described the fortifications as between waist high and breast high and composed of large pine logs with dirt thrown over them. The picket or skirmish line was just to the south of his house. The house was thus between the picket line and the main Confederate line on the White Oak Road.

Gillian noticed several Union cavalry charges during the day, but they were stopped at the picket line.

During the late afternoon, time unspecified, Lee and Gillian were located at the northwest corner of the Gillian field. Lee noted that no couriers were available and asked Gillian if he would carry a dispatch to General Pickett. Gillian said that he would try and asked where Pickett was. Lee replied that he was at Five Forks. Lee gave a written dispatch to Gillian and Gillian set out. He did not know the contents of the message. He rode eastward behind the Confederate line along the White Oak Road. He passed individual Confederates streaming to the rear, but no organized retreat. Upon reaching Five Forks, he encountered a mounted Pickett. He said that he knew and recognized Pickett but did not explain how this was possible.

As Gillian handed Pickett the dispatch, the cannon were still firing to the southeast, but within the brief time that Pickett read the dispatch, the situation changed radically. The cannon ceased firing, some of the horses had been killed, and the cannoneers were cutting the spokes of the wheels with an ax. Gillian also noted a line of troops moving down the Ford Road. At first he thought that they were Confederates, but then recognized their flag and uniforms as Union. Gillian asked Pickett if he had any reply. Pickett said no and then said, "You go away from here slowly and quietly; sir."[9] Perhaps he did not want to stimulate panic. Gillian left slowly, riding away until he encountered Lee where he had left him.

The Confederate picket line was still holding at this time. Later, Lee led a charge across Gillian field and beyond the house. He brought an ambulance. Gillian's mother, sister, and two women were still in the house. Gillian's sister and two ladies who were with her came out with some baggage and got in the ambulance. His mother walked up to the ambulance but then, for some reason, returned to the house. Here she met oncoming Union cavalrymen. Here the story became unclear. It is not known if she departed with the others in the ambulance or remained behind.

Later, Lee retired up the White Oak Road to the Roper Road and rode up the Roper Road to the railroad. He was unmolested in his retreat.

Warren Testifies

The big day finally arrived. It was July 1, 1880, when Warren took the stand. He had waited fifteen years for this moment.

Warren's testimony was only relevant to the issue at hand from March 31, 1865, so we will skip forward to that date. We will start with the battle of the White Oak Road, which took place during the day of the 31st.

On the morning of March 31, there was some adjustment between Humphreys and Warren that resulted in Griffin being moved to a position behind a branch of Gravelly Run that was located between the Boydton Plank Road and the White Oak Road. The positions of the three divisions of the Fifth Corps were thus: Ayres closest to the White Oak Road, Crawford en echelon behind and to the right of Ayres, and Griffin further behind, at the east side of the Gravelly Run branch (see map 16).

Warren's headquarters with the telegraph wagon was located on the Quaker Road. The distance from the headquarters to Ayres's front was about two miles. Warren was tied to the telegraph during the early morning, responding to Meade's messages.

At 8:55 a.m., Warren received a message from Meade stating that, as a result of the weather, no changes would be made in the position of the troops that day. Wagons would be brought up and the troops given three days' rations.

At 9:40 a.m., Warren advised Meade that he had just received a report from Ayres that the enemy had pickets on the east side of the White Oak Road. Thus, the White Oak Road was not the front, but rather, within control of the Confederates. Warren further advised Meade that he had directed Ayres to drive the pickets off and develop the strength of the enemy.

Meade responded with a 10:30 a.m. message that read: "Your dispatch giving Ayres position is received. General Meade directs that should you determine by your reconnaissance that you can get possession of and hold the White Oak Road, you are to do so, notwithstanding the order to suspend operations today."[10]

Before Warren received Meade's reply, he vacated his headquarters to proceed to

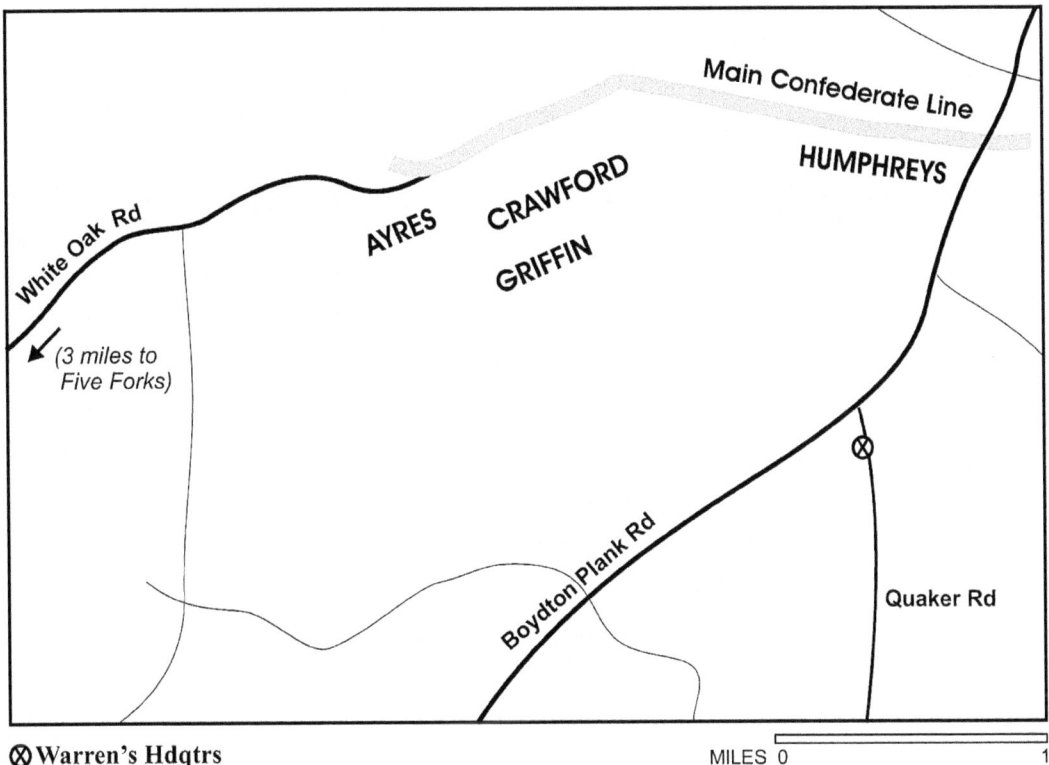

Map 16. Position of Fifth Corps prior to Confederate attack.

the front and supervise the reconnaissance. Warren had proceed no farther than Griffin's position on this side of the run when he encountered chaos. Ayres and Crawford's men were coming back in a rushing, disorganized crowd. Furthermore, Warren was amazed at the Gravelly Run tributary. When he last saw it, it was an insignificant creek. Now it was sixty feet wide and four to five feet deep. Warren considered that his presence was required here and he proceeded no farther to the front at this time.

The enemy pursued the fleeing men as far as the run and no farther. They contented themselves in shooting across from the far side. Warren and Griffin helped organize the crowd into their original formations. This, and getting them back across the run, took at least two hours before Ayres, Crawford, and the undamaged Griffin were ready to counterattack.

In the meantime, General Miles's division from Humphreys' command struck the oncoming Confederates in their left flank.

As soon as Warren's corps was ready to advance and the Confederates were cleared from the roadway on the far side of the run, Warren's engineers finished construction of a bridge suitable for wheeled vehicles.

Warren arranged the Fifth Corps for the counterattack, as indicated in figure 13. The three divisions from left to right were Ayres, Griffin, and Crawford. The innovation was that Chamberlain's brigade of Griffin's division was pushed out front and center, thus making a flying wedge.

At 1 p.m. Warren sent a message to Mead advising him of the situation, telling him that he (Warren) was preparing to counterattack and that the attack would be delivered at about 1:45 p.m.

At about 2:50 p.m. Warren's troops were in motion and, by 3:40, they were on the White Oak Road. They had succeeded in part in pushing the enemy back beyond his original position of that morning.

At 3:40 p.m. Warren sent a message to Meade advising Meade that he had pushed the enemy back into their works on the far side of the White Oak Road, but that the enemy in their main line, a mile to the north, was firing artillery into his right flank (see map 17).

	CHAMBERLAIN	
AYRES	GRIFFIN	CRAWFORD

Figure 13. Fifth Corps deployment for counterattack.

At the time, Warren was personally on the White Oak Road supervising operations. He maintained pickets on the far side of the White Oak Road until dark. In short, Warren managed to reverse the situation. At dawn, the Confederates had pickets on his

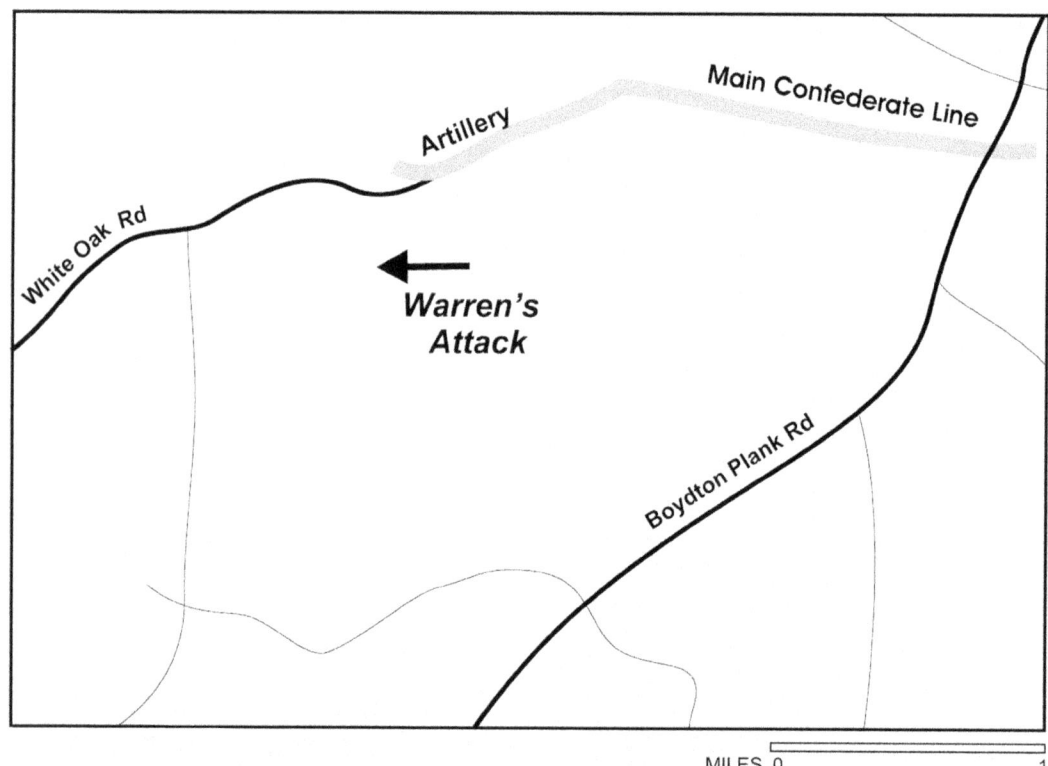

Map 17. Warren's attack enfiladed by Confederate Main Line.

side and thus controlled the road. At dark, he had pickets on their side and thus the road was his.

Sometime after 4:30 p.m. Warren, while talking to Chamberlain on the White Oak Road, received a dispatch from General Meade. Among other things, it said that Sheridan was "pushing up the White Oak Road … take care not to fire into him."[11] Warren immediately recognized that this dispatch demonstrated that Meade was out of touch with reality. Warren and Chamberlain had been hearing the sound of battle to their south. It was receding to the east. Both recognized that, not only was Sheridan not "pushing up the White Oak Road," but was himself being pushed back to Dinwiddie Courthouse.

Warren, acting on his own initiative, ordered Bartlett's brigade of Griffin's division to proceed cross country to the sound of the guns and aid Sheridan. Very soon after that, Warren received another message from Meade ordering him, in essence, to do what he had already done; that is, send a brigade to aid Sheridan. Warren received this order at 5:45 p.m. Bartlett had already departed.

Within minutes, an officer from Sheridan's command appeared and told Warren that Sheridan had been attacked, was being pushed back, and that he and his men had been cut off. Warren advised Meade of this development and also that he had ordered Bartlett's brigade to Sheridan's assistance.

At about 6:30 p.m. Warren received a dispatch from Meade stating that the enemy had penetrated between Sheridan and Warren, and that Warren should redirect the brigade that he had ordered to aid Sheridan to proceed via the Boydton Plank Road. Warren replied that it was too late to redirect the brigade that he had dispatched to aid Sheridan, as it had already departed. He, however, had three regiments on the Boydton Plank Road guarding his artillery, and he would order them, under General Pearson, to proceed down the road to join Sheridan. He further advised Meade that he was personally inspecting the enemy installations along the White Oak Road and assessed that, if they were well manned, he could not carry them.

Warren further testified that he came within 200 yards of the enemy installations in his inspection that evening, and personally drew enemy artillery fire, so that he could ascertain the location of the artillery.

Warren and Meade continued to exchange messages during the eve of March 31. Warren's responses to Meade's orders up to 10:15 that night were beyond criticism. Where he could not obey the orders to the letter or could better meet the spirit by exercising the normal discretion of a corps commander, he did so. At 10:50 p.m. Warren received the following message from Meade:

To Maj Genl Warren
U.S.M.T. Hdqtrs A of P
1015 p.m. Mar 31, 1865

Send Griffin promptly as ordered by the Boydton P. R. but move the balance of your command by the road Bartlett is on, and strike the enemy in rear who is between him and Dinwiddie. General Sheridan reported his last position as north of Dinwiddie Court House, near Dr. Smiths, the enemy holding the cross roads at that point. Should the enemy turn on you, your line of retreat will be by J. M. Boisseau's on the Boydton Plank Rd. See one inch maps. You must be very prompt in the movement, and get the forks of the road at J. M. Brooks before the enemy.... Don't encumber yourself with anything that will impede your progress....

Geo. G. Meade[12]

Prior to receipt of this message and in response to an earlier order, Warren had ordered Ayres, Griffin, and Crawford to move back from the White Oak Road to the positions they had occupied before the battle. Now, in response to the new order, he ordered Ayres to continue down the Boydton Plank Road to Dinwiddie, and Crawford and Griffin to stop and mass where they were and await further orders. Crawford and Griffin then spent the night where they were, and not until dawn were they ordered to proceed on to Bartlett's old position at J. M. Boisseau's in the enemy's rear.

Warren's testimony continued Friday, July 2, 1880. As justification for holding Crawford and Griffin back during the night, Warren testified: "I did not think it advisable, under the circumstances, to attempt to make the rear attack until I was sure Sheridan was re-enforced, but to leave the infantry of Griffin and Crawford where they were until we could get further light on that subject."[13]

He further testified: "If re-enforcements were to be sent to Sheridan, they were to go by way of the Quaker Road, so as to cross Gravelly Run at the pontoon bridge I had built there. If they moved for a rear attack, they would have to take a southwest course towards Crump's. Having decided what was best to do, I thought it best to let them remain where they were until we could get more positive information about how to proceed."[14]

Warren also testified that a problem of telegraph outages that night caused confusion. For example, a message would arrive indicating ignorance of something already explained in a preceding telegram. In a sense, he believed he was on his own.

Warren heard from Ayres at about 4:30 a.m. that Ayres was in contact with Sheridan. Shortly thereafter, Colonel Forsyth of Sheridan's staff arrived with a message from Sheridan to Warren. It read:

Major Gen Warren
Commanding 5th A. C.

Headquarters Middle
Military Division
Dinwiddie C. H. April 1, 1865

I am holding in front of Dinwiddie CH, on the road leading to Five Forks, for three quarters of a mile with General Custer's division. The enemy are in his immediate front, lying so as to cover the road just this side of A. Adams house, which leads out across Chamberlains bed or run. I understand that you have a division at J. Boisseau's: If so you are in the rear of the enemy's line. Possibly they may attack Custer at daylight; if so have this division attack instantly and in full force. Attack at daylight anyway. I will make an effort to get the road this side of Adams house, and if I do, you can capture the whole of them....

P. H. Sheridan[15]

(At the time Warren received Sheridan's message, Warren had no troops at J. Boisseau's. The divisions of Crawford and Griffin were still encamped at the site of the battle of the White Oak Road and Ayres had just entered the Brooks road en route to Sheridan. The Confederates were already in the process of withdrawing from the vicinity of Dinwiddie to Five Forks, and any opportunity to cut them off had already passed. See map 18.)

Upon reading this, Warren left his headquarters immediately accompanied by Captain Wadsworth and headed for the encampments of Griffin and Crawford. Both Griffin and Crawford were encamped at the White Oak Road where the battle ended. Neither

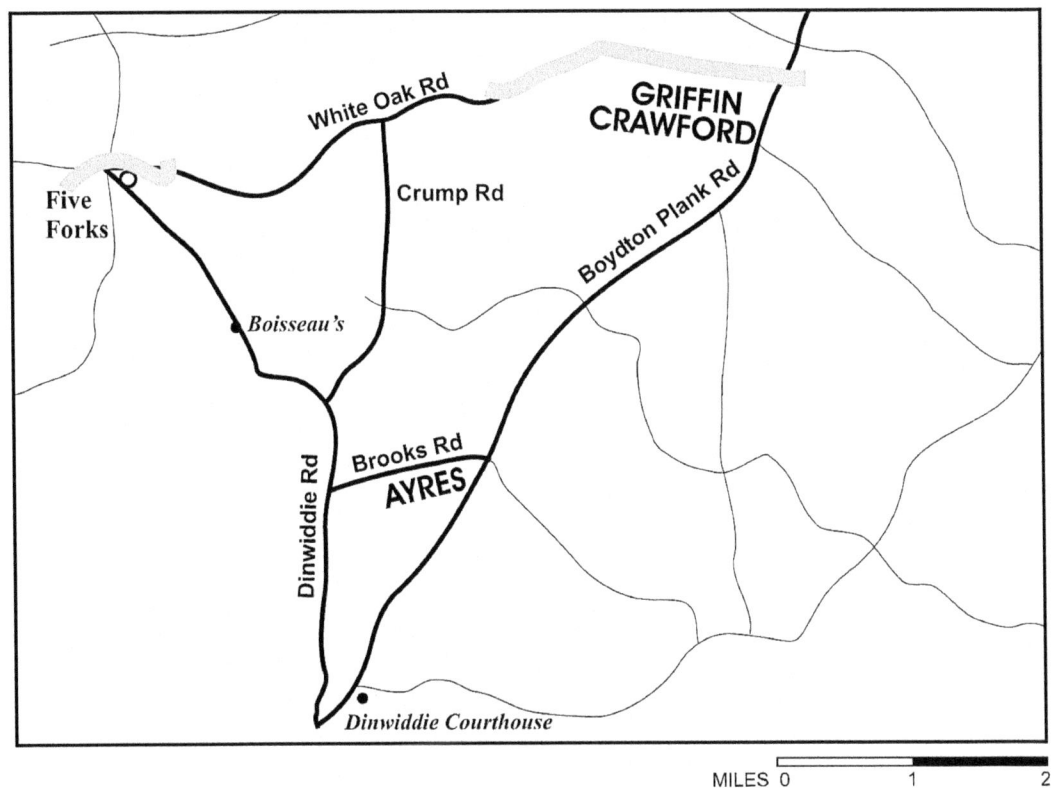

Map 18. Situation at daylight, April 1.

had succeeded in moving back to their pre-battle locations when the second order to stand pat reached them.

Warren reached Griffin first and ordered him to proceed immediately to J. Boisseau's. He then reached Crawford, who was closest to the enemy. There was a real danger that the enemy would attack Crawford once they realized he was withdrawing, so that Warren had him withdraw in line of battle. Warren accompanied Crawford to J. Boisseau's.

When Warren reached J. Boisseau's at the intersection of the Crump and Five Forks–Dinwiddie Roads, he met Griffin, who told him that Sheridan directed that they remain there until he sent for them.

It was about 8 a.m. when Warren met Griffin at J. Boisseau's. At about 9 a.m., while Warren was still with Griffin, he was handed a dispatch from Meade. It advised Warren that, upon his junction with Sheridan, he and his corps would be under Sheridan's orders. Warren waited about two hours, that is, to about 11 a.m., and decided that he would seek out Sheridan to ascertain if Sheridan had any orders for him. Warren found Sheridan's headquarters farther up the Five Forks Road, closer to Five Forks. Sheridan had been lying on a blanket and sat up as Warren approached.

Warren's conversation with Sheridan was brief and ended when an aide gave Sheridan a message and Sheridan rode off. Warren could recall nothing unusual or unpleasant about the meeting, and Sheridan showed no displeasure with the time of arrival of Warren's corps.

Warren waited at Sheridan's headquarters, assuming that Sheridan would soon return. Around 1 p.m. Major Gillespie of Sheridan's staff arrived with orders. They were that Warren was to bring his entire corps up to Gravelly Run Church and deploy for action. Warren immediately dispatched his inspector general, General Bankhead, to go to Generals Crawford, Griffin, and Ayres, in that order, and to bring their divisions up as rapidly as possible.

Warren then set out to find Sheridan to get elaboration on the orders. He rode up the road to Five Forks and met Sheridan coming back. They rode together about fifteen minutes while Sheridan explained his plan. Warren testified:

> He told me that the enemy was in line of battle along the White Oak road, their left resting about where the road that I was to turn off on crossed the White Oak Road [intersection of Crump Road with the White Oak Road]; and that he wanted me to form my line so that I should strike with the right extreme on the angle of the works, and let the left engage the front, and place one division behind the right to support the attack on the angle where we thought the fighting would be the heaviest. And to so place the men oblique to the road as to bring this heaviest force of mine on the angle of the works—give it a direction whose obliquity to the road would correspond with the supposed position of the enemy and his works.[16]

(Here we can see that Sheridan's plan was near fatally flawed because it was based on faulty intelligence. It presumed that the left flank of the Confederate line with its refuse was at the intersection of the Crump Road with the White Oak Road. It was not. It was several hundred feet short of the Crump intersection.)

Warren planned his dispositions in accordance with Sheridan's faulty intelligence. Let us turn to Warren's words:

> I decided to put General Crawford's division on the right of the road, to strike the angle first, and put General Griffin's division behind that. They were the two heaviest divisions by considerable—larger than the other one. I placed the smaller division on the left of the road, which was General Ayres, as I supposed, from the position of the enemy as given to me, that General Crawford's center would fall right on the angle of their line, and that, if he was not able to carry it, General Griffin would be right there to sustain him, and to take advantage of any success. General Ayres being the weakest division, I left on the left to engage the front and prevent the enemy there re-enforcing the angle.[17]

(Warren made his plans in accordance with Sheridan's faulty intelligence, and all the bad things that happened were a direct result of this. Crawford, supported by Griffin, was supposed to hit the angle and fight the major battle. Instead, Ayres, the weakest division, fought the battle of the angle while Crawford, followed by Griffin, marched off away from the battle. See figure 14.)

After departing from Sheridan, Warren deployed his escorts as pickets so as to conceal from the enemy the deployment of his corps at Gravelly Run Church. Warren then proceeded to Gravelly Run Church and supervised the placing of each brigade in the manner we have previously described.

General Sheridan arrived shortly after the troops began to arrive. Warren had sketched the placement of his troops and, upon Sheridan's arrival, showed the sketch to Sheridan. Sheridan concurred that the placement met his wishes. Warren estimated that the distance across his front from the left of Ayres to the right of Crawford was 1,000 yards.

As the troops were forming up, Sheridan commented to Warren several times that he was anxious to get started, as his cavalrymen were running short of ammunition. Warren responded that they were forming as fast as they could, and even offered to move forward before all of his troops had joined. Sheridan rejected this offer, and said he would wait until all of the corps was ready.

Warren spent his entire time at Gravelly Run Church, from the time he arrived at about 2 p.m. until the corps stepped off at about 4 p.m. in organizing the troops, briefing the division and brigade commanders, and periodically sending staff officers off to hurry up the oncoming troops.

Warren submitted the diagram that he used to brief his generals. The refuse angle of the enemy line was incorrectly placed at the intersection of the Crump and the White Oak Roads, and in the diagram, Crawford's division, followed by Griffin's, was headed directly for the misplaced angle.

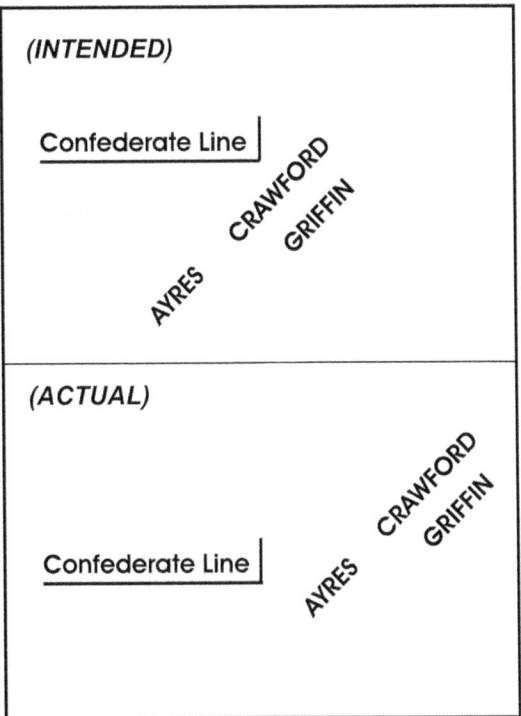

Figure 14. Sheridan's faulty intelligence.

Much of Warren's testimony related to his movements about the battlefield at Five Forks during the hostilities. In general, he attempted to maintain a position where he could be found if required. He devoted his energies into managing the entire corps and to bringing all components into effective action. He managed to redirect Griffin, whose division was moving away from the action, into an extension of Ayres's division as it swept down the White Oak Road. He redirected Crawford, who was proceeding westward across the Ford Road, to turn south on the Ford Road so as to strike the enemy in the rear. He ended by describing the action at Gillian field where, in the final phases of the battle, he led a charge.

Warren testified as to his interaction with Sheridan during the battle. In the early phases, Sheridan approached him and exclaimed, "We have flanked them gloriously."[18] Sheridan then remarked that Griffin and Crawford were moving away from the action and must be brought back. Warren assured him that he was sending staff officers to do just that. He added that Sheridan need not worry, as Crawford and Griffin were experienced and competent officers and would soon find the action. Warren's next transaction with Sheridan involved an exchange of messages. While proceeding down the Ford Road to hit the enemy in the rear, Warren sent Colonel Locke with a message for Sheridan. It was to the effect that Warren had gained the enemy's rear and requested any further instructions. Locke returned with an insulting message for Warren. Warren preferred not to repeat the words, but stated that it contained an insulting gesture and an oath. This message was delivered before Warren led the charge across Gillian field. Warren's last transactions with Sheridan occurred in Gillian field in the final phases of the battle, when it had already been won. Colonel Forsyth of Sheridan's staff approached him and handed him written orders. They were as follows:

> Cavalry Hdqtrs, April 1st, 1865
> Maj Gen Warren, commanding 5th A. C. is relieved from duty and will report at once for orders to Lt Gen Grant, cmdg Armies of the U. States. By command of Maj Genl Sheridan.
> Jas. W. Forsyth[19]

Warren sought out Sheridan for an explanation. Sheridan simply replied: "Obey the order."[20]

In cross examination, Major Gardner, Sheridan's attorney, zeroed in on two actions of Warren. The first was Warren's response to Meade's order dated 10:15 p.m. March 31, and the second was Warren's tardy response in reporting in to General Sheridan on the morning of April 1.

As we will recall, the 10:15 p.m. order directed Warren to send one division down the Boydton Plank Road to join Sheridan at Dinwiddie and two overland to J. Boisseau's to strike the enemy in the rear. The order called for promptness and included the phrases: "You must be very prompt in movement" and "Don't encumber yourself with anything that will impede your progress."

Warren received the order at 10:50 p.m. March 31. He promptly ordered Ayres's division (in place of Griffin's division) to proceed down the Boydton Plank Road to Dinwiddie, but did not order the other two divisions to proceed to J. Boisseau's until daylight on April 1. They did not arrive until about 8:00 a.m. on the 1st. Thus, despite the fact that the order demanded promptness, Warren did not order the two divisions to move until after daylight on the 1st, and the first of the troops did not cover the four miles to J. Boisseau's until nine hours after the receipt of the order.

Warren's attempted explanation of why he waited until daylight to order Crawford and Griffin to proceed to J. Boisseau's was convoluted and obviously did not satisfy Gardner and was unlikely to satisfy the court.

The other incident of special interest to Gardner was Warren's delay in reporting to Sheridan after arriving at J. Boisseau's. Warren arrived at about 8:00 a.m. the 1st with Crawford; Griffin had arrived shortly before. About 9:00 a.m., Warren received a message from Meade specifically placing the Fifth Corps under Sheridan's command and ordering Warren to report to Sheridan. Warren finally reported to Sheridan at about 11 a.m. What was Warren's reason (or excuse) for the delay in reporting? He contended that when Griffin arrived, he reported to Sheridan. Sheridan ordered that Griffin remain where he was and await further orders. Warren contended that Griffin's reporting to Sheridan constituted the arrival and reporting of the Fifth Corps, and that Sheridan's order to Griffin to remain where he was and await further orders also applied to him. Be that as it may, Warren's delay in personally reporting to Sheridan, although it could be considered a slight, had no bearing on future operations.

Warren, in his testimony, provided some significant statistics. The losses of the Fifth Corps for the battle of Five Forks were:

Escort	1
Artillery	0
Griffin	125

Ayres	208
Crawford	300
Total	633

The losses of the Fifth Corps for March 31, that is, the battle of the White Oak Road, were:

Griffin	178
Ayres	663
Crawford	558
Artillery	7
Escort	1

The number of effectives on March 31 was Griffin, 5985; Ayres, 3308; and Crawford, 4698.

From the above we can see that the Fifth Corps alone had over one and one half the number of men as Pickett, and Sheridan's cavalry had at least as many men as Pickett. Thus, at the battle of Five Forks, the Union outnumbered the Confederates by two or three to one.

Warren finally completed his testimony on July 5, 1880. The court devoted the days until July 14 to procedural matters. It then recessed until at least September 1880 to permit Sheridan to attend to business. It was now the turn of Sheridan's witnesses.

Chapter 11

Sheridan Responds

The court re-convened on October 1, 1880, in the Army Building in Manhattan. All subsequent witnesses were called at the request of General Sheridan. The first was Brigadier General Ranald S. MacKenzie.

Brigadier General Ranald S. MacKenzie

At the time of the battle of Five Forks, Brigadier Ranald S. MacKenzie was in command of the cavalry division of the Army of the James. During the night of March 31–April 1, while guarding the wagon park at the rail head, MacKenzie, with his command, was ordered to report to General Sheridan in the vicinity of Dinwiddie Courthouse. He was subsequently ordered by Sheridan to operate on the right flank of Crawford's division. Crawford wandered so far to the north that MacKenzie was pushed all the way up to Hatchers Run and beyond. Thus, he played no significant part in the battle, and his testimony had no relevance to the issues under investigation by the court.

Captain Henry C. Erich

The next to testify was Captain Henry C. Erich of MacKenzie's command. Although he presented some details of MacKenzie's moves, he, like his commander, presented nothing of relevance to the issues before the court.

Captain Henry E. Alford

Captain Henry E. Alford was attached to the reserve cavalry brigade, which reported to Sheridan. During the early afternoon of the 1st, while Warren's troops were gathering at Gravelly Run Church, he was used as a messenger by Sheridan. Part of the time he was accompanied by Colonel Bankhead of Warren's staff. In his own words, the messages they carried were always the same; "His [Sheridan's] orders were repeated directions to hurry up the infantry, it was the sum and substance of all the orders."[1]

During the afternoon of the 1st, Alford overheard a conversation between Sheridan and Warren. In Alford's words: "I heard General Sheridan express great displeasure at the length of time it was taking the infantry to get into action, and speak in a more than emphatic way of the length of time that the cavalry had been obliged to wait for it, and the rapidity with which the day was passing, and unless greater haste could be made by the Fifth Corps, that the plan of the day would be lost, and that he had been waiting all day for the infantry."[2] Alford thus affirmed that Sheridan was unhappy with the rate of formation of the Fifth Corps, but gave no testimony as to whether he himself considered it slow.

The remainder of Alford's testimony related to General Ayres's operations against the refuse and beyond. He affirmed that Sheridan was active at the front.

Captain Henry Wood

Captain Henry Wood was yet another cavalry officer. As of April 1, 1865, Wood was acting regimental adjutant of the Seventeenth Pennsylvania Calvary. Wood described his unit's attack against the Confederates on the White Oak Road, but said nothing relevant to the issues before the court.

Major Vanderbilt Allen

As of April 1, 1865, Major Vanderbilt Allen was a first lieutenant on the staff of General Sheridan. He spent the pre-battle hours at Gravelly Run Church with Sheridan and was with Sheridan during much of the battle. Allen described the meeting between Sheridan and Warren at the Gravelly Run Church thusly: "General Sheridan appeared to be very impatient in regard to the delay by the troops coming up. General Warren, I thought, appeared to be—did not show the energy that we had been in the habit of seeing with other corps commanders, in getting his troops up. That was only in his manner, that was all that I judged from."[3] When asked if he had any prior association with Warren, Allen replied in the affirmative. Warren had been one of his instructors at West Point.

Allen also testified to the gallantry of Sheridan at the battle at the angle. He testified that, when Ayres's men faltered before the refuse, "General Sheridan took his headquarters flag, rode to the head of the division, and took them in."[4]

During the early phases of the battle, Sheridan ordered Allen to find General Warren. Allen spent about one-half hour searching for Warren but had to report to Sheridan that he was unable to find him.

Major E. M. Baker

At the time of the battle of Five Forks, Major E. M. Baker was a captain serving as acting adjutant general of the cavalry of the Middle Military Division under General Wesley Merritt.

The orders that the cavalry received from Sheridan at Five Forks were to move over the Confederate works on the White Oak Road as soon as they heard heavy musketry firing from the infantry on their right. Baker crossed over the works at the intersection of the White Oak Road and the Ford Road. The infantry had not yet arrived but were approaching from the right with Sheridan carrying a flag.

The cavalry and infantry intermingled and then followed the retreating enemy westward along the White Oak Road for about two miles when darkness ended the chase. Baker noticed no major combat on Gillian field as they passed.

Baker was present when Griffin reported to Sheridan to assume command of the corps. This occurred just after sundown. Griffin asked Sheridan if he should form a new line, as the infantry and cavalry were all intermingled. He did not specify what Sheridan's reply was.

Baker and other staff members spent the night after the battle in the Gillian house.

Brevet Major General Wesley Merritt

Merritt was a division commander in Sheridan's cavalry force and second in command to Sheridan. There had been some complaints that led horses impeded the march of Warren's corps to Gravelly Run Church. Merritt did not think it likely that there were any there and, if so, stated that they could have easily been moved out of the way. In this regard, he mentioned a previous instance involving General Warren: "Complaints had been made by General Warren himself, and particularly in the wilderness. I think that every man knew better than to leave led horses on the road; the cavalry had an interest in having a good reputation in that as well as other things."[5] (Merritt's gratuitous comment about Warren's earlier complaint suggests that Warren's actions remained a sore spot with Sheridan and Merritt.)

Merritt observed the meeting between Sheridan and Warren at Gravelly Run Church and commented: "He [Sheridan] was impatient restless, apparently anxious…. General Warren's manner impressed me. It may not have been his manner alone, it may have been something he said, but I have a firm recollection that he was reluctant, quiet, and uninterested with what might possibly be the results of the day."[6]

Merritt acknowledged that he had known Warren almost since the beginning of the war and occasionally worked with him, but was never close to him. He also elaborated some on Warren's previous criticism of Sheridan for blocking the road ahead of him with led horses. It happened at Spotsylvania Courthouse, and Merritt learned of it either from General Sheridan or General Meade. Merritt would not, however, admit that he had any animosity towards Warren.

Merritt described the Union cavalry attack against the Confederate barrier on the White Oak Road during the battle of Five Forks. He testified that he himself crossed over the barrier at the juncture of the White Oak Road and the Ford Road, and arrived before the infantry. He testified that the Union infantry was still to his right, coming down toward the intersection, and it was the cavalry that captured the cannon at the intersection. Surprisingly, Merritt knew nothing of Crawford, who was coming down the Ford Road to the intersection at the time.

Merritt further testified that their task was simplified because the Confederates had expected that the main attack would be on their right flank, rather than their left. The left flank was less than four miles up the White Oak Road to the main Confederate defense line before Petersburg and, had the Confederates sent reinforcements down the White Oak Road, they would have struck the Union attack force in the rear and, in Merritt's estimation, disaster would have resulted.

Brigadier General H. E. Davies, Jr.

Brigadier General H. E. Davies, Jr., was a brigade commander under Sheridan. His testimony provided nothing of relevance to the issues before the court.

Brigadier General Francis T. Sherman

At the time of Five Forks, Brigadier General Francis T. Sherman was inspector general of the Middle Military Division on the staff of Sheridan. Between 3 and 4 p.m. on April 1, General Sheridan directed Sherman to take a message to Warren. The message was that Warren should put his corps in position and attack at once. At the time, Sheridan was with his cavalry south of the White Oak Road.

Sherman reached Warren at about 4 p.m. where Warren's corps had formed up at Gravelly Run Church. Here are Sherman's own words:

> I came up to where General was—found General Warren dismounted and sitting at the front of a tree, with a memorandum or field book in his hand. I rode up, dismounted, saluted General Warren, and delivered the message. General Warren took no notice of my salute or of the message which I gave him. Thinking that he may possibly not have heard, I repeated it. General Warren then failed to recognize me as a staff officer, or the message I bore him. I thought this was very surprising and very singular, and waiting a few moments, rode up to what was known as Gravelly Run Church.[7]

Near here, Sherman encountered an enemy picket, who fired at him. Sherman decided to return to Warren and try once again. He found Warren still in the position where he had left him and no indication of the movement of the corps. At this, Sherman decided to return to Sheridan. He quickly encountered Sheridan, who was en route to Gravelly Run Church.

Sherman recounted his experience with Warren to Sheridan: "I told General Sheridan I had been received very discourteously by General Warren who did not appear to desire to take any action upon his, General Sheridan's, message or the orders that I bore him."[8] Sherman then fell in behind Sheridan, who continued on to Warren. They found Warren in the place where Sherman had last left him. Sheridan dismounted and engaged in a short conversation with Warren. Sherman could not hear what they said but, almost instantly, the Fifth Corps was put in motion.

When the Fifth Corps skirmish line encountered enemy skirmishers, the skirmish line almost immediately fell down. General Sheridan rode between the lines and rallied them, and the advance continued. Before Ayres hit the refuse, Sheridan sent Sherman off with a message for Griffin. Sherman conducted a lengthy search and found MacKenzie but not Griffin. He then set out to return to Sheridan. By the time he found Sheridan near Gillian field to report his lack of success, the battle was over. Sherman had seen none of it. Sherman estimated that the time he spent away from Sheridan looking for Griffin was not more than about forty minutes. Judging by known factors, it must have been closer to two hours.

Brevet Brigadier General Charles S. Fitzhugh

At the time of Five Forks, Charles S. Fitzhugh was a colonel in command of the Second Brigade of Devin's cavalry division in Sheridan's command. Fitzhugh described how, on April 1, they followed the retiring Confederates back from the vicinity of Dinwiddie to Five Forks. They departed at about 8 a.m., were stopped just once and had to fight their way through, and arrived opposite the Confederate defenses on the White Oak Road at 11 a.m. or 12 p.m.

The dismounted Union cavalry lined up opposite the Confederate works with Fitzhugh's brigade near the middle. His left flank rested on the Dinwiddie–Five Forks Road. The plan was for the dismounted cavalry to storm the Confederate line once they had determined that the infantry attack against the angle was in progress.

The Union cavalry inched up to within sixty to eighty yards of the Confederate line prior to the final storming. When they heard the sound of battle to their right and saw the Union infantry sweeping down the White Oak Road, the attack came. The attack came at 4:30 or 5 p.m. and swept right over the Confederate works. As far as Fitzhugh was concerned, the battle was now over for him, and it was up to the mounted cavalry to conduct the pursuit of the fleeing enemy.

Crossing the enemy barricade, Fitzhugh found that he was at the intersection of the Ford Road and the only mounted man present. He saw a Confederate battle flag and went to seize it as a trophy, but someone else beat him to it. There were two abandoned cannon at the intersection and some Union men commandeered one and aimed it to the northwest, in the direction of what appeared to be fleeing Confederates. However, General Ayres came along and ordered them to desist, as he thought Union troops were in the area of aim.

Fitzhugh testified that he saw nothing of Crawford, and he saw neither Warren nor Sheridan.

Brevet Brigadier General Brayton Ives

Brayton Ives was a colonel and in command of the First Connecticut Cavalry in Pennington's brigade of Custer's division at Five Forks.

During the night of March 31–April 1, Ives's regiment was located one-half to one mile north of Dinwiddie Courthouse. Soon after daylight on the 1st, they began a move cross country toward the Confederate position on the White Oak Road. Ives's regiment was on the extreme right of Custer's division.

They encountered only minor resistance until they neared the Gillian house. Here, the enemy fire became severe. The regiment had apparently wandered too far to the west and there was no connection on the right flank (that is, to the east). Here, they received orders from Custer to close up to their right; that is, to close on Fitzhugh's brigade to the east. While moving across the enemy front to the east, the regiment was subjected to artillery fire from Rebel cannon at the intersection of the White Oak Road and the Dinwiddie Road. Captain Parmelee, who was near Ives, was struck in the chest and killed. The regiment finally closed on Fitzhugh's brigade at about 11 a.m. and awaited the orders to attack. Ives's regiment's right flank and Fitzhugh's left flank rested on the Five Forks–Dinwiddie Road.

It was between 4 and 5 p.m. when the attack on the Confederate position was undertaken. Ives's regiment was repulsed twice but succeeded in crossing the barrier on the third try. Ives could give no estimate of his losses, but they were considerable.

Once across the barrier, the enemy fled and surrendered, and Ives considered the victory won. He testified that the Confederate cannons continued to fire to very near the final crossing of the barrier. Once across the barrier, Ives could not recollect seeing any organized body of infantry, neither Ayres to the east nor Crawford to the north.

Ives made no mention of having seen either Sheridan or Warren at any time.

Lieutenant Colonel Mortimer B. Birdseye

On April 1, 1865, Mortimer B. Birdseye was lieutenant colonel of the Second New York Cavalry of Pennington's brigade of Custer's division. Birdseye's regiment and Colonel Ives's regiment set out for Five Forks at daylight on April 1. They took the route via Chamberlain's Bed rather that the Dinwiddie–Five Forks Road. After a couple of miles, the two regiments dismounted and formed a skirmish line and proceeded on toward the White Oak Road. The remaining two regiments of the brigade followed behind in column.

As Birdseye's and Ives's regiments approached the Gillian house, two pieces of enemy artillery opened fire on them. Birdseye's headquarters bugler was killed and he understood that an officer in Ives's regiment was also killed.

Colonel Whitaker of Custer's staff rode up and told them that they were to close up to General Devin's division to their right. They ultimately connected with Devin and then advanced and drove the enemy skirmishers before them. The area was thickly wooded, and Birdseye could not see the breastworks along the White Oak Road. However, they apparently came within rifle range, received a heavy fire, and were driven back. It was now about noon.

They advanced again to the extent that Birdseye could plainly see the enemy breastworks and the men behind them. This time, Major O'Keele was shot and left on the field. Birdseye took four men and went to retrieve O'Keele. Two of them were killed, although the others did succeed in bringing O'Keele back. He was, however, shot and wounded again on the way out.

The final charge of the Union line occurred when "the sun was from an hour to half an hour high."[9] This time they went over the barrier and captured many prisoners as well as two cannon. Upon crossing the barrier, Birdseye noticed friendly infantry to his right. He saw General Sheridan on a black horse with a flag in his hand with a crowd of dismounted men around him.

Birdseye attempted to gather his scattered men and proceeded north (up the Ford Road) to pursue the fleeing enemy. Altogether, he gathered 120 to 140 men. As he proceeded north up the Ford Road toward the Boisseau house, he came across a Union column of infantry crossing the road from his right to his left. The general in charge objected to the dismounted Union cavalry men passing through his column and rode back along the marching column, waving his saber and shouting, "Stop the cavalry; don't let them through your ranks."[10] Birdseye did not recognize the general nor know the unit identity of the marching troops. He did note, though, that they wore the Maltese Cross symbol, indicating that they were from the Fifth Corps.

Birdseye's men passed over to the west side of the Ford Road and made their way back to the White Oak Road through the woods. They hit the White Oak Road farther to the west than their original crossing of the barrier. Here, he met a mounted General Custer. Birdseye inquired of Custer where their horses were. One of Custer's staff spoke up, indicating they were three to four miles off and were still where the regiment left them that morning.

Major William R. Mattison

William R. Mattison was a captain at Five Forks and commanded a battalion of four companies in Colonel Birdseye's Second New York Cavalry. His testimony added nothing of relevance to that of Birdseye, so we will not recount it here.

Brevet Brigadier General Orville Babcock

As of March 31–April 1, 1865, Orville Babcock was a lieutenant colonel and aide de camp to General Grant. During the day of the 1st, Babcock was ordered by General Grant to carry a verbal message to General Sheridan. As near as Babcock could recollect, the exact words were: "Tell General Sheridan that, if in his judgment, the Fifth Corps would do better under one of the division commanders, he is authorized to relieve General Warren, and order him to report to him, General Grant."[11] Babcock left General Grant's headquarters about 10 a.m. on the 1st and delivered the message to Sheridan between 11 and 12 a.m.

Babcock found Sheridan passing along his line from left to right giving instructions. After giving his message, Babcock, at Sheridan's request, rode along with him to General Devin's headquarters. Devin commanded a division of cavalry in Sheridan's command. Babcock heard Sheridan tell Devin that he intended to throw the infantry upon the enemy left and, at the same time, the cavalry would attack the right. He then gave Devin instructions that, when he saw the engagement actually taking place, Devin would withdraw his command. Devin remonstrated, stating that he would make a charge. Sheridan remarked to him that he did not have ammunition enough. Devin replied that he had "ammunition enough to give them one more surge."[12] Sheridan then gave Babcock his plans for Babcock to give to Grant.

Babcock was questioned as to whether he observed the movement of the Fifth Corps from their bivouacs to Gravelly Run Church. Although Babcock must have passed marching Fifth Corps units on his way back to Grant, he had no recollection of seeing any.

Babcock testified that he did not see Warren on either March 31 or April 1. Babcock did not participate in the battle of the White Oak Road, the battle of Dinwiddie Courthouse, or the Battle of Five Forks, and provided no testimony on these events.

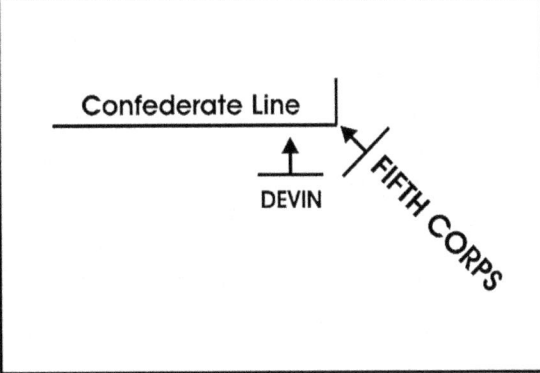

Figure 15. Devin's and Fifth Corps' positions.

(Devin, whose division was at the eastern end of Sheridan's cavalry line, that is, closest to the Fifth Corps, did participate in the attack. The reason that Sheridan wanted Devin to pull out was apparently the fear that the Fifth Corps would fire into Devin's troops [see figure 15].)

Major William Thompson

William Thompson was a major of the Seventeenth Pennsylvania Cavalry in Fitzhugh's brigade of Devin's division at the time of Five Forks. His testimony provided nothing of significance and little new except some additional details of Sheridan's activity once the barrier was crossed: "I saw General Sheridan with his corps flag; saw General Forsyth alongside of him; heard Forsyth remark that we were going pell mell, cavalry, infantry and artillery all mixed up: and I heard General Sheridan distinctly remark that it did not matter how we went—the enemy were so demoralized that it made no difference."[13]

Brevet Brigadier General Horace Porter

Horace Porter was a lieutenant colonel and aide de camp to General Grant at the time of the battle of Five Forks. His testimony proved to be one of the most comprehensive of the entire hearing.

On the afternoon of March 31, Grant's headquarters were at the widow Butler's on the Boydton Plank Road. This was close to Warren's headquarters. Warren had been engaged that morning and driven back. Grant also learned that, some four to five miles to the south, Sheridan had also been attacked and was having a hard time of it. Grant directed Porter to go to Sheridan, have a conference with him, find out what the situation was, and what Sheridan proposed to do.

Porter proceeded down the Boydton Plank Road and found Sheridan to the north of Dinwiddie Courthouse. It was now about 4 p.m. Sheridan told Porter that he had a strong force of enemy infantry before him. He had been pushed back, but thought he could hold out at Dinwiddie. If not, and he were pushed beyond the Boydton Plank Road, he could still maintain contact with Grant via the Vaughan Road.

Sheridan said that this had created a situation that he and Grant had looked forward to. They had now succeeded in drawing a large force of the enemy out of his entrenchments and into the open. Furthermore, since the Union forces to the north were farther west than the enemy before Sheridan, the opportunity was now presented to hit this force in the flank and rear, as well as in the front. Sheridan emphasized that time was of the essence. Once the enemy force before Sheridan recognized that it could be taken in flank and rear, the enemy would retreat and the opportunity would be lost. Sheridan emphasized that tomorrow morning might be too late. They must act now.

Porter hurried back with Sheridan's message. In the meantime, Grant had moved his headquarters from Mrs. Butler's to Dabney Mills to bring it closer to the southern force's area of operations. Porter reached Grant a little after dark and delivered Sheridan's assessment of the situation. Grant took a very favorable view of the situation and reiterated that he had always hoped to confront a large group of Confederates in the open, that is, outside of their entrenchments.

Shortly after Porter's conference with Grant, Captain Sheridan, Philip Sheridan's younger brother and aide, arrived. He had stopped off at Meade's headquarters to ascertain where Grant was located and brought a message from Meade. Porter did not know its contents. Captain Sheridan repeated what Porter had already told Grant and brought him up to date as to what had transpired since Porter had departed.

Grant had visualized and hoped for the situation now before him, and had planned to send the Sixth Corps to join Sheridan. The Sixth Corps had been under Sheridan during Sheridan's Valley Campaign and worked well with him. However, time would not now allow this. The only corps that could join Sheridan that night was the Fifth Corps, and that would have to do.

Porter was questioned extensively about the crossing of Gravelly Run. He crossed it twice on horseback during the day of March 31, once down to Dinwiddie and once back from Dinwiddie. Both crossings took place while the bridge was down and before the construction of a new bridge began.

Porter testified that he crossed in essentially the same place coming and returning. Upon confronting the downed bridge, Porter rode upstream looking for a suitable crossing. He testified that reaching the stream was more of a problem than crossing it. The banks were steep, muddy, and slippery. Porter found what he considered to be a suitable entrance to the water a few hundred yards upstream. The depth of the water was higher than his horse's belly. Porter thought it was at about the maximum depth where a horse could still walk and not swim. Both crossings by Porter took place while it was still light, while Ayres had to cross by night.

When pressed for answers, Porter admitted that the run could be forded by infantry, but declined to speculate as to whether time would actually be gained by waiting for the construction of a bridge. (All questioning as to the problem of crossing Gravelly Run was moot, as we now know that the construction of the bridge was actually complete before Ayres arrived at the crossing.)

Grant and Meade exchanged messages during the night regarding the transfer of the Fifth Corps to Sheridan. The next morning, April 1, 1865, Grant directed Porter to return to Sheridan and send him (Grant) frequent bulletins during the day on the progress of the operation. Porter took a dozen orderlies with him to send back reports. He then proceeded down the Boydton Plank Road to the Brooks Road and down the Brooks Road where he found Sheridan. It was now about 10 a.m.

Porter told Sheridan of the importance Grant placed on the operation; that is, the destruction of the Rebel force by the augmented Sheridan. He told Sheridan that Grant thought Sheridan was on the spot and would have to make the decisions, but he would be held strictly accountable for their outcome.

Sheridan responded that he fully appreciated the importance of the operation but expressed disappointment that the Fifth Corps had not arrived earlier. As of the time Porter talked to Sheridan, Warren still had not reported to him in person. Sheridan said that the enemy was falling back, that he had lost the opportunity to strike them in the flank and rear, and now he would have to fight them behind their barricades at Five Forks.

About noon, General Babcock arrived at Sheridan's headquarters. Porter was present when Babcock delivered his message to Sheridan that Sheridan was authorized to relieve Warren if he considered it advisable.

Sheridan explained his battle plan to Porter and Porter passed it on to Grant. Porter was with or near Sheridan when Sheridan ordered the Fifth Corps to proceed to Gravelly Run Church, while the corps formed up at Gravelly Run Church, and when the corps stepped off to the attack.

Surprisingly, Porter said nothing about Warren's initial reporting in to Sheridan. He did observe Warren and Sheridan conferring at Gravelly Run Church, but either did not hear or could not remember most of what they said. He did, however, overhear Sheridan expressing concern that Lee would send reinforcements down the White Oak Road while the attack was in progress. Porter did notice Sheridan's exasperation with what Sheridan considered the slow pace of formation of the Fifth Corps and did overhear him more than once say that he feared that the sun would set before he could attack. Porter himself made no comment on the rate of formation of the Fifth Corps.

When the Fifth Corps did step off, Sheridan, his staff, and Porter accompanied Ayres's division. Ayres's division was preceded by a line of skirmishers. As they moved over the open ground, they were met by a very heavy fire from an enemy line of skirmishers. Some of the men were shot down and others lay on the ground. General Sheridan seized his battle flag and rushed forward, and by shouting and gesticulating, the advance was taken up again. The men reached the barricade, met a very heavy fire and fell back some distance. General Sheridan was with the troops giving his personal supervision, and by shouting and encouraging, the men, moved forward a second time, and this time carried the works.

Once inside, Sheridan turned to Porter and asked if he had seen General Warren. Porter responded that he had not, since he had seen them conferring prior to the attack. Sheridan requested that, if Porter saw him, to tell Warren to report to him. Porter, of course, being a member of Grant's staff, was not subordinate to Sheridan, and Sheridan put this in the form of a request and not an order.

Porter set out to find Warren. After an extensive search, he found not Warren but Crawford. This was before Warren joined Crawford. Porter stayed with Crawford's command for a time, but then departed for Sheridan before Warren arrived.

Porter finally found Sheridan on the White Oak Road west of the intersection with the Ford Road. It was already getting dark and the battle was winding down. Porter told Sheridan that he had been unable to find Warren. Sheridan replied that he had already relieved Warren and replaced him with Griffin, and had directed Warren to report to General Grant. Sheridan said nothing about the reason for relieving Warren. Porter immediately departed to inform Grant of the good news of victory and Warren's fate. By the time Porter arrived at General Grant's headquarters, he discovered that Warren had already reported and departed.

Lieutenant Colonel Theodore W. Bean

At the time of Five Forks, Theodore W. Bean was a captain on the staff of General Merritt as acting provost marshal of the First Cavalry Division. His testimony added nothing relevant to the issues under consideration.

Lieutenant Colonel George L. Gillespie

At the time of Five Forks, George L. Gillespie was a captain and chief engineer of the Army of the Shenandoah under Sheridan. Much of Gillespie's testimony was devoted to the maps he had drawn up for the court and to events prior to Warren's involvement.

Between 10 and 10:30 a.m. on April 1, General Sheridan gave Gillespie the following instructions: "I want you to select ground which will hold Warren's corps close under the flank of Devin's command and beyond observation of the enemy."[14] In response to this order, Gillespie selected the open area at Gravelly Run Church. When Gillespie returned to Sheridan to report his selection, Sheridan was talking to General Warren. Sheridan told Gillespie to take Warren to the ground and let him look it over. Gillespie and Warren reached the ground around 11 a.m. After an examination that lasted about twenty minutes, Warren declared it satisfactory. Warren and Gillespie then rode down the Crump Road (on which the church ground was located) to the intersection with the Five Forks–Dinwiddie Road. Warren requested that Gillespie remain there until the head of the column of troops arrived, so as to direct them up the Crump Road.

Gillespie waited about one-half hour, no troops arrived, and he was relieved by another officer. Gillespie rode back to Sheridan and reported that the location was satisfactory to Warren. He then returned to Gravelly Run Church and found Warren, sitting about where he left him, and writing in a notebook. No troops had yet arrived and it was now about noon.

Gillespie was not present when Sheridan ordered the Fifth Corps to proceed to Gravelly Run Church, and he did not know the time at which Sheridan did so.

About fifteen minutes after Gillespie rejoined Warren, Sheridan himself arrived to inspect the ground. Sheridan and Warren conferred, but Gillespie had no idea what they said. They then heard firing in the distance and Sheridan dispatched Gillespie to General Merritt to instruct Merritt to save his ammunition.

Gillespie spent some considerable time looking for General Merritt and, when he returned, troops were forming up and Sheridan was in conversation with Warren. Although Gillespie did not know what they said, Sheridan appeared animated and Warren was cool and collected.

When the corps was finally formed up, Sheridan said to his staff: "Gentleman, you will mount."[15] Sheridan and his staff rode behind the picket line of Ayres's division. It was now about 4 p.m. When they reached the White Oak Road, Sheridan halted and let the main line pass in front of him. Gillespie did not recollect where General Warren was at this time.

Ayres's division wheeled to the left to face the enemy in the refuse. Gillespie largely recounted the heroics of Sheridan wherein he rode to the front and rallied the troops. Gillespie noticed that there was a widening interval between Ayres and Crawford's division and suggested to Sheridan that Griffin's division, which was following Crawford, should move up and fill the gap. Sheridan curtly replied that he had already ordered this.

Gillespie noticed, as Crawford's division moved off to the north, a general and staff following. He assumed that this was Warren. Once Sheridan and Gillespie crossed the enemy refuse, Gillespie remained with Sheridan as far as the intersection with the Ford Road. The only order that Gillespie received from Sheridan at that time was to go find General Merritt and tell him to suspend the pursuit.

It was now already dark. While en route to find Merritt, Gillespie encountered two horsemen riding down the White Oak Road from the west toward Five Forks. Gillespie asked if they knew where Merritt was. One proved to be Warren himself, and the other, Captain Vanderbilt Allen. They instructed him as to Merritt's whereabouts.

Gillespie was asked by the court if he had any prior personal acquaintance with Warren. He replied in the affirmative. He had known Warren since he (Gillespie) was a cadet at West Point and had several interactions with him since. He was then asked to describe Warren's mannerisms. Gillespie described them thusly: "I do not think he is a man who is given to especial animation—extreme animation."[16]

The next two witnesses to testify were Lieutenant Colonel Durand and Brevet Major General Capehart. Both testified to the cavalry movements that could have no relationship to the question of Warren's performance.

Captain C. Mason Kinne

At the time of Five Forks, Captain C. Mason Kinne was acting as aide to General Devin. On the afternoon of April 1, Sheridan's three cavalry divisions were deployed in front of the Confederate barrier on the White Oak Road from left to right as follows: Custer, Merritt, and Devin. It was thus Devin's division that was to connect with the Fifth Corps at the Confederate refuse. Stagg's brigade was at the far right. It was part facing the Confederate line and part refused. The part facing the Confederate line was dismounted and the part refused was mounted. Prior to the attack, the Fifth Corps, forming up at Gravelly Run Church, could not be seen from Devin's position.

Kinne understood the plan as follows. The Fifth Corps would march forward and connect with Stagg's right. It would then swing around so as to be perpendicular to the Confederate line on the White Oak Road and face to face with the Confederate refuse. When the Fifth Corps stormed the refuse, the cavalry would attack from the front.

Kinne was sent to the extreme right by Devin. His job was to watch for the infantry (the Fifth Corps) and, when it had swung in position to attack, was to inform Devin. Kinne saw the Fifth Corps advance, connect with Stagg's left, and swing around. He saw, however, only one division and thus was unsure whether this was the main attack. In order to gain clarification, he rode to the rear of the Union infantry seeking the corps commander but he was unable to find him. He saw the single division attack, driven back and then rally. He encountered a division staff officer and asked if this was the general advance. The staff officer replied that he thought so, and Kinne then returned to report to General Devin. The cavalry then attacked, and the cavalry and the infantry went over simultaneously.

We will now skip over the testimony of Captain Charles H. Miller and go to that of Captain William Marks.

Captain William Marks

Captain William Marks was a first lieutenant of the Twentieth Pennsylvania Cavalry of Fitzhugh's brigade of the First Cavalry Division in Sheridan's command at Five Forks.

On the afternoon of the 1st, Marks was directed by one of Sheridan's staff officers to take twenty-five mounted men, return to the ammunition wagons in the rear, and to bring a case of ammunition on the pommel of the saddle of each man. It was a little after 4 p.m. when they started. They began from a point one quarter mile south of the Rebel line on the White Oak Road, and proceeded approximately one-half mile back down the Five Forks–Dinwiddie Road to the ammunition wagons. Soon after starting, they met a column of infantry coming toward Five Forks, but it turned off to the right (presumably on the Crump Road). The column was headed by a general who someone said was Warren. However, when Warren was pointed out to Marks in the courtroom, Marks could not say that he was the man.

When Marks was challenged as to the time he claimed he met the marching column, he responded that he had kept a journal at the time, and that he had it with him now. (It is difficult to reconcile Marks's testimony with that of other witnesses. We know from multiple witnesses that the Fifth Corps was assembled for advance at Gravelly Run Church at around 4 p.m. and stepped off to the attack shortly thereafter. The last to arrive was Ayres's division that arrived and deployed just before the advance. What Marks saw must have been Ayres's division.) Marks commented on the rate of the march of the column as "very easy."[17]

We will skip over the next six witnesses to come to the high point of Sheridan's case: the testimony of General Grant. It had been three years since Grant completed his second term as president and he had just five more years to live.

Ulysses Simpson Grant

Grant took the stand on October 23, 1880, almost a year after the court first convened. It was the seventy-second day the court conducted business.

If one expected to hear a crisp, coherent explanation as to why Warren was relieved, one was to be sorely disappointed. Rather, the hearing broke down into interminable arguments by the opposing lawyers as to what was admissible and what was not. The court finally decreed as follows: "The court is of the opinion that the conduct of General Warren or any opinion formed upon his conduct previous to the operations of 31st, August, ought not be made the matter of record here. We are required simply to investigate General Warren's conduct on March 31 and April 1. Anything that may have occurred on March 31st in General Warren's conduct that influenced General Grant might properly be made a matter of record, but anything previous to that date not."[18]

Grant testified that he was dissatisfied with Warren's performance at the battle of the White Oak Road on March 31, and with his delay in reporting to Sheridan on the 1st.

Stickney, Warren's attorney, tried to elicit from Grant that, just possibly, Grant's evaluation of Warren might be wrong. Grant replied no, that although he admitted that he had made many mistakes, he was not wrong in his evaluation of Warren. Grant also described his meeting with Warren when Warren reported to him after he was relieved:

> General Warren came to my headquarters and stated that he had been relieved by General Sheridan. My answer to General Warren was substantially this: that I was not surprised, and I informed him that I had given the authority for his removal, and I also stated to General Warren that while I had a very great regard for his capacity and personal courage, yet he had certain defects which I then told him of a subordinate commander. I believe I expressed the opinion to him that he might succeed very much better in a different sphere or command, where he would have no superior, and expressed the willingness to assign him to duty elsewhere.[19]

(In Grant's testimony as to his meeting with Warren, he says that he told Warren of his defects but he did not give details in his testimony. However, he did describe the perceived defects in his memoirs. They were twofold. First, when Warren was given an order, he considered what everyone else related to the situation should do. That was not his responsibility. It was the responsibility of the superior issuing the order, and Warren should restrict his efforts and concerns to accomplishing what he was tasked with doing. Second, Warren was loath to delegate authority. He tended to believe that he could accomplish each of his division commander's tasks better than they could and, instead of handling the corps as a whole, handled it piecemeal.)

It would appear that the interrogators of General Grant, Mr. Stickney for Warren and Major Gardner for Sheridan, thought time stood still for Grant as of the night of March 31–April 1, 1865, that every detail of what transpired that night was fresh in his mind and on the tip of his tongue. In the intervening fifteen years, Grant had since presided over the Union Army in the final climactic days of the war; had presided over Reconstruction; had served two terms as president of the United States; and finally, had travelled around the world.

Now Grant was being bombarded for details that many would not remember after twenty-four hours. Of the numerous dispatches exchanged that night, at precisely what time did he see or send each; by telegraph or courier; did he see this one before that one; if by courier, who brought it, and other details. Predictably, Grant often replied that he did not know or could not remember.

Nothing that Grant said impacted on the facts already established: That it was unrealistic for the Fifth Corps in toto to arrive by midnight; that Ayres arrived as fast as reasonably possible; that Griffin and Crawford could have arrived earlier than they did; that it was actually Meade who first proposed that the Fifth Corps be sent to aid Sheridan.

What Grant added were items of human interest, such as his version of meeting with Warren after Warren's relief.

And so, the hearing dragged on. Witness after witness rehashed what had already been said. Finally, Stickney summed up for Warren and Major Gardner for Sheridan. The court then consulted, debated, discussed, and finally, on Tuesday, November 8, 1881, almost two years after the court convened and in its 107th meeting, finally issued its findings. They were not published for another year, until November 1882. In the meantime, Warren died of complications from diabetes on August 8, 1882.

Before we look at the court's findings, let us see what we can conclude from the testimony.

Chapter 12

Some Conclusions

On the basis of the evidence, we may draw the following conclusions:

(1) General Warren could not be held responsible for his temporary setback in the battle of the White Oak Road on March 31. At the time of the attack, his troops were deployed as directed, and, contrary to the allegations of General Grant, when attacked, were not attempting to seize the White Oak Road, but were conducting a reconnaissance of the Confederate position. Warren subsequently counterattacked and seized all the lost ground and more.

(2) No reinforcements were sent to Pickett on March 31. Pickett fought the battle of Five Forks with the troops that were sent down to Five Forks on March 29 and 30.

(3) Warren's sending of Bartlett's brigade to assist Sheridan on the afternoon of March 31 was counterproductive. It not only provided no aid to Sheridan, but alerted the Confederates to Union forces in their rear, causing them to withdraw to Five Forks.

(4) The downed bridge on the Boydton Plank Road over Gravelly Run was of no significance and did not delay Ayres. He arrived at the crossing after the bridge was replaced.

(5) The only significant delay in Ayres's march down the Boydton Plank Road to join Sheridan was caused by Sheridan himself. He failed to notify Ayres to turn off at the Brooks Road until Ayres was past the intersection.

(6) The earliest suggestion to transfer the entire Fifth Corps to Sheridan came from Meade, not Grant.

(7) Crawford's and Griffin's divisions could have and should have arrived in Pickett's rear at J. Boisseau's much earlier than they did. Warren received the order from Meade to send the two divisions at 10:50 p.m. on March 31. Despite the phrase "You must be very prompt in the movement," Warren did not order the two divisions to proceed until daylight on April 1. Warren's reasons (or excuses) were not convincing.

(8) Warren was tardy in reporting in to Sheridan the morning of April 1. He received Meade's 6 a.m. order to report to Sheridan no later than 9:30 a.m., and did not report to Sheridan until after 11 a.m. In the intervening time between receipt of the order and the actual reporting, Sheridan was within a mile or two of Warren.

(9) The best evidence is that there was no unnecessary delay in the Fifth Corps moving up to Gravelly Run Church and then forming up for the attack on April 1.

(10) The initial momentary confusion of Ayres's division of the Fifth Corps in attacking the Confederate refuse can be attributed to Sheridan, not Warren. Sheridan

believed that the refuse at the end of the Confederate line along the White Oak Road was at the junction of the Crump Road with the White Oak Road. Sheridan intended that Crawford's division, followed by that of Griffin, hit the angle of the main line with the refuse. However, Sheridan's intelligence was faulty. The angle was not at the junction with the Crump Road, but was several hundred feet to the west of the junction. This resulted in the entire Fifth Corps missing the angle and hitting open road beyond the angle. In consequence, the left flank of the Fifth Corps (Ayres) was subjected to Confederate fire into its flank, which caused the confusion. It was the responsibility of the Union cavalry to provide correct intelligence, and the cavalry reported to Sheridan and not to Warren.

(11) Warren acted properly during the battle by devoting all his efforts to bringing all components of the Fifth Corps into action rather than personally directing combat in one area.

(12) Crawford's wide swing to the north, away from the action, and then return south down the Ford Road actually proved beneficial. By doing so, he cut off the possibility of the Confederates retreating up the Ford Road, crossing Hatchers Run, and joining Rosser. Had the Confederates been permitted to do so, Sheridan may have been required to fight a second battle to reach the railroad, and, in this instance, the Confederates would have had a more favorable position than Five Forks.

(13) Sheridan's exasperation with Crawford's marching off to the north, away from the battle at the refuse, was unjustified. He did not know that Crawford was confronted with Munford's Confederate cavalry division.

(14) It was Crawford's division that actually suffered the largest number of casualties of any Union unit.

(15) Warren's leading of the charge across Gillian Field was no more than a footnote to a battle already won. The last Confederates were already fleeing to safety in the west.

(16) It would be more correct to say that the Fifth Corps, aided by Sheridan's cavalry, won the battle of Five Forks than to say that Sheridan's cavalry, aided by the Fifth Corps, won the battle of Five Forks. The casualties tell the whole story: Fifth Corps—634, cavalry—196.

(17) Sheridan's tribute to the performance of the Fifth Corps under Griffin in the closing days of the war was actually a compliment to Warren. It is the responsibility of a general not only to conduct battle management, but to train and discipline his troops for the next combat.

(18) General Warren's performance met the approval of General Warren. It did not meet the approval of his superiors, Generals Sheridan and Grant.

Chapter 13

The Findings

We might liken the results of the Court of Inquiry to a female elephant about to give birth. With a mighty, earthshaking trumpet, she brought forth a mouse. Considering the time and expense expended, the results were, well, insignificant.

The court crystallized its task into resolving four so-called "imputations." Each imputation was a written document casting dispersions on Warren. One was written by Grant and three by Sheridan. The court was to resolve whether each of the four imputations was justified.

Imputation 1

General Grant wrote:

> On the morning of the 31st, General Warren reported favorably to getting possession of the White Oak Road, and was directed to do so. To accomplish this, he moved with one division instead of his whole corps, which was attacked by the enemy in superior force and driven back on the Second Division before it had time to form, and it, in turn, forced back upon the Third Division, when the enemy was checked. A division of the Second Corps was immediately sent to Warren's support, the enemy driven back with heavy loss, and the possession of the White Oak Road gained.[1]

To summarize Grant's imputation in the most simplistic terms: Warren was ordered to seize the White Oak Road and set out to do so with a single division, followed by a second, and was beaten in detail. That is, the First Division was beaten, and then the second. Grant's point was that, once ordered to seize the White Oak Road, Warren should have committed all three divisions acting in unison.

The court determined that, up to the Confederate attack on Ayres's division, Warren, in fact, had not been ordered to seize the White Oak Road. In fact, Ayres was merely conducting a reconnaissance to determine the strength of the enemy defending the White Oak Road. Thus, Grant's entire imputation was based on erroneous information.

This was a favorable determination by the court for Warren, but it was immediately negated by what followed. The court concluded by stating:

> The court is further of the opinion that, considering the Fifth Corps constituted the extreme left wing of the armies operating against Richmond, and that the corps was in a delicate position and liable to be attacked at any moment, of which General Warren had been repeatedly warned, he should have been with his advanced division, guiding and directing

them, and that he should have started earlier to the front than he did and not have waited at the telegraph office to keep in communication with General Meade's headquarters, unless he had direct orders that morning to do so, which however does not appear in the evidence.[2]

Imputation 2

General Sheridan wrote: "Had General Warren moved according to the expectations of the Lieutenant-General, there would appear to have been but little chance for the escape of the enemy's infantry in front of the Dinwiddie Court House."[3]

The court's opinion was as follows:

It is supposed that the "expectations of the lieutenant-general" referred to in the imputation, are those expressed in his dispatch to General Sheridan of 10:45 p.m. of March 31, 1865, as follows:

> Dabney's Mills
> March 31, 1865–10:45 p.m.
>
> Major General Sheridan
>
> The Fifth Corps has been ordered to your support. Two divisions will go by J. Boisseau's and one down the Boydton Road. In addition to this I have sent McKenzie's cavalry, which will reach you by the Vaughn Road. All these forces, except the cavalry, should reach you by 12 tonight.
>
> You will assume command of the whole force sent to operate with you and use it to the best of your ability to destroy the force which your command has fought so gallantly to-day.
>
> U. S. Grant
> Lieutenant General

In which he says "all these forces except the cavalry should, reach you by 12 tonight." If this supposition be correct, the court is of the opinion, considering the condition of the roads and surrounding country over which part of the troops had to march, the darkness of the night, the distance to be traveled, and the hour at which the order for the march reached General Warren, that it was not practicable for the Fifth Corps to have reached General Sheridan at 12 o'clock on the night of March 31.

Notwithstanding that dispositions suitable for the contingency of Sheridan falling back from Dinwiddie might well have occupied and perplexed General Warren's mind during the night, the court is of the opinion that he should have moved the two divisions by the Crump Road in obedience to the orders and expectations of his commander, upon whom alone rested the responsibility of the consequences.

It appears from the dispatches and General Warren's testimony, that neither Generals Meade, Sheridan, or Warren expressed an intention of having this column attack before daylight.

The court is further of the opinion that General Warren should have started with two divisions, as directed by General Meade's dispatch as early after its receipt, at 10:50 p.m. as he could be assured of the prospect of Ayres' departure down the Boydton Plank Road, and should have advanced on the Crump Road as far as directed in that dispatch, or as far as might be practicable or necessary to fulfill General Meade's intention: whereas the evidence shows that he did not start until between five and six in the morning of the 1st of April, and did not reach J. Boisseau's with the head of the column till about seven o'clock in the morning.

The dispatches show that Generals Meade and Warren anticipated a withdrawal during the night of the enemy's forces fronting General Sheridan, which was rendered highly probably from the known position in their rear of a portion of the Fifth Corps (Bartlett's brigade) at J. Boisseau's, and the event justified the anticipation.[4]

The court's findings on imputation 2 were a partial victory for Warren. They concluded that:

(1) Warren could not have joined Sheridan by midnight on March 31.
(2) Warren's two division that were to arrive via J. Boisseau's could have and should have started and arrived earlier than they did.
(3) Even had they arrived earlier, they would have arrived too late to serve the intended purpose, that is, to trap Pickett's force between the Sheridan-Ayres force at Dinwiddie and the two divisions (Crawford and Griffin) at J. Boisseau's.

Imputation 3

General Sheridan wrote: "General Warren did not exert himself to get up his corps as rapidly as he might have done, and his manner gave me the impression that he wished the sun to go down before dispositions for the attack could be completed."[5]

The court's findings were as follows:

> The court is of the opinion that there was no unnecessary delay in the march of the Fifth Corps, and that General Warren took the usual methods of a corps commander to prevent delay.
> The question regarding Warren's manner appears to be too intangible and the evidence on it too contradictory for the court to decide, separate from the context, that he appeared to wish "the sun to do down before dispositions for the attack would be completed"; but his actions, as shown by the evidence, do not appear to have corresponded with such wish, if even he entertained it.[6]

Imputation 4

General Sheridan wrote: "During this attack I again became dissatisfied with General Warren. During the engagement portions of his line gave way when not exposed to heavy fire, and simply from want of confidence on the part of the troops, which General Warren did not exert himself to inspire."[7]

The court's findings were: "General Warren's attention appears to have been drawn, almost immediately after Ayres received the flank fire from the 'return' and his consequent change of front, to the probability of Crawford with Griffin diverging too much from and being separated from Ayres, and by continuous exertions of himself and staff substantially remedied matters; and the court thinks that this was for him the essential point to be attended to, which also exacted his whole efforts to accomplish."[8]

D. G. Swain, the judge advocate-general of the army, was required to endorse the findings. Swain made a comprehensive summation of the evidence, but the last paragraph of his endorsement said it all. It read: "I think it will be seen from the evidence that reasonable grounds existed in justifying the statements contained in the reports of Generals Grant and Sheridan affecting General Warren, and that the act of General Sheridan in relieving General Warren from command as he did was the exercise of a discretion with which he was clothed, and in so doing there is nothing to show that he was activated by other than patriotic and justifiable motives."9

Thus, in a stroke, Swain came down solidly on the side of Sheridan and undid whatever Warren may have gained in the findings. Swain made the obvious point that the determination of who was best qualified to head the Fifth Corps was a matter of discretion, and Sheridan clearly was authorized to exercise that discretion. The supreme authority in the military was, of course, President Abraham Lincoln, and Lincoln affirmed Sheridan's decision by his silence.

CHAPTER 14

Sherman's Endorsement

If the judge advocate-general's endorsement was considered to have wounded Warren, Sherman's endorsement was the coup de grace. Let us recount Sherman's endorsement verbatim:

REPORT OF THE GENERAL OF THE ARMY

HEADQUARTERS OF THE ARMY,
Washington, D.C., July 15, 1882

The opinion of the court of inquiry in various branches of the case of Gouverneur K. Warren, lieutenant-colonel of engineers, brevet major-general United States Army, and the elaborate review of the same by Judge-Advocate-General Swain, having been submitted to me for consideration, I have to state that my official action is in no sense necessary to give strength to the conclusions reached or effect to whatever Executive action the case may call for.

The court of inquiry was ordered by President Hayes, on the urgent and repeated request of General Warren, and although General Warren could not have been tried by a general court-martial because of the prohibition as to time in the one hundred and third Article of War, yet the power and right of the President of the United States to order an inquiry into "the nature of any transactions of, or accusations or imputations against, any officer" is clearly given by the one hundred and fifteenth Article of War without any limitation as to time or circumstance, and it is for the President of the United States alone to make such application of the results of this inquiry as his judgment may approve. To aid him in this I venture to condense a few points in this most elaborate record.

In the month of March 1865, Abraham Lincoln was President of the United States, and constitutional Commander-in-Chief of the Army and Navy. The United States were engaged in a war involving the existence of the government, and had vast armies in the field, one of which—the Army of the Potomac—under the immediate command for Major-General Meade, was operating south of the James River, near Petersburg, against the enemy's capital, and against his chief army commanded by General Lee.

The Army of the Potomac was organized into corps, divisions, and brigades. The corps commanders were always appointed by the President, whilst the division and brigade commanders were usually designated by the commanding general. On the 31st of March 1865, General G.K. Warren commanded the Fifth Corps, composed of three division—Griffin, Ayres, and Crawford—on the extreme left of the Army of the Potomac.

At that date there were other armies operating against the same enemy, viz, the Army of the James and a corps of cavalry under General Sheridan. Lieutenant-General Grant commanded all the armies of the United States, but was personally present with the Army of the Potomac. He possessed the absolute confidence of the President, and was vested with every power necessary to success. About that date he had sent General Sheridan to feel for and attack the extreme right flank of the enemy's line at or near the Five Forks. He, General

Sheridan, March 30, encountered a force too large to overcome with cavalry alone and called for re-enforcement. This was promptly ordered by Lieutenant-General Grant, through General Meade, who ordered the nearest corps—Fifth, General Warren's—which corps was ordered to report to General Sheridan at or near Dinwiddie by daylight of April 1, and be subject to his orders. The court of inquiry does not state that the President had deputed to General Grant his undoubted authority to appoint and remove corps commanders, but this is inferred and unquestioned. Yet it is clearly found that General Grant had deputed to General Sheridan the right to remove General Warren and give the command of the Fifth Corps, if he saw fit, to General Griffin, one of the division commanders.

The court found that the Fifth Corps did not reach General Sheridan as early on the 1st of April, as he had reason to expect, or as it might have done.

On that 1st day of April, under the immediate command of General Sheridan, was fought the battle of Five Forks—one of infinite importance. The history of it is given in great detail in the proceedings of this court, and the findings are that the tactical handling of the Fifth Corps by General Warren was unskillful, and that though the general result was a success and victory, yet the victory resulted in spite of the misdirection of two of the three divisions of the Fifth Corps, for which the corps commander was held responsible.

General Sheridan, then using the authority vested in him, relieved General Warren of his command, and devolved it on the next in rank, General Griffin. He had full authority for so doing; was sustained at the time by his immediate superior, Lieutenant-General Grant, and his action was never questioned by the then President Lincoln, or his immediate successor, Johnson. There the matter ought to have ended.

But General Warren appealed to the successive Presidents for a court of inquiry, but did not succeed until 1881, when by President Hayes he was granted the opportunity for a full hearing before an impartial court of inquiry, whose proceedings contain a complete history of these important events, and whose findings confirm substantially what was officially reported on the dates of the occurrences.

It would be an unsafe and dangerous rule to hold the commander of an army in battle to a technical adherence to any rule of conduct for managing his command. He is responsible for results, and holds the lives and reputations of every officer and soldier under his orders as subordinate to the great end—victory. The most important events are usually compressed into an hour, a minute, and he cannot stop to analyze his reasons. He must act on the impulse, the conviction, of the instant, and should be sustained in his conclusions, if not manifestly unjust. The power to command men and give vehement impulse to their joint action is something which cannot be defined by words, but it is plain and manifest in battles, and whoever commands an army in chief must choose his subordinates by reason of qualities which can alone be tested in actual conflict.

No one has questioned the patriotism, integrity, and great intelligence of General Warren. These are attested by a long record of most excellent service, but in the clash of arms at and near Five Forks, March 31 and April 1, 1865, his personal activity fell short of the standard fixed by General Sheridan, on whom alone rested the great responsibility for that and succeeding days.

My conclusion is that General Sheridan was perfectly justified in his action in this case, and he must be fully and entirely sustained if the United States expects great victories by her armies in the future.

All the other branches settled by this court belong to the domain of history rather than of military inquiry.

W.T. Sherman,
General[1]

Sherman's endorsement stated that, not only did Sheridan have the authority to remove Warren, but that his removal was fully justified.

Warren's persistence in seeking the court of inquiry ultimately proved injurious to him. He would have fared far better in history had he graciously accepted his removal and moved on with his career.

Warren's case is often incorrectly linked with that of Major General Fitz John Porter. Porter, unlike Warren, was actually accused of a crime, convicted, and sentenced. Justice demanded that he be exonerated. Warren was never accused of a crime, much less tried, convicted, and sentenced. His removal was the result of the judgment of those who, history unanimously agrees, contributed more to final victory than he did.

CHAPTER 15

The Nature of Warren

We tend to think of Sheridan removing Warren as commander of the Fifth Corps in a fit of anger. This is not exactly correct. Had Sheridan simply "removed" Warren, Brigadier General Crawford, the next senior general in the corps, would have become the commander. Sheridan "replaced" Warren with Griffin, thus jumping over Crawford.

Griffin had graduated from West Point in 1847, three years before Warren. Unlike Warren, he did not enter the Corps of Engineers, but became an artillerist. Thus, Griffin spent his thirteen prewar years in military matters, while Warren spent his ten prewar years in civil engineering matters.

Griffin's wartime rise in rank was even more meteoric that that of Warren. He became brigadier general in June 1862, while Warren did not become a brigadier general until September 1862. Warren, however, leapfrogged Griffin when he was promoted to major general. Up to Five Forks, Griffin's wartime record rivaled that of Warren. Warren, in fact, was sufficiently impressed with Griffin to recommend him for promotion to major general. Even at the time of Warren's

Major General Charles Griffin, First Division commander, Fifth Corps. Sheridan's choice to replace Warren.

150

replacement with Griffin, Griffin outranked Warren in the regular army, Warren being a major and Griffin a colonel.

What about Crawford? Crawford had an unusual background in that he had been a medical doctor. Up to the outbreak of hostilities, he had served as a surgeon in the Medical Corps. After the outbreak of hostilities, he transferred from the Medical Corps to the infantry. Thus, in an era when a clique of West Pointers controlled both the Union and Confederate Armies, Crawford was an outsider who had not attended West Point at all.

Crawford's wartime record could not match that of either Warren or Griffin, in large part because he had been seriously wounded early in the war and had spent much time on the sidelines recuperating.

The fact that Sheridan "replaced" Warren with Griffin, rather than merely removing Warren and letting Crawford assume command, indicates that he must have given some serious thought to the matter, rather than merely acting on the spur of the moment.

For all practicable purposes, the war ended in April 1865. Tens of thousands had their lives tragically altered. Many had suffered material losses. Men had lost their arms, legs, and sight. Women had lost their husbands and bread winners, children their fathers, and mothers their sons. Many now had only the bleakest futures.

The war had cost Warren nothing. It is true that he had suffered three minor wounds, but all healed and had no impact on his future life. At the war's conclusion, he returned to the position in the Corps of Engineers that he would have occupied had there been no war, that of major. This was the work that he enjoyed, in which he excelled, and in which he was duly appreciated. His superior was once again his friend and mentor Andrew Humphreys.

Although Warren was now a major rather than a major general, the position of major in the regular army was one that was to be envied by most. It placed him firmly in the upper middle class, both socially and economically. In addition to these assets, Warren had another plus to look forward to. He had acquired a wartime bride and could now look forward to a settled and normal family life.

Actually, the war had been a plus to Warren. Had there been no war, he would have never risen to the exalted rank of major general, would never have entered the nation's history books, and never had national name recognition. This latter was an invaluable asset for his peacetime life. This asset could be employed to benefit him in a number of ways; one was writing, another was politics.

After the war, there was a great public thirst for inside information on all that had happened. The rock stars of the day were the Civil War generals, and they re-fought their battles in the press. Almost all the top generals cashed in on this bonanza with newspaper articles, magazine articles, and books. Warren did not.

There was another avenue that name recognition opened up. This was politics. Many of the generals went on to brilliant political careers. For example, fellow corps commander Ambrose Burnside, who left the army in disgrace after being unjustly blamed for the crater fiasco, went on to become twice governor of Rhode Island and a U.S. senator. Fellow corps commander Winfield S. Hancock went on to receive the nomination for president by the Democratic Party in the election of 1880. Opposing Confederate corps commander John Brown Gordon went on to become a U.S. senator and governor of Georgia, and opposing Confederate cavalry corps commander Wade Hampton went on to become governor of South Carolina and a U.S. senator. Warren did not pursue a political career.

Although Warren had been humiliated, he had never even been accused of a crime, much less convicted of one. He had received no fine, no punishment, no censure, and no reduction in rank.

When Warren appeared before Grant on April 1, 1865, Grant did not shout at him, censure him, or berate him. He merely reassigned him. The real cause of Warren's relief was Grant. Had not Grant gratuitously given Sheridan the authority to relieve Warren, there is no doubt that Sheridan would not have done so. We may question the wisdom of Grant's authorizing Warren's relief. We may not question his right to do so. In fact, it was Grant's duty to see that the round pegs were put into the round holes. Also, there is no doubt that, up to this point, he was adept in doing just that. It is easy to cite instances wherein he replaced mediocrities or even incompetents with talented individuals. If indeed he was wrong in Warren's case, we can say that, however competent, no one is right in every case. Grant was not a mean man. To the contrary, he was invariably considerate. When he found it necessary to criticize someone in writing, he usually included some ameliorating statement such as "the fault was beyond the subject's control."

Grant was a forty-three year old man at the time of the battle of Five Forks. He was a man who had learned to live with failure and humiliation. As a young man, he resigned from the army under duress because of a drinking problem. He then failed at both farming and business, and was compelled to return to his father for menial employment in his father's business.

During the war, in 1862, after his successes at Forts Henry and Donelson, he was unceremoniously relieved of command by his superior, Henry Halleck, and replaced by a subordinate. The charge was disobedience of an order that was totally unjustified. Grant watched his army march off to its next campaign under a previous subordinate. Thus, Grant's experience had many similarities to that of Warren. Grant was ultimately restored to command and, later in the war, became the superior of Halleck. Despite Grant's experience under Halleck, he was able to work harmoniously and constructively with him for the remainder of the war. Grant thus knew failure and humiliation and was able to move on. Warren was not. Up to Five Forks, Warren had known nothing but success, praise, and even adulation. Here, he met one of life's bumps and could not accept it. He had to have redress, however long it took.

We could cite many cases where a Civil War general suffered unjust treatment but was able to put the cause above his ego and move on.

Confederate Brigadier General Richard Garnett was unjustly relieved from command by "Stonewall" Jackson at the battle of Kernstown for conducting an unauthorized retreat that all could see then and now was inevitable. Garnett was not only relieved on the battlefield, but was placed under arrest. When he returned to duty, he served with great distinction until he was killed while gallantly leading his brigade in Pickett's charge at Gettysburg.

Confederate General Joseph Johnston was unceremoniously relieved of command of the Army of Tennessee at the gates of Atlanta after conducting a masterful retreat

before a greatly superior force. He was replaced by "in over his head" General Hood, who led the Confederate Army to destruction in just six months. Johnston was then recalled when it was too late, but served with his usual competence to the end.

We could cite many other cases where generals were unjustly treated but were able to put the cause above their egos and move on, but can cite no other case wherein a general persisted for over fifteen years after the war to redress what he considered a slight.

Had Warren ever unjustly abused a subordinate? You bet! And we have cited a few of many such cases.

Had Warren been accused of a crime, he would have been entitled to a trial—in the military a court-martial. However, he was not accused of a crime and wanted a court of inquiry. A court of inquiry is merely an investigative body that uses judicial procedures. Its purpose is to establish the facts of a situation. No one is entitled to a court of inquiry. In the case at hand, the purpose would be to establish if the facts justified Warren's relief. Of course, if the court concluded that the facts did not justify Warren's relief, it would necessarily conclude that Sheridan and Grant unjustifiably relieved him. In a sense then, the court of inquiry would really be a trial of Sheridan and Grant.

By 1877, Warren had already won his case in the public mind. Those familiar with the case overwhelmingly were of the opinion that Warren had been unjustifiably removed. As early as May 1865, it was clear that the rank and file sided with Warren. On May 3, 1865, the Fifth Corps was to pass through Petersburg, Warren's current duty station, on its way back to Washington to participate in the grand victory parade. Griffin advised Warren that the corps wished to give him a salute of honor. Warren took the salute standing on the balcony of the Bolingbroke Hotel in Petersburg as the corps passed before him.

In May 1874, Warren attended a Ninth Corps reunion in Harrisburg, Pennsylvania. A reporter noted that when Warren entered there "was the signal for uproarious applause, and when he attempted to take a seat in the body of the hall, he was carried enthusiastically to the platform where the general officers were seated."[1]

When Warren suffered an early death in 1882 at the age of fifty two and left a financially distressed widow, veterans of the Army of the Potomac and the Fifth Corps took up a collection to buy her a house. If there was still any doubt as to where veterans' sympathies lay, it was dispelled at the actual court of inquiry where veteran after veteran of the old Fifth Corps testified in Warren's favor.

As of March 1865, the leadership of the Army of the Potomac was dominated by officers who had served in the prestigious Corps of Engineers before the war. These included Meade, the commander of the army, and all four of his corps commanders—Warren, Humphreys, Wright, and Parke. The members of the Corps considered themselves part of an elite group and in a sense they were.

When Grant came east in 1864 to take charge, he brought his protégé, Sheridan, and his indispensable assistant and chief of staff, General Rawlins. None had been members of the Corps of Engineers, and Rawlins was a pariah in that he was not only not an engineer, but did not even attend West Point.

Warren had a tendency to arrogance and undoubtedly looked down on the new arrivals as his academic inferiors. This in fact they were, but they far exceeded him in another form of intelligence—so called "street smarts." We know Warren's true feelings toward Grant and Rawlins from his private correspondence. As we have previously pointed out, he referred to Grant as a worthless drunk in a letter to his wife, and to Rawlins as a liar and coward in a letter to his brother. In all probability, Grant, Rawlins, and Sheridan perceived Warren's true feelings toward them and responded in kind. Under the circumstances, it was almost inevitable that, sometime in the future, an open clash of personalities would occur, and so it did.

Grant, Rawlins, Sheridan, and Warren were all talented generals and all contributed greatly to the final victory. We may call the relieving of Warren by Grant and Sheridan unfortunate, but there was blame on both sides. There is no black and white, no hero and no villain.

Warren had been unfairly treated. Was he capable of seeking unfair advantages for himself? Indeed he was. In an 1864 letter to his wife, he advised her to cultivate people like the Hamilton Fishes or Governor Morgan or the Seymours, people "of the highest respectability and wealthy"[2] whose friendship might be of service to him.

Warren's finest hour was his refusal to order his men to a useless death at Mine Run. His finest hour could have been simply accepting his dismissal from the command of the Fifth Corps and continuing on with his army career the best he could.

The Fifth Corps alone suffered 634 casualties during the battle of Five Forks in killed, wounded, and missing. Most of the missing undoubtedly ended up in unmarked graves. It is doubtful if any of those killed or maimed believed they suffered for the reputation of General Warren, who sustained not a scratch. Indeed, in all probability, none thought of General Warren at all.

This was an era when Congress adhered to the few responsibilities allocated to it in the Constitution. It commonly made appropriations in the tens of thousands of dollars rather than in the billions. Was it then in the national interest to appropriate tens of thousands of dollars for a court of inquiry whose sole purpose was to punish General Warren's detractors? Was Warren's reputation of more value than the lives of his troops?

Warren had received a bad break. Had he received unearned good breaks? Indeed he had. The sure ticket to high rank in the U.S. Volunteer Army was to be a West Point graduate. At the time, one entered West Point not by merit but by political connections. Had not Warren's father been politically connected, he never would have entered West Point. Had he not entered West Point, it is beyond question that he never would have risen to the rank of major general in the Volunteer Army. We can consider it all but certain that many of Warren's subordinates were his subordinates only because their fathers were not politically connected.

If Warren were a bigger man, he would have concluded: I have done my best. There is nothing to be gained in the public interest by further expenditures to assuage my feelings. Let the chips fall where they may. General Sheridan undoubtedly contributed more to the final victory than I did. My vindication could come only at his expense.

Warren made a significant contribution to final victory but, in the final analysis, indeed he was a small man.

Chapter 16

*The Aftermath—
What Happened to Them?*

Warren died on August 8, 1882, at the age of fifty-two. His death was attributed to acute liver failure caused by diabetes. His death came less than three months prior to the publication of the conclusions of the Court of Inquiry. Had he read the final report with its endorsements, he would have been disappointed. It was less than a complete vindication, a partial victory at best.

Warren's death occurred in Newport, Rhode Island, his home. In accordance with his wishes, he was buried in civilian clothes, without military honors, in the local Island Cemetery.

Warren left a widow, Emily Chase Warren, a fifteen year old son, Sydney, and a six year old daughter, Emily. Due to Warren's large expenditures relative to the court, including attorney fees and expenditures for mapping the battlefield, the family was left in tight financial circumstances. This was in part ameliorated by a collection from Fifth Corps veterans.

Warren's wife lived quietly and unobtrusively in Newport until her death on December 27, 1928, at the age of eighty-eight. Unlike the widows of Pickett and Custer, she did not devote her time to writing or lecturing to embellish the reputation of her deceased husband. Today she lies side by side with Warren in the local Island Cemetery.

Today Warren is barely remembered except by Civil War buffs. There are, however, two exceptions. A seventeen foot statue of Warren stands atop Little Round Top at Gettysburg, reminding visitors of Warren's contribution to the victory. A duplicate statue stands in the Grand Army Plaza in Brooklyn, New York.

Warren's son, Sydney, died in 1907 at the age of forty-one. His daughter reached the ripe old age of ninety and died in 1965. Warren's younger sister, Emily, to whom he was always very close, lived to eclipse her brother in both fame and fortune. More about her later.

Let us now look at the fate of Warren's three division commanders—Griffin, Crawford, and Ayres.

Major General Charles Griffin

Major General Charles Griffin, the commanding general of the First Division of the Fifth Corps and the man Sheridan chose to replace Warren, was the first of the principals of the Warren–Five Forks saga to die.

As a result of Griffin's contribution to the victory at Five Forks, he received a brevet as major general in the regular army. A brevet is, of course, an honorary rank, and the holder acquires none of the emoluments or authority of the rank. Upon dissolution of the Volunteer Army, Griffin returned to his true rank in the regular army, that of colonel.

Griffin's brief postwar career was closely intermingled with that of Sheridan. He first served as commanding officer of the 35th Infantry Regiment, then under Sheridan as assistant commissioner of the Freedman's Bureau. Lastly, he was ordered to proceed to New Orleans to relieve Sheridan as commander of the Fifth Military District. He never arrived. He died en route of yellow fever on September 15, 1867, at the age of forty-one. He is buried in Oak Hill Cemetery in Washington, D.C.

Major General Samuel Crawford

At the time of Five Forks, the physician-soldier Samuel Crawford was in command of the Third Division of Warren's Fifth Corps.

It was Crawford's division that marched away from the action at the refuse that infuriated Sheridan and ultimately led to Warren's relief. And yet, Sheridan specifically commended Crawford in his official report for Crawford's performance at Five Forks.

Crawford was a regular army officer and, at the dissolution of the Volunteer Army, reverted to his regular army rank of lieutenant colonel. In February 1873, he was given a disability retirement as a result of his wartime wounds. He was placed on the retirement roster as brigadier general, and thus was the only of Warren's three division commanders to achieve the rank of general in the regular army.

Crawford had participated in the battle of Gettysburg and spent much of the remainder of his life in an effort to preserve the battlefield. In this he succeeded and, in fact, he may be the single individual most responsible. This may be his greatest legacy.

Crawford died on November 3, 1892, at the age of sixty-four and is buried at Laurel Hill Cemetery in Philadelphia.

Major General Romeyn Ayres

The third of Warren's three divisions was commanded by Major General Romeyn Ayres. In Sheridan's eyes, it was Ayres's division that stormed the refuse that was most responsible (next to himself, of course) for the victory at Five Forks. And yet, he chose not Ayres but Griffin as Warren's successor.

Ayres was a regular army officer and, at the dissolution of the Volunteer Army, reverted to his rank of lieutenant colonel in the regular army. He served in garrisons in Arkansas, Louisiana, and Florida before being promoted to colonel of the 2nd Artillery in 1879. Ayres died on active duty on December 4, 1888, at Ft. Hamilton, New York, at the age of sixty-three. He is buried in Arlington National Cemetery.

Washington Roebling

Warren's young aide de camp was Washington Roebling. During many of Warren's younger sister's visits, she became acquainted with Roebling and the two fell in love. They were married in January 1865, and thus Roebling became not only Warren's aide de camp, but his brother-in-law.

Roebling was the son of a prominent bridge builder, and to this profession he returned at the end of the war. With the assistance of his young wife, he went from success to success, and finally undertook the ultimate challenge of the day—the construction of the Brooklyn Bridge, connecting Manhattan with Long Island. This required the largest suspension bridge of the time. The result proved to be a masterpiece, which stands strong, beautiful, and useable into the future as far as one can see to this day. This accomplishment provided the Roeblings with fame and fortune far exceeding that accomplished by any other Fifth Corps veteran.

Most remarkable was the fact that the sickly Roebling was often replaced by his wife as chief engineer. Her technical expertise and management acumen was such that, in an age when this seemed impossible, the workers readily accepted her management. The prominent and wealthy Roeblings were able to help the proud Warren financially from time to time, albeit discreetly.

Emily died on February 28, 1903, at the age of sixty. Against all odds, her sickly husband lived on another twenty-three years and finally died on July 21, 1926, at the age of eighty-nine.

Major General Philip Sheridan

Let us now look at Warren's nemesis, General Philip Sheridan. Sheridan was already a hero in the eyes of the Union populace at the conclusion of the Civil War. A factor that greatly increased his prominence and popularity was the publication of the poem "Sheridan's Ride" shortly after his victory at Cedar Creek. It depicted an absent Sheridan riding toward the battlefield, rallying his fleeing troops, and transforming a disastrous defeat into a resounding victory.

Sheridan entered the postwar regular army third in seniority, being junior only to Grant and Sherman. He was subsequently promoted to lieutenant general, only the fourth officer to achieve that exalted rank after Washington, and then to full general with only Grant and Sherman preceding him.

Sheridan presided over the Indian Wars as the head of the Department of Missouri and, in 1883, supplanted Sherman as commanding general of the army. He remained in this capacity until his unexpected and premature death from heart failure on August 5, 1888, at the age of fifty-seven. He died in Nonquitt, Massachusetts, and is buried in Arlington National Cemetery.

Sheridan's accomplishments extended into the civilian world. He was instrumental in founding Yellowstone National Park. He even made it into *Bartlett's Familiar Quotations* with a saying that is often corrupted into "the only good Indian is a dead Indian." What he actually said was, "The only good Indians I ever saw were dead."

Sheridan's prominence waxed while Warren's waned. Today he has entered the pantheon of American notables; his name is familiar to almost all Americans while that of Warren is largely forgotten. Sheridan's picture has appeared on stamps, and his name on schools, counties, townships, a city, a mountain, and even a glacier.

Sheridan's young widow gave him the ultimate tribute. When queried as to whether she would remarry, she replied: "I would rather be the widow of Phil Sheridan than the wife of any man living."[1]

Major General George Pickett

We now turn to Warren's adversary at Five Forks, Confederate Major General George Pickett.

We have previously noted that Pickett had been a central figure in two of the Army of Northern Virginia's biggest fiascos and, in both instances, managed to emerge unscathed while his men were slaughtered.

Pickett, with the remainder of his division, managed to escape from Five Forks and rejoin Lee's army for the final week of the war.

Upon Lee's surrender, most Confederate officers were simply permitted to return to their homes and resume their lives unmolested. Pickett, however, had reason to be worried. After Gettysburg, he had been assigned to command the Department of North Carolina. While there, his troops captured a number of Union soldiers who had previously served in the Confederate Army. Pickett had ordered them court-martialed as traitors, and twenty-two were subsequently executed. Pickett feared that, upon surrender, he might be singled out as a war criminal. Consequently, he and his young wife fled to Canada.

After less than a year, it became evident to the Picketts that it was safe for them to return, and they resumed life in Virginia. Pickett engaged in the insurance business with very modest success. He received a full pardon in 1874 and died on July 30, 1875, at the age of fifty from a liver abscess. He was initially interred in the Cedar Grove Cemetery in Norfolk, but was soon exhumed and reburied in the Confederate Valhalla, the Hollywood Cemetery in Richmond. Here a large monument adorns his grave.

Pickett's young widow outlived her husband by fifty-five years, and died on March 31, 1931. During the fifty-five years, she devoted much time to writing and lecturing, embellishing the reputation of her husband. Pickett has thus come down to us as Pickett the "gallant" rather than Pickett the "loser."

Major General Christopher Columbus Augur

Lastly, we will turn to the officer who presided over the court of inquiry, Major General Christopher Columbus Augur. Of all the principals, Augur was to suffer the strangest death. Having survived the Mexican War, the Civil War, and the Indian Wars, he was murdered.

Augur ended the Civil Was as a major general of the Volunteer Army, and then reverted to his rank in the regular army as lieutenant colonel. He was promoted to colonel in 1866 and to brigadier general in 1869. He continued in that rank until his retirement in 1885.

In retirement, Augur resided in Georgetown, Washington, D.C. On January 15, 1898, he remonstrated with a black man in front of his house for using profane language. The man, in turn, shot him. Augur expired from his wound the following day at the age of seventy-six. He is buried in nearby Arlington National Cemetery.

Appendix A:
Sheridan's Official Report

Army regulations required that all officers commanding units of regimental size or larger submit reports of their unit's participation in each campaign. The purpose was twofold—for instruction and for history. Thus, both Sheridan and Warren were required to submit reports for their commands' involvement in the events occurring between March 29 and April 1, 1865.

It was widely believed that Sheridan relieved Warren under the intense pressure of the stressful, exhausting, and exhilarating events of April 1, 1865, and that the subsequent report would present a calmer and more measured account of events, and thus might, to a degree, exonerate Warren. It was not to be.

In modern parlance, Sheridan's report did a hatchet job on Warren. If there had been any doubt as to Sheridan's true feelings toward Warren, there could be none after reading the report.

Sheridan actually submitted two reports. The first was submitted on April 2, within twenty-four hours of the battle, and contained only a bare bones description of the battle and nothing for or against Warren. The second and far more detailed report was submitted more than a month later, on May 16, and excoriated Warren. The latter report is presented verbatim below.

Cavalry Headquarters,
May 16, 1865

General: I have the honor to submit the following narrative of the operations of my command during the recent campaign in front of Petersburg and Richmond, terminating with the surrender of the rebel Army of Northern Virginia at Appomattox Court-House, Va., on April 9, 1865:

On March 26 my command, consisting of the First and Third Cavalry Divisions, under the immediate command of Bvt. Maj. Gen. Wesley Merritt, crossed the James River by the bridge at Jones' Landing, having marched from Winchester, in the Shenandoah Valley, via White House, on the Pamunkey River.

On March 27 this command went into camp near Hancock's Station, on the military railroad, in front of Petersburg, and on the same day the Second Cavalry Division, which had been serving with the Army of the Potomac, reported to me, under the command of Maj. Gen. George Crook.

The effective force of these three divisions of cavalry was as follows: General Merritt's command, First and Third Divisions, 5,700; General Crook's command, Second Division, 3,300; total effective force, 9,000.

With this force I moved out on the 29th of March, in conjunction with the armies operating against Richmond, and in the subsequent operations I was under the immediate orders of the lieutenant-general commanding. I moved by the way of Reams' Station, on the Weldon railroad, and Malone's Crossing, on the Rowanty Creek, where we were obliged to construct a bridge. At this point our advance encountered a small picket of the rebel cavalry, and drove it to the left across Stony Creek, capturing a few prisoners, from whom and from my scouts I learned that the enemy's cavalry was at or near Stony Creek Depot, on the Weldon railroad, on our left flank and rear. Believing that it would not attack me, and that by pushing on to Dinwiddie Court-House I could force it to make a wide detour, we continued the march, reaching the Court-House about 5 p.m. encountering only a small picket of the enemy, which was driven away by our advance.

It was found necessary to order General Custer's division, which was marching in rear, to remain near Malone's Crossing, on the Rowanty Creek, to assist and protect our trains, which were greatly retarded by the almost impassable roads of that miry section.

The First and Second Divisions went into camp, covering the Vaughan, Flat Foot, Boydton plank, and Five Forks roads, which all intersect at Dinwiddie Court-House, rendering this an important point, and from which I was expected to make a cavalry raid on the South Side Railroad, and thence join General Sherman or return to Petersburg, as circumstances might dictate. However, during the night the lieutenant-general sent me instructions to abandon the contemplated raid and act in concert with the infantry, under his immediate command, and turn the right flank of Lee's army if possible.

Early on the morning of the 30th of March I directed General Merritt to send the First Division, Brigadier-General Devin commanding, to gain possession of the Five Forks, on the White Oak road, and directed General Crook to send General Davies' brigade of his division to the support of General Devin. Gregg's brigade, of Crook's division, was held on the Boydton plank road, and guarded the crossing of Stony Creek, forcing the enemy's cavalry, that was moving from Stony Creek Depot to form a connection with the right of their army, to make a wide detour, as I had anticipated, on the road south of Stony Creek and west of Chamberlain's Bed—a very fatiguing march in the bad condition of the roads. A very heavy rain fell during this day, aggravating the swampy nature of the ground, and rendering the movements of troops almost impossible. General Merritt's reconnaissance developed the enemy in strong force on the White Oak road, in the vicinity of the Five Forks, and there was some heavy skirmishing throughout the day.

Next morning, March 31, General Merritt advanced toward the Five Forks with the First Division, and, meeting with considerable opposition, General Davies' brigade, of Crook's division, was ordered to join him, while General Crook, advancing on the left with the two other brigades of his division, encountered the enemy's cavalry at Chamberlain's Creek, at a point a little north and west of Dinwiddie, making demonstrations to cross. Smith's brigade was ordered to hold them in check, and Gregg's brigade to a position on his right. The advance of the First Division got possession of the Five Forks, but in the meantime the Fifth Army Corps, which had advanced toward the White Oak road from the Vaughan road, was attacked and driven back, and withdrawing from that point, this force of the enemy marched rapidly from the front of the Fifth Corps to the Five Forks, driving in our cavalry advance, and moving down on roads west of Chamberlain's Creek, attacked General Smith's brigade, but were unable to force his position. Abandoning the attempt to cross in his front, this force of the enemy's infantry succeeded in effecting a crossing higher up the creek, striking General Davies' brigade, of the Second Division, which, after a gallant fight, was forced back upon the left flank of the First Division, thus partially isolating all this force from my main line covering Dinwiddie Court-House. Orders were at once given to General Merritt to cross this detached force over to the Boydton plank road and march down to Dinwiddie Court-House and come into the line of battle. The enemy, deceived by this movement, followed it up rapidly, making a left wheel and presenting his rear to my line of battle. When his line was nearly parallel to mine, General Gibbs' brigade, of the First Division, and

General Irvin Gregg's brigade, of the Second Division, were ordered to attack at once, and General Custer was directed to bring up two of his brigades rapidly, leaving one brigade of his division with the trains, that had not yet reached Dinwiddie Court-House. In the gallant attack made by Gibbs and Gregg the enemy's wounded fell into our hands, and he was forced to face by the rear rank and give up his movement, which, if continued, would have taken in flank and rear the infantry line of the Army of the Potomac. When the enemy had faced to meet this attack, a very obstinate and handsomely contested battle ensued, in which, with all his cavalry and two divisions of infantry, the enemy was unable to drive five brigades of our cavalry, dismounted, from an open plain in front of Dinwiddie Court-House. The brunt of their cavalry attack was borne by General Smith's brigade, which had so gallantly held the crossing of Chamberlain's Creek in the morning. His command again held the enemy in check with determined bravery, but the heavy force brought against his right flank finally compelled him to abandon his position on the creek and fall back to the main line immediately in front of Dinwiddie Court-House. As the enemy's infantry advanced to the attack, our cavalry threw up slight breast-works of rails at some points along our lines, and when the enemy attempted to force this position, they were handsomely repulsed and gave up the attempt to gain possession of the Court-House. It was after dark when the firing ceased, and the enemy lay on their arms that night not more than 100 yards in front of our lines.

The commands of Generals Devin and Davies reached Dinwiddie Court-House without opposition by way of the Boydton plank road, but did not participate in the final action of the day.

In this well-contested battle the most obstinate gallantry was displayed by my entire command. The brigades commanded by General Gibbs and Colonels Stagg and Fitzhugh, in the First Division, Generals Davies, Gregg, and Smith, in the Second Division, Colonels Pennington and Capehart, in the Third Division, vied with each other in their determined efforts to hold in check the superior force of the enemy, and the skillful management of their troops in this peculiarly difficult country entitles the brigade commanders to the highest commendation.

Generals Crook, Merritt, Custer, and Devin, by their courage and ability, sustained their commands and executed the rapid movements of the day with promptness and without confusion.

During the night of the 31st of March my headquarters were at Dinwiddie Court-House, and the lieutenant-general notified me that the Fifth Corps would report to me and should reach me by midnight. This corps had been offered to me on the 30th instant, but very much desiring the Sixth Corps, which had been with me in the Shenandoah Valley, I asked for it, but on account of the delay which would occur in moving that corps from its position in the lines in front of Petersburg it could not be sent me. I respectfully submit herewith my brief account of the operations of the day, the response to which was the ordering of the Fifth Corps to my support and my command, as also the dispatch of the lieutenant-general notifying me of his action. I understood that the Fifth Corps, when ordered to report to me, was in position near S. Dabney's house, in the angle between the Boydton road and the Five Forks road. Had General Warren moved according to the expectations of the lieutenant-general, there would appear to have been but little chance for the escape of the enemy's infantry in front of Dinwiddie Court-House. Ayres' division moved down the Boydton plank road during the night, and in the morning moved west by R. Boisseau's house, striking the Five Fords road about two miles and a half north of Dinwiddie Court-House. General Warren, with Griffin's and Crawford's divisions, moved down the road by Crump's house, coming into the Five Forks road near J. Boisseau's house between 7 and 8 o'clock on the morning of the 1st of April. Meantime I moved my cavalry force at daylight against the enemy's lines in my front, which gave way rapidly, moving off by the right flank, and crossing Chamberlain's Creek. This hasty movement was accelerated by the discovery that two divisions of the Fifth Corps were in their rear, and that one division was moving toward their left and rear.

The following were the instructions sent to General Warren:

> CAVALRY HEADQUARTERS,
> Dinwiddie Court-House, April 1, 1865—3 a.m.
>
> Major-General WARREN,
> Commanding Fifth Army Corps:
>
> I am holding in front of Dinwiddie Court-House, on the road leading to Five Forks, for three-quarters of a mile, with General Custer's division. The enemy are in his immediate front, lying so as to cover the road just this side of A. Adams' house, which leads out across Chamberlain's bed or run. I understand you have a division at J. Boisseau's; if so, you are in rear of the enemy's line and almost on his flanks. I will hold on here. Possibly they may attack Custer at daylight; if so, attack instantly and in full force. Attack at daylight anyhow, and I will make an effort to get the road this side of Adams' house, and if I do you can capture the whole of them. Any force moving down the road I am holding, or on the White Oak road, will be in the enemy's rear, and in all probability get any force that may escape you by a flank attack. Do not fear my leaving here. If the enemy remains I shall fight at daylight.
>
> P.H. SHERIDAN,
> Major-General.

As they fell back the enemy was rapidly followed by General Merritt's two divisions—General Devin on the right and General Custer on the left; General Crook in rear. During the remainder of the day General Crook's division held the extreme left and rear and was not seriously engaged.

I then determined that I would drive the enemy with the cavalry to the Five Forks, press them inside of their works, and make a feint to turn their right flank, and meanwhile quietly move up the Fifth Corps with a view to attacking their left flank, crush the whole force, if possible, and drive westward those who might escape, thus isolating them from their army at Petersburg. Happily, this conception was successfully executed. About this time General Mackenzie's division of cavalry, from the Army of the James, reported to me, and consisted of about 1,000 effective men. I directed General Warren to hold fast at J. Boisseau's house, refresh his men; and be ready to move to the front when required; and General Mackenzie was ordered to rest in front of Dinwiddie Court-House until further orders. Meantime General Merritt's command continued to press the enemy, and by impetuous charges drove them from two lines of temporary works, General Custer guiding his advance on the Widow Gilliam's house and General Devin on the main Five Forks road. The courage displayed by the cavalry officers and men was superb, and about 2 o'clock the enemy was behind his works on the White Oak road, and his skirmish line drawn in. I then ordered up the Fifth Corps on the main road, and sent Brevet Major Gillespie, of the Engineers, to turn the head of the column off on the Gravelly Church road, and put the corps in position on this road obliquely to and at a point but a short distance from the White Oak road and about one mile from the Five Forks. Two divisions of the corps were to form the front line, and one division was to be held in reserve, in column of regiments, opposite the center. I then directed General Merritt to demonstrate as though he was attempting to turn the enemy's right flank, and notified him that the Fifth Corps would strike the enemy's left flank, and ordered that the cavalry should assault the enemy's works as soon as the Fifth Corps became engaged, and that would be determined by the volleys of musketry. I then rode over to where the Fifth Corps was going into position, and found them coming up very slowly. I was exceedingly anxious to attack at once, for the sun was getting low, and it would have been shameful to have gone back with no results to compensate for the loss of the brave men who had fallen during the day.

In this connection I will say that General Warren did not exert himself to get up his corps as rapidly as he might have done, and his manner gave me the impression that he wished the sun to go down before dispositions for the attack could be completed. As soon as the corps was in position I ordered an advance in the following formation; Ayres' division on the left, in double lines; Crawford's division on the right, in double lines; and Griffin's division in reserve, behind Crawford; and the White Oak road was reached without opposition.

While General Warren was getting into position I learned that the left of the Second Corps of the Army of the Potomac, on my right, had been swung around from the direction of its line of battle until it fronted on the Boydton road and parallel to it, which afforded an opportunity to the enemy to march down the White Oak road and attack me in right and rear. General Mackenzie was therefore sent up the Crump road with directions to gain the White Oak road if possible, but to attack at all hazards any enemy found, and if successful then march down that road and join me. General Mackenzie executed this with courage and skill, attacking a force of the enemy on the White Oak road and driving it toward Petersburg. He then countermarched and joined me on the White Oak road just as the Fifth Corps advanced to the attack, and I directed him to swing round with the right of the infantry and gain possession of the Ford road at the crossing of Hatcher's Run. The Fifth Corps on reaching the White Oak road made a left wheel and burst on the enemy's left flank and rear like a tornado, and pushed rapidly on, orders having been given that if the enemy was routed there should be no halt to reform broken lines. As stated before, the firing of the Fifth Corps was the signal to General Merritt to assault, which was promptly responded to, and the works of the enemy were soon carried at several points by our brave cavalrymen. The enemy were driven from their strong line of works and completely routed, the Fifth Corps doubling up their left flank in confusion, and the cavalry of General Merritt dashing on to the White Oak road, capturing their artillery, and turning it upon them and riding into their broken ranks so demoralized them that they made no serious stand after their line was carried, but took to flight in disorder. Between 5,000 and 6,000 prisoners fell into our hands, and the fugitives were driven westward, and were pursued until long after dark by Merritt's and Mackenzie's cavalry for a distance of six miles.

During this attack I again became dissatisfied with General Warren. During the engagement portions of his line gave way when not exposed to a heavy fire, and simply from want of confidence on the part of the troops, which General Warren did not exert himself to inspire. I therefore relieved him from the command of the Fifth Corps, authority for this action having been sent to me before the battle, unsolicited.

When the pursuit was given up I directed General Griffin, who had been ordered to assume command of the Fifth Corps, to collect his corps at once, march two divisions back to Gravelly Church, and put them into position at right angles to the White Oak road, facing toward Petersburg, while Bartlett's division (Griffin's old) covered the Ford road to Hatcher's Run. General Merritt's cavalry went into camp on the Widow Gilliam's plantation, and General Mackenzie took position on the Ford road at the crossing of Hatcher's Run.

I cannot speak too highly of the conduct of the troops in this battle and of the gallantry of their commanding officers, who appeared to realize that the success of the campaign and fate of Lee's army depended upon it. They merit the thanks of the country and reward of the Government. To Generals Griffin, Ayres, Bartlett, and Crawford, of the Fifth Corps, and to Generals Merritt, Custer, Devin, and Mackenzie, of the cavalry, great credit is due, and to their subordinate commanders they will undoubtedly award the praise which is due to them for the hearty co-operation, bravery, and ability which were everywhere displayed.[1]

The remainder of the report describes events occurring after the battle of Five Forks and consequently is omitted here.

On the afternoon of March 31, both Warren's and Sheridan's forces were attacked. Warren suffered an initial reversal, having two of his three divisions routed before recouping and then pushing the Confederates back across the White Oak Road. Sheridan, in turn, was pushed all the way back from Five Forks to Dinwiddie Courthouse by an inferior Confederate force, from where he called for help. In Sheridan's report, he blames this reversal on Warren. He contends that when Warren was initially pushed back, this freed Confederate forces to march down the White Oak Road to Five Forks to assist those already there, and that these reinforcements made the difference in forcing him back to Dinwiddie. This is, of course, nonsense. The Confederates fighting Warren and Sheridan were at all times separate and distinct.

As we have previously noted, on March 31 at 10:05 p.m. Grant sent a message to Sheridan advising him that the Fifth Corps had been ordered to his support and would reach him by midnight that night. Grant's assessment of the time of arrival was based on false information, and there is absolutely no way the Fifth Corps could have reached Sheridan by midnight, regardless of who was in charge. Sheridan almost certainly knew this by the time he submitted his report. Nevertheless, in his report, Sheridan, referring to Grant's dispatch, stated that "had Warren moved according to the expectations of the lieutenant general, there would appear to have been little chance for the escape of the enemy's infantry in front of Dinwiddie Court House." This was yet another gratuitous dig at Warren, and totally unfair at that.

Sheridan even purports to read Warren's mind, and he does not like what he sees. In describing Warren's lining up his troops for the attack, Sheridan writes: "In this connection I will say that General Warren did not exert himself to get up his corps as rapidly as he might have done, and his manner gave me the impression that he wished the sun to go down before dispositions for the attack could be completed." He of course cites no specific actions of Warren, for if Warren, in fact, had deliberately delayed the attack, he would have been guilty of treason.

Sheridan was not only dissatisfied with Warren's preparation for the attack, but with Warren's subsequent actions during the attack. Sheridan wrote: "During the attack, I again became dissatisfied with General Warren. During the engagement portions of his line gave way when not exposed to a heavy fire, and simply from want of confidence on the part of the troops, which General Warren did not exert himself to inspire." This charge is so nebulous that it does not merit comment.

Sheridan ends his report of the battle by specifically commending the actions of all three of Warren's division commanders without mentioning Warren. He thus concludes by throwing salt in the wound.

Appendix B:
Warren's Official Report

Now let us look at Warren's report. Inasmuch as Warren prepared his report after that of Sheridan, we might expect that it would be in the form of a rebuttal. However, it contains no blame and no animosity, but, as far as a human can do, presents a detailed, objective look at the events as they transpired. The blanks are Warren's.

> Reports of Maj. Gen. Gouverneur K. Warren, U.S. Army,
> commanding Fifth Army Corps.
>
> NEW YORK, February 21, 1865 [1866].
>
> General GEORGE D. RUGGLES,
> Assistant Adjutant-General, Military Division of the Atlantic:
> GENERAL: I forward herewith my report of the operations of the Fifth Corps during the 29th, 30th, and 31st of last March. The long time consumed was unavoidable, for I am without any assistance in my work, the War Department being unable to grant me an assistant or even to pay for copying my report. This copy I send you is not very neat, and it is the only one I have made. If you have force enough in your office will you not please have a fair copy made for yourself and return this one to me for my own file. I will compare and sign the copy you make if you wish it.
>
> REPORT.
>
> The initial movement of the final campaign was made by the Fifth Corps at 3 a.m. on the 29th of March, no other portions of the army moving till 6 a.m. The Fifth Corps was at the time composed as follows:
>
> First. The First Division, commanded by Bvt. Maj. Gen. Charles Griffin, contained 6,547 men. It was divided into three brigades: The Third Brigade was under General J.J. Bartlett, being composed of veteran regiments, and numbered -----; the Second Brigade was under General Gregory, and numbered -----; the First Brigade was under General J.L. Chamberlain, and numbered -----.
>
> Second. The Second Division, Bvt. Maj. Gen. R.B. Ayres commanding, contained about 3,980 men, divided up as follows: The Maryland Brigade (the Second), ----- strong, under General Denison; the Third Brigade, ----- strong, under General Gwyn; and the First Brigade, General Fred. Winthrop commanding, ----- strong. Both Generals Griffin and Ayres were officers of the regular artillery and graduates of West Point.
>
> Third. The Third Division, which was 5,260 strong and commanded by Bvt. Maj. Gen. S.W. Crawford. It was composed of all the regiments that had belonged to the old First Army Corps prior to its consolidation with the Fifth. This division had been organized for General Crawford by General Meade's order, after the battle of the Weldon Railroad, where General Crawford's previous command suffered a heavy loss in prisoners. The three brigades

of this division were commanded—the First, ----- strong, by Colonel Kellogg; the Second, ----- strong, by General Baxter; the Third, ----- strong, by General Coulter.

The artillery of the corps consisted of two rifled-gun batteries of four guns each and three light 12-pounder batteries of four guns each, the whole under command of Bvt. Brig. Gen. C.S. Wainwright. The staff of the corps was full of experienced and educated officers: Col. H.C. Bankhead, inspector-general, and Maj. William T. Gentry, commissary of musters, were graduates of the Military Academy. Col. F.T. Locke, the adjutant-general, had held his position from the first organization of the corps in May 1862. Col. A.L. Thomas, chief quartermaster; Col. D.L. Smith, chief commissary; Dr. T.R. Spencer, medical director; Dr. Charles K. Winne, medical inspector; Captain Malbon, chief ambulance officer, and Capt. George B. Halsted, assistant adjutant-general, were all experienced and [of] unquestioned ability in their departments. Maj. E.B. Cope, my principal aide-de-camp, was a very skillful topographer, an indispensable officer in the column having the advance over a country like that we were upon. Capt. James W. Wadsworth, son of the lamented general, and Capt. Gordon Winslow, son of the lamented the Rev. Gordon Winslow, were my personal aides. Capt. W.H.H. Benyaurd, of the regular engineers, was detached from General Meade's staff to accompany me, and gave most important assistance. Major Van Brocklin, of the Engineer Brigade, with a light pontoon train of canvas boats, also accompanied me. Captain Horrell commanded my escort of about forty mounted men, which constituted the cavalry of the corps.

The map which we possessed of the country into which the Fifth Corps was about to operate, was what was known as the Dinwiddie County map, prepared many years ago, and republished for our use on a scale of one inch to the mile. It gave no topography except the main streams and main roads. The names of the occupants of the houses did not now all correspond to those on the map; some of them, too, had disappeared, and others had been erected in places not noted. The map contained no distinction of the forest and clearings or swamps, all of which have ever played a most important part in the Virginia campaigns. I give a copy of the map with which we set out and one on the same scale of the country as we found it.

The country in which we were to operate was of the forest kind common to Virginia, being well watered by swampy streams. The surface is level and the soil clayey or sandy, and, where these mix together, like quicksand. The soil, after the frosts of winter first leave it, is very light and soft, and hoofs and wheels find but little support.

The following extracts are from the order for the general movement directed by General Meade, dated March 27, but received by me during the afternoon of the 28th:

> The following movements of the corps of this army are ordered:
>
> 1. At 3 a.m. of the 29th instant the Fifth Army Corps, Major-General Warren commanding, will move to the crossing of Hatcher's Run at W. Perkins' house; thence west to the junction of the old stage road and the Vaughan road, and *from* this point will open communication with the Second Corps on the Vaughan road. This accomplished, the Fifth Corps will be moved to occupy a position in the vicinity of Dinwiddie Court-House.
>
> ***
>
> 8. The chief engineer Army of the Potomac will detail a pontoon train of about 100 feet of bridge to accompany the Fifth Corps to Hatcher's Run.
>
> ***
>
> 10. Each corps will be prepared to move with five four-gun batteries—three smooth-bore and two rifled.

On the receipt of the above the following order was prepared and issued by me:

HEADQUARTERS FIFTH ARMY CORPS,
March 28, 1865.

GENERAL ORDERS, No. 22

The following will be the order of march to-morrow:

1. At 3 a.m. General Ayres, with his division, will cross Arthur's Swamp; proceed south, via the

Goshen house and B.W. Kelly's, to the stage road; thence along the stage road to the crossing of Rowanty Creek and seize the crossing. General Ayres will be followed immediately by the pontoon train, and that by two batteries of artillery, all under the orders of General Ayres. The part that does not cross until after the bridge is laid will mass and park. As soon as the crossing is gained a double bridge will be laid, and General Ayres will proceed (as soon as the two batteries can cross) to the junction of the stage road with the Vaughan road, at Miss Hargrave's, keeping the column stretched out on the road after crossing, so as to lose no time in so doing.

2. General Ayres' batteries will be immediately followed by General Griffin's division.

3. The remaining artillery and intrenching tools will follow General Griffin.

4. General Crawford will follow the artillery.

5. The train designated to accompany the troops and the bridge train not already in use will follow General Crawford's division, and with these will be sent all the pack animals and servants, and they will not be allowed to accompany the troops.

6. The command in this order will proceed as rapidly as possible, via J. Hargrave's and J. Kidd's, to Dinwiddie Court-House, promptly attacking the enemy if found opposing the advance, and keeping well closed up to the front. The troops must by all means be kept in the ranks of their respective companies, and any man may be justifiably shot who leaves without permission from division commander.

7. Headquarters of the corps will be with the advance division.

8. The trains authorized to accompany the corps across Rowanty Creek are—one medical wagon; one army wagon, with hospital supplies to each brigade; one army wagon with forage for each division; ambulance train (one-half the ambulances); ammunition wagons sufficient to carry twenty rounds per man; one wagon for each brigade for sales to officers; forage for one day must be carried in the spring wagons or on the horses.

9. The remaining wagons will be parked under the direction of the corps quartermaster near W. Perkins', and after the day's operations are completed, on application at corps headquarters, other supplies can be brought up at night if needed.

10. As a battle is expected the command must be as little encumbered as possible and prepared for action so that nothing will have to be sent to the rear when the fighting begins.

11. The musicians will be left in camp to sound reveille as usual, not at the hour of march, but as sounded under ordinary circumstances. Commanders are requested to give the matter their particular attention. After the usual hour of reveille has been sounded the musicians can join their respective commands.

By command of Major-General Warren:

FRED T. LOCKE,
Brevet Colonel and Assistant Adjutant-General.

After the above order was issued the following was received from General Meade's adjutant-general:

[Extract.]

2. Major-General Warren will move at the hour designated, but will not proceed beyond the junction of the Vaughan and Quaker roads till notified that Major-General Humphreys is in position, or nearly so. On being so notified Major-General Warren will advance on the Boydton plank road, taking position with his right in connection with General Humphreys and reserving sufficient force to refuse and guard his left. Major-General Warren will also advance skirmishers, well supported; and in case the enemy is found outside his works attack and endeavor to force him back to them. Corps commanders are notified the cavalry will be occupied on the left of the Fifth Corps.

About 8.25 p.m. March 28 I also received the following dispatch from General Meade's chief of staff:

General Humphreys is not certain that he can reach the Quaker road. He is instructed to place his right within supporting distance of General Ord and to form his line and determine his left by his formation of his corps. He is informed that you will probably move up the Quaker road to connect with his left after being informed of his position.

It will be noticed that these two dispatches differ about the road I was to move upon—the one saying the Boydton road, and the other the probability of the Quaker road. As General Humphreys was not to move till 9 a.m. it was obvious that, unless I was greatly impeded by the enemy, I should reach the junction of the Vaughan and Quaker roads much in advance of his getting into position, so as "to determine his left." I should therefore have to take up a position while waiting his movements. From my previous acquaintance with this locality, gained in the movement made in February, I knew that to get a good position for my troops I should have to extend my left to include a high ridge at H. Hargrave's. This would place me within half a mile of the Boydton road should I be directed ultimately to move out on that road, and leave the remainder of my force near the junction of the Vaughan and Quaker roads, so as to move up the latter if required to. In obedience to the orders the head of the column (General Ayres' division) moved out precisely at 3 a.m. The excitement of moving and the necessary preparations kept almost everyone from sleeping any of the preceding portion of the night.

At 4.45 a.m. the head of the column reached the crossing of Rowanty Creek. A few shots were fired by the enemy's lookouts there, probably as an alarm signal, but no opposition was made to our crossing. The engineers speedily laid a canvas pontoon bridge, and meanwhile the troops were scrambling across on fallen trees and the wrecks of a former bridge. As soon as the bridge was passable for horses I passed over with my escort, and we again began to advance. For the first mile our progress was somewhat impeded by trees which the enemy had cut down, and which were removed as we went along. The roads were dry except in the swampy places.

At 8 a.m. the head of the column reached the junction of the Vaughan and stage roads. This information I communicated to General Humphreys, along the Vaughan road, by Captain Winslow and an escort of ten mounted men. I then went with the troops to superintend the taking up the position required, while awaiting the movement of General Humphreys. At 10.20 I received the following dispatch by Major Jay, written by General Webb at 8.45 a.m.:

> Major-General Meade directs you to move up the Quaker road to Gravelly Run crossing. By throwing out parties on your right you will be able to find General Humphreys in the direction of J. Slaughter's (the most northerly). He is feeling out in that direction.

To this I sent back by Major Jay the following reply:

> I have just received the dispatch by Major Jay. I think my skirmishers are out on the Quaker road as far as Gravelly Run. They had been ordered there, and I'll see that it is done. My command will be posted as follows: One brigade, with the trains, at the junction of the Vaughan and stage roads; two brigades at the crossing of the Quaker and Vaughan roads; a brigade up the Quaker road; one on the road leading to R. Boisseau; Griffin's division near Chapel, Scott, and Hargrave. Skirmish lines will be put well out, and as soon as things are in hand I will push out a force to R. Boisseau's on the plank road. Barringer's brigade, and perhaps a division of cavalry, passed down the Quaker road to Stony Creek yesterday. No enemy met; a few scouts seen.

At 12 m. I received the following from General Webb, written 11.20 a.m.:

> From your last dispatch the major-general commanding would infer that you did not understand his last order by Major Jay. Your disposition to cover your left flank and rear are approved, but this must not prevent your moving your corps up the Quaker road across Gravelly Run, and then facing north, with your right connecting with General Humphreys. This done, you can make disposition to cover your left, and you will cover and hold the plank road, if possible, with your corps.

I immediately ordered General Griffin's division up the Quaker road, and sent the following dispatch to General Webb, by Captain Emory, the bearer of the last dispatch received:

I did not understand till Captain Emory came that I was to move my corps up the Quaker road. My dispositions were preliminary to feeling out from my assigned position here. I have sent my escort out toward R. Boisseau, and they have not yet returned. General Griffin's division is now moving up the Quaker road, as directed and I will send Crawford after him and dispose of the troops according to developments and as directed in the dispatch just received.

General Meade himself joined me at the junction of the Vaughan and Quaker roads, and we proceeded with the troops north to Gravelly Run. Here we found the bridge broken, and the stream too deep to be easily forded. The skirmish line, however, got over and engaged a small force of the enemy trying to stop our advance, but they were speedily driven back and followed up.

The pioneers of General Griffin's division commenced at once to construct a bridge, which, in the usual time, they rendered practicable, though somewhat difficult for artillery.

During the afternoon Major Van Brocklin added here a pontoon bridge. The north bank of Gravelly Run presented an excellent position for the enemy to dispute the advance up the Quaker road, and breast works had been thrown up for that purpose. But had they been occupied in force possession of them could have been gained by a flank and rear attack by the Second Corps, a division of which might have soon been disposed for that purpose.

My advance, soon after crossing Gravelly Run, passed the left flank of the Second Corps, which, moving up in extended line through difficult woods, did so more slowly. The resistance of the enemy gradually increased till, in the vicinity of Wilson's and Arnold's old saw mill, between 3 and 4 p.m. his line of battle was met, and a sanguinary encounter took place. The road was found seriously obstructed with fallen trees, but the pioneers labored with energy and a way was soon cleared, and a 12-pounder battery was brought up and opened on the enemy.

Captain Horrell, commanding my escort, was sent out on the road which leaves the Quaker road one mile north of Gravelly Run and goes to the plank road, and engaged the skirmishers on the enemy's right, and General Crawford was ordered to form behind Captain Horrell's skirmishers and on General Griffin's left.

The fire of General Griffin's division was, however, so effective that the enemy gave way in his front, and the enemy fell back everywhere on his line, leaving about 100 prisoners and the dead and wounded in our hands. Our loss was about 370 killed and wounded; among the former was the lamented Major Maceuen, of the One hundred and ninety-eighth Pennsylvania Volunteers. The brave General Chamberlain, of Maine, was slightly wounded and his clothes quite riddled with bullets; General Sickel, of Pennsylvania, was also wounded. At the time of writing this, I have not received General Griffin's report. I, however, quote the following from General Chamberlain's report of First Brigade, First Division:

On reaching Gravelly Run Major-General Griffin directed me to form my brigade in order of battle and advance against some works which were in sight on the opposite bank. Crossing the run, I sent Maj. E.A. Glenn, commanding second battalion of the One hundred and ninety-eighth Pennsylvania Volunteers, forward with his command as skirmishers, and formed my lines, with Bvt. Brig. Gen. H.G. Sickel, One hundred and ninety-eighth Pennsylvania Volunteers, on the right, and Col. G. Snipes, One hundred and eighty-fifth New York, on the left of the road. Major Glenn pushed forward vigorously and drove the enemy's skirmishers out of their works without any difficulty, and succeeded in pushing them through the woods and as far as the Lewis house. The enemy making considerable show of force in the edge of wood beyond, I halted Major Glenn and brought my line of battle up to supporting distance. Here I was directed to halt. In a short time I was ordered by General Griffin to resume the advance. There being at that time no firing of any consequence on the skirmish line I brought my line of battle up to that point, reformed it on the buildings, reenforced the skirmishers by a company from the One hundred and eighty-fifth New York, and commenced a rapid advance with my whole command. The skirmishers reached the edge of the woods before the firing became at all severe. I was exceedingly anxious that the troops should gain the cover of the woods before receiving the shock of the fire, but the obstacles to be overcome were so great that this could not be fully accomplished, and my men were obliged to gain the woods against a heavy fire. They advanced, however, with great steadiness and drove the enemy from their position and far into the woods. It was not long, however, before another attack was made upon us, evidently by a greatly superior force, and we became completely enveloped in a withering fire. We replied with spirit and persistency, holding our ground, taking rather the defensive at this stage of the action. In the course of half an hour my left became so heavily pressed that it gradually gave way, and at last was fairly turned, and driven entirely out of the woods to a direction parallel with the road by which we advanced. This position could not be held ten minutes, and nothing but the most active exertions of field and staff officers kept the men where they were, the fire all the time being very severe. At this moment I sent a request for General Gregory, commanding Second Brigade, on my left, to attack the enemy in flank in their newly gained position. I was assured by Major-General Griffin, who was on the line, that if we could hold on five minutes he could bring up the artillery. Upon this I succeeded in rallying the men, and they once more gained the woods. Battery B of the Fourth U.S. Artillery now came into position and opened a most effective fire. By this assistance we held the line until the enemy fell heavily upon our right and center, and my men being by this time out of ammunition, many of them absolutely without a cartridge, began to yield ground. Seeing that this was inevitable I dispatched an aide to General Gregory asking him for a regiment, and at the same time Major-General Griffin ordered up three regiments of the Third Brigade. These regiments came promptly to our assistance. I was at that moment endeavoring to reform my broken line, so as, at all events, to cover the artillery. The line was falling back in front of the Lewis house when Lieutenant-Colonel Doolittle, of the One hundred and eighty-eighth New York, came up, gallantly leading his regiment, as also Colonel Partridge, Sixteenth Michigan; the One hundred and fifty-fifth Pennsylvania and First Michigan came on in the most handsome manner, passing to my front, Brevet Brigadier-General Pearson, of the One hundred and fifty-fifth, grasping his colors and dashing straight against the enemy's line. This assistance and the admirable service of the artillery compelled the enemy to abandon their position; otherwise I must have been driven entirely from the field.

This action lasted nearly two hours before any support reached us. I need not speak of the severity of the engagement, nor of the conduct of my officers and men, inasmuch as it was all under the eye and direction of the major-general commanding, who shared the dangers, as well as the responsibilities, of that field; but I may be permitted to mention the fact that more than 400 of my men and 18 officers killed and wounded marked our line with too painful destructiveness. Nor can I fail to speak of the steadfast coolness and courage of Brevet Brigadier-General Sickel, whose example and conduct made my efforts needless on that part of the line, until he was borne from the field severely wounded; the unflinching tenacity of Colonel Sniper at his perilous post, and the desperate bravery with which he rallied his men, seizing his colors after it had fallen from the hands of three color-bearers and a captain, and bearing it into the very ranks of the enemy; the fiery courage of Major Glenn, which could scarcely be restrained; and of the heroic spirit of Major Maceuen, who fell dead foremost in the ranks of honor; nor shall I forget to name the young gentlemen of my staff—Lieutenants Walters and Vogel, my personal aides, both painfully wounded, but keeping the field to the last; Lieutenant Mitchell, my adjutant-general, and Lieutenant Fisher, pioneer officer—who rendered me essential aid in the hottest of the fire. Private Kelsey, my orderly, rode upon the enemy's line and captured, under my own eyes, an officer and five men, and brought them in. Remaining on the field that night and the next day, we buried our dead and 130 of the enemy's, and brought in the wounded of both parties.

General Griffin's skirmish line was advanced by my order as soon as the enemy gave way, myself accompanying it, and did not stop till it drew the fire of the enemy's artillery from breast-works about half a mile north of the junction of the Quaker road with the plank road to Boydton. This position of the enemy was then thought by us to be his main line. The One hundred and eighteenth Pennsylvania Volunteers drove the last of the enemy out of the position where the two roads join, but a farther advance could not be made across the large, open field, occupied as it was by the enemy on the farther side. The difficult woods through which General Humphreys' troops had to move prevented his left getting up to join with my right.

General Crawford's troops, on the left of General Griffin's, mistook the direction given them, so that neither got up into position till after dark. A farther advance against the enemy could not be made that night, and it was believed we had accomplished what was expected by our instructions.

In different dispatches to General Meade the above facts were reported.

In a dispatch from General Webb, written at 7 p.m. I had the gratification to find the following:

> The major-general commanding directs me to congratulate you and General Griffin upon your success to-day.

I communicated a copy of this to General Griffin, who was eminently deserving praise.

During the night I intrenched a brigade and two batteries at J. Stroud's, the most advanced position we had gained, and place General Crawford's division on and facing west from the plank road, his left resting on Gravelly Run, the plank road bridge over it having been destroyed by the enemy. General Ayres was held in reserve and to picket the rear, a measure rendered necessary for the security of our position and trains, which latter might be attacked by the enemy's cavalry (Barringer's) that had been reported to have passed south of us.

The following sketch shows the location of the Fifth Corps and the enemy on the night of March 29, 1865—scale one inch per mile. *[Sketch not provided]*

I give here the report of casualties in the Fifth Army Corps, March 29, 1865:

Command	Killed Officers	Killed Men	Wounded Officers	Wounded Men	Missing Officers	Missing Men	Total Officers	Total Men	Aggregate
Cavalry escort, headquarters Fifth Army Corp	—	—	—	3	—	—	—	3	3
Artillery	—	1	1	3	—	—	1	4	5
First Division	5	47	18	275	—	22	23	344	367
Second Division	—	—	—	—	—	—	—	—	—
Third Division	—	—	—	6	—	—	—	6	6
Total	5	48	19	287	—	22	24	357	381

During the evening of the 29th the following dispatch was received from General Meade's assistant adjutant-general—Colonel Ruggles:

> Major-General Warren will advance his line at 6 a.m. to-morrow, letting his right rest over and across the Quaker road and his left extending as far as is consistent with a due covering and guarding of his flank.
>
> Major-General Humphreys will at the same time advance his line, keeping his left connected with Major-General Warren and throwing his right forward as far as Crow's. The object of this movement is to force the enemy into his line of works and develop the same, and, if he is found out of his line, to give battle. Corps commanders will endeavor to have reserves suitably posted along their lines, and will render each other such mutual support as the exigencies of the hour may demand.

This was succeeded by the following from General Webb, chief of staff, written at 9.20 p.m. received at 11 p.m.

> The major-general commanding directs me to state that from your dispatch he infers that the main points of the order now sent to you have been practically carried out by General Griffin. You will, however, determine this definitely in the morning, and the enemy being driven within his works, you will extend your line to the left and will determine the position of his works. General Humphreys will push on, and will do the same in his front. You will develop to your left as far as possible consistent with the instructions to protect your flank.

In accordance with the above I issued the following order at 11.20 p.m.:

> Division commanders will hold their commands in readiness at 6 a.m. to-morrow either to advance upon the enemy or to repel any attempt upon his part. The order is to advance.

It began to rain during the night, and continued on throughout the 30th, sometimes falling heavily. This made the roads and fields almost impracticable for artillery and filled the swamps with water. Heavy details had to be sent back to assist the trains, which were nearly immovable in the mud.

At 5.50 a.m. I sent the following to General Webb:

> I have my command all in readiness, but my advance is so far ahead of General Humphreys and in sight of the enemy across the open ground that I do not think it advisable to attempt anything more northward until General Humphreys gets into position on my right. My left, on the plank road, cannot be extended with propriety till I can get some idea of General Sheridan's movement, and now rests on Gravelly Run, and, if I move, it will be in the air. I believe I am now in the best position I can be, unless an assault is intended on the enemy's lines near the Quaker road. I cannot move forward, and it does not appear a favorable place in front of Griffin.

At 6 a.m. I sent the following to General Humphreys, commanding Second Corps:

> I do not think it best to advance any farther till General Miles gets up in position on my right, which, as the woods are difficult, will take some time. A broad, open field is in my front, with the enemy in force last night on the opposite side. Will you let me know as soon as your line is established as near the enemy's line as may be without assaulting it.

To this I received the following reply from General Humphreys:

> Your dispatch of 6 a.m. is just received. My Third and Second Divisions are moving, but through a dense and most impenetrable swamp, and their progress is necessarily slow. General Miles has orders to keep moving, keeping his connection with you. I have just repeated these orders to him.

At 6 a.m. I also sent the following order to General Griffin, commanding First Division:

> Have General Bartlett's skirmish line feel the enemy in his front and ascertain if they are in the same position as last night, if he has not already determined it, and send me a report in writing.

At 7.30 a.m. I received the following from General Griffin:

> Since the fog has lifted a little I find the right of my skirmish line within 150 yards of a complete line of rifle-pits, now held in, as far as developed, the usual force for such a line. I have made a demonstration with my skirmish line, which is in the open field, and am satisfied the position will be hotly contested. I send a diagram of my lines and the lines of the enemy, with the supposed line of advance of the Second Corps. No connection has yet been made with me on my right or left, either by line of battle or skirmish line.
>
> Very respectfully, your obedient servant,
>
> Jos. J. Bartlett,
Brevet Major-General, Commanding Brigade.
>
> Since the above was written it has been reported that the Second Corps connects.
>
> Chas. Griffin,
Brevet Major-General

I then sent this to General Webb, chief of staff, with the following remarks:

> I send the above for your information. General Crawford is in force across a swamp on Griffin's left. We have a corporal from Johnson's division, captured this morning on the skirmish line. From the shape of the enemy's line I think there must be a considerable salient or bend near Dabney's Mill.

At this time my information was that the enemy held Dabney's Mill. At 8.30 a.m. I received the following dispatch from General Webb, written, probably, on the receipt of my dispatch to him of 5.50 a.m.:

> General Meade does not think you hold as much of the front line as the strength of your command would warrant. He desires to have you make use of both Crawford's and Ayres' to develop to the left. He cannot give you any more definite information of General Sheridan's movements than to state that he is ordered to attack or turn the enemy's right. You must act independently of Sheridan, and, protecting your flanks, extend to the left as far as possible. If the enemy comes out and turns your left you must attack him. You will be supported with all the available force to be procured.
>
> A. S. Webb,
Chief of Staff

Preparations were immediately made to carry out this order "to extend to the left as far as possible," and General Ayres' division was moved up to my most advanced position on the left, and reconnoitering parties were sent out to gain a knowledge of the country to my left. This dispatch placed me in much perplexity. I had already stated that I could not extend farther with safety to my remaining in position, and yet this dispatch required me to extend farther; and yet did not define how far, nor for what object. I had no desire but to comply with instructions; but leaving the limit of extension discretionary with me, while being dissatisfied with my use of this discretion and requiring me to extend father, and not saying how far nor what for, was most embarrassing. The fault of these unlimited extensions were inevitable exposure of the flanks. It was a system that, notwithstanding what we had suffered from it, the orders to the corps commanders constantly required, and the enemy were so aware of this prevailing plan that they constantly provided to attack the flank as soon as we had fairly exposed it, as we were required to do in closing upon the enemy's intrenchments. These intrenchments, from their artificial strength, enabled the enemy to hold with comparatively weak force, and to detach, notwithstanding his inferiority in numbers, a force to operate on our flank, where a blow could be given with even a small body.

Illustrations of the weakness of our lines from extension and of consequent disastrous swoops of the enemy upon them are numerous throughout the war. Our flanks could only be secure, either in moving into position or advancing to attack, by providing a heavy mass of troops at that always threatened point. If the enemy came out and turned my flank it was inevitable that I would have to receive his attack, provided I extended my lines "as far as possible." I therefore sent the following questions to General Webb, at 8.30 a.m.:

> I have just received your dispatch dated 7.50 a.m. If I extend my line to the left as far as "possible," using "both Crawford and Ayres," and "the enemy turns my left," what will I have to attack him with?

I would further remark here that in almost every instance orders from above me so disposed of my troops that they could not be kept together or moved together as General Grant's report says mine should have moved on the 31st.

At 9 a.m. I received the following dispatch from General Webb, written 8.40 a.m.:

> From deserters and prisoners we learn that the enemy's line runs along the White Oak Ridge road to Boydton plank road; then back on the road to Burgess' Mill, and then down Hatcher's Run. Humphreys has possession of Dabney's Mill. Their picket-line was a rifle-pit and easily taken.

At 9.20 a.m. I sent the following dispatch to General Webb:

> Your dispatch 8.40 a.m. (No. 3) just received. The information I have received is of the same effect as that you send me. Two deserters report the line immediately in front of General Griffin as what they think a strong one, with two lines of obstructions in front. They had a large number of negroes to work upon it yesterday. General Crawford is at present making a temporary line near the plank road on which we can reform in case of a reverse after advancing. I will then extend my left as far as practicable.

At 9.55 a.m. I received the following from General Webb, written 9.30 a.m.:

> General Meade directs that you send Colonel Walsh to his position at the junction of the old stage and Quaker roads, and direct him to report from that point to General Macy, provost-marshal-general. He is very anxious to have you cover as much of the front line as possible consistent with the safety of your command, and his idea was that you would put both Griffin and Crawford in front, keeping a portion of each as a reserve, and keeping Ayres to cover your left flank.

At 9.50 a.m. I sent the following to General Webb:

> Captain Gillespie has just come from General Sheridan's headquarters, at Dinwiddie Court-House, on his way to General Grant. He came up the Boydton plank road. When he left Dinwiddie Court-House one division of the cavalry was to move out on the road due north of Dinwiddie, and mass at Boisseau's, then feel out toward the White Oak road. General Sheridan remains at Dinwiddie with one other division, and the other division is upon Stony Creek, where the Vaughan road crosses. I shall soon send out General Ayres' division on a reconnaissance from Mrs. Butler's northwesterly toward S. Dabney's. He will be in position to develop the enemy's line, and where I can support him with General Crawford, and where he can co-operate with General Sheridan if he comes within reach.

At 10.15 a.m. I sent the following dispatch to General Webb:

> My idea of the way I should extend my line I have indicated in my dispatch of 9.50. Having my troops all well in hand I can move out Ayres in column to-day as I did Griffin yesterday, and if he meets the enemy give him battle. I can support him, if needed, with nearly the whole corps, and follow up any advantage gained, and if I am worsted I have a good place to reform on. This may seem a little slow, but it is the only way we can keep our troops working together and conduct operations with certainty. The amount of line I can occupy will depend upon the character of the country I develop. The roads and fields are getting too bad for artillery, and I do not believe General Sheridan can operate advantageously. If General Humphreys is able to straighten out his line between my right and the vicinity of the Crow house, he will hold it in pretty strong force, but the woods are so bad they alone will keep him nearly all day finding out how matters stand. The order about the cavalry reporting to General Macy has been sent out.

Having made all the necessary preparation at 10.30 a.m. I sent the following order to General Ayres by Major Cope:

> I wish you would take your division (with a battery of artillery, if you think it practicable), and move out on a reconnaissance northwest from Mrs. Butler's, or as near that direction as may be practicable, keeping with your own men a connection with our present picket-line, which must remain as it is. Major Cope, of my staff, will accompany you. If within a mile beyond the plank road you find any enemy drive him back, but do not advance your main force farther than that, unless to procure some obvious advantage gained, till you report to me the result. With your main body thus in good position, protecting your own flanks, advance your skirmishers out as far as prudent to reconnoiter and develop the character of the country and the enemy's position. A portion of my escort will accompany you. General Merritt's cavalry division is massed at J. Boisseau's, and are feeling on the road north from that toward the White Oak road. If you become engaged with a superior force, and can hold on, I will re-enforce you with Crawford's division as soon as called for.

At 11.15 a.m. the following dispatch was also sent to General Griffin by Colonel Locke, my adjutant-general:

> The major-general commanding wishes you to swing around on the left as General Ayres moves out.

At 11.20 a.m. I received the following dispatch from General Humphreys:

> My line of battle now extends in a straight line past the Crow house to your right. I have ordered the skirmishers of the two divisions and those on the right of Miles' division to be advanced and get to Hatcher's Run if they can. Please let me know if you are going to advance your skirmishers or line of battle, that I may have my movements conform to yours. The enemy's main line of works on the other side of Hatcher's Run is in view, the Crow house being 600 or 800 yards distant there.

To this I sent, at 11.20 a.m., the following reply:

> My position on the plank road at the junction of the Quaker road cannot be advanced any farther, the enemy being reported strongly intrenched. There may be a little portion of my extreme right, retired last night for want of connection, which can be thrown out if your line can be advanced. Any straightening out in that portion of the line that General Miles thinks practicable shall be done. I am about sending out a division from the plank road north northwest from Mrs. Butler's, to reconnoiter and drive back the enemy, and shall follow up any engagement that may take place outside of the enemy's line of works with nearly all the corps. Your line must now be very much shorter than it was when first taken up yesterday. Telegraph line is at my headquarters.

At 11.30 a.m. I sent the following to General Webb:

> General Ayres is now moving out to extend my line. If he meets more force within a mile than he can dispose of Crawford will go to his support, and I can also use a brigade from Griffin. If the enemy is outside of his line, or comes out, we shall have a considerable fight pretty soon.

At 12 a.m. I received the following dispatch from General Grant to General Meade, forwarded to me by General Webb:

> HEADQUARTERS ARMY OF THE POTOMAC,
> March 30, 1865.
>
> Major-General MEADE:
>
> My idea was that we should try to extend our left so as to cross to White Oak road, say at W.

Dabney's, or as near up to the enemy as we can. This would seem to cover all the roads up to Ford's road, by which Sheridan might then go and get on the South Side road, and possibly double up the enemy and drive him north of Hatcher's Run.

U.S. GRANT,
Lieutenant-General.

General WARREN:
This dispatch is forwarded to you for your information simply. Your dispatch has been received. The commanding general sees no reason for any change in his previous orders to you. He has no information of General Sheridan's movements beyond the general statement that General S. is to turn the enemy's right.

ALEX S. WEBB,
Brevet Major-General.

It did seem to me that on General Meade's receiving this dispatch he should have signified to me whether or not I was to extend my left so as to cross the White Oak road; if not, how far I should extend it; for in this latter case I should not be carrying out General Grant's expectations. Had I been in communication with General Grant I should certainly have solicited from him some definite information on this point. But General Meade so far differed in judgment with me that he did not think a movement for a specific object which might be impracticable did not require any modification of instructions, arriving at no apparent consummation. It seemed to me all the difference imaginable. I therefore, at 12 a.m., addressed the following dispatch to General Webb:

> I received your dispatch inclosing one from General Grant, in which you say "the commanding general sees no reason to change his previous orders." Your instructions have never said definitely how far I was expected to extend, nor the object desired. General Grant's is definite on both points, and if I am to attempt that myself at all hazards I don't shrink from it. General Humphreys can, perhaps, extend farther to the left, if required. Common experience requires that I should extend my left toward the White Oak road with strong force and precaution against an attack from the enemy. I am very glad to know the object and extent of my farther movement to the left. I have seen General Sheridan. He has ordered a division to move north to the White Oak road, which greatly simplifies my movement.

The receiving of dispatches and giving necessary orders had kept me almost continuously engaged at my headquarters so that I had had no opportunity to examine the condition of affairs personally along my front.

I now went up the Quaker road to where General Griffin's advance was, and arrived there just as his skirmish line was advancing, that of the enemy having fallen back. What this act on their part was due to I am not aware of, but think it probable that the advance of General Humphreys' skirmish line some distance to my right had made the position of those in front of General Griffin untenable. Finding by personal examination that our line of battle could be now advanced across the open field to a good position, and also open the direct road to Dabney's Mill, it was directed to move forward. General Miles' division, of the Second Corps, also moved forward, connecting with my right. During this movement the enemy opened with artillery from some breast-works near the Burgess house. It was for some time uncertain whether this was on the north or south side of Hatcher's Run, but reconnaissances which we made and prisoners taken showed it to be at the junction of the plank road with the White Oak road.

I went out on our picket-line, after it had been advanced, to see the enemy's breast-works, and found these were well located and constructed, and defended by infantry and artillery, wherever the trees enabled us to see them. The timber had been well slashed to give effect to their fire, and where the fallen trees did not obstruct the ground abatis had been laid. It rained very hard during these operations.

While occupied in the above manner, I sent, at 12.40 p.m. the following:

> I have just received notice from General Humphreys that deserters inform him that Heth's and Wilcox's divisions left Petersburg this morning, and are now in the lines this side of Hatcher's

Run. P.S.—Prisoners just captured (four of them) in front of First Division picket-line report that they understood that two of the divisions that came down were Heth's and Pickett's.

About 1.20 p.m. I received the following dispatch from General Webb, written at 1 p.m.:

> In view of the information received from the cavalry, and of the state of the weather, General Meade directs me to state you are not to shorten any line you may have developed, but you will push that well up to the enemy, and, having intrenched, you will await orders. Your dispatch of 12.40 is received.

At 1.20 p.m. I received from General Webb the following from Col. E.S. Parker, on Lieutenant-General Grant's staff, written 12.45 p.m.:

> The lieutenant just in from General Merritt's with dispatches from Sheridan. Merritt says that the reconnaissance sent out from near Boisseau's encountered the enemy in considerable force. They went to about two miles of the Five Forks; found the enemy occupying the road. Those going north proceeded to about a mile of the White Oak road, and found the road also occupied by the enemy. Nearly all the forces met these cavalry. All the roads leading toward the White Oak road are covered by the enemy. No engagement reported.

At 2.30 p.m. I sent the following report to General Webb—the first paragraph relating to General Griffin's front; the latter, to General Ayres, from whom I had just heard:

> I have advanced my line of battle to cover the junction of the Dabney Mill road with the plank road, and made a heavy advance with my skirmishers. The enemy opened with artillery from a fort near Burgess' Tavern, and also from a point near T. Pentecoast's. General Ayres' advance is near S. Dabney's, meeting that far with no opposition. From his advanced point he saw infantry moving west on the White Oak road. Soon as our attack began near the plank road there was a movement of their troops back toward Burgess' Mill. The reports about their late movements are a little uncertain. I have received the report of General Merritt's operations. His skirmishers could be heard due west from J. Stroud's.

At 3.15 p.m. I sent the following to General Webb:

> We have captured one officer of Pickett's division near S. Dabney's. He was in charge of a guard to the train that was passing west. I was mistaken about Griffin's firing causing these troops to return; they have all gone on. Cannot General Humphreys extend a little more to the left, and let me have Griffin's division to move out with, as well as Ayres and Crawford? I am already advanced as far as I think it would be prudent to take up a continuous line. The cavalry skirmishing is now heard southwest from Dabney's.

At 4 p.m. I again addressed General Webb on the same subject, as follows:

> General Ayres' advance now sees the White Oak road near W. Dabney's for three-quarters of a mile. There is a difficult swamp between the plank road and that place. I have now a continuous intrenched line from my right across Griffin's front, and along the plank road nearly down to Gravelly Run. If General Humphreys can take charge of Griffin's front, about 500 yards west of plank road, with the return down it, I can take my corps and block the White Oak road.

At about 4.30 p.m. the enemy made an advance against General Griffin's skirmishers, and forced them back on Griffin's left; but his attack was not made in much force, and was quickly driven back, and we took a few prisoners. This was probably a mere reconnaissance by the enemy to ascertain our position. The prisoners taken were perfectly raw, drafted men from North Carolina.

At 4.50 p.m. I sent the following to General Webb:

> A portion of Wilcox's division made a demonstration against Griffin about twenty minutes ago, and were easily driven back into their lines. We took a few prisoners—broken-down men lately forced into the service. They don't know much, but think Johnson's division moved to their right when they came down this morning. General Heth is here, but they do not think his division is. They think Heth commands the corps, and Hill all the defenses south of the James.

When the above was received by General Webb, he, at 7.20 p.m. sent the following, which I received at 7.30 p.m.:

> Your dispatch dated 5 p.m. has just been received. Please find out and telegraph, if possible, what brigades of Wilcox's are in your front. What grounds have those men for thinking more of his brigades than their own are there?

At 8.15, having obtained full information, I sent the following in answer to the above:

> General Griffin has taken no prisoners to-day, except from Scales' brigade. One of them, Thirty-fourth North Carolina, states his brigade was led by Major Norman [Norment]. There are four brigades in Wilcox's division, commanded by General Scales, Colonels Howe [Hyman], Gallaway, and Stowe. They left the works in front of our signal tower at 3 o'clock this morning. Thinks all the brigades of his division were present to-day, but is not sure. General Wilcox is absent on leave.

I have quoted the last two dispatches out of the order of time, so that they may all appear here together, relating to the same subject.

While still with General Griffin's division, I, at about 5.30 p.m. received the following copy of a dispatch from Lieutenant-General Grant to General Meade; the hour it was written not stated:

> GRAVELLY CREEK, March 30, 1865.
>
> Major-General MEADE:
> General Merritt met the enemy's cavalry at J. Boisseau's and drove him on the right and left roads, and pushed on himself, driving the enemy, and now occupies the White Oak road at Five Forks, and also where the right-hand branch intersects it. Merritt lost 150 men wounded.
>
> U.S. GRANT,
> Lieutenant-General.

Having given General Griffin instructions to endeavor to find out everything possible in his front, and to make a dash with his skirmishers and their supports, and try to develop any weak points of the enemy, so that we might be prepared for any order during the night to make a grand assault at daybreak, I set out personally to visit the advance position of General Ayres in the daylight that yet remained. I found that he had been unable with propriety to move his artillery and headquarters farther than the swampy branch of Gravelly Run, as this stream was flooded and difficult to cross; that the ground was very soft and muddy, and the road along which his advance was made was nearly all the way through woods, affording but little chance for observation; that his picket-line was advanced nearly up to the White Oak road; and that no opposition had compelled them to stop short of it. I then gave directions to the officer in charge of the pickets to have them advanced at sunset, and then rode back to my headquarters, which I reached some time after dark.

The only casualties reported to-day were 3 men killed and 9 wounded in the First Division, and 1 man killed in the artillery—a total of 13.

The following sketch shows the location of the troops at the close of the day, March 30, 1865: *[Sketch not provided]*

The whereabouts of Pickett's division that we had seen to pass along the White Oak road going west was explained by the following:

At 11 p.m. I received the following dispatches by telegraph from General Webb:

> The accompanying dispatch from Major-General Sheridan is sent to you for your information. In consequence of the state of affairs here reported, it will be necessary General Ayres should be put on his guard, and that he should be re-enforced without delay, as the enemy may attack him at daylight. As General Humphreys will hold the right and relieve General Griffin, it is presumed that Crawford can be sent to Ayres' support, if not there now. Acknowledge receipt of this.

The following at the same time:

> General Humphreys has been ordered to relieve General Griffin with General Miles and one brigade of General Mott's division—in all, 10,000 men—and is directed to hold the plank road and General Griffin's line. Griffin relieved, you will support General Ayres in his position, and strengthen yourself at this point. You will hold your corps ready to attack and await further orders.

The following is the dispatch from General Sheridan:

> CAVALRY DIVISION, March 30, 1865—7 p.m.
>
> Lieutenant-General GRANT:
> Pickett's division is developed along the White Oak road, its right at Five Forks, and extending

toward Petersburg. After the small force at Five Forks was driven back, no attempt was made to follow up, and the enemy did not appear to be in strong force there. Pickett's division is on the White Oak road, his right extending as far as Five Forks. Prisoners report the enemy's cavalry concentrated at Five Forks. I have, however, no positive information of this. General Merritt pickets nearly up to the White Oak road, and is encamped at J. Boisseau's house.

P. SHERIDAN,
Major-General

About 11 p.m. I also received the following dispatch from General Griffin:

> I regret to say that I have been unable to form any definite opinion as to the practicability of an assault upon the enemy's works. My skirmish line was unable to press forward, as they encountered a skirmish line of the enemy in superior numbers, and to-morrow things may be changed.

At 11 p.m. I informed General Webb of the contents of General Griffin's dispatch in the following, which also acknowledged the receipt of his dispatch, as requested:

> Your dispatch referring to General Ayres being re-enforced and dispatch of General Sheridan's received. General Griffin reports that he has been unable to form any definite opinion as to the practicability of making an assault.

Colonel Locke, my adjutant-general, at 11 p.m. March 30, issued the following order:

> General Ayres will re-enforce his advance at daylight to-morrow morning with his whole division. General Crawford will hold his command ready to follow General Ayres. General Griffin, as soon as relieved by General Humphreys' troops, will move down the Boydton plank road to where General Ayres now is.

It will be seen now that General Crawford was still in position on the Boydton plank road, as I had wished to use him where necessity might require, either to the right or left. The point at which General Ayres' headquarters were was the point designated for Griffin's division. I directed the advance of General Ayres to be re-enforced at daybreak, as it could not well be done in the night without a great consumption of time and loss of rest to the men; and, beside, that, on account of the darkness and bad road, and want of knowledge of the position, the troops would not be in as good order to meet an attack at daybreak as if fresh and moving up to the point. No attack at daybreak was made by the enemy, nor any attack ordered for me to make, as intimated might be in General Webb's dispatch of 11 p.m.

At 12.10 a.m. the following dispatch was received from General Webb, time of writing not given:

> General Griffin will be relieved as soon as possible. General Humphreys will be instructed to report to you when the division starts.

And at the same time the following from General Humphreys:

> I am directed to relieve General Griffin with Miles' division, and take up the line now held by Griffin, and take up the return on Boydton plank road. I am to send a brigade from Mott's division to support the left of the line after Griffin leaves. I have given the necessary orders to carry this out as soon as possible. Can you send me some description of the position held by Griffin, indicated in the instructions I have received, as above stated?

To this last Colonel Locke, adjutant-general, sent the following reply, at 12.25 a.m. March 31:

> In reply to your dispatch of 12 p.m. General Warren having retired, I have the power to state that General Griffin occupies a line of works from the left of your line on the Boydton plank road, running one-fourth of a mile west, then refused to the rear until it again strikes the plank road near the junction of the Quaker road, from thence south on the plank road a few hundred yards. The left of his picket line rests near a large branch of Gravelly Run.

At 6.10 a.m. March 31 the following dispatch was received from General Ayres, written at an hour not named:

> I have the honor to request that the line of pickets now extending to the Dabney house may be relieved by other troops as soon as my division takes up its new position. I would relieve them by other troops of this division, but those troops now on are so well tired out (having been on picket

at the last position on the Vaughan road) that I can't expect much service from them to-day, and the effective force of the division would thus be reduced.

The following directions were consequently sent at 7 a.m. to General Crawford:

> Withdraw all your pickets south of those established by General Ayres; then move with your whole division and mass it by a house occupied by a colored man; then replace General Ayres' pickets from left of General Humphreys up to a point north of negro house. Make your headquarters at that house. Leave the pioneers of two brigades to begin to make a bridge across the stream for the passage of artillery. Major Cope will go with you and assist you in carrying out this order.

Instructions were also sent to General Crawford to support General Ayres, and it was my intention to go in person to superintend operations at the point as soon as the giving and receiving instructions necessary for the operations of the day would permit. On this morning, as on the preceding one, the dispatches received and orders rendered thereby necessary to be issued retained me at the vicinity of the telegraph office till nearly 9 a.m.

At 7.35 a.m. the following dispatch was received from General Webb, per U.S. military telegraph, written at 7.30 a.m. March 31, 1865:

> Major-General WARREN:
> The general commanding desires you to report the position of your troops this a.m.

In answer to which the following was sent:

> General Griffin's troops will be massed near Mrs. Butler's; General Ayres' near S. Dabney's; General Crawford about half way between. They are along a wood road running from near Mrs. Butler's to W. Dabney's, on the White Oak road; it is not practicable now for wheels, and there is a very difficult branch of Gravelly Run that runs south from the White Oak Ridge, joining the main stream at the crossing of the plank road, which will take a long time to make practicable for wagons. I have all the pioneers I can spare to work on it. I will send you a sketch.

Finding myself still delayed in going to General Ayres position, the following dispatch was sent to him at 8.15 a.m. March 31:

> During the night I received a dispatch, of which the inclosed is a copy. I infer from that that the small force of General Merritt which gained the White Oak road fell back again a short distance. The point called Five Forks, alluded to, is on the White Oak road, about four miles due west from S. Dabney's. You must, therefore, have your dispositions made to look out for any force coming against your left flank from the west, as well as from the north. General Crawford is to mass at the negro house in a field which you passed on your way out, and Griffin is where you camped last night. I send you a tracing.

At 8.40 a.m. I received the following dispatch from General Webb, written 8.25 a.m.:

> There is firing along Humphreys' front. The major-general commanding desires you be ready to send your reserve, if it should be called for, to support Humphreys. There will be no movement of troops to-day.

To this I at once sent the following:

> Your dispatch of 8.25 is just received. There is a good deal of musketry firing going on in our lines by the men firing off their guns to put in fresh loads. Unless I break loose entirely from General Humphreys, I think the force he sent to relieve General Griffin is much more than under any circumstances could be needed there. My troops are, however, at all times as ready to move as it is possible to keep them for a long time. If the enemy break General Humphreys' line at any time, or threaten to do so, I shall not wait for orders to assist him if I can.

At 8.50 a.m. the following was received from General Humphreys, written 7.40 a.m.:

> Please let me know where your right will rest, that I may connect with you. General Miles has already relieved General Griffin, and I find a vacant space on his left.

At 8.55 a.m. the following order was received from General Meade's headquarters, and the necessary orders consequent upon it were given to the chief of artillery, chief quartermaster, and chief commissary:

> Owing to the weather no change will to-day be made in the present position of the troops. Three days' rations of subsistence and forage will be brought up and issued to the troops and the artillery,

and every one authorized to accompany them. The empty supply wagons will be sent to the rear, to be refilled at the railroad terminus. The chief engineer and corps commanders will use every exertion to make practicable the roads to the rear, and communicating with their several commands.

At 9 a.m. the following dispatch was sent to General Humphreys in reply to this:

> I send you a sketch of the country west of the plank road and a copy of my communication to General Webb as to my position. I cannot take up any regular line of battle on account of the woods and swamps, but have assembled each division at a point so they can fight in any direction with the line refused. I had a portion of Griffin and a battery stationed at Stroud's for support. I don't think your left could be turned, even if I moved away, without your having full information; but as my troops now are, I could move Griffin right upon your flank along with my artillery. I shall work hard all day to get the road through the woods in order.

At 9.40 a.m., from information received, I sent the following dispatch:

> General WEBB,
> Chief of Staff:
> I have just received report form General Ayres that the enemy have their pickets still this side of the White Oak road, so that their communication is continuous along it. I have sent out word to him to try and drive them off or develop with what force the road is held by them.
> This operation I deemed essentially necessary to the safety of our position, and only rendered the more so by the suspension of a further movement of troops, as this pause would give time to the enemy to gain a knowledge of our force and position. And in order that the troops might gain rest while operations were suspended a greater distance would be required between our picket-line and line of battle to give the latter time to fully get under arms so soon as any pressure of the advancing enemy showed itself at the advance posts. To prevent any relaxation of vigilance till our position should be made secure, I gave no notice to my command of the order suspending movements. General Webb on receiving the above-quoted dispatch sent me the following, written 10.30 a.m.:
> Your dispatch giving Ayres' position is received. General Meade directs that should you determine by your reconnaissance that you can get possession of and hold the White Oak road you are to do so, notwithstanding the order to suspend operations to-day.

The following sketch exhibits position of troops at this time, General Griffin being in position to support either my advance or the Second Corps as required: *[Sketch not provided]*

General Winthrop, with his brigade, of General Ayres' division, advanced about 10.30 a.m. and was repulsed, and simultaneously an attack which had been preparing against General Ayres was made by the enemy in heavy force, both from the north and west, and he was forced back. General Ayres and General Crawford did all that was in their power to stay the enemy. I hastened toward the point of attack, but on arriving near General Crawford's division it was also being forced back, and all our efforts to hold the men in the woods were unavailing. I am unable to give a more detailed account of this affair, not having reports of it from General Ayres and General Crawford. I then directed the formation of General Griffin's division along the branch of Gravelly Run, with Mink's battery on his right. General Crawford's and General Ayres' divisions formed behind and in this line, and many of them took part in the engagement there. There Colonel Sergeant, of the Two hundred and tenth Pennsylvania Volunteers, of Ayres' division, was mortally wounded.

Severe fighting at the creek now ensued and the advance of the enemy completely checked.

I had early in these occurrences sent word of them to General Humphreys, on my right. He at once ordered up General Miles' division on my right, and a brigade of this advanced gallantly against the enemy, but was at first driven back.

The temporary result of this attack by the enemy was such as different portions of our army had experienced on many former occasions in taking up new and extended lines, but our loss was not great, and was probably quite equaled by the enemy.

The prospect of fighting the enemy outside of his breast-works, instead of having to assail him behind his defenses and through his obstructions, was one sufficiently animating to our hopes to more than compensate for the partial reverse we had sustained, and preparations were at once instituted for an advance with the whole corps.

At 1 p.m. I made the following report to General Webb:

> General Ayres made an advance with a small force at 10 a.m., which the enemy drove back and followed up in heavy force, compelling both Ayres and Crawford to fall back on Griffin, and, of course, in much confusion. Griffin's troops held the enemy at the run, west of the plank road. General Miles' division (a brigade of it) afterward attacked the enemy and were forced back on my right. My skirmish line in front of Griffin (most of it) has advanced on my left. I am going to send forward a brigade, supported by all I can get of Crawford and Ayres, and attack, swinging on our right. Arrangements are being made for this, and it will take place about 1.45 p.m. if the enemy does not attack sooner.

Owing to some difficulties in crossing the run this advance, which was thus made with the whole corps available, took place a little after the time specified above.

General Humphreys' division, under General Miles, also advanced against the enemy about the same period on our right, but his movement was not made in close connection with mine. While my corps was moving the following dispatch, written 2.50 p.m. was received from General Webb:

> General WARREN:
>
> The following is received from General Humphreys:
> "From the prisoners taken it is apparent that the left of Pickett's division is opposite the center of Miles. An advance of the Fifth Corps, swinging round, must necessarily take Pickett on his right flank. Pickett is the right of their line.
>
> "A.A.H.,
> "Major-General."
>
> Since Miles is already well forward from your right flank the general commanding considers that that must be secure. Miles is ordered to take the enemy's works, supported by his own corps. You will see the necessity of moving as soon as possible.

This dispatch evidently implied a want of promptness in my movements, and yet my troops had been urged and moved as fast as possible. The information about Pickett's division was erroneous, and was worse than useless to me. According to subsequent information his division was at that time some three or four miles away driving General Sheridan. Nor did Miles assault the enemy's breast-works as the dispatch led me to infer he would. General Chamberlain's brigade led my advance, and finding the opposition less than we expected, General Crawford's division was brought to my right, so as to be in support there, as we approached the White Oak road, the direction of our movements being such as to present that flank first to the enemy's position along that road. I quote the following from General Chamberlain's report:

> I was desired by General Griffin to regain the field which these troops had yielded. My men forded a stream nearly waist deep, formed in two lines, Major Glenn having the advance, and pushed the enemy steadily before them. Major-General Ayres' division supported me on the left en echelon by brigade, the skirmishers of the First Division, in charge of General Pearson, in their front. We advanced in this way a mile or more into the edge of the field it was desired to retake. Up to this time we had been opposed by only a skirmish line, but quite a heavy fire now met us, and a line of battle could be plainly seen in the opposite edge of the woods, and in a line of breast-works in the open field, in force at least equal to our own. I was now ordered by Major-General Warren to halt and take the defensive. My first line had now gained a slight crest in the open field, where they were subjected to a severe fire from the works in front and from the woods on each flank. As it appeared that the enemy's position might be carried with no greater loss than it would cost us merely to hold our ground, and the men were eager to charge over the field, I reported this to General Griffin and received permission to renew the attack. My command was brought into line and put in motion. A severe oblique fire on my right, together with the artillery which now opened from the enemy's works, caused the One hundred and ninety-eighth to waver for a moment. I then requested General Gregory, who reported to me with his brigade, to move rapidly into the woods on our right by battalion en echelon by the left, so as to break this flank attack, and possibly to turn the enemy's left at the same moment that I should charge the works directly in front at a run. This plan was so handsomely executed by all that the result was completely successful. The woods and the works were carried, with several prisoners and one battle-flag, and the line advanced some 300 yards across the White Oak road.

My loss in this action was not more than 75, but it included some of my best officers and men.

It would be unjust not to mention the services of Major Glenn and Colonel Sniper in this affair, whose bravery and energy I relied upon for the successful execution of my plans. I would also express my obligations to General Gregory for his quick comprehension of my wishes, and for his efficient aid. I may be permitted also to mention the gallantry of Captain Fowler, assistant adjutant-general of division, who rode into the hottest fire to bring my orders, having his horse killed under him in doing so, and who by his conduct and bearing showed an example worthy of all praise.

During the night we buried our dead and cared for our wounded, and bivouacked in the line.

The temporary halt was necessitated by the threatening attitude the enemy's position exhibited, as above described by General Chamberlain, and in order to get the remainder of the corps up and well in hand for a weighty assault. This having been effected, the order to advance was given, with the result as described in the quotation from General Chamberlain's report.

At 3.40 p.m. I wrote from the White Oak [road] the following dispatch to General Webb:

> We have driven the enemy, I think, into his breast-works. The prisoners report General Lee here to-day, and also that their breast-works are filled with troops. We have prisoners from a portion of Pickett's and Johnson's divisions. General Chamberlain's brigade acted with much gallantry in this advance, capturing nearly the entire Fifty-sixth Virginia Regiment with its flag.

With the elation due to our success, I thought we might be able to carry the enemy's breast-works at once, and thus force in their right flank and carry all their line south of Hatcher's Run. I at once commenced a personal reconnaissance for this purpose, and superintended personally the advance of our skirmishers to gain points of observation. We thus drew a very severe fire from the line, particularly of artillery. The examination showed me that the enemy's defenses were as complete and as well located as any I had ever been opposed to. Thus far my operations had been quite independent of those of General Sheridan.

About 5 p.m. March 31 I received, while on the White Oak road, the following from General Webb, chief of staff, written 4.30 p.m.:

> Secure your position and protect as well as possible your left flank. Word has been sent to Sheridan, and it is believed that Sheridan is pushing up. General Humphreys will be ordered to push up and to connect with your right. You might, if you think it worthwhile, push a small force down the White Oak road and try to communicate with Sheridan, but they must take care and not fire into his advance.

The rattle of musketry could now be heard southwest from us, which seemed to us to be receding, and which led us to think the enemy was driving our cavalry. I then ordered General Griffin to send General Bartlett, with his brigade, directly across the country, so as to attack the enemy on the flank, and I sent Major Cope, of my staff, with him.

At 5.15 p.m. I received the following from General Webb, written 5.15 p.m. which directed what before had only been suggested:

> The major-general commanding directs that you push a brigade down the White Oak road, to open it for General Sheridan, and support the same, if necessary. The firing is so near that the general presumes that the command will not have far to go. The distance you will push out must depend on the circumstances of the movement and the support you can give them.

Thus at the time that to General Meade it seemed "the firing is so near" it plainly sounded to us more and more distant, indicating that our cavalry was falling back, of which I soon had confirmation.

At 5.50 p.m. I sent the following to General Webb:

> I have just seen an officer and a sergeant from General Sheridan's command who were cut off in an attack by the enemy and escaped. From what they say our cavalry was attacked about noon by

cavalry and infantry and rapidly driven back, two divisions—Crooks' and Devin's—being engaged. The firing seems to recede from me toward Dinwiddie Court-House. I have sent General Bartlett and my escort in that direction, but I think they cannot be in time. I hear cannonading that I think is from near Dinwiddie Court-House.

About 6.30 p.m. I received the following from General Webb:

> A staff officer of General Merritt has made a report that the enemy has penetrated between Sheridan's main command and your position. This is a portion of Pickett's division. Let the force ordered to move out the White Oak road move down the Boydton plank road as promptly as possible.

The force I had sent under General Bartlett had now been gone an hour, and to recall it would have required two hours at least for it to reach the Boydton plank road, and make it too late for use before dark. My artillery had all been left on the Boydton plank road on account of the mud, which had compelled me to do so, and General Griffin had left Brevet Brigadier-General Pearson there with three regiments of infantry of Brevet Major-General Bartlett's brigade to support it.

I therefore sent the following dispatch to General Webb at 6.30 p.m. which explains what I did:

> I have ordered General Pearson, with three regiments that are now on the plank road, right down toward Dinwiddie Court-House. I will let Bartlett work and report result, as it is too late to stop him.

It was then nearly dark. Having reconnoitered the enemy's breast-works on the White Oak road, I added the following concerning them to my dispatch of 6.30 p.m.:

> We can see the enemy's breast-works for two miles east along the White Oak road. If they are well manned they cannot be carried. I am within 200 yards of where they turn off northward from the White Oak road.

I then gave directions to secure the position we had gained, by intrenching, and proceeded with my staff back about two miles to the Boydton plank road, at which place I could communicate by telegraph with General Meade during the night. General Meade's headquarters were distant four miles and a half, near where the Vaughan road crosses Hatcher's Run; General Grant's were near Dabney's Mills, about four miles from me; General Sheridan's at Dinwiddie Court-House, distant five miles and a half, and separated from me by a stream not fordable for infantry, where it crossed the Boydton plank road, and the bridge broken down.

At 8 p.m. I received the following dispatch from General Meade, written 7.30 p.m.:

> Dispatch from General Sheridan says he was forced back to Dinwiddie Court-House by strong force of cavalry, supported by infantry. This leaves your rear and that of the Second Corps on the Boydton plank road open, and will require great vigilance on your part. If you have sent the brigade down the plank road it should not go farther than Gravelly Run, as I don't think it will render any service but to protect your rear.

General Pearson had been compelled to stop at Gravelly Run on account of the swollen stream and broken bridge.

At 8.20 p.m. I wrote to General Webb:

> I sent General Bartlett out on the road running from the White Oak road and left him there. He is nearly down to the crossing of Gravelly Run. This will prevent the enemy communicating by that road to-night. I have about two regiments and the artillery to hold the plank road toward Dinwiddie Court-House. It seems to me the enemy cannot remain between me and Dinwiddie Court-House if Sheridan keeps fighting them, and I believe they will have to fall back to the Five Forks. If I have to move to-night I shall leave a good many men who have lost their way. Does General Sheridan still hold Dinwiddie Court-House?

At 8.40 p.m. I received by telegraph the following from General Webb, marked "confidential," written 8.30 p.m.:

> The probability is that we will have to contract our lines to-night. You will be required to hold, if possible, the Boydton plank road, and to Gravelly Run; Humphreys and Ord along the run. Be prepared to do this at short notice.

I regretted exceedingly to see this step foreshadowed, for I feared it would have the morale of giving a failure to our whole movement, as similar orders had done on previous occasions. It would besides relieve the enemy in front of Sheridan from the threatening attitude my position gave me, and I therefore sent the following by telegraph, at 8.40 p.m. to General Webb:

> The line along the plank road is very strong. One division, with my artillery, I think can hold it if we are not threatened south of Gravelly Run east of the plank road. General Humphreys and my batteries, I think, could hold this securely, and let me move down and attack the enemy at Dinwiddie Court-House on one side and Sheridan on the other. On account of Bartlett's position they (the enemy) will have to make a considerable detour to re-enforce their troops at that point from the north. Unless General Sheridan has been too badly handled I think we have a chance for an open field fight that should be made use of.

The following sketch represents the position of the Fifth Corps at dark March 31, 1865:
[Sketch not provided]
The following is the report of casualties in Fifth Army Corps March 31, 1865:

Command	Killed Officers	Killed Men	Wounded Officers	Wounded Men	Missing Officers	Missing Men	Total Officers	Total Men	Aggregate
Cavalry escort	—	—	—	1	—	—	—	1	1
Artillery	—	1	—	6	—	—	—	7	7
First Division	2	21	7	143	—	5	9	169	178
Second Division	1	50	25	249	3	335	29	634	663
Third Division	1	50	20	360	3	124	24	534	558
Total	4	122	52	759	6	464	62	1,345	1,407

My desire to retain the position we had gained after so much hard fighting, and which I considered under the circumstances so advantageous to us, was not accomplished, and orders came to fall back.

At 9.17 p.m. I received the following by telegraph dispatch, written by General Webb at 9 p.m.:

> You will, by the direction of the major-general commanding, draw back at once to your position within the Boydton plank road. Send a division down to Dinwiddie Court-House to report to General Sheridan. This division will go down the Boydton plank road. Send Griffin's division. General Humphreys will hold to Mrs. Butler's.

Whereupon I issued with following order to my command, which was sent out 9.35 p.m.:

> I. General Ayres will immediately withdraw his division back to where it was massed yesterday, near the Boydton plank road.
> II. General Crawford will follow General Ayres, and mass his troops behind the intrenchments near Mrs. Butler's.
> III. General Griffin will immediately withdraw General Bartlett to his present position; then move back to the plank road and down to Dinwiddie Court-House, and report to General Sheridan.
> IV. Captain Horrell, with the escort, will remain where General Griffin's headquarters now are till daybreak, and then come back to the plank road, bringing in all stragglers.
> V. Division commanders in executing this movement, which is ordered by General Meade, will take care to see that none of their pickets or any portion of the troops are left behind.
> VI. General Ayres and General Crawford will have their troops under arms at daylight, and the chief of artillery will have all the batteries in readiness to move.

At 9.50 p.m. I received by telegraph the following from General Webb, written 9.20 p.m.:

> The division to be sent to Sheridan will start at once. You are to be held free to act within the Boydton plank road. General Humphreys will hold to the road and the return.

To this I immediately replied:

> Your dispatch of 9.20 is just received. I had already sent out my orders, of which I send you a copy. You directed General Griffin to be sent to General Sheridan at once. It will take so much time to get his command together that I withdrew the other divisions first, they being unengaged, but this will not retard General Griffin. The bridge is broken on the plank road, and will take I

hardly know how long to make practicable for infantry. I sent an officer (Captain Benyaurd, engineers) to examine it as soon as your first order was received. He now reports it not fordable for infantry. It requires a span of forty feet to complete the bridge, and the stream is too deep to ford. Nevertheless, I will use everything I can get to make it passable by the time General Griffin's division reaches it.

General Griffin's division, in addition to the delay of assembling General Bartlett's brigade, had to withdraw his picket-line in front of the enemy, and if he moved first, the others, pending it, had to relieve his picket-line.

The bridge over Gravelly Run we had found broken by the enemy on our occupation of the plank road on the 29th. As I was required to operate independently of the cavalry and protect my own flanks, it was desirable to me, being in my rear, as I forced the enemy on the White Oak road, that it should remain so. Even the dispatch this evening from General Meade, which I received at 8 p.m. (previously given), would have justified me in destroying it had it yet been standing intact.

I had no pontoons with me now. The supply with which I had started on the 29th had been used in bridging Rowanty Creek and the Quaker road crossing of Gravelly Run, and the boats and engineers were kept there for the service of the trains. I directed a house to be torn to pieces to supply materials. At 10.15 p.m. I received by telegraph the following dispatch from General Webb, written 9.40 p.m.:

> Since your dispatch of 8.20 p.m. the general commanding finds that it is impossible for Bartlett to join Griffin in time to move with any promptitude down the Boydton plank road. He therefore directs that you send another good brigade to join Griffin in the place of Bartlett's in this movement.

Sheridan was attacked by five brigades from Gordon's corps—three from Pickett's, possibly by two from Gordon's, one of them being Hoke's old brigade.

This dispatch showed that my previous one, giving the condition of the bridge at Gravelly Run, had not yet been received. I deemed it would show when it was that General Bartlett could join General Griffin before the bridge would be passable, and that Griffin could thus reach Sheridan as soon as anyone and require no change in my previous order, and while waiting the result of the reception of the knowledge of the state of the crossing by General Meade, I, at 10.50 p.m. received the following dispatch from him, written 10.15 p.m.:

> Send Griffin promptly as ordered by the Boydton plank road, and move the balance of your command by the road Bartlett is on and strike the enemy in rear, who is between him and Dinwiddie Court-House. General Sheridan reports his position as north of Dinwiddie Court-House, near Dr. Smith's, the enemy holding the crossroads at that point. Should the enemy turn on you your line of retreat will be by J.M. Brooks' and R. Boisseau's, on the Boydton plank road (see 1-inch map). You must be very prompt in this movement, and get the forks of the road at J.M. Brooks' before the enemy, so as to open to R. Boisseau's. The enemy will probably retire toward Five Forks, that being the direction of their main attack this day. Don't encumber yourself with anything that will impede your progress or prevent your moving in any direction. Let me know when Griffin starts and when you start.

This dispatch also showed that mine concerning the crossing of Gravelly Run was still not received. That I did not overestimate the effect of this dispatch when it should reach, is proved by General Meade's dispatch, written 11.45 p.m. It also showed complete ignorance of the position of the enemy along the road Bartlett is (was) on, for the enemy already held this road on the south side of Gravelly Run, and if not themselves at J.M. Brooks', occupied our approach to it. The condition of affairs here is given by Major Cope in his report, as follows:

> About 5 p.m. you directed me to lead General Bartlett's brigade, by a direct road, if possible, toward the sound of firing in the direction of Dinwiddie Court-House, and attack the enemy in the rear. I immediately reported to General Bartlett, who had his column put in motion. The left of the corps rested in open ground. We came out from the left and crossed this ground for half a mile, then we came to a small branch of Gravelly Run, on the edge of the timber. Here we found a wood road that ran in the right direction. We followed it one mile through this wood, over rolling ground, crossing three branches of Gravelly Run. At the south edge of this timber and in

open ground on a hill stands Doctor -----'s house, and here our skirmishers became engaged with the enemy's pickets. The ground slopes from here to Gravelly Run, and is open in front all the way down. The enemy, after considerable skirmishing, were driven down the slope and across the run, three-quarters of a mile from the house. The house is near a main road leading north from Dinwiddie Court-House to the White Oak road. General Bartlett established a line of pickets along Gravelly Run, crossing this road. He also kept vedettes out on his right watching this road and other approaches in the rear. It was much after dark when he had made the proper disposition of his troops, and then we began to turn our attention to the number and extent of the enemy's camp-fires. They seemed to stretch for miles on the south side of the run, and we could distinctly hear them chopping, moving wagons, and talking.

In addition to this the enemy held a point on the road Bartlett was on where it joins the White Oak road, as had been ascertained by Major Gentry, of my staff, while endeavoring to communicate with General Bartlett. The major lost his orderly by capture while he narrowly escaped himself.

It was now an hour and a half since my order had been sent withdrawing the divisions to the plank road, so that I supposed they were all moving back toward the plank road along the forest road, with its single bridge across the branch of Gravelly Run, and in the order of Ayres, Crawford, Griffin, with General Bartlett's brigade nearly rejoined to the latter. To prevent the confusion and delay that would occur by bringing General Griffin to the plank road and sending back General Ayres, one of which would have to leave the road for the other to pass, and to save the time that would be lost by each division in changing their relative places I determined to send General Ayres' division instead of General Griffin's, as it greatly simplified and expedited the operation and saved the men's strength, so sorely tried. It had besides the effect to prevent the separation of brigades from their proper divisions and keep each intact, a matter of importance.

As quickly as I could write it, I, at 11 p.m. issued the following order:

> I. General Ayres, instead of halting his command as directed in his last order (see mine of 9.35 p.m.), will proceed down the plank road to Dinwiddie Court-House and report to General Sheridan. He will send a staff officer to report here when the head of the column arrives.
> II. General Crawford and General Griffin will mass their divisions at the point where this order reaches them, and report their position by the officer that brings it. A change of plan makes this change of order necessary.

I note here, a little out of the order of time, that I did not learn the position of General Crawford and General Griffin till 1 a.m., and so difficult had it been to get the troops in motion on this intensely dark and stormy night that although this order from me was sent one hour and a half after the one for them to fall back to the plank road, yet it found them still in the same position.

It must be remembered that our troops, so near the enemy, could not be roused by drums and bugles and loud commands, but each order had to be communicated from each commander to his subordinate—from the general till it reached the non-commissioned officers, which latter could only arouse each man by shaking him. The obstacles to overcome in carrying out so many orders and changes of orders in the darkness of a stormy, starless night, when the moon had set, requires a statement of them in detail.

In order to comply with General Meade's first order I had first to send an officer to each division; then Major Cope was the only officer capable of taking an order to General Bartlett's brigade, and he was sent. I had sent Major Gentry to ascertain General Bartlett's position, but he, taking the White Oak road, found the enemy holding the junction of it with the one General Bartlett was on, and he failed, as before stated, to find a way to him.

I had to send another officer for the pioneers, and go with them at once to the crossing of Gravelly Run to make the bridge. I had to send another to the bridge itself to report the condition of the crossing. I had, with my full complement of staff officers, the following available, all the others being engaged in their appropriate departments: Colonel Bankhead, Major Gentry, Major Cope, Captain Banyaurd, Captain Wadsworth, and Captain Winslow.

Having, under these circumstances, made my dispositions to execute one order for a general movement promptly, it is easy to see what strait I would be placed in to countermand those orders before the officers sent out with the first orders returned. After I had sent the order last quoted, I informed General Meade what I had done, as follows:

> I issued my orders on General Webb's first dispatch to fall back, which made the divisions retire in the order they could most readily move in, viz, Ayres, Crawford, and Griffin. I cannot change them to-night without producing confusion that will render all my operations nugatory. I will now send General Ayres to General Sheridan, and take General Griffin and General Crawford to move against the enemy, as this last dispatch directs I should. Otherwise, I cannot accomplish the apparent objects of the orders I have received.

I proceeded to make the necessary orders and arrangements to move with the two divisions as soon as I could. The movement had to be made without artillery or ambulances or ammunition wagons, and instructions had to be given in the two latter cases for special provisions. The chief of artillery had to be informed and relations established between him and General Humphreys, commanding the Second Corps, whose troops were required to take my place along the plank road.

At twenty minutes past 12 I received the following from General Humphreys:

> I am directed to resume my position of this morning, etc., etc. At what time do you propose to move? I propose to move simultaneously with you.

To this I sent the following reply:

> I have just received your dispatch by Captain Wister. Under the order to withdraw at once (viz, that received at 9.17 p.m. I thought we each could do so individually, under cover of darkness, and so ordered. I have since received orders to attack the enemy with two divisions, sending one down the plank road to report to General Sheridan. My artillery, five four-gun batteries, under General Wainwright, will remain on the line of the plank road. I think the enemy that drove General Sheridan must withdraw to-night. I had a brigade on the road north from J. Boisseau's. I have now orders to move against the force that attacked Sheridan, and shall send all the force I have to move there, or wherever the firing of battle near us may indicate.

At 1 a.m. I received reports from my officers who had returned from carrying my orders of 11 p.m. and learned the position of Generals Crawford and Griffin.

At this time I received the following dispatch from General Meade, written by him at 11.45 p.m.:

> A dispatch, partially transmitted, is received, indicating the bridge over Gravelly Run is destroyed, and time will be required to rebuild it. If this is the case, would not time be gained by sending the troops by the Quaker road? Time is of the utmost importance. Sheridan cannot maintain himself at Dinwiddie without re-enforcements, and yours are the only ones that can be sent. Use every exertion to get troops to him as soon as possible. If necessary, send troops by both roads and give up the rear attack. If Sheridan is not re-enforced and compelled to fall back he will retire by the Vaughan road.

On receiving this dispatch showing so much solicitude for General Sheridan's position and the necessity of re-enforcing him directly, even if I had to countermand the previous order and forego entirely the rear attack, and which also left the question for me determine, I felt much anxiety about what to do. The night was far advanced. The distance to Dinwiddie Court-House by the Quaker road from the location of my troops was over ten miles. It was impossible for them to reach there by that road before 8 a.m. By that time they could be of no use in holding Dinwiddie Court-House.

In this case the most direct route for the rear attack would be down the plank road, where General Ayres was marching. This attack, too, would be then the most effective, as the whole corps would be together in making it, and all in communication with headquarters and General Sheridan, which might be of great importance. If General Sheridan retired by the Vaughan road the rear and right flank of General Humphreys would be left exposed, as stated in General Meade's dispatch, received by me 8 p.m. (already given here). To send the division around by the Quaker road was to break my command up in three pieces, and if it had been done it is doubtful if the success of the 1st of April would have been gained, as the men thus sent would have been too exhausted to reach the Five Forks that day. I therefore determined that it was best to abide the movements already begun, and keep the two division—Griffin's and Crawford's—where they were, till I could hear that General Ayres had certainly re-enforced General Sheridan. The men of the two divisions were gaining, while waiting the result, a little of that rest they stood so much in need of on this their fourth night of almost continual deprivation of it, and we had but a short distance to move before reaching the enemy near J. Boisseau's. Having determined this, at 1.20 a.m. I wrote the following dispatch to General Meade:

> I think we will have an infantry bridge over Gravelly Run sooner than I could send troops around by the Quaker road, but if I find any failure I will send that way. I have sent Captain Benyaurd (two hours ago) with what he thought was necessary to make it practicable in one hour, and trust to that. I am sending to General Sheridan my most available force.

At 2.05 a.m. I learned the following, which I sent General Webb:

> The bridge over Gravelly Run Captain Benyaurd reports now practicable for infantry, and General Ayres advancing across it toward Dinwiddie Court-House. I have given General Ayres orders to report to General Sheridan.

At 4.30 a.m. I received information that General Ayres had communicated with General Sheridan, and while I was just mounting to join Generals Griffin and Crawford, to move across the country against the enemy at J. Boisseau's, I received the following from General Sheridan at 4.50 a.m., which is published with his report, and there stated to be written at 3 a.m.:

> I am holding in front of Dinwiddie Court-House, on the road leading to Five Forks, for three-fourths of a mile, with General Custer's division. The enemy are in his immediate front, lying so as to cover the road just this side of the Adams house, which leads across Chamberlain's run or bed. I understand you have a division at J. Boisseau's; if so, you are in rear of the enemy's line and almost on his flank. I will hold on here. Possibly they may attack Custer at daylight; if so, have this division attack instantly and in full force. Attack at daylight anyway, and I will make an effort to get the road this side of Adams' house, and if I do you can capture the whole of them. Any force moving down the road I am holding, or on the White Oak road, will be in the enemy's rear, and in all probability get any force that may escape you by a flank attack. Do not fear my leaving here. If the enemy remain I shall fight at daylight.

This supposititious state of affairs given above promised most brilliant results if true, but it was not. The enemy occupied the position at J. Boisseau's on the preceding night, and instead of my having a division there, the nearest to it I had was Bartlett's brigade, three-fourths of a mile north of Gravelly Run, the crossing of which the enemy guarded. Even this brigade of mine I had to withdraw, by General Meade's order, at 9.35 p.m. I fully expected, if the enemy had not retired, to have to fight a battle in order to get across Gravelly Run to J. Boisseau's, and if the enemy had designed to stay we undoubtedly must have done so. I so anticipated in my instructions to General Griffin, who, about 5 a.m., left his position near the enemy on the White Oak road and moved directly and rapidly across the country to Crump's. He found the enemy had left the crossing of the run open, and he moved on to J. Boisseau's, meeting at the forks of the road our cavalry, under General Devin. At this point General Griffin reported to General Sheridan, as I had directed, should such a state of affairs as was found be developed. I remained with General Crawford's division, which we formed to retire in line of battle to meet the enemy should he pursue us from his breastworks, as I confidently expected he would as soon as he discovered our movements. I also deployed my escort to retire toward the plank road to take back any men or supplies which might be coming to that point through ignorance of the change that had been made in the night. General Griffin's march having been unmolested I did not reach him until he had met our cavalry. I then ascertained that General Ayres' division was massed about half a mile south of us, near J.M. Brooks'. It will be remembered that General Ayres began to move back from the White Oak road by an order from me, sent at 9.35 p.m. and which was the first intimation of sending troops to General Sheridan. No orders stopped him, nor did anything delay him but physical obstacles, such as the darkness, bad roads, and broken bridge. I will now quote (from his report) the result:

The division was ordered to move down the Boydton pike during the night of March 31, and report to General Sheridan at Dinwiddie Court-House. Before arriving there it was met by a staff officer of General Sheridan's, with instructions to turn off on a road leading west into a road leading from Dinwiddie Court-House to the White Oak road (i.e., from R. Boisseau's to J.M. Brooks') and come upon the left and rear of the enemy, who was facing General Sheridan's command, near Dinwiddie Court-House. As we approached just after daylight the enemy hastily decamped.

This actual trial disposes of the question of the ability of my troops to reach General Sheridan by midnight. It took General Ayres till daybreak. It may be said in support of the "expectations" that the state of this bridge and stream were not known when the expectations were formed, but they should have been, as the route was used for communications between General Grant and General Sheridan the two preceding days. But let us suppose the two divisions that General Grant directed to be moved by J. Boisseau's were expected to reach General Sheridan by midnight. The order which I received was written by General Meade 10.15 p.m. five minutes after General Grant's to General Sheridan. It reached me 10.50 p.m. thirty-five minutes after being written. Supposing all possible dispatch used, twenty minutes at least would be required for me to make the necessary arrangements; twenty more minutes would be required to carry my order to the divisions; twenty more minutes for them to transmit them to the brigades, and forty minutes at least for the troops to get ready to move, for it must be remembered that no bugles nor drums could be used to sound calls or arouse the men. No general could make plans based on greater rapidity of execution than here allowed, and our experience rarely realized it on the most favorable occasions, while this was one of the least so. Summing up these intervals of time we have two hours to add to the time of General Grant's writing to General Sheridan. I venture to say it took nearly this time for the note itself to reach General Sheridan. Adding these two hours would make it at least 12 o'clock before my two divisions could move. They then had four miles to traverse, taking the White Oak road, before reaching the crossing of Gravelly Run, which would occupy till 2 a.m. I had then to cross the stream and strike the rear of the enemy attacking General Sheridan, enumerated by him as follows:

> The opposing force was Pickett's division, Wise's independent brigade of infantry, and Fitzhugh Lee's, Rosser's, and W.H. Lee's cavalry commands. This force is too strong for us.

To join General Sheridan by midnight on this route I then had to capture or destroy whatever of this force was between me and General Sheridan. Any expectation more unreasonable could not have been formed, nor would I attribute them to any one not wholly ignorant of the true state of the case.

In regard to intercepting the enemy, the facts show it was impossible, under the circumstances. I learned from deserters that they had begun to move toward Five Forks as early as 10 p.m. the night before, believing their position would be untenable the next morning. They had consequently withdrawn in the night, carrying off their wounded and leaving only a cavalry picket in General Sheridan's front, which, as General Ayres says, "hastily decamped as he approached at daylight."

It will be seen by the following dispatch of General Meade to General Grant, dated 6 a.m. April 1, that General Sheridan himself must have been aware of this withdrawal of the enemy early in the night:

> The officer sent to Sheridan returned between 2 a.m. and 3 a.m. without any written communication, but giving General S[heridan]'s opinion that the enemy were retiring from his front. The absence of firing this morning would seem to confirm this. I was asleep at the time this officer returned and did not get the information until just now. Should this prove true, Warren will be at or near Dinwiddie soon with his whole corps and will require further orders.

Now, the officer that brought General Meade this information from General Sheridan, "between 2 and 3 a.m.," could not have left General Sheridan less than two hours previous, the distance being about ten miles, over the worst possible roads; so that General Sheridan thought the enemy was retiring as early, at least, as between 12 and 1, and the information could scarce have reached General Sheridan from his picket-line in less than one hour's time; so that the enemy's movements in retiring must have become apparent as early, at least, as between 11 and 12. This conclusion confirms the report that deserters gave me in the morning, and the completeness of the withdrawal further sustains it.

While awaiting with General Griffin for instructions from General Sheridan, who had advanced with the cavalry toward Five Forks, I received, about 9.30 a.m., the following order, written by General Webb, at 6 a.m.:

> General Meade directs that in the movements following your junction with General Sheridan you will be under his orders and will report to him. Please send in a report of progress.

At 9.30 a.m. I sent the following to General Webb, as directed:

> I reached the crossing of Gravelly Run early this morning and met General Sheridan there. We are massed at that point by his order. I did not meet General Sheridan personally; General Griffin, leading the column, saw him. If we remain in this vicinity we can get rations up by the Boydton plank road; we were unable, except in part, to replenish yesterday. The enemy did not follow with a single man when we left the White Oak road this morning.

It was a matter of wonder at the time, and has been ever since, how the enemy permitted our thus withdrawing without following us up to see the way we took, even if it had been with only a regiment. He would thus early have gained the knowledge that our infantry was moving toward his detached force, under General Pickett, which we beat so badly toward evening. General Lee could then have re-enforced his detached troops or timely warned them to withdraw. I kept my skirmish line halted a long while after my advance set out in the morning, so as to cover the movement as late as possible, and deployed my escort to fall back on the Boydton plank road and delude any pursuing force, if possible, into the belief that we had all retired in that direction. It was a want of vigilance that was most rare on their part and betokened that apathy which results from a hopelessness as to the use of further resistance.

The following dispatch from Colonel Locke to General Webb, written 11 a.m. April 1, describes an achievement which deserves mention, and which seems alike indicative of the sinking spirits of the Confederates:

> I have the honor to send the following report:
>
>   Capt. B.C. Clement, with one sergeant and thirteen men of the Sixteenth North Carolina Cavalry, Roberts' brigade, Lee's division, have just been received. They were captured this morning by three men of the First Division sharpshooters, Major Jacklin commanding. These three men went through the lines of the Second Corps to find the First Division (which had moved early this morning from its former position), and after passing around the picket-line of the Second Corps came upon these men in two squads and captured them. The names of the captors are W.M. Cronkite, A. McCrory, and William Stubel, all of the Sixteenth Michigan Veteran Volunteers detailed as sharpshooters. The horses of the prisoners were brought in with them. Our escort being short of horses they have been retained here. The prisoners will be sent up at once.
>
>   P.S.—General Warren being absent at the front, I send the above.

The battle of Five Forks, in the evening, was the last serious engagement of the Fifth Corps. I have made the report of this to Colonel Bowers, headquarters armies of the United States.

The operations of my command, just recounted, were of a most wearying and sanguinary character. The order to move at 3 a.m. on March 29 was of the deepest moment to everyone. The arrangements to be made and the excitement of the hopes and fears of the campaign kept all from sleeping that night. We were moving during all the 29th, and the day closed with a sharp and successful engagement. The night brought rain, and much destroyed the opportunity of the men to rest. Continuous operations throughout the heavy rains of March 30 resulted in much extension of our lines, with new intrenchments to build, and closer contact with the defenses into which the enemy was driven. Another rainy night, with the ground now soaking wet, allowed of little sleep, except to those overpowered with weariness. Movements early commenced on the morning of March 31 were succeeded by a fierce engagement and heavy losses, resulting in the defeat of the enemy and a still closer investure of his defenses, and the wresting from him of the use of the White Oak Ridge. Disasters to our cavalry corps compelled my men to move to its succor during the night, many of them moving the whole night through. All this was done in a section of country quite new to us, where swamps and heavy forests abounded, and yet I can testify it was done as cheerfully and promptly as it was possible for us to do.

As usual we lost heavily in battle, but the enemy suffered more, and on every occasion the conflict closed with ourselves the masters of the field. The following is the aggregate loss from March 29 to 31, inclusive: Killed, 183; wounded, 1,206; missing, 492; aggregate, 1,881.

It is not in my power to speak in adequate terms of those who did their duty. Many of them had risked their lives on all our former battle-fields. This I shall endeavor to recapitulate when I have finished all the detailed reports.

At present I will but make my acknowledgments of the faithful service of my command in general, and of my division commanders and staff officers, whose names, rank, and positions I gave at the commencement of this report.

Respectfully submitted.

G.K. WARREN,
Late Major-General Volunteers, Comdg. Fifth Army Corps.
NEW YORK, February 21, 1866.

Col. T.S. BOWERS,
Assistant Adjutant-General, Hdqrs. Armies of the Unites States:

COLONEL: I respectfully forward herewith my report of the battle of Five Forks. I beg you will excuse any want of neatness in the copy, as I have no one to assist me, and I send it as it is to prevent any further delay.

Very respectfully, your obedient servant,

G.K. WARREN,
Major Engineers, etc.
NEW YORK, December 1, 1865.

SIR: I respectfully submit this report and map of the operations of the Fifth Army Corps at the battle of Five Forks.

About 9 a.m. April 1 (having effected a junction with General Sheridan at about 7 a.m.) I received the following order from General Meade:

HEADQUARTERS ARMY OF THE POTOMAC,
April 1, 1865—6 a.m.

Major-General WARREN:

General Meade directs that in the movements following your junction with General Sheridan you will be under his orders, and will report to hm. Please send a report of progress.

ALEX. S. WEBB,
Brevet Major-General and Chief of Staff.

In compliance with the above, I served under General Sheridan during that day and until the winning of the victory at Five Forks in the evening. At 7 p.m. I received from him the following:

FIELD ORDER)   CAVALRY HEADQUARTERS,
No.)   April 1, 1865.

Major-General Warren, commanding Fifth Army Corps, is relieved from duty, and will report at once for orders to Lieutenant-General Grant, commanding Armies of the United States.

By command of Major-General Sheridan:

JAS. W. FORSYTH,
Brevet Brigadier-General and Chief of Staff.

In consequence of this order I address this report to you. General Sheridan gave no reason for this order of his, but I at once set out to obey it, reaching General Grant about midnight. The next morning I was assigned another command. Deeming, by the comments of the public prints, that the removing of me from the command of the Fifth Corps at the close of an eventful battle was, in the ignorance and misrepresentation concerning it, causing me an injury in the estimation of my countrymen, I requested a full investigation of it in a communication to you, written on April 22. In the rapid sequence of important events this communication remained unacted upon till May 6, at which time it was disapproved as being "impossible at this time to give the court and witnesses necessary to an investigation." I had a few days previous been appointed to the command of the Department of Mississippi, which, it was given me to believe, was regarded as an evidence of confidence in me, removing any unfavorable inferences to be drawn in the taking of me from the command of the Fifth Corps. That this was fully satisfactory to my feelings it could not be said; but the war was ended in Virginia, while yet the Confederate flag and forces kept the field in the department assigned me, and this made the change of command at that time acceptable. The surrender, however, of all the organized troops of the enemy in the limits of my new command took place while on my way to it, and my military operations there were confined to capturing the few still defiant fugitives on their way to Texas and Mexico. The war being closed, duty no longer required me in the field. Wearied as I was with long and continuous service, I felt unable to endure the summer climate of Mississippi. To request to be relieved would place me with the "unemployed generals" whose resignations had been solicited by the War Department order of May 1. I therefore tendered my resignation, and it was accepted.

The report of General Sheridan concerning the battle of Five Forks, dated May 16, I first saw in the official Army and Navy Gazette of June 13. In this he states his reasons for relieving me from command of the Fifth Corps. That he should have given his reasons for this removal was to be expected, but I cannot but think it an additional hardship to me that these should have been given to the public, without my first having a chance to explain or justify my conduct on the points in question, especially as I had sought in every way to arrive at these reasons and to submit my conduct to the severest scrutiny. In justice I but ask that this report shall be given the same publicity.

Report.

The order of General Meade in the morning of April 1, to serve under General Sheridan, gave me much satisfaction at the time of its receipt. I was then completely ignorant of his having a preference for another corps, or the slightest object to myself. I had never served with him before. When I met him at about 11 a.m. his manner was friendly and cordial. After talking with me a short time at the place where I found him (during which time he was occasionally receiving reports from his cavalry commanders) he mounted and rode off to the front. At 1 p.m. an officer brought me an order to bring up the infantry. I at once dispatched Col. (now brevet brigadier-general) H.C. Bankhead to give the orders to the division commanders to bring up their commands, specifying the relative order in which I thought they could move the most rapidly. I then went up the Five Forks road, in advance of the infantry, to see General Sheridan, and to inform myself of the use to be made of my troops, so that no time would be lost on their arrival. General Sheridan explained to me the state of affairs and what his plan was for me to do. This I entered upon most cordially. He had placed a staff officer back on the road to mark the point where my command was to turn off. I then rode back to the point indicated, turned up the road (which led by Gravelly Run Church), and examined the ground, using my escort to picket the front I was to take up, so as to prevent the enemy discovering the presence of the infantry. General Sheridan's order was to form the whole corps before advancing, so that all of it should move simultaneously. He specially stated that the formation was to be oblique to the road, with the right advanced, with two divisions in front, and the third in reserve behind the right division. The number of lines and consequent extent of front he left me to decide. Upon examination I determined on an equivalent of three lines of battle for each of the front divisions, arranged as follows: Each division was to place two brigades in front, each brigade in two lines of battle, and the third brigade in two lines of battle behind the center of the two front lines; the Third Division to be posted in column of battalions in mass behind the right. To General Ayres I assigned my left; General Crawford, my right; and General Griffin, my reserve, behind the right. In moving they were instructed to keep closed to the left and to preserve their direction in the woods, by keeping the sun, then shining brightly, in the same position over their left shoulders. General Ayres placed the Maryland Brigade on his left, in two lines, and General Gwyn's brigade on his right. This last brigade was formed in three lines, instead of two, as the regiments could not be well disposed in two lines. General Winthrop's brigade General Ayres formed as his reserve. General Crawford formed his line so as to place Colonel Kellogg's brigade on his left, General Baxter's brigade on his right, and General Coulter's brigade as his reserve. The length of the front we occupied was about 1,000 yards. The casualties of battle of the three preceding days, together with the loss of those who had given out from weariness or were absent on detached duty, had probably reduced our effective force at least 1,000 men in each division below that with which we set out on the 28th, so that we had then present about 12,000 men. While the troops were forming I prepared the accompanying sketch, with explanations, for each division commander, and directed them, as far as time would admit, to explain it to the brigade commanders.

April 1–3 p.m.

> The following is the movement now about to be executed:
> *[Sketch not provided]*
> The line will move forward as formed till it reaches the White Oak road, when it will swing round to the left perpendicular to the White Oak road. General Merritt's and General Custer's cavalry will charge the enemy's line as soon as the infantry get engaged. The cavalry is on the left of the infantry, except Mackenzie's, which is moving up the White Oak road from the right.

General Griffin in his report says the formation prior to the attack was as follows:

> The First Division, on the right flank, formed in three lines, with one brigade on its right in echelon.

I supplied General Griffin with the same sketch and plan of operations as I had General Ayres and General Crawford, in which I thought I indicated General Griffin's position in rear of the right. But the necessity for him to protect his own flank, and the wedge-like shape of the formation, as a whole, led General Griffin to regard his division as on the right.

General Sheridan says in his report that he directed "one division to be formed in reserve, opposite the center." This is a mistake. His order was to form it in rear of the right. The line was to be formed "obliquely to and at a point a short distance from the White Oak road." This threw the right in the advance, and it was supposed by him would strike the enemy first and need the support.

During the formation of my troops I used all the exertions possible to hasten their arrival, and everything was so prepared for them that they marched at once to their assigned position without a halt. General Sheridan expressed to me the apprehension that the cavalry, which continued to fire on the enemy, would use up all their ammunition before my troops would be ready. I informed him that they would not all be in position before 4 p.m. but that I was ready to move at once with whatever was at hand if he directed, and let the rest follow, but he did not. His impatience was no greater apparently than I felt myself, and which I strove to repress and prevent any exhibition of, as it would tend to impair confidence in the proposed operations. When everything possible is being done, it is important to have the men think that it is all that success requires, if their confidence is to be retained.

Against General Sheridan's most ungenerous statement that I gave him the impression that I wanted the sun to go down, I simply place my denial, and trust that my whole conduct in life, and especially in this war, sustains me in it. The sun did not set until two hours and a half after the formation was completed.

In proof of the efforts I made to get the troops in position and the rapidity with which they did move, I present the following communications from Brevet Brigadier-General Bankhead, of my staff; Brevet Major-General Crawford, commanding Third Division;

Brevet Major-General Griffin, commanding First Division; Brevet Major-General Ayres, commanding Second Division:

General Bankhead writes, under date of June 27:

> Sir: In reply to your letter of the 17th instant, received the 25th, I have the honor to state that I was with you April 1, at the time you received some instructions from General Sheridan through one of his staff officers. As to the nature of the order I am not aware, further than that you immediately turned to me and directed me "to bring up the corps at once" along the road we were at the time, and that you would meet the column yourself; that the division would march in the following order, viz: Third, First, Second. I immediately galloped back and gave the order in person to Generals Griffin and Crawford. As I was directed to see the head of the column was started on the right road, I sent the order to General Ayres, commanding Second Division (who was farther off to the right), by one of your aides, either Major Cope or Captain Wadsworth. The orders were obeyed promptly, and the troops moved out as expeditiously as the nature of the road and the crowded state it was in (being blocked up with led cavalry horses) would admit. Every exertion appeared to be made by General Crawford, who had the advance, to keep the road clear for the infantry to pass. I remained with the head of the column until within a short distance of the place it was halted and placed in position to make the attack.
>
> H.C. Bankhead,
> Brevet Colonel and Assistant Inspector-General.

The following is from General Crawford, dated July 17:

> General: In reply to your communication of June 17, asking if my division did not move with all practicable dispatch in forming prior to our attack on the enemy at the battle of Five Forks, I have the honor to state that the troops under my command moved at once upon receipt of the order, and that, in my opinion, no unnecessary time was lost from that time till they were formed as you directed.
>
> S.W. Crawford,
> Brevet Major-General.

The following is from General Griffin, dated June 26:

> General: In reply to your communication of the 17th instant, in reference to the movement of the First Division just prior to the battle of Five Forks, April 1, 1865, I have to state I was in command of that division on that day, and, about 2 p.m. received, though Colonel Bankhead, corps inspector, an order to move down the road leading northward with all possible dispatch, as the cavalry and infantry were to attack the enemy at once. I moved my troops as promptly as I could, and on arriving near the place where the corps was formed for the attack was met by yourself. You immediately pointed out the ground that my troops were to form on, remarking in substance that you wished me to be as expeditious as possible. The order was executed at once, and I then reported in person to you. In my opinion the division was formed without any halting or unnecessary delay.
>
> Charles Griffin,
> Brevet Major-General.

The following is from General Ayres, dated June 24:

> Sir: I have the honor to acknowledge the receipt of yours of the 17th instant, last evening, asking an official statement concerning the movement of the Fifth Corps on the 1st of April, from the position where it was massed to that where the lines of battle were formed previous to the attack. I do not know at what time the order was given to commence the movement. I was ordered to follow the First Division. This was done, and my division was kept well closed up on the troops in front. On arriving near the position where the lines were forming you requested me to form my troops as expeditiously as possible, as General Sheridan desired to attack the enemy immediately. Once again during the formation you desired me to be expeditious. My division being a very small one, was soon formed, whereupon I reported to you that I was ready. The order was then given, and the troops moved at once to the attack.
>
> R.B. Ayres,
> Brevet Major-General.

In view of this testimony it is apparent that General Sheridan had left out of his calculations the necessary time to make the formation he directed, and that, in his own opinion, his plan was endangered thereby. The propriety of an army all moving at once presupposes, in order that the general who so employs it should be entitled to the credit of the results obtained, that he should have his information so exact that the mass falls directly upon a vulnerable and vital point of the enemy's position. If there should be a mistake in this, the chief merit belongs to those exertions and arrangements by which this mistake is corrected or in the new dispositions which the occasion demands as requisite and which are not impracticable. But this calculation as to the position of the left flank of the enemy's line was faulty, and to a very serious extent, considering that he had placed all the troops in position for the move. The changes we had to make afterward required the greatest exertion of myself and staff, when everything was in motion and in woods of the difficult nature usually found in Virginia, no one of the command being at all acquainted with the ground over which we were moving.

After the forward movement began a few minutes brought us to the White Oak road, distant about 1,000 yards. There we found the advance of General Mackenzie's cavalry, which, coming up the White Oak road, had arrived there just before us. This showed us for the first time that we were too far to our right of the enemy's left flank. General Ayres' right crossed the road in the open field, and his division commenced changing front at once, so as to bring his line on the right flank of the enemy's position. Fortunately for us the enemy's left flank so rested in the woods that he could not fire at us as we crossed this open field, and the part of it that faced us formed a very short line. This General Ayres attacked at once, the firing being heavy, but less than usually destructive, on account of the thick woods. The rapid change of front by General Ayres caused his right flank at first to get in advance of General Crawford's, owing to the greater distance the latter had to move, and exposed the former to being taken in flank by the enemy. Orders were sent by me to General Crawford to oblique his division to the left and close up this interval. As soon as I had found the enemy's left flank orders were sent to General Griffin by several staff officers to move also obliquely to the left and come in to the support of General Ayres. But as Griffin's division was moving out of sight in the woods the order only reached him in the neighborhood of the place marked "Chimneys" on the map.

While giving orders thus I did not think it proper to leave my place on the open field, because it was one where my staff officers, sent to different parts of the command, could immediately find me on their return, and thus I could get information from all points at once, and utilize the many eyes of my staff and those of my commanders, instead of going to some special point myself and neglect all others. The time had not arrived, in my judgment, for me to do that. It may be that at this time it was that General Sheridan thought I did not exert myself to inspire confidence in the troops that broke under a not very severe fire. There was no necessity for my personal presence for such purpose reported from any part of the field. The time which elapsed before hearing from General Crawford or General Griffin convinced me that they must have passed on beyond the right of General Ayres. Leaving sufficient means to send any important information after me, I then rode rapidly to the right near the Chimneys, and was received with a considerable fire from the enemy across the open field. As I afterward learned, this fire occasioned some unsteadiness in General Ayres' right and also caused the left of General Crawford to oblique to the right, so as to keep the protection of the ridge and trees. I remained here until General Griffin arrived with his division, when I directed him to attack the enemy on the right of General Ayres, and this he proceeded to do. I then rode back to General Ayres' position and found that he had captured the enemy's extreme right [left] and some thousand prisoners. This information I sent to General Griffin, and then rode as rapidly as possible to direct General Crawford as circumstances might require. Before proceeding further I will give quotations from Major Cope's report relating to the proceeding:

You sent me to General Griffin with an order to bring his division toward the White Oak road, by the flank, in order to be in better supporting distance of the Second Division, also to inform General Crawford that he was going somewhat too far to the right. I found Generals Griffin and Crawford to the right of the Chimneys, and gave them your orders. At this time the enemy had a line of skirmishers running from the left of their line of works by the Sidney [Sydnor] house toward Hatcher's Run. You came to where General Griffin was, and then returned to the White Oak road, where I joined you a few minutes after. The part of the enemy's line where you were had been carried by General Ayres, and you sent me again to General Griffin with this information and with an order to push forward as fast as possible. He had already reached the Sidney [Sydnor] house and was pushing forward across the field. I delivered your order and gave him the direction to advance, which was west.

I also annex an extract from General Ayres' report describing his operations after the forward movement began:

> Advancing through a wood into an opening, the skirmishers engaged those of the enemy, pushing them back. Soon after crossing the White Oak road, finding the enemy's fire to come from the left, I changed front to the left, by facing the Second Brigade to the left and filing to the left. Not to lose time I also threw the First Brigade (his reserve) into the front line, on the left of the Second. The Third Brigade soon after engaging the enemy, finding its right flank in the air (I must confess that I experienced anxiety also on this account), portions of it were very unsteady, but subsequently moved up and bore their part in the action in a handsome manner. After this change of front the troops were pushed forward and soon came upon the left flank of the enemy, which was thrown back at right angles with his mainline and covered by a strong breast-work, screened behind a dense undergrowth of pine and about 100 yards in length. This breast-work my troops charged and took at the bayonet's point, capturing in carrying it over 1,000 prisoners and several battle-flags. Halting there a short time by General Sheridan's order, till it was apparent the enemy were giving way generally, I pushed forward rapidly, holding my men in hand and marching steadily in line of battle.

I have italicized "halting there, etc.," because it shows that General Sheridan modified his own order not to halt. No order to halt was given by me. What caused the general giving way of the enemy while General Ayres was halted by General Sheridan's order was due to the operations elsewhere directed.

It will be seen that the rapid change of front by General Ayres, necessitated by the unexpected condition of things, unavoidably threw his flank temporarily in the "air." Had the line gradually swung round General Crawford would have been on his right, but as it was the change had the momentary effect to leave General Crawford "in echelon" in rear of General Ayres' right. It happened also that the right of General Ayres became exposed to a fire from the enemy across the open field around Sidney's [Sydnor's]. General Crawford's left encountered the same fire as it came up on General Ayres' right, and the effect was to cause the line to oblique somewhat to the right to gain the cover of the woods and ridges; but it kept steadily moving on in the enemy's rear, a threatening movement which made the position of the enemy no longer tenable, assailed as he was both in front and flank beside. I will now extract from General Crawford's report. After giving a copy of the order of attack that I had furnished him with, he says:

> In obedience to this order we crossed Gravelly Run, crossed the White Oak road, and changed direction to the left and advanced directly west. We encountered the enemy's skirmishers shortly after moving, driving them steadily back. Our way led through bogs, tangled woods, and thickets of pine, interspersed with open spaces here and there. The connection between the Second Division and my line could not be maintained. I received orders from both General Sheridan and General Warren to press rapidly forward. I urged on the entire command. General Coulter's brigade, from being in support in my rear, was brought to fill the gap between me and Second Division. I pressed immediately on and found myself in the enemy's rear, on the Ford road, which I crossed. Just at this point the enemy opened upon my center and left flank a very heavy fire. Major General Warren arriving on the field at that moment directed me to advance immediately down the Ford road, and General Coulter's brigade was selected for that purpose. Two regiments, commanded by Major Funk, [were] placed on what was then the left of the road, and the rest of the brigade were on the right, supported by the other two brigades in echelon. I advanced at once and captured a battery of four guns and the battle-flag of the Thirty-second Virginia Infantry. We then changed direction and advanced again in a southwest direction, the enemy flying before us, though keeping up a desultory firing.

General Griffin's report says:

> Immediately after the order to advance against the enemy was given, with instructions to the division that after it had crossed the road it was to change direction to the left, so as to strike the

enemy in flank and rear. After advancing about a mile, and finding nothing in front save a few cavalry vedettes, and there being heavy volleys of musketry to the left and rear, the division was halted.

This halting, under the circumstances, was a commendable exercise of discretion. He says that, a personal examination showing him the enemy on his left, he marched in that direction. To effect this same thing I had sent Major Cope to him, as already stated. A small portion of General Griffin's division became separated in the woods from the rest and continued on with General Crawford's division, and was used by me on the Ford road. General Griffin moved against the enemy at "double-quick," taking his breast-works and 1,500 prisoners. As stated by General Crawford I came up with his division near B. Boisseau's after he had crossed the Ford road. He had been driving back the enemy's skirmish line all the way and continually turning the left of any force opposing Generals Ayres and Griffin.

> NOTE.—General Sheridan's report states that he directed General Mackenzie to swing round on the right of the infantry and gain the Ford road, so as to cut off the enemy's escape that way. As General Mackenzie did not succeed in getting there till after the infantry had gained the road I asked of him the nature of his operations. He informed me that in attempting to execute his order he found himself north of Hatcher's Run and moving directly away from the battle, which seemed heavy. He therefore (as General Griffin had done) moved back toward the White Oak road so as to take part in the action.

I at once directed his line to swing round to face southward, as we had now closed up the outlet for the enemy's escape northward, and move down upon the position of the enemy at the forks of the road, a point well indicated to us by the firing of some pieces of artillery there by the enemy. General Crawford's troops soon encountered a stiff line of the enemy, formed to meet him, and from the fire of which General Coulter's brigade suffered severely. The contest, however, was short, for the enemy, now pressed front, flank, and rear, mostly threw down their arms. Three guns of the captured battery were found on the road where they had been stopped in their attempt to escape northward. Immediately after the forks were gained I directed General Crawford to change front again to the right and march toward the sound of the firing, so as again to take the enemy in flank and rear, and this he at once did. I also directed a cavalry brigade, which had been kept mounted and which now came rapidly along the Ford road toward me, not to move along it farther, but to file to their left and proceed in the direction General Crawford had taken. I then passed down the Ford road, reached the forks and turned to the right along the White Oak road. The troops were joyous and filled with enthusiasm at their success, but somewhat disorganized thereby and by their marching and fighting so long in the woods. On my arriving at the point E (see map), I found that our advance there was stayed by the enemy, who had formed a new line for their left flank near the position F, while they yet maintained their line against our cavalry on the south. Though the orders had been not to halt, and many officers were then urging their men forward, the disordered men, not feeling the influence of their commanders, continued to fire without advancing. Accompanied by Captain Benyaurd and the portion of my staff then present, I rode out to the front and called those near me to follow. This was immediately responded to. Everywhere along the front the color-bearers and officers sprang out, and, without more firing, our men advanced, capturing all the enemy remaining. During this last charge my horse was fatally shot within a few paces of the line where the enemy made his last stand, an orderly by my side was killed, and Colonel Richardson, of the Seventh Wisconsin, who sprang between me and the enemy, was severely wounded. I sent General Bankhead, after the last of the enemy had been captured, to General Sheridan to report the result and receive his instructions. He returned with the reply that my instructions had been sent me. At 7 p.m. they reached me, and were as follows:

> Major-General Warren, commanding Fifth Army Corps, is relieved from duty, and will report at once for orders to Lieutenant-General Grant, commanding Armies of the United States.

The Fifth Corps in this battle captured 3,244 men, with their arms, 11 regimental colors, and 1 four-gun battery, with its caissons. It lost in killed and wounded 634 men, of which

300 were in General Crawford's division, 205 in General Ayres' division, and 125 in General Griffin's division.

The conduct of my command, officers and men, in these last four days' operations, was characterized by unqualified obedience to orders and resolve to do their duty as it was required of them. Their exertions are deserving of highest commendation.

If it be not too invidious to mention the names of a few where many deserve to be, I will here speak of my division commanders and of my staff, as these were immediately subordinate to me. Bvt. Maj. Gen. S.W. Crawford commanded my Third Division, Bvt. Maj. Gen. Charles Griffin my First Division, and Bvt. Maj. Gen. R.B. Ayres my Second Division, and performed their duties bravely and ably, meeting the varying requirements of their commands on the battle-field with judgment and energy, and always striving to carry out the orders they received, according as the nature of the ground and dispositions of the enemy's forces permitted or required. My staff did not fail me in one instance, in the multifarious, arduous, and dangerous duties of their positions. The following is an enumeration of them: Bvt. Brig. Gen. C.S. Wainwright, chief of artillery; Col. H.C. Bankhead, inspector-general; Col. F.T. Locke, adjutant-general; Col. A.L. Thomas, chief quartermaster; Col. D.L. Smith, chief commissary of subsistence; of Surg. T. Rush Spencer, medical director; of Maj. William T. Gentry, U.S. Army, commissary of musters; Dr. Charles K. Winne, U.S. Army, medical inspector; Capt. George B. Halsted, assistant adjutant-general. My aides-de-camp were: Maj. E.B. Cope, Capt. James W. Wadsworth, and Capt. Gordon Winslow, and in the operations herein reported Capt. William H.H. Benyaurd, U.S. Engineers. Capt. Napoleon J. Horrell, Fourth Pennsylvania Cavalry, one of the most brave and energetic of officers, commanded my personal escort, consisting of about forty men.

In nearly every one of the numerous battles we have had with the enemy, my command had to lament the loss of some of its bravest and best, and the battle of Five Forks was not an exception to our former experience. Bvt. Brig. Gen. Frederick Winthrop, colonel of the Fifth New York Volunteers, commanding First Brigade, Second Division, was mortally wounded at the head of his command while making a successful assault. His conduct had always been distinguished for gallantry of action and coolness of thought, and no one carried with him more of the confidence and inspiration that sustains a command in trying scenes. His countrymen have lost no one of their soldiers who more deserves a lasting place in their memory.

In this battle I claim to have done my duty myself, and I believe a perusal of this report and of those of my subordinates will show that the opinion of General Sheridan, that I did not exert myself as he thought I should, must have arisen from some misapprehension or misconception of my efforts. His implied charge of neglect, in stating that I failed to reach Dinwiddie Court-House by midnight, as expected, the lieutenant-general must now know is unjust, for it was impossible for my troops to get there before daybreak. I trust, therefore, that I may yet receive some unequivocal acknowledgment of my faithful services at the battle of Five Forks, that will forever free me from opprobrium even among the superficial.

Very respectfully, your obedient servant,

G.K. WARREN,
Late Major-General of Volunteers, Comdg. Fifth Army Corps.

Col. T.S. BOWERS,
Asst. Adjt. Gen., Headquarters Armies of the United States.

ADDENDA.

PETERSBURG, April 13, 1865.

Major-General WARREN;

GENERAL: I beg leave to submit statement of the operations of the Fifth Army Corps on April 1, 1865, at the battle of Five Forks, as seen by me.

About 8 o'clock on the morning of the 1st I started out from headquarters to join you on the White Oak road, near the Dabney house. I reached there at 8.30 a.m. and found the troops in motion. They marched in a southwest direction, and in one mile came to the Dinwiddie Court-House road, near Doctor Boisseau's; then proceeded down this road to its junction with Ford's road. This point was reached by the First and Third Divisions about 9.30. The Second Division had come up by the Boydton plank road the night before, and was massed half a mile beyond. The cavalry was passing on Ford's road toward Five Forks. About 12 o'clock the corps was ordered to move in the direction of the Five Forks, the First Division leading, followed by the Third, then came the Second. In two miles and a half the head of the column turned to the right and proceeded to the vicinity of Gravelly Run Church. The troops were then formed in the following order: The Third Division on the right of the road leading north by the church and crossing the White Oak road, the Second Division on the left, and the First in reserve. There each division commander was furnished with a plan and written explanation of the movement about to be made. About 4 o'clock, all being ready, the line was ordered to advance. In one-fourth of a mile it crossed the White Oak road, wheeled to the left perpendicular to the road. This movement brought the First and Third Divisions in the woods, and as the line advanced they went too much to the right and lost the connection with the Second Division. After the line had passed through the open fields to the edge of timber, the Second Division became engaged with the enemy's skirmishers. You sent me to General Griffin with an order to bring his division toward the White Oak road, by the left flank, in order to be in better supporting distance of the Second, also to inform General Crawford that he was going somewhat too far to the right. I found Generals Griffin and Crawford to the right of the burned chimneys, and gave them your orders. At this time the enemy had a line of skirmishers running from the left of their line of works by the Sidney [Sydnor] house toward Hatcher's Run. You came to where General Griffin was, and then returned to the White Oak road, where I joined you a few minutes after. This part of the enemy's line where you were had been carried by the Second Division, and you sent me again to General Griffin with the information and with an order to push forward as fast as possible. He had already reached the Sidney [Sydnor] house and was pushing forward across the field. I delivered your order and gave him the direction....[1]

Appendix C:
Horace Porter's Narrative

Horace Porter was a colonel on Grant's staff. He was with Grant from the beginning of the operation on March 28 until the morning of April 1, when Grant sent him to accompany Sheridan during the forthcoming battle of Five Forks. Thus, Porter was not only an eye witness, but a participant at the top level in the events recounted in this book. Herewith is Porter's account of the events.

Five Forks and the Pursuit of Lee.
by Horace Porter, Brevet Brigadier-General, U.S.A.

It was 9 o'clock in the morning of 29th of March 1865. General Grant and the officers of this staff had bidden good-bye to President Lincoln and mounted the passenger car of the special train that was to carry them from City Point to the front, and the signal was given to start; the train moved off, Grant's last campaign had begun. Since 3 o'clock that morning the columns had been in motion and the Union Army and the Army of Northern Virginia were soon locked in a death-grapple. The President remained at City Point, where he could be promptly informed of the progress of the movement.

The military railroad connecting headquarters with the camps south of Petersburg was about thirteen miles long, or would have been if it had been constructed on a horizontal plan, but as the portion built by the army was a surface road, up hill and down dale, if the rise and fall had been counted in, its length would have defied all ordinary means of measurement. Its undulations were so striking that a train moving along it looked in the distance like a fly crawling over a corrugated washboard. The general sat down near the end of the car, drew from his pocket the flint and slow-match that he always carried, which, unlike a match, never missed fire in a gale of wind, and was soon wreathed in the smoke of the inevitable cigar. I took a seat near him with several other officers of the staff, and he at once began to talk over his plans in detail. They had been discussed in general terms before starting out from City Point. It was his custom, when commencing a movement in the field, to have his staff-officers understand fully the objects he wished to accomplish, and what each corps of the army was expected to do in different emergencies, so that these officers, when sent to distant points of the line, might have a full comprehension of the general's intentions, and so that, when communication with him was impossible or difficult, they might be able to instruct the subordinate commanders intelligently as to the intentions of the general-in-chief.

For a month or more General Grant's chief apprehension had been that the enemy might suddenly pull out from his intrenchments and fall back into the interior, where he might unite with General Joe Johnston against Sherman and force our army to follow Lee to a great distance from its base. General Grant had been sleeping with one eye open and one foot out of bed for many weeks, in the fear that Lee would thus give him the slip. He did not dare delay his movements against the enemy's right until the roads became dry enough to permit an army to move comfortably, for fear Lee would himself take advantage of the good roads to start first. Each army, in fact, was making preparations for either a fight or a foot-race—or both. Sheridan, with his cavalry command, had been ordered to move out in the direction of Dinwiddie Court-House, and to be ready to strike the enemy's right and rear. It was the intention, as soon as he could take up a good position for this purpose, to reinforce him with a corps of infantry, and cut off Lee's retreat in the direction of Danville, in case we should break through his intrenched lines in front of Petersburg, and force him from his position there.

The weather had been fair for several days, and the roads were getting in good condition for the movement of troops; that is, as good as could be expected, through a section of country in which the dust in summer was generally so thick that the army could not see where to move, and the mud in winter was so deep that it could not move anywhere. The general, in speaking of what was expected of Sheridan, said: "I had a private talk with Sheridan after I gave him his written instructions at City Point. When he read that part of them which directed him, in certain contingencies, to proceed south along the Danville railroad and cooperate with Sherman by operating in Joe Johnston's rear, he looked so unhappy that I said to him, as I followed him out of the tent, that that part of the instructions was put in only as a blind, so that if he did not meet with entire success the people of the North, who were then naturally restless and apt to become discouraged, might not look upon a temporary check as an entire defeat of a definite plan,—and that what I really expected was that he would remain with the armies operating against Lee, and end matters right here. This made him happy, and he has started out perfectly confident of the success of the present movement." Referring to Mr. Lincoln, he said: "The President is one of the few visitors I have had who has not attempted to extract form me a knowledge of my plans. He not only never asked them, but says it is better he should not know them, and then he can be certain to keep the secret. He will be the most anxious man in the country to hear the news from us, his heart is so wrapped up in our success, but I think we can send him some good news in a day or two." I never knew the general to be more sanguine of victory than in starting out on this campaign.

When we reached the end of the railroad we mounted our horses, which had been carried on the same train, started down the Vaughan road, and went into camp for the night in a field just south of that road, close to Gravelly Run. That night (March 29th) the army was disposed in the following order from right to left: Weitzel in front of Richmond, with a portion of the Army of the James, Parke and Wright holding our works in front of Petersburg, Ord extending to the intersection of Hatcher's Run and the Vaughan road, Humphreys stretching beyond Dabney's Mill, Warren on the extreme left reaching as far as the junction of the Vaughan road and the Boydton plank-road, and Sheridan at Dinwiddie Court-House. The weather had become cloudy, and toward evening rain began to fall. It fell in torrents during the night and continued with but little interruption all the next day. The country was densely wooded, and the ground swampy, and by evening of the 30th whole fields had become beds of quicksand in which horses sank to their bellies, wagons threatened to disappear altogether, and it seems as if the bottom had fallen out of the roads. The men began to feel that if anyone in after years should ask them whether they had been through Virginia, they could say, "Yes, in a number of places." The road had become sheets of water; and it looked as if the saving of that army would require the services, not of a Grant, but of a Noah. Soldiers would call out to officers as they rode along: "I say, when are the gun-boats coming up?" The buoyancy of the day before was giving place to gloom, and some began to fear that the whole movement was premature.

While standing in front of the general's tent on the morning of the 30th, discussing the situation with several others on the staff, I saw General Sheridan turning in from the Vaughan road with a staff-officer and an escort of about a dozen cavalrymen, and coming toward our headquarters camp. He was riding his white pacer, a horse which had been captured from General Breckinridge's adjutant-general at Missionary Ridge. But, instead of striking a pacing gait now, it was at every step driving its legs knee-deep into the quicksand with the regularity of a pile-driver. As soon as Sheridan dismounted, he was asked with much eagerness about the situation on the extreme left. He took a decidedly cheerful view of matters, and entered upon a very animated discussion of the coming movements. He said he could drive in the whole cavalry force of the enemy with ease, and if an infantry force were added to his command he would strike out for Lee's right and either crush it or force him so to weaken his intrenched lines that the troops in front of them could break through and march into Petersburg. He warmed up with the subject as he proceeded, threw the whole energy of his nature into the discussion, and his cheery voice, beaming countenance, and impassioned language showed the earnestness of his convictions.

"How do you propose to supply your command with forage if this weather lasts?" he was asked by one of the group.

"Forage?" said Sheridan; "I'll get all the forage I want. I'll haul it out if I have to set every man in the command to corduroying roads, and corduroy every mile of them from the railroad to Dinwiddie. I tell you I'm ready to strike out tomorrow and go to smashing things." And, pacing up and down, he chafed like a hound in the leash. We told him this was the kind of talk we liked to listen to at headquarters, and while General Grant fully coincided in these views it would still further confirm him in his judgment to hear such words as had just been spoken; we urged Sheridan to go and talk in the same strain to the general-in-chief, who was in his tent with General Rawlins. Sheridan, however, objected to obtruding himself unbidden upon his commander. Then we resorted to a bit of strategy. One of us went into the general's tent and told him Sheridan had just come in from the left and had been telling us some matters of much interest, and suggested that he be invited in and asked to state them. This was assented to, and Sheridan was told the general wanted to hear what he had to say. Sheridan then went in and began to speak to General Grant as he had been speaking to the staff. Several persons soon after came into the tent, and General Sheridan stepped out and accompanied General Ingalls to the latter's tent. A few minutes later General Grant went to this tent, General Ingalls came out, and Grant and Sheridan fully discussed the situation. In spite of the opposition which had arisen in some quarters to continuing offensive operations, owing to the state of the weather and the deplorable condition of the roads, General Grant decided to press the movement against the enemy with all vigor.

After his twenty-minutes talk with Grant, Sheridan mounted his horse, and, waving us a good-bye with his hand, rode off to Dinwiddie. The next morning, the 31st, he reported that the enemy had been hard at work intrenching at Five Forks and to a point about a mile west of there. Lee had been as prompt as Grant to recognize that Five Forks was a strategic point of great importance, and, to protect his right, had sent Pickett there with a large force of infantry and nearly all the cavalry. The rain continued during the night of the 30th, and on the morning of the 31st the weather was cloudy and dismal.

General Grant had expected that Warren would be attacked that morning, and had warned him to be on the alert. Warren advanced his corps to ascertain with what force the enemy held the White Oak road and to try to drive him from it; but before he had gone far he met with a vigorous assault. When news came of the attack General Grant directed me to go to the spot and look to the situation of affairs there. I found Ayres's division had been driven in, and both he and Crawford were falling back upon Griffin. Miles, of Humphreys's corps, was sent to reinforce Warren, and by noon the enemy was checked. As soon as General Grant was advised of the situation, he directed General Meade to take the offensive vigorously. Miles made a movement to the left and attacked in flank the troops in front of Warren, and the enemy soon fell back. General Grant had now ridden out to the front, and hearing that he was at Mrs. Butler's house near the Boydton plank-road, I joined him there. It was then a little after 1 o'clock. He had in the meantime ordered the headquarters camp to be moved to Dabney's Mill, on a cross-road running from the Boydton plank to the Vaughan road, and about two miles from Meade's headquarters, which were near the crossing of the Vaughan road and Hatcher's Run. The general was becoming apprehensive lest the infantry force that had moved against Warren might turn upon Sheridan, who had only cavalry with which to resist, as the weather had rendered it impracticable thus far to send him a corps of infantry as intended, and the general-in-chief was urgent that a strong forward movement should be made by the Fifth Corps for the purpose of deterring the enemy from detaching infantry from that portion of his line. This advance was made later in the afternoon, and with decided success. When this movement had been decided upon, General Grant directed me to go to Sheridan and explain what was taking place in Warren's and in Humphreys's front, and have a full understanding with him as to further operations in his vicinity. I rode rapidly down the Boydton plank-road, and soon came to Gravelly Run. Hearing heavy firing in the direction of Five Forks road, I hurried on in that direction. Crossing by the Brooks road from the Boydton plank to the five Forks road, which runs north from Dinwiddie, I saw a portion of our cavalry moving eastward, pressed by a heavy force of the enemy, and it was found that Devin and Davies, after holding on tooth and nail for hours, had been driven in by the force of superior numbers and were falling back toward the Boydton plank-road. The brigades of Gibbs and J.I. Gregg had rushed in on the right and rear of the enemy, and got in some very good work, but were soon after compelled to fall back toward Dinwiddie. I turned the corner of the Brooks cross-road and the Five Forks road just as the rear of our cavalry was passing it, and encountered one of Sheridan's bands, under a heavy fire, playing "Nellie Bly" as cheerily as if it were furnishing music for a country picnic.

I found Sheridan a little north of Dinwiddie Court-House, and gave him an account of matters on the left of the Army of the Potomac. He said he had had one of the liveliest days in his experience, fighting infantry and cavalry with cavalry only, but that he was concentrating his command on the high ground just north of Dinwiddie, and would hold that position at all hazards. He did not stop here, but becoming more and more animated in describing the situation and stating his views and intentions, he declared his belief that with the corps of infantry he expected to be put under his command he could take the initiative the next morning and cut off the whole of the force that Lee had detached. He said: "This force is in more danger than I am—if I am cut off from the Army of the Potomac, it is cut off from Lee's army, and not a man in it should ever be allowed to get back to Lee. We at last have drawn the enemy's infantry out of its fortifications, and this is our chance to attack it." He begged me to go to General Grant at once and again urge him to send him the Sixth Corps, because it had been under him in the battle in the Valley of Virginia, and knew his way of fighting. I told him, as had been stated to him before, that the Sixth Corps was next to our extreme right, and that the only one which could reach him by daylight was the Fifth. I started soon after for General Grant's headquarters at Dabney's Mill, a distance of about eight miles. I reached there at 7 o'clock p.m., and gave the general a full description of Sheridan's operations. He at once telegraphed the substance of my report to Meade, and preparations soon after began looking to the sending of the Fifth Corps to report to Sheridan. About 7:40 Captain M.V. Sheridan, of Sheridan's staff, brought still later news from Dinwiddie, saying that the cavalry had had more fighting but was holding its position.

It was finally decided that Warren should send Ayres down the Boydton plank and across by the Brooks road, and Griffin and Crawford by the Crump road, which runs from the White Oak road south to J. Boisseau's. Mackenzie's small division of cavalry was ordered to march to Dinwiddie and report to Sheridan. All haste was urged, in the hope that at daylight the enemy might be caught between Warren's two divisions of infantry on one side and Ayres's division and Sheridan's cavalry on the other, and be badly beaten. It was expected that the infantry would reach its destination in ample time to take the offensive at break of day, but now one delay after another was met with, and Grant, Meade, and Sheridan spent a painfully anxious night in hurrying forward the movement. Ayres had to rebuild a bridge over Gravelly Run, which took till 2 a.m. Warren, with his other two divisions, did not get started from their position on the White Oak road till 5 a.m., and the hope of crushing the enemy was hourly growing less. This proved to be one of the busiest nights of the whole campaign. Generals were writing dispatches and telegraphing from dark till daylight. Staff-officers were rushing from one headquarters to another, wading through swamps, penetrating forests, and galloping over corduroy roads, engaged in carrying instructions, getting information, and making extraordinary efforts to hurry up the movement of the troops.

The next morning, April 1st, General Grant said to me: "I wish you would spend the day with Sheridan's command, and send me a bulletin every half-hour or so, advising me fully as to the progress of his movements. You know my views, and I want you to give them to Sheridan fully. Tell him the contemplated movement is left entirely in his hands, and he must be responsible for its execution. I have every confidence in his judgment and ability. I hope there may now be an opportunity of fighting the enemy's infantry outside of its fortifications."

I set out with half a dozen mounted orderlies to act as couriers in transmitting field bulletins. Captain Peter T. Hudson, of our staff, went with me. After traveling again by way of the Brooks road, I met Sheridan, about 10 a.m., on the Five Forks road not far from J. Boisseau's house. Ayres had his division on this road, having arrived about daylight, and Griffin had reached J. Boisseau's between 7 and 8 a.m. I had a full conference with Sheridan. He told me the force in front of him had fallen back early in the morning, that he had pursued with his cavalry and had had several brushes with the enemy, and was driving him steadily back; that he had his patience sorely tried by the delays that had occurred in getting the infantry to him, but he was going to make every effort to strike a heavy blow with all the infantry and cavalry, as soon as he could get them into position, provided the enemy should make a stand behind his intrenchments at Five Forks, which seemed likely. General Warren, who had accompanied Crawford's division, arrived at 11 o'clock and reported in person to Sheridan.

A few minutes before noon Colonel (afterward General) Babcock, of General Grant's staff, came over from headquarters and said to Sheridan: "General Grant directs me to say to you, that if in your judgment the Fifth Corps would do better under one of the division commanders, you are authorized to relieve General Warren, and order him to report to General Grant, at headquarters." General Sheridan replied, in effect, that he hoped such a step as that might not become necessary, and then went on to speak of his plan of battle. We all rode on farther to the front, and soon met General Devin, who was considerably elated by his successes of the morning, and was loudly demanding to be permitted to make a general charge on the enemy. Sheridan told him he didn't believe he had enough ammunition, to which Devin replied: "I guess I've got enough to give 'em one surge more."

General Babcock now left us to return to headquarters. About 1 o'clock it was reported by the cavalry that the enemy was retiring to his intrenched position at Five Forks, which was just north of the White Oak road, and parallel to it, his earth-works running from a point about three-quarters of a mile east of Five Forks to a point a mile west, with an angle or crotchet about one hundred yards long thrown back at right angles to his left to protect that flank. Orders were at once given to the Fifth Corps to move up the Gravelly Run Church road to the open ground near the church, and form in order of battle, with Ayres on the left, Crawford on his right, and Griffin in rear as a reserve. The corps was to wheel to the left, and make its attack upon the "angle," and then, moving westward, sweep down in rear of the enemy's intrenched line. The cavalry, principally dismounted, was to deploy in front of the enemy's line and engage his attention, and, as soon as it heard the firing of our infantry, to make a vigorous assault upon his works.

The Fifth Corps had borne the brunt of the fighting ever since the army had moved out on the 29th, and the gallant men who composed it, and had performed a conspicuous part in nearly every battle in which the Army of the Potomac had been engaged, seemed eager once more to cross bayonets with their old antagonists. But the movement was slow, the required formation seemed to drag, and Sheridan, chafing with impatience and consumed with anxiety, became as restive as a racer when he nears the score and is struggling to make the start.

He made every possible appeal for promptness, he dismounted from his horse, paced up and down, struck the clenched fist of one hand into the palm of the other, and fretted like a caged tiger. He said at one time: "This battle must be fought and won before the sun goes down. All the conditions may be changed in the morning; we have but a few hours of daylight left us. My cavalry are rapidly exhausting their ammunition, and if the attack is delayed much longer they may have none left." And then another batch of staff-officers were sent out to gallop through the mud and hurry up the columns.

At 4 o'clock the formation was completed, the order for the assault was given, and the struggle for Pickett's intrenched line began. The Confederate infantry brigades were posted from right to left as follows: Terry, Corse, Steuart, Ransom, and Wallace. General Fitzhugh Lee, commanding the cavalry, had placed W.H.F. Lee's two brigades on the right of the line, Munford's division on the left, and Rosser's in rear of Hatcher's Run to guard the trains. I rode to the front in company with Sheridan and Warren, with the head of Ayres's division, which was on the left. When this division became engaged, Warren took up a more central position with reference to his corps. Ayres threw out a skirmish-line and advanced across an open field, which sloped down gradually toward the dense woods, just north of the White Oak road. He soon met with a fire from the edge of this woods, a number of men fell, and the skirmish-line halted and seemed to waver. Sheridan now began to exhibit those traits that always made him such a tower of strength in the presence of an enemy. He put spurs to his horse and dashed along in front of the line of battle from left to right, shouting words of encouragement and having something cheery to say to every regiment. "Come on, men," he cried. "Go at 'em with a will. Move on at a clean jump or you'll not catch one of them. They're all getting ready to run now, and if you don't get on to them in five minutes, they'll every one get away from you! Now go for them." Just then a man on the skirmish-line was struck in the neck; the blood spurted as if the jugular vein had been cut. "I'm killed!" he cried, and dropped on the ground. "You're not hurt a bit," cried Sheridan; "pick up your gun, man, and move right on to the front." Such was the electric effect of his words that the poor fellow snatched up his musket and rushed forward a dozen paces before he fell never to rise again. The line of battle of weather-beaten veterans was now moving right along down the slope toward the woods with a steady swing that boded no good for Pickett's command, earth-works or no earth-works. Sheridan was mounted on his favorite black horse "Rienzi" that had carried him from Winchester to Cedar Creek, and which Buchanan Read made famous for all time by his poem of "Sheridan's Ride." The roads were muddy, the fields swampy, the undergrowth dense, and "Rienzi," as he plunged and curveted, dashed the foam from his mouth and the mud from his heels. Had the Winchester pike been in a similar condition, he would not have made his famous twenty miles without breaking his own neck and Sheridan's too.

Mackenzie had been ordered up the Crump road with directions to turn east on the White Oak road and whip everything he met on that route. He met only a small cavalry command, and having whipped it according to orders, now came galloping back to join in the general scrimmage. He reported to Sheridan in person, and was ordered to strike out toward Hatcher's Run, then move west and get possession of the Ford road in the enemy's rear.

Soon Ayres's men met with a heavy fire on their left flank and had to change direction by facing more toward the west. As the troops entered the woods and moved forward over the boggy ground and struggled through the dense undergrowth, they were staggered by a heavy fire from the angle and fell back in some confusion. Sheridan now rushed into the midst of the broken lines, and cried out: "Where is my battle-flag?" As the sergeant who carried it rode up, Sheridan seized the crimson and white standard, waved it above his head, cheered on the men, and made heroic efforts to close up the ranks. Bullets were humming like a swarm of bees. One pierced the battle-flag, another killed the sergeant who had carried it, another wounded Captain A.J. McGonnigle in the side, others struck two or three of the staff-officers' horses. All this time Sheridan was dashing from one point of the line to another, waving his flag, shaking his fist, encouraging, threatening, praying, swearing, the very incarnation of battle. It would be a sorry soldier who could help following such a leader. Ayres and his officers were equally exposing themselves at all points in rallying the men, and soon the line was steadied, for such material could suffer but a momentary check. Ayres, with drawn saber, rushed forward once more with his veterans, who now behaved as if they had fallen back to get a "good-ready," and with fixed bayonets and a rousing cheer dashed over the earth-works, sweeping everything before them, and killing or capturing every man in their immediate front whose legs had not saved him.

Sheridan spurred "Rienzi" up to the angle, and with a bound the horse carried his rider over the earth-works, and landed in the midst of a line of prisoners who had thrown down their arms and were crouching close under their breastworks. Some of them called out, "Whar do you want us-all to go to?" Then Sheridan's rage turned to humor, and he had a running talk with the "Johnnies" as they filed past. "Go right over there," he said to them, pointing to the rear. "Get right along, now. Drop your guns; you'll never need them any more. You'll all be safe over there. Are there any more of you? We want every one of you fellows." Nearly 1,500 men were captured at the angle.

An orderly here came up to Sheridan and said: "Colonel Forsyth of your staff is killed, sir." "It's no such thing," cried Sheridan. "I don't believe a word of it. You'll find Forsyth's all right." Ten minutes after, Forsyth rode up. It was the gallant General Frederick Winthrop who had fallen in the assault and had been mistaken for him. Sheridan did not even seem surprised when he saw Forsyth, and only said: "There! I told you so." I mention this as an instance of a peculiar trait of Sheridan's character, which never allowed him to be discouraged by camp rumors, however disastrous.

The dismounted cavalry had assaulted as soon as they heard the infantry fire open. The natty cavalrymen, with tight-fitting uniforms, short jackets, and small carbines, swarmed through the pine thickets and dense undergrowth, looking as if they had been especially equipped for crawling through knot-holes. Those who had magazine guns created a racket in those pine woods that sounded as if a couple of army corps had opened fire.

The cavalry commanded by the gallant Merritt made a final dash, went over the earth-works with a hurrah, captured a battery of artillery, and scattered everything in front of them. Here Custer, Devin, Fitzhugh, and the other cavalry leaders were in their element, and vied with each other in deeds of valor. Crawford's division had advanced in a northerly direction, marching away from Ayres and leaving a gap between the two divisions. General Sheridan sent nearly all of his staff-officers to correct this movement, and to find General Warren, whom he was anxious to see.

After the capture of the angle I started off toward the right to see how matters were going there. I went in the direction of Crawford's division, passed around the left of the enemy's works, then rode due west to a point beyond the Ford road. Here I met Sheridan again, just a little before dark. He was laboring with all the energy of his nature to complete the destruction of the enemy's forces, and to make preparation to protect his own detached command from an attack by Lee in the morning. He said he had relieved Warren, directed him to report in person to General Grant, and placed Griffin in command of the Fifth Corps. I had sent frequent bulletins during the day to the general-in-chief, and now dispatched a courier announcing the change of corps commanders and giving the general result of the round-up.

Sheridan had that day fought one of the most interesting technical battles of the war, almost perfect in conception, brilliant in execution, strikingly dramatic in its incidents, and productive of immensely important results.

About half-past seven o'clock I started to general headquarters. The roads in places were corduroyed with captured muskets. Ammunition trains and ambulances were still struggling forward for miles; teamsters, prisoners, stragglers, and wounded were choking the roadway. The coffee-boilers had kindled their fires. Cheers were resounding on all sides, and everybody was riotous over the victory. A horseman had to pick his way through this jubilant condition of things as best he could, as he did not have the right of way by any means. I traveled again by way of the Brooks road. As I galloped past a group of men on the Boydton plank, my orderly called out to them the news of the victory. The only response he got was from one of them who raised his open hand to his face, put his thumb to his nose, and yelled: "No, you don't—April fool!" I then realized that it was the 1st of April. I had ridden so rapidly that I reached headquarters at Dabney's Mill before the arrival of the last courier I had dispatched. General Grant was sitting with most of the staff about him before a blazing campfire. He wore his blue cavalry overcoat, and the ever-present cigar was in his mouth. I began shouting the good news as soon as I got in sight, and in a moment all but the imperturbable general-in-chief were on their feet giving vent to wild demonstrations of joy. For some minutes there was a bewildering state of excitement, grasping of hands, tossing up of hats, and slapping of each other on the back. It meant the beginning of the end—the reaching of the "last ditch." It pointed to peace and home. Dignity was thrown to the winds. The general, as was expected, asked his usual question: "How many prisoners have been taken?" This was always his first inquiry when an engagement was reported. No man ever had such a fondness for taking prisoners. I think the gratification arose from the kindness of his heart, a feeling that it was much better to win in this way than by the destruction of human life. I was happy to report that the prisoners this time were estimated at over five thousand, and this was the only part of my recital that seemed to call forth a responsive expression from his usually impassive features. After having listened to the description of Sheridan's day's work, the general, with scarcely a word, walked into his tent, and by the light of a flickering candle took up his "manifold writer," a small book which retained a copy of the matter written, and after finishing several dispatches handed them to an orderly to be sent over the field wires, came out and joined our group at the campfire, and said as coolly as if remarking upon the state of the weather: "I have ordered an immediate assault along the lines." This was about 9 o'clock.

General Grant was anxious to have the different commands move against the enemy's lines at once, to prevent Lee from withdrawing troops and sending them against Sheridan. General Meade was all activity and so alive to the situation, and so anxious to carry out the orders of the general-in-chief, that he sent word that he was going to have the troops make a dash at the works without waiting to form assaulting columns. General Grant, at 9:30 p.m. sent a message saying he did not mean to have the corps attack without assaulting columns, but to let the batteries open at once and to feel out with skirmishers....[1]

The remainder relates to events occurring beyond the subject of this book.

Chapter Notes

ABBREVIATIONS: OR—U.S. War Department, *The War of the Rebellion: A Compilation of the Official Records of the Union and Confederate Armies*. Series I, Vol. 46, Part I; FCI—*Findings of the Court of Inquiry and Reviews of the Judge Advocate-General and the General of the Army in the Case of Major General G. K. Warren*; BL—*Battles and Leaders of the Civil War*; PFO—*Proceedings, Findings and Opinions of the Court of Inquiry, Convened by Order of the President of the United States ... In the Case of Gouverneur Kemble Warren and United States, Army. Court of Inquiry (Warren: 1879–1881)*. Part 1; PFO2—*Proceedings, Findings and Opinions of the Court of Inquiry, Convened by Order of the President of the United States ... In the Case of Gouverneur Kemble Warren and United States, Army. Court of Inquiry (Warren: 1879–1881)*. Part 2.

Chapter 2

1. OR, 797.
2. Ibid., 807.

Chapter 4

1. OR, 1116.
2. David W. Lowe, *Meade's Army: The Private Notebooks of Lt. Col. Theodore Lyman*, 353.
3. FCI, "Grant's Dispatch to Lincoln at City Point of 10:30 AM, April 1, 1865," 15.
4. OR, 1110.
5. OR, 796.

Chapter 6

1. Ulysses S. Grant, *The Personal Memoirs of Ulysses S. Grant*, 657.
2. David S. Heidler and Jeanett Heidler, *Encyclopedia of the American Civil War*, 1334.
3. David M. Jordan, *Happiness Is Not My Companion*, 208.
4. Ibid., 238.
5. "Letter of Warren to S. W. Crawford of April 24, 1882," *The Warren Papers*.
6. Ulysses S. Grant, *The Personal Memoirs of Ulysses S. Grant*, 466.
7. Ibid., 465.
8. David W. Lowe, ed., *Meade's Army: The Private Notebooks of Lt. Col. Theodore Lyman*, 151.
9. David M. Jordan, *Happiness Is Not My Companion*, 224.
10. OR, 829.
11. Horace Porter, "Five Forks and the Pursuit of Lee," *Battles and Leaders of the Civil War*, 713.
12. "Letter of Warren to His Brother of November 22, 1877," *The Warren Papers*.
13. "Letter of Warren to His Wife of February, 1869," *The Warren Papers*.
14. Allan Nevins, ed., *A Diary of Battle: The Personal Journals of Colonel Charles S. Wainwright 1861–1865*, 364.
15. Ibid., 368.
16. Ibid., 378.
17. Ibid., 387.
18. Ibid., 390.
19. Ibid., 396.
20. Ibid., 404–405.
21. Ibid., 409.
22. Ibid., 436.
23. Ibid., 476.
24. Ibid., 508–509.
25. David W. Lowe, *Meade's Army: The Private Notebooks of Lt. Col. Theodore Lyman*, 356.

Chapter 9

1. "Testimony of Capt. E. R. Warner," PFO, 38.
2. "Testimony of Lt. Gen. H. Sheridan," PFO, 52.
3. Ibid.
4. Ibid.
5. Ibid.
6. Ibid., 53.
7. Ibid., 54.
8. Ibid., 55.

9. Ibid., 56.
10. Ibid.
11. Ibid., 72.
12. Ibid., 73.
13. Ibid., 128.
14. "Testimony of Frederick C. Newhall," PFO, 147.
15. "Testimony of James W. Forsyth," PFO, 142.
16. "Testimony of Col. John A. Kellog," PFO, 219.
17. "Testimony of Brig. Gen. Joshua L. Chamberlain," PFO, 201.
18. Ibid., 231.
19. Ibid., 204.
20. Ibid., 236.
21. "Testimony of Maj. Gen. Romeyn B. Ayres," PFO, 269.
22. "Testimony of Col. W. W. Swan," PFO, 294.
23. "Testimony of Col. R. M. Brinton," PFO, 302.
24. "Testimony of Col. E. B. Cope," PFO, 326–27.
25. "Testimony of Brig. Gen. Frederick Locke," PFO, 366.
26. "Testimony of Brig. Gen. C. E. LaMotte," PFO, 377.
27. "Testimony of Col. Walter T. Chester," PFO, 385.
28. "Testimony of Lt. Col. James P. Mead," PFO, 398.

Chapter 10

1. "Testimony of Col. Harrison Adreon," PFO, 429.
2. Ibid.
3. "Testimony of Joseph Mayo," PFO, 499.
4. "Testimony of W. Gordon McCabe," PFO, 513.
5. "Testimony of Lt. Col. Theodore Lyman," PFO, 519.
6. Ibid.
7. "Testimony of Rev. Edmund R. Sanborn," PFO, 530.
8. "Testimony of Maj. Gen. Samuel Crawford," PFO, 584.
9. "Testimony of Samuel Y. Gilliam," PFO, 678.
10. "Testimony of Maj. Gen. G. K. Warren," PFO, 716.
11. Ibid., 720.
12. Ibid., 728.
13. Ibid., 735.
14. Ibid.
15. Ibid., 739.
16. Ibid., 744.

17. Ibid., 744–745.
18. Ibid., 750.
19. Ibid., 753.
20. Ibid., 757.

Chapter 11

1. "Testimony of Capt. Henry E. Alford," PFO2, 21.
2. Ibid., 9.
3. "Testimony of Maj. Vanderbilt Allen," PFO2, 18.
4. Ibid.
5. "Additional Testimony of Maj. Gen. Wesley Merritt," PFO2, 23.
6. Ibid.
7. "Testimony of Brig. Gen. Frances T. Sherman," PFO2, 30.
8. Ibid., 32.
9. "Testimony of Lt. Col. Mortimer B. Birdseye," PFO2, 48.
10. Ibid., 49.
11. "Testimony of Brig. Gen. Orville Babcock," PFO2, 55.
12. Ibid., 56.
13. "Testimony of Maj. William Thompson," PFO2, 57.
14. "Testimony of Lt. Col. George L. Gillespie," PFO2, 73.
15. Ibid., 75.
16. Ibid., 81.
17. "Testimony of Capt. William Marks," PFO2, 101.
18. "Testimony of Lt. Gen. Ulysses Simpson Grant," PFO2, 129.
19. Ibid., 131.

Chapter 13

1. FCI, "General Grant's Report on page 1137 of the report of the Honorable Secretary of War to the first session of the 39th Congress," 3.
2. FCI, 7.
3. Ibid., 8.
4. Ibid., 16–17.
5. OR, General Sheridan's Report, 1105.
6. FCI, 17.
7. OR, General Sheridan's Report, 1105.
8. FCI, 18–19.
9. Ibid., 58.

Chapter 14

1. FCI, 59–60.

Chapter 15

1. David M. Jordan, *Happiness Is Not My Companion*, 257.

2. "Letter of Warren to Emily Warren of December 3, 1864," *The Warren Papers*.

Chapter 16

1. *Generals South Generals North*, 292.

Appendix A

1. OR, 1101–07.

Appendix B

1. OR, 796–837.

Appendix C

1. Horace Porter, "Five Forks and the Pursuit of Lee," *Battles and Leaders of the Civil War*, 708–722.

Bibliography

An Account of Operations of the Fifth Army Corps, Commanded by Maj. G. K. Warren at the Battle of Five Forks, April 1, 1865. New York: D. Van Nostrand, 1866.
Commager, Henry Steele, ed. *Living History of the Civil War.* New York: Tess, 2000.
Dispatches of Meade, Grant, Warren and Sheridan that relate to Warren's activity March 30–April 1, 1865, are contained in Warren's report in the *Official Records of the Union and Confederate Armies*, Series 1, Vol. 46, Part I.
Findings of the Court of Inquiry and Reviews of the Judge Advocate-General and the General of the Army in the Case of Major General G. K. Warren. Washington, D.C.: Government Printing Office, 1883.
"General Grant on the Siege of Petersburg." *Battles and Leaders of the Civil War*, Vol. 4. New York: Thomas Yoseloff, 1952. 574–579.
Generals South Generals North. Guilford, CT: Globe Pequiat, 2011.
Grant, Ulysses S. *The Personal Memoirs of Ulysses S. Grant.* New York: Konecky and Konecky, 1992.
Heidler, David S., and Jeanett Heidler. *Encyclopedia of the American Civil War.* New York: W. W. Norton, 2000.
Jordan, David M. *Happiness Is Not My Companion.* Bloomington: Indiana University Press, 2001.
"Letter of Warren to Emily Warren of December 3, 1864." *The Warren Papers.* New York State Library.
"Letter of Warren to His Brother of November 22, 1877." *The Warren Papers.* New York State Library.
"Letter of Warren to His Wife of February, 1869." *The Warren Papers.* New York State Library.
"Letter of Warren to S. W. Crawford of April 24, 1882." *The Warren Papers.* New York State Library.
Livermore, Thomas. *Numbers and Losses in the Civil War.* Carlisle, PA: John Kallmann, 1996.
Lowe, David W., ed. *Meade's Army: The Private Notebooks of Lt. Col. Theodore Lyman.* Kent, OH: Kent State University Press, 2007.
McPherson, James. *Atlas of the Civil War.* Philadelphia: Courage, 2005.
Miller, Francis Trevelyan. *The Armies and the Leaders.* New York: Castle, 1957.
Nevins, Allan, ed. *A Diary of Battle: The Personal Journals of Colonel Charles S. Wainwright 1861–1865.* New York: Da Capo Press, 1962.
Porter, Horace. *Campaigning with Grant.* New York: Konecky and Konecky, 1992.
Porter, Horace. "Five Forks and the Pursuit of Lee." *Battles and Leaders of the Civil War*, Vol. 4. New York: Thomas Yoseloff, 1956.
Proceedings, Findings and Opinions of the Court of Inquiry, Convened by Order of the President of the United States ... In the Case of Gouverneur Kemble Warren and United States, Army. Court of Inquiry (Warren: 1879–1881). Parts 1 and 2. Washington, D.C.: Government Printing Office, 1883.
Report of the General of the Army. Washington, D.C.: Headquarters of the Army, July 15, 1882.
Rodenbouch, Theo F. *The Photographic History of the Civil War: The Cavalry.* New York: Fairfax, 1983.
Sheridan, P. H. *The Personal Memoirs of P. H. Sheridan.* Reprint. New York: Da Capo, 1992.
"Sheridan's Official Report of Operations Mar 29–April 1, 1865." U.S. War Department. *The War of the Rebellion: A Compilation of the Official Records of the Union and Confederate Armies.* Series I, Vol. 46, Part I. Harrisburg, PA: National Historical Society, 1971.
U.S. Army Military Institute. *The Official Military Atlas of the Civil War.* New York: Barnes and Noble, 1983.
"Warren's Official Report of Operations Mar 29–April, 1865." U.S. War Department. *The War of the*

Rebellion: A Compilation of the Official Records of the Union and Confederate Armies. Series I, Vol. 46, Part I. Harrisburg, PA: National Historical Society, 1971.

The West Point Atlas of the Civil War. New York: Tess, 1995.

Testimony, Court of Inquiry

"Additional Testimony of Maj. Gen. Wesley Merritt." *Proceedings, Findings and Opinions of the Court of Inquiry, Convened by Order of the President of the United States ... In the Case of Gouverneur Kemble Warren and United States, Army. Court of Inquiry (Warren: 1879–1881).* Part 2. Washington, D.C.: Government Printing Office, 1883. 22–26.

"Testimony of Brig. Gen. Brayton Ives." *Proceedings, Findings and Opinions of the Court of Inquiry, Convened by Order of the President of the United States ... In the Case of Gouverneur Kemble Warren and United States, Army. Court of Inquiry (Warren: 1879–1881).* Part 2. Washington, D.C.: Government Printing Office, 1883. 42–44.

"Testimony of Brig. Gen. C. E. LaMotte." *Proceedings, Findings and Opinions of the Court of Inquiry, Convened by Order of the President of the United States ... In the Case of Gouverneur Kemble Warren and United States, Army. Court of Inquiry (Warren: 1879–1881).* Part 1. Washington, D.C.: Government Printing Office, 1883. 371–381.

"Testimony of Brig. Gen. Francis T. Sherman." *Proceedings, Findings and Opinions of the Court of Inquiry, Convened by Order of the President of the United States ... In the Case of Gouverneur Kemble Warren and United States, Army. Court of Inquiry (Warren: 1879–1881).* Part 2. Washington, D.C.: Government Printing Office, 1883. 29–39.

"Testimony of Brig. Gen. Frederick Locke." *Proceedings, Findings and Opinions of the Court of Inquiry, Convened by Order of the President of the United States ... In the Case of Gouverneur Kemble Warren and United States, Army. Court of Inquiry (Warren: 1879–1881).* Part 1. Washington, D.C.: Government Printing Office, 1883. 363–371.

"Testimony of Brig. Gen. H. C. Bankhead." *Proceedings, Findings and Opinions of the Court of Inquiry, Convened by Order of the President of the United States ... In the Case of Gouverneur Kemble Warren and United States, Army. Court of Inquiry (Warren: 1879–1881).* Part 1. Washington, D.C.: Government Printing Office, 1883. 337–348.

"Testimony of Brig. Gen. Hollon Richardson." *Proceedings, Findings and Opinions of the Court of Inquiry, Convened by Order of the President of the United States ... In the Case of Gouverneur Kemble Warren and United States, Army. Court of Inquiry (Warren: 1879–1881).* Part 1. Washington, D.C.: Government Printing Office, 1883. 314–320.

"Testimony of Brig. Gen. Horace Porter." *Proceedings, Findings and Opinions of the Court of Inquiry, Convened by Order of the President of the United States ... In the Case of Gouverneur Kemble Warren and United States, Army. Court of Inquiry (Warren: 1879–1881).* Part 2. Washington, D.C.: Government Printing Office, 1883. 59–68.

"Testimony of Brig. Gen. Joshua L. Chamberlain." *Proceedings, Findings and Opinions of the Court of Inquiry, Convened by Order of the President of the United States ... In the Case of Gouverneur Kemble Warren and United States, Army. Court of Inquiry (Warren: 1879–1881).* Part 1. Washington, D.C.: Government Printing Office, 1883. 228–237, 271–288.

"Testimony of Brig. Gen. Orville Babcock." *Proceedings, Findings and Opinions of the Court of Inquiry, Convened by Order of the President of the United States ... In the Case of Gouverneur Kemble Warren and United States, Army. Court of Inquiry (Warren: 1879–1881).* Part 2. Washington, D.C.: Government Printing Office, 1883. 55–56.

"Testimony of Brig. Gen. Richard Coulter." *Proceedings, Findings and Opinions of the Court of Inquiry, Convened by Order of the President of the United States ... In the Case of Gouverneur Kemble Warren and United States, Army. Court of Inquiry (Warren: 1879–1881).* Part 1. Washington, D.C.: Government Printing Office, 1883. 348–357.

"Testimony of Brig. Gen. Ranald MacKenzie." *Proceedings, Findings and Opinions of the Court of Inquiry, Convened by Order of the President of the United States ... In the Case of Gouverneur Kemble Warren and United States, Army. Court of Inquiry (Warren: 1879–1881).* Part 2. Washington, D.C.: Government Printing Office, 1883. 1–3.

"Testimony of Capt. C. Mason Kinne." *Proceedings, Findings and Opinions of the Court of Inquiry, Convened by Order of the President of the United States ... In the Case of Gouverneur Kemble Warren and United States, Army. Court of Inquiry (Warren: 1879–1881).* Part 2. Washington, D.C.: Government Printing Office, 1883. 96–99.

"Testimony of Capt. Charles F. Sawyer." *Proceedings, Findings and Opinions of the Court of Inquiry, Convened by Order of the President of the United States ... In the Case of Gouverneur Kemble Warren and United States, Army. Court of Inquiry (Warren: 1879–1881)*. Part 1. Washington, D.C.: Government Printing Office, 1883. 410–416.

"Testimony of Capt. E. G. Sherley." *Proceedings, Findings and Opinions of the Court of Inquiry, Convened by Order of the President of the United States ... In the Case of Gouverneur Kemble Warren and United States, Army. Court of Inquiry (Warren: 1879–1881)*. Part 1. Washington, D.C.: Government Printing Office, 1883. 416–419.

"Testimony of Capt. E. R. Warner." *Proceedings, Findings and Opinions of the Court of Inquiry, Convened by Order of the President of the United States ... In the Case of Gouverneur Kemble Warren and United States, Army. Court of Inquiry (Warren: 1879–1881)*. Part 1. Washington, D.C.: Government Printing Office, 1883. 36–39.

"Testimony of Capt. Henry C. Erich." *Proceedings, Findings and Opinions of the Court of Inquiry, Convened by Order of the President of the United States ... In the Case of Gouverneur Kemble Warren and United States, Army. Court of Inquiry (Warren: 1879–1881)*. Part 2. Washington, D.C.: Government Printing Office, 1883. 5–7.

"Testimony of Capt. Henry E. Alford." *Proceedings, Findings and Opinions of the Court of Inquiry, Convened by Order of the President of the United States ... In the Case of Gouverneur Kemble Warren and United States, Army. Court of Inquiry (Warren: 1879–1881)*. Part 2. Washington, D.C.: Government Printing Office, 1883. 7–11.

"Testimony of Capt. Henry Wood." *Proceedings, Findings and Opinions of the Court of Inquiry, Convened by Order of the President of the United States ... In the Case of Gouverneur Kemble Warren and United States, Army. Court of Inquiry (Warren: 1879–1881)*. Part 2. Washington, D.C.: Government Printing Office, 1883. 12–15.

"Testimony of Capt. William Marks." *Proceedings, Findings and Opinions of the Court of Inquiry, Convened by Order of the President of the United States ... In the Case of Gouverneur Kemble Warren and United States, Army. Court of Inquiry (Warren: 1879–1881)*. Part 2. Washington, D.C.: Government Printing Office, 1883. 100–103.

"Testimony of Col. D. L. Smith." *Proceedings, Findings and Opinions of the Court of Inquiry, Convened by Order of the President of the United States ... In the Case of Gouverneur Kemble Warren and United States, Army. Court of Inquiry (Warren: 1879–1881)*. Part 1. Washington, D.C.: Government Printing Office, 1883. 603–613.

"Testimony of Col. E. B. Cope." *Proceedings, Findings and Opinions of the Court of Inquiry, Convened by Order of the President of the United States ... In the Case of Gouverneur Kemble Warren and United States, Army. Court of Inquiry (Warren: 1879–1881)*. Part 1. Washington, D.C.: Government Printing Office, 1883. 320–333.

"Testimony of Col. Harrison Adreon." *Proceedings, Findings and Opinions of the Court of Inquiry, Convened by Order of the President of the United States ... In the Case of Gouverneur Kemble Warren and United States, Army. Court of Inquiry (Warren: 1879–1881)*. Part 1. Washington, D.C.: Government Printing Office, 1883. 428–435.

"Testimony of Col. John A. Kellog." *Proceedings, Findings and Opinions of the Court of Inquiry, Convened by Order of the President of the United States ... In the Case of Gouverneur Kemble Warren and United States, Army. Court of Inquiry (Warren: 1879–1881)*. Part 1. Washington, D.C.: Government Printing Office, 1883. 218–228.

"Testimony of Col. R. M. Brinton." *Proceedings, Findings and Opinions of the Court of Inquiry, Convened by Order of the President of the United States ... In the Case of Gouverneur Kemble Warren and United States, Army. Court of Inquiry (Warren: 1879–1881)*. Part 1. Washington, D.C.: Government Printing Office, 1883. 301–314.

"Testimony of Col. Walter T. Chester." *Proceedings, Findings and Opinions of the Court of Inquiry, Convened by Order of the President of the United States ... In the Case of Gouverneur Kemble Warren and United States, Army. Court of Inquiry (Warren: 1879–1881)*. Part 1. Washington, D.C.: Government Printing Office, 1883. 381–389.

"Testimony of E. M. Baker." *Proceedings, Findings and Opinions of the Court of Inquiry, Convened by Order of the President of the United States ... In the Case of Gouverneur Kemble Warren and United States, Army. Court of Inquiry (Warren: 1879–1881)*. Part 2. Washington, D.C.: Government Printing Office, 1883. 20–21.

"Testimony of Fitzhugh Lee." *Proceedings, Findings and Opinions of the Court of Inquiry, Convened by Order of the President of the United States ... In the Case of Gouverneur Kemble Warren and United*

States, Army. Court of Inquiry (Warren: 1879–1881). Part 1. Washington, D.C.: Government Printing Office, 1883. 466–484.

"Testimony of Frederick C. Newhall." *Proceedings, Findings and Opinions of the Court of Inquiry, Convened by Order of the President of the United States ... In the Case of Gouverneur Kemble Warren and United States, Army. Court of Inquiry (Warren: 1879–1881)*. Part 1. Washington, D.C.: Government Printing Office, 1883. 141–154.

"Testimony of Holman S. Melcher." *Proceedings, Findings and Opinions of the Court of Inquiry, Convened by Order of the President of the United States ... In the Case of Gouverneur Kemble Warren and United States, Army. Court of Inquiry (Warren: 1879–1881)*. Part 1. Washington, D.C.: Government Printing Office, 1883. 455–466.

"Testimony of James W. Forsyth." *Proceedings, Findings and Opinions of the Court of Inquiry, Convened by Order of the President of the United States ... In the Case of Gouverneur Kemble Warren and United States, Army. Court of Inquiry (Warren: 1879–1881)*. Part 1. Washington, D.C.: Government Printing Office, 1883. 189–211.

"Testimony of James W. Wadsworth." *Proceedings, Findings and Opinions of the Court of Inquiry, Convened by Order of the President of the United States ... In the Case of Gouverneur Kemble Warren and United States, Army. Court of Inquiry (Warren: 1879–1881)*. Part 1. Washington, D.C.: Government Printing Office, 1883. 181–189.

"Testimony of Joseph Mayo." *Proceedings, Findings and Opinions of the Court of Inquiry, Convened by Order of the President of the United States ... In the Case of Gouverneur Kemble Warren and United States, Army. Court of Inquiry (Warren: 1879–1881)*. Part 1. Washington, D.C.: Government Printing Office, 1883. 496–511.

"Testimony of Joseph P. Cotton." *Proceedings, Findings and Opinions of the Court of Inquiry, Convened by Order of the President of the United States ... In the Case of Gouverneur Kemble Warren and United States, Army. Court of Inquiry (Warren: 1879–1881)*. Part 1. Washington, D.C.: Government Printing Office, 1883. 327–346.

"Testimony of Lt. Col. Ellis Spear." *Proceedings, Findings and Opinions of the Court of Inquiry, Convened by Order of the President of the United States ... In the Case of Gouverneur Kemble Warren and United States, Army. Court of Inquiry (Warren: 1879–1881)*. Part 1. Washington, D.C.: Government Printing Office, 1883. 400–410.

"Testimony of Lt. Col. George L. Gillespie." *Proceedings, Findings and Opinions of the Court of Inquiry, Convened by Order of the President of the United States ... In the Case of Gouverneur Kemble Warren and United States, Army. Court of Inquiry (Warren: 1879–1881)*. Part 1. Washington, D.C.: Government Printing Office, 1883. 72–86.

"Testimony of Lt. Col. James P. Mead." *Proceedings, Findings and Opinions of the Court of Inquiry, Convened by Order of the President of the United States ... In the Case of Gouverneur Kemble Warren and United States, Army. Court of Inquiry (Warren: 1879–1881)*. Part 1. Washington, D.C.: Government Printing Office, 1883. 389–400.

"Testimony of Lt. Col. M. V. Sheridan." *Proceedings, Findings and Opinions of the Court of Inquiry, Convened by Order of the President of the United States ... In the Case of Gouverneur Kemble Warren and United States, Army. Court of Inquiry (Warren: 1879–1881)*. Part 1. Washington, D.C.: Government Printing Office, 1883. 289–290.

"Testimony of Lt. Col. Mortimer B. Birdseye." *Proceedings, Findings and Opinions of the Court of Inquiry, Convened by Order of the President of the United States ... In the Case of Gouverneur Kemble Warren and United States, Army. Court of Inquiry (Warren: 1879–1881)*. Part 2. Washington, D.C.: Government Printing Office, 1883. 47–51.

"Testimony of Lt. Col. Theodore Bean." *Proceedings, Findings and Opinions of the Court of Inquiry, Convened by Order of the President of the United States ... In the Case of Gouverneur Kemble Warren and United States, Army. Court of Inquiry (Warren: 1879–1881)*. Part 2. Washington, D.C.: Government Printing Office, 1883. 68–71.

"Testimony of Lt. Col. Theodore Lyman." *Proceedings, Findings and Opinions of the Court of Inquiry, Convened by Order of the President of the United States ... In the Case of Gouverneur Kemble Warren and United States, Army. Court of Inquiry (Warren: 1879–1881)*. Part 1. Washington, D.C.: Government Printing Office, 1883. 517–523.

"Testimony of Lt. Col. West Funk." *Proceedings, Findings and Opinions of the Court of Inquiry, Convened by Order of the President of the United States ... In the Case of Gouverneur Kemble Warren and United States, Army. Court of Inquiry (Warren: 1879–1881)*. Part 1. Washington, D.C.: Government Printing Office, 1883. 435–439.

"Testimony of Lt. Gen. Philip H. Sheridan." *Proceedings, Findings and Opinions of the Court of Inquiry, Convened by Order of the President of the United States ... In the Case of Gouverneur Kemble Warren and United States, Army. Court of Inquiry (Warren: 1879–1881)*. Part 1. Washington, D.C.: Government Printing Office, 1883. 51–128.

"Testimony of Lt. Gen. Ulysses Simpson Grant." *Proceedings, Findings and Opinions of the Court of Inquiry, Convened by Order of the President of the United States ... In the Case of Gouverneur Kemble Warren and United States, Army. Court of Inquiry (Warren: 1879–1881)*. Part 2. Washington, D.C.: Government Printing Office, 1883. 126–138.

"Testimony of M. D. Corse." *Proceedings, Findings and Opinions of the Court of Inquiry, Convened by Order of the President of the United States ... In the Case of Gouverneur Kemble Warren and United States, Army. Court of Inquiry (Warren: 1879–1881)*. Part 1. Washington, D.C.: Government Printing Office, 1883. 419–428.

"Testimony of Maj. Gen. G. K. Warren." *Proceedings, Findings and Opinions of the Court of Inquiry, Convened by Order of the President of the United States ... In the Case of Gouverneur Kemble Warren and United States, Army. Court of Inquiry (Warren: 1879–1881)*. Part 1. Washington, D.C.: Government Printing Office, 1883. 707–801.

"Testimony of Maj. Gen. Romeyn B. Ayres." *Proceedings, Findings and Opinions of the Court of Inquiry, Convened by Order of the President of the United States ... In the Case of Gouverneur Kemble Warren and United States, Army. Court of Inquiry (Warren: 1879–1881)*. Part 1. Washington, D.C.: Government Printing Office, 1883. 246–271, 290–291.

"Testimony of Maj. Gen. Samuel Crawford." *Proceedings, Findings and Opinions of the Court of Inquiry, Convened by Order of the President of the United States ... In the Case of Gouverneur Kemble Warren and United States, Army. Court of Inquiry (Warren: 1879–1881)*. Part 1. Washington, D.C.: Government Printing Office, 1883. 566–588.

"Testimony of Maj. Gen. Wesley Merritt." *Proceedings, Findings and Opinions of the Court of Inquiry, Convened by Order of the President of the United States ... In the Case of Gouverneur Kemble Warren and United States, Army. Court of Inquiry (Warren: 1879–1881)*. Part 1. Washington, D.C.: Government Printing Office, 1883. 589–602.

"Testimony of Maj. Richard Esmond." *Proceedings, Findings and Opinions of the Court of Inquiry, Convened by Order of the President of the United States ... In the Case of Gouverneur Kemble Warren and United States, Army. Court of Inquiry (Warren: 1879–1881)*. Part 1. Washington, D.C.: Government Printing Office, 1883. 357–363.

"Testimony of Maj. Vanderbilt Allen." *Proceedings, Findings and Opinions of the Court of Inquiry, Convened by Order of the President of the United States ... In the Case of Gouverneur Kemble Warren and United States, Army. Court of Inquiry (Warren: 1879–1881)*. Part 2. Washington, D.C.: Government Printing Office, 1883. 18–20.

"Testimony of Maj. W.H.H. Benyaurd." *Proceedings, Findings and Opinions of the Court of Inquiry, Convened by Order of the President of the United States ... In the Case of Gouverneur Kemble Warren and United States, Army. Court of Inquiry (Warren: 1879–1881)*. Part 1. Washington, D.C.: Government Printing Office, 1883. 154–181.

"Testimony of Maj. William R. Mattison." *Proceedings, Findings and Opinions of the Court of Inquiry, Convened by Order of the President of the United States ... In the Case of Gouverneur Kemble Warren and United States, Army. Court of Inquiry (Warren: 1879–1881)*. Part 2. Washington, D.C.: Government Printing Office, 1883. 51–55.

"Testimony of Maj. William Thompson." *Proceedings, Findings and Opinions of the Court of Inquiry, Convened by Order of the President of the United States ... In the Case of Gouverneur Kemble Warren and United States, Army. Court of Inquiry (Warren: 1879–1881)*. Part 2. Washington, D.C.: Government Printing Office, 1883. 56–59.

"Testimony of Rev. Edmund R. Sanborn." *Proceedings, Findings and Opinions of the Court of Inquiry, Convened by Order of the President of the United States ... In the Case of Gouverneur Kemble Warren and United States, Army. Court of Inquiry (Warren: 1879–1881)*. Part 1. Washington, D.C.: Government Printing Office, 1883. 524–530.

"Testimony of Samuel Y. Gilliam." *Proceedings, Findings and Opinions of the Court of Inquiry, Convened by Order of the President of the United States ... In the Case of Gouverneur Kemble Warren and United States, Army. Court of Inquiry (Warren: 1879–1881)*. Part 1. Washington, D.C.: Government Printing Office, 1883. 663–682.

"Testimony of Thomas Munford." *Proceedings, Findings and Opinions of the Court of Inquiry, Convened by Order of the President of the United States ... In the Case of Gouverneur Kemble Warren and United*

States, Army. Court of Inquiry (Warren: 1879–1881). Part 1. Washington, D.C.: Government Printing Office, 1883. 439–455.

"Testimony of W. Gordon McCabe." *Proceedings, Findings and Opinions of the Court of Inquiry, Convened by Order of the President of the United States ... In the Case of Gouverneur Kemble Warren and United States, Army. Court of Inquiry (Warren: 1879–1881)*. Part 1. Washington, D.C.: Government Printing Office, 1883. 511–517.

"Testimony of W.H.F. Lee." *Proceedings, Findings and Opinions of the Court of Inquiry, Convened by Order of the President of the United States ... In the Case of Gouverneur Kemble Warren and United States, Army. Court of Inquiry (Warren: 1879–1881)*. Part 1. Washington, D.C.: Government Printing Office, 1883. 530–538.

"Testimony of W. W. Wood." *Proceedings, Findings and Opinions of the Court of Inquiry, Convened by Order of the President of the United States ... In the Case of Gouverneur Kemble Warren and United States, Army. Court of Inquiry (Warren: 1879–1881)*. Part 1. Washington, D.C.: Government Printing Office, 1883. 484–496.

Index

Adams House 120, 164, 190
Adreon, Col. Harrison 96–97
Alford, Capt. Henry E. 126–127
Allen, Maj. Vanderbilt 65, 127, 137
Antietam, Battle of 16, 33
Appomattox 16, 47, 71, 161
Appomattox River 7, 10, 18
Army Corps 32
Army of the James 7, 18, 35, 126, 147, 164, 203
Army of the Potomac 1, 3, 7, 10, 12, 16, 22, 32, 33–38, 48, 51–52, 55–56, 147, 153, 161, 163, 165, 168, 176, 193, 205–206
Augur, Brig. Gen. G.C. 51–53, 158–159
Ayres, Maj. Gen. R. 16–17, 20, 22–23, 26–28, 30, 47, 56–70, 72–79, 82–84, 86–91, 93, 96–97, 100–101, 111–113, 116–117, 120, 122–125, 127, 129–131, 134–135, 137–138, 140–145, 147, 155–156, 163, 165, 167–170, 173–176, 178–183, 186, 188–191, 194 200, 204–208

Babcock, Lt. Col. Orville 62
Babcock, Brig. Gen. W. 60, 67, 132–133, 135, 206
Baker, Maj. E.M. 127–128
Bankhead Col. H.C. 66, 82–84, 122, 126, 168, 188, 194–196, 199–200
Barringer's Brigade 110, 170, 173
Bartlett, Brig. Gen. C.G. 56, 72, 78, 80–81, 91–92, 109–110, 119–120, 141, 145, 165, 167, 174, 184–188, 190
Battery B of Fourth U.S. Artillery 172
Baxter, Brig. Gen. 70–71, 84–86, 88–90, 93, 113–114, 168, 195
Beale 110–111
Bean, Lt. Col. Theodore W. 136

Beardslee 9
Benyaurd, Maj. W.H. 64–65, 75, 90, 168, 187, 190, 199–200
Big Bethel, Battle of 33
Birdseye, Lt. Col. Mortimer B. 131–132
Boisseau 8, 26, 59, 73, 81, 86, 89–91, 93–94, 98, 132, 175, 178
Boisseau, Dr. 80–81, 88, 90, 92, 109–110, 113–114, 201
Boisseau, G. 56
Boisseau, J. 24, 57, 59, 64, 66–67, 71, 78, 119–121, 124, 141, 144–145, 163–164, 176, 179–180, 189–191, 205–206
Bolingbroke Hotel 153
Bowerman, Col. 74–76, 78, 93, 96
Boydton Plank Road 4, 9–10, 18–20, 22, 24, 45, 54–57, 59–60, 64–69, 71–72, 74–77, 80–82, 86–87, 89, 100–101, 116, 119–120, 124, 133–135, 141, 144, 162–163, 165, 169–170, 172, 175, 180, 185–187, 191–192, 201, 203–205, 209
Brinton, Col. R.M 78–79
Brooks Road 75, 77, 86–87, 96, 101, 120, 135, 141, 205–206, 209
Bull Run, Battle of 16, 33, 48
Burgess House 177, 178
Burke 4, 10
Burnside, Maj. Gen. Ambrose 3, 35, 44, 151
Butler, Mrs. R. 8, 71–73, 109, 133–134, 175–176, 181, 186, 204

Capehart, Brig. Gen. 137, 163
Cedar Mountain, Battle of 52
Cemetery Ridge 34
Chamberlain, Brig. Gen. Joshua 31, 38, 71–73, 76, 100, 117, 119, 167, 171, 183–184
Chamberlain's Bed 120, 131, 162, 164, 190

Chester, Lt. Col. Walter T. 88–89
Chickamauga, Battle of 49
chimneys 26, 63, 66, 82–83, 85–86, 89–91, 93, 113, 197, 202–203
City Point 6, 10–11, 19, 22
Claiborne Road 81
Clement, Capt. B.C. 192
Cold Harbor, Battle of 3–4
Cope, Col. E.B. 13, 79–81, 168, 176, 181, 184, 187–188, 196–197, 199–200
corduroy road 10, 22
Corps of Engineers 41, 47, 51–52, 150–151, 153
Corse, Brig. Gen. M.D. CSA 25, 28, 95–96, 98–99, 105–107, 110–111, 115, 207
Cotton, Joseph P. 73, 115
Coulter, Brig. Gen. Richard 31, 70, 84–86, 88–90, 113, 168, 195, 198–199
court martial 48, 50, 147, 153, 158
court of inquiry 1, 17, 48–53, 143, 147–148, 153–155, 158
Crater, Battle of the 49, 151
Crawford, Maj. Gen. Samuel 16–17, 20, 23, 26–28, 30, 36, 39, 47, 57–58, 61–68, 70, 72–91, 98, 100–102, 111–114, 116–117, 120–126, 128, 130–131, 136–137, 140–142, 145, 147, 150–151, 155–156, 163, 165, 167, 169–176, 178–183, 186, 188–190, 194–201, 204–206, 208
Cronkite, W.M. 192
Crook, Maj. Gen. George 161–164, 185
Crow House 176
Crump Road 88, 120–123, 136, 138, 142, 144, 165, 190, 205, 207
Custer, Maj. Gen. G.A. 51, 120,

219

130–132, 137, 155, 162–165, 190, 195, 208

Dabney, A. 8
Dabney, S. 8, 163, 175, 181
Dabney, W. 8, 178, 181
Dabney's Mill 24, 54–55, 57, 108, 134, 144, 174–175, 177–178, 185, 203–205, 209
Dakotas 33
Danville Railroad 4, 10, 203
Davies, Brig. Gen. H.E. 129, 162–163, 205
Davis, Jefferson 33
Denslow, Lt. Col. W.J. 82
Department of West Virginia 37
Dinwiddie 8, 25–26, 38–39, 56, 59–60, 64, 67–69, 72, 74–78, 81–82, 86–87, 91, 95–96, 100–101, 107–109, 111, 115, 119–121, 124, 130–131, 134, 136, 138, 144–145, 148, 162, 166, 168, 175, 189, 191, 204–205
Dinwiddie Court House 10, 22–24, 38, 55–57, 59–60, 62, 66, 69–70, 72–73, 75, 77, 80–81, 89, 95–96, 98, 102–103, 105, 107, 109–111, 119–120, 126, 130, 133–134, 144, 162–166, 168–169, 175, 185–191, 200–201, 203, 205
Doolittle, Lt. Col. 172
Durand, Lt. Col. 137
Duryee, Abram 33

Early, Maj. Gen. Jubal CSA 49
Emory, Capt. 170
Erich, Capt. Henry C. 126
Esmond, Maj. Richard 85–86

Farnham, Col. 85, 88, 90
Fifth Corps 7–9, 14–17, 19, 21, 24–27, 30, 32, 34, 36–38, 44, 48–49, 54, 57–59, 61–64, 67, 69–70, 74, 83, 86–87, 89–91, 95–96, 100–101, 105, 109, 111–113, 116–118, 124–125, 127, 129, 132–138, 140–148, 150, 153–157, 162–169, 173, 183, 186, 192–194, 196, 199, 205–206, 208
Fifth New York Cavalry 93
Fifty-Sixth Virginia 184
First Cavalry Division 136, 138
First Connecticut Cavalry 130
First Maine Sharpshooters 92
Fish, Hamilton 154
Fisher, Lt. 172
Fitzhugh, Brig. Gen. Charles S. 96, 130–133, 138, 163, 208

Five Forks, Battle of 1, 18, 25–26, 28, 32, 38–39, 50, 54, 62–64, 77, 79, 82, 86–87, 89, 91–92, 95–96, 101–107, 109–110, 114–115, 123–133, 135–138, 141–142, 147–148, 150, 152, 154–156, 158, 162–166, 178–181, 185, 187, 189–194, 196, 200, 202, 204–206
Ford Road 10, 25–29, 39, 62, 65–68, 71, 79, 80–82, 84–86, 89–93, 98–99, 101–103, 105–108, 110–111, 114, 116, 123, 128, 130, 132, 136–137, 142, 165, 198–199, 207–208
Forsyth, Col. James W. 62, 66–71, 75, 78, 83, 120, 124, 133, 193, 208
Fort Donelson 152
Fowler, Capt. 184
Franklin, Battle of 5
Fredericksburg, Battle of 16, 33
Funk, Maj. 97, 198

Gaines Mill, Battle of 33
Gallaway, Col. 179
Gardner, Maj. Asa B. 100, 124, 139–140
Garnett, Brig. Gen. Richard CSA 152
Gentry, Maj. Wiliam T. 81, 168, 188, 200
Georgia 5, 152
Gettysburg, Battle of 15–16, 29, 33–34, 36, 49, 51, 71, 152, 155–156, 158
Gibbon, Maj. Gen. John 37
Gibb's Brigade 162–163, 205
Gillespie, Lt. Col. George L. 122, 136–137, 175
Gillian, Samuel Y. 115–116
Gillian Farm 25
Gillian Field 25, 66, 82, 85–87, 89, 91, 96, 101–102, 105, 107, 111, 114, 115, 123–124, 128, 130, 142
Glenn, Maj. E.A. 171–172, 183–184
Gordon, Maj. Gen. John Brown CSA 151, 187
Governors Island 53, 55, 60, 95, 97, 109, 115
Grant, Lt. Gen. U.S. 3–13, 16, 18–19, 21–25, 27, 29, 34–42, 45, 47–49, 51–61, 66–70, 76, 83, 108–109, 124, 132–136, 138–148, 152–154, 157, 166, 175–179, 185, 191, 193, 199, 202–206, 209
Gravelly Run 19–24, 45, 54, 56–57, 60, 62, 64, 68–69, 73, 75–

76, 78, 87, 90, 96, 100, 108, 116–117, 120, 134, 141, 170–171, 173–174, 178–182, 185–192, 198, 203, 205
Gravelly Run Church 25–26, 31, 57–58, 60–61, 63–64, 66–67, 69–71, 73, 75–77, 79–85, 87–88, 91–93, 96, 101, 110, 113, 122–123, 126–129, 133, 135–138, 141, 164–165, 194, 201, 206
Gregg, Brig. Gen. J.I. 162–163, 205
Gregory, Brig. Gen. 31, 167, 172, 183–184
Griffin, Maj. Gen. Charles 16–17, 23, 26–28, 30, 38, 42, 47, 50, 56–58, 61, 63–64, 66–67, 70–84, 88, 91–92, 98, 100, 108–110, 112–114, 116–117, 119–125, 128, 130, 136–137, 140–142, 145, 147–148, 150–151, 153, 155–156, 163, 165, 167, 169–190, 192, 194–201, 204–206, 208
Gwynn, Brig. Gen. James 30, 74–76, 78, 93

Halleck, Maj. Gen. Henry 152
Halsted, Capt. George B. 168, 200
Hampton, Maj. Gen. Wade CSA 152
Hancock, Maj. Gen. W.S. 14, 19, 34, 36, 51–52, 151
Hargrave, Miss 8, 169
Hargrave, Mrs. 8
Hargraves, H. 170
Harrisburg 153
Hatchers Run 25–27, 29, 39, 68–69, 80–81, 85, 91–92, 98–99, 102, 108, 111, 126, 142, 165, 168, 175–177, 184–185, 197, 199, 201, 203, 205, 207
Hayes, Rutherford B. 49–50, 147–148
Hood, Gen. John B. CSA 5, 153
Hooker, Maj. Gen. Joseph 3, 16, 33–34
Horrell, Capt. 168, 171, 186, 200
Howe, Col. 179
Hudson, Capt. Peter T. 206
Humphreys, Maj. Gen. Andrew 13, 19, 24, 32, 34, 37, 47, 52, 56, 72, 74, 108–109, 116–117, 151, 153, 169–170, 172–186, 189, 203–205

Imputation 1 143
Imputation 2 144
Imputation 3 145
Imputation 4 145

Ives, Brig. Gen. Brayton 130–131

Jacklin, Maj. 192
Jackson, Lt. Gen. "Stonewall" CSA 14, 32, 152
James River 3, 147, 161
Jay, Maj. 170
Jerusalem Plank Road 4, 9
Johnson, President 148
Johnston, Gen. J.E. CSA 5–6, 10, 152–153, 202–203
Jones Landing 161

Kellogg, Col. John A. 30, 66, 69–71, 82, 84–86, 88–90, 93–94, 113, 168, 195
Kelsey, Pvt. 172
Kernstown, Battle of 152
Kinne, Capt. L. Mason 137–138

Lamotte, Brig. Gen. C.E. 87–88
Lee, Maj. Gen. Fitzhugh CSA 23, 25, 53, 98, 101–103, 106, 191, 207
Lee, Gen. Robert E. CSA 3, 5–7, 10, 12, 18–19, 21, 29, 36, 38–39, 42, 58, 63, 71, 95, 147, 158, 162, 165, 184, 192, 202–205, 207–209
Lee, Maj. Gen. W.H.F. CSA 53, 95–96, 98, 102, 105–107, 110–111, 115–116, 191, 207
Lewis House 171–172
Lincoln, Pres. Abraham 3, 22, 146–148, 202–203
Little Round Top 34, 51, 71, 155
Locke, Lt. Col. Frederick T. 17, 45, 47, 49, 54, 83, 86–87, 90, 101, 123, 168–169, 176, 180, 192, 200
Longstreet, Lt. Gen James CSA 14, 32, 49
Lyman, Lt. Col. Theodore 22, 37, 45, 108–109

MacKenzie, Maj. Gen. R.S. 24, 57, 60–61, 93, 126, 130, 164–165, 195, 197, 199, 205, 207
Macy, Brig. Gen. 175–176
Malbon, Capt. 168
Malones Crossing 162
maps 8
Marks, Capt. William 138
Mattison, Maj. William R. 132
Mayo, Col. Joseph CSA 25, 28, 98, 105–106, 114
McCabe, W. Gordon 106–108
McClellan, Maj. Gen. George B. 3, 14–16, 33, 41–42
McCrory, A. 192

McGonnigle, Capt. A.J. 207
McMillan, Maj. James 51
Mead, Lt. Col. James P. 89–91
Meade, Maj. Gen. George 1, 3, 12–13, 15–16, 19, 22–24, 34–39, 44–45, 50, 54–58, 60, 64, 67, 69, 71–72, 81, 108–109, 116, 118–119, 121, 124, 128, 134–135, 141, 144, 147–148, 153, 167–170, 173–179, 181–182, 184–194, 204–205, 209
Melcher, Capt. Holman S. 87, 100–101
Merritt, Maj. Gen. Wesley 21–23, 53, 70, 127–129, 136–137, 161–165, 176, 178–181, 185, 195, 208
Miles, Maj. Gen. Nelson 108–109, 117, 174, 176–177, 179–183, 204
Military Division of the Atlantic 167
military railroad 11, 22, 161, 202
Miller, Capt. Charles H. 138
Mine Run Campaign 36
Mink's Battery 182
Mississippi 5, 52, 194
Mitchell, Lt. 172
Morgan, Governor 154
Mott, Brig. Gen. 87, 179–180
Munford, Maj. Gen. Thomas CSA 25, 30, 62, 95–99, 101–102, 104, 107, 113, 142, 207

Nashville 5
Nebraska 33
Newhall, Lt. Col. Frederick C. 62–63, 90
Newton, Col. John 52–53
Ninety-first New York Volunteers 82, 94
Ninth Corps 35, 153
Norman, Maj. 179
North Anna, Battle of 3

O'Keele, Maj. 131
One Hundred Eighteenth PA 172
One Hundred Eighty-Eighth N.Y. 172
One Hundred Eighty-Fifth N.Y. 171
One Hundred Fifty-Fifth PA 172
One Hundred Ninety-Eighth PA 171, 183
Ord, Maj. Gen. E.O. 18

Pamunkey River 161
Parke, Maj. Gen. John G. 47, 153, 203

Parker, Col. E.S. 178
Parmelee, Capt. 131
Partridge, Col. 172
Pearson, Brig. Gen. 119, 172, 183, 185
Pennington's Brigade 130–131, 163
Pentecoast, T. 178
Perkins, W. 168–169
Petersburg 3–4, 6–7, 9–10, 38, 44, 79, 101, 111, 129, 147, 153, 161–165, 177, 180, 200, 202–204
Pickett, Maj. Gen. George CSA 19, 23–27, 29, 36, 38–39, 51, 59–60, 66, 92, 95–96, 98–99, 101–107, 110–111, 114–116, 125, 141, 145, 152, 155, 158, 178–180, 183–185, 187, 191–192, 204, 207
Plank Road 4, 9–10, 18–22, 24, 45, 54–56, 59–60, 64–69, 71–72, 74–77, 80–82, 86–87, 89, 96, 100–101, 116, 119–120, 124, 133–135, 141, 144, 162–163, 169–183, 185–190, 192, 201, 203–205
Porter, Maj. Gen. Fitz John 16–17, 48
Porter, Col. Horace 39, 55, 62, 70, 83, 133–136, 149, 202–209

Quaker Road 19–20, 45, 116, 120, 169–177, 180, 187, 189–190

radio 8–9
railroads 5, 9–11
Ransom, Brig. Gen. M.W. CSA 25, 95–96, 98, 104–107, 111, 207
Rapidan 36
Rawlins, Maj. Gen. John 40, 54–55, 69, 153–154, 204
Reams Station 162
Richardson, Col. 199
Richmond 3–7, 9, 10, 15, 107, 143, 158, 161–162, 203
Rienzi 207–208
roads 9
Roberts Brigade 192
Roebling, Washington 47, 157
Rosecrans, Maj. Gen. W.S. 49
Rosser, Maj. Gen. T.L. CSA 25, 29, 92, 95, 98–99, 102, 111, 142, 191, 207
Rowanty Creek 19, 162, 169–170, 187
Ruggles, Brig. Gen. George D. 167, 173

Index

Sanborn, Rev. Edmund R. 109–110
Sawyer, Capt. Charles F. 92–93
Scales Brigade 179
Schofield, Maj. Gen. John 5
Second Corps 7, 18–19, 34, 36, 51–52, 100, 113, 143, 165, 168, 171, 174, 177, 182, 185, 189, 192
Second New York Cavalry 131–132
Sedgwick, Maj. Gen. John 36
Sergeant, Col. 182
Seventeenth Pennsylvania Cavalry 127, 133
Seventh Wisconsin 199
Shenandoah Valley 6–7, 161, 163
Shenandoah Valley Army 4, 6, 18, 25, 52, 136
Sheridan, Capt. Michael Vincint 68–70
Sheridan, Maj. Gen. Phillip 1, 4, 6–7, 10, 12–13, 18–19, 21–31, 35–39, 41–42, 45–81, 83–91, 95–97, 100–103, 107–111, 113, 119–148, 150–158, 161–167, 174–180, 183–200, 202–209
Sherley, Capt. E.G. 93–94
Sherman, Brig. Gen. Francis T. 129–130
Sherman, Maj. Gen. William T. 5–6, 41, 48–49, 51, 147–148, 157, 162, 202–203
Sickel, Brig. Gen. H.G. 171–172
Sixteenth Michigan 172, 192
Sixteenth North Carolina Cavalry 192
Sixth Corps 36, 134, 163, 205
Smith, Col. D.L. 168, 200
Sniper, Col. G. 172, 184
Southside Railroad 4, 10, 25, 102, 115
Spear, Col. Ellis 91–92
Spencer, Dr. T.R. 168, 200
Spotsylvania, Battle of 3, 42, 128
Stage Road 168–170
Staggs Brigade 137–138, 163
Steuart, Brig. Gen. G.H. CSA 25, 27–28, 95–96, 98, 102–103, 105–106, 110–111, 207
Stickney, Mr. Albert 55, 58–62, 100, 139–140
Stony Creek 162, 170, 175
Stowe, Col. 179
Stroud, J. 173, 178, 182
Stubel, William 192
Swain, D.G. 145–146
Swan, Col. W.W. 77–78
Syndor 26, 82, 85–86, 92, 101, 113

telegraph communication 8, 13
telegraph wagon 9
Thirty Second Virginia Infantry 198
Thomas, Col. A.L. 168, 200
Thomas, Maj. Gen. George H. 5
Thompson, Maj. William 133
topographical engineers 32, 47
Tower, Col. Z.B. 51–52
Twentieth Pennsylvania Cavalry 138
Two Hundred and Tenth Pennsylvania Volunteers 182

U.S. Volunteer Army 6, 14–15, 17, 32–33, 40–41, 47–48, 74, 84, 154

Van Brocklin, Maj. 168, 171
Vaughan Road 24, 144
Virginia 3, 8, 12, 29, 36, 158, 168, 194, 197, 203, 205
Vogel, Lt. 172

Wadsworth, Capt. James W. 65–66, 120, 168, 188, 196, 200
Wainwright, Brig. Gen. Charles 16–17, 42, 54, 168, 189, 200
Wallace, Brig. Gen. W.H. CSA 25, 98, 104–105, 207
Walsh, Col. 175
Walters, Lt. 172
Warner, Capt. E.R. 54–55, 111
Warren, Maj. Gen. Gouverneur 1, 8–9, 13, 16–25, 27–74, 76–101, 108–109, 111–133, 135–158, 161–169, 173, 177, 180–181, 183, 191–193, 198–200, 203–208
weather 12
Webb, Brig. Gen. A.S. 170, 173–187, 189–190, 192–193
Weldon Railroad 4, 11, 19, 22, 162, 167
West Point 17, 32–33, 38, 41–42, 47, 49, 52, 68, 127, 137, 150–151, 153–154, 167
Whitaker, Col. 131
White House 15, 161
White Oak Road 7, 16, 19, 21–28, 30, 38–39, 56, 58, 61–63, 65–72, 74–93, 95–116, 118–120, 122–123, 125, 127–139, 141–143, 162, 164–166, 175–185, 187–188, 190–192, 195, 197–201, 204–207
Wilcox, Maj. Gen. CSA 177–179
Wilderness, Battle of the 36–38
Wilson House 65–66, 71, 74, 81–82, 86, 100
Winne, Dr. Charles K. 168, 200
Winslow, Rev. Gordon 168, 170, 188, 200
Winthrop, Brig. Gen. Frederick 65, 74–76, 78, 167, 182, 195, 200, 208
Wister, Capt. 189
Wood, Capt. Henry 127
Wood, Lt. Col. W.W. 102–105
Wright, Maj. Gen. H.G. 47, 153, 203

Zouaves 33